THE DALAI LAMA

Celebrating
30 Years of Publishing
in India

ALSO BY ALEXANDER NORMAN

Secret Lives of the Dalai Lama:
The Untold Story of the Holy Men Who Shaped Tibet,
from Pre-History to the Present Day

THE DALAI LAMA

AN EXTRAORDINARY LIFE

ALEXANDER NORMAN

HarperCollins *Publishers* India

First published in hardback by HarperCollins *Publishers* 2020
4th Floor, Tower A, Building No. 10, Phase II, DLF Cyber City,
Gurugram, Haryana – 122002
www.harpercollins.co.in

This edition published in India by HarperCollins *Publishers* 2022

2 4 6 8 10 9 7 5 3

P ISBN: 978-93-5629-294-9
E ISBN: 978-93-5357-651-6

Book design by Greta D. Sibley

Map by Mapping Specialists, Ltd.

Printed and bound at
Thomson Press (India) Ltd

MIX
Paper
FSC FSC® C010615

This book is produced from independently certified FSC® paper
to ensure responsible forest management.

For my children:

M.R.N.

E.A.N.

T.F.H.N.

CONTENTS

A Note on Language and Spelling

Most would agree that the Tibetan alphabet, in each of its forms, is highly attractive on the page. Its use in a nonspecialist book such as this is out of the question, however. Moreover, the standard (Wylie) method of transcription into European characters, although it renders the Tibetan accurately, produces almost equally baffling results for the general reader. Who would guess that *bstan 'dzin rgya mthso* (the name of the present Dalai Lama) is pronounced "Tenzin Gyatso"?

In view of this difficulty, I have given phonetics (often my own) for all Tibetan words and names. Where they occur more than once, I have — in most cases — included them in the glossary at the end, together with the correct Wylie transliteration.

It is also worth noting that Tibetan uses different tones, so words that are phonetically similar may have an entirely different meaning. Notoriously, the words for "ice," "shit," and "fat" are pronounced exactly alike, save for tonal register.

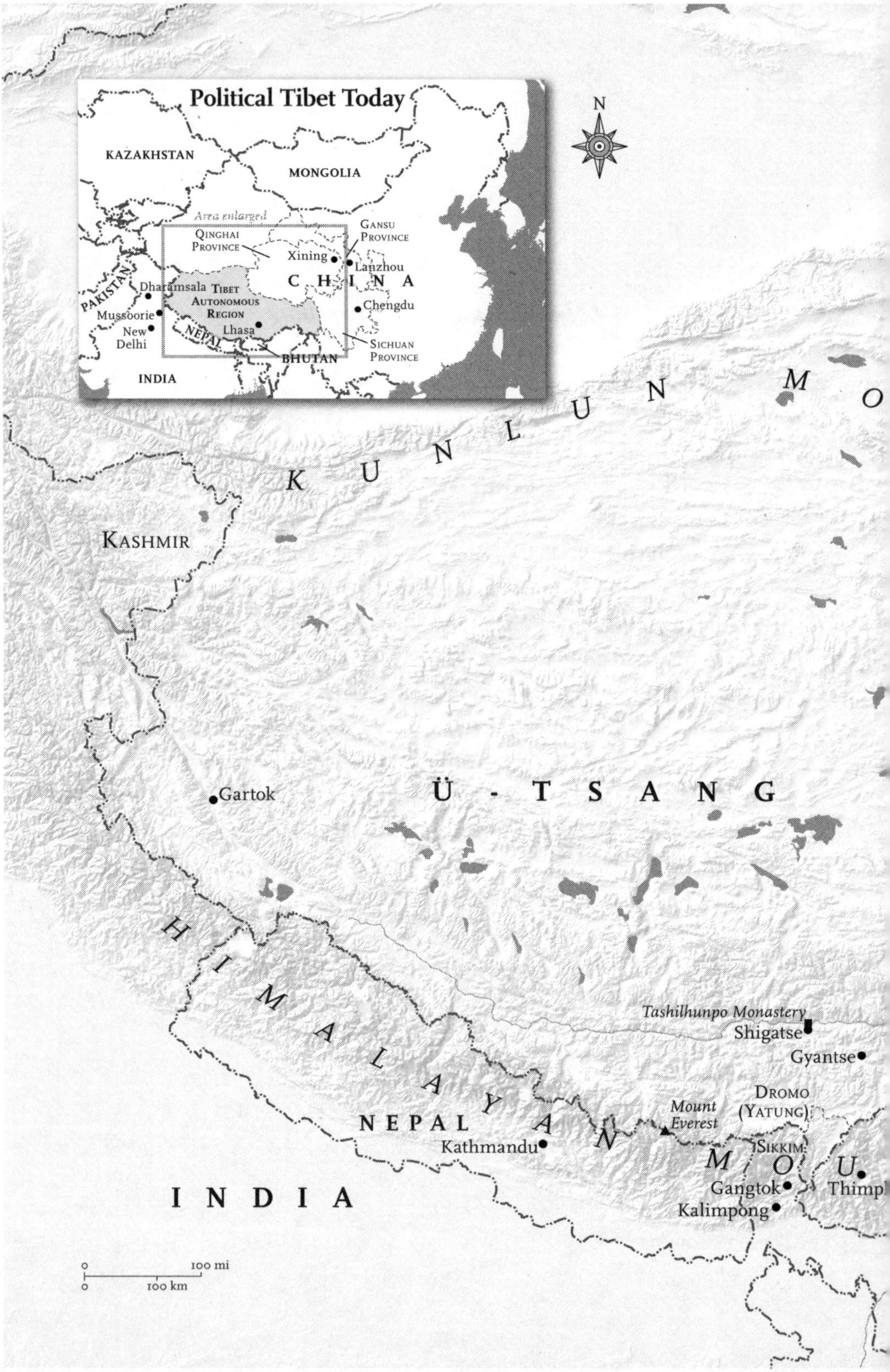

Political Tibet Today
KAZAKHSTAN
MONGOLIA
Area enlarged
QINGHAI PROVINCE
GANSU PROVINCE
Xining
Lanzhou
CHINA
PAKISTAN
Dharamsala
TIBET AUTONOMOUS REGION
Chengdu
Mussoorie
New Delhi
Lhasa
NEPAL
SICHUAN PROVINCE
BHUTAN
INDIA
N
KUNLUN MO
KASHMIR
Gartok
Ü-TSANG
HIMALAYAN MOU
Tashilhunpo Monastery
Shigatse
Gyantse
DROMO (YATUNG)
Mount Everest
NEPAL
Kathmandu
SIKKIM
Gangtok
Kalimpong
INDIA
0 100 mi
0 100 km

Cultural Tibet

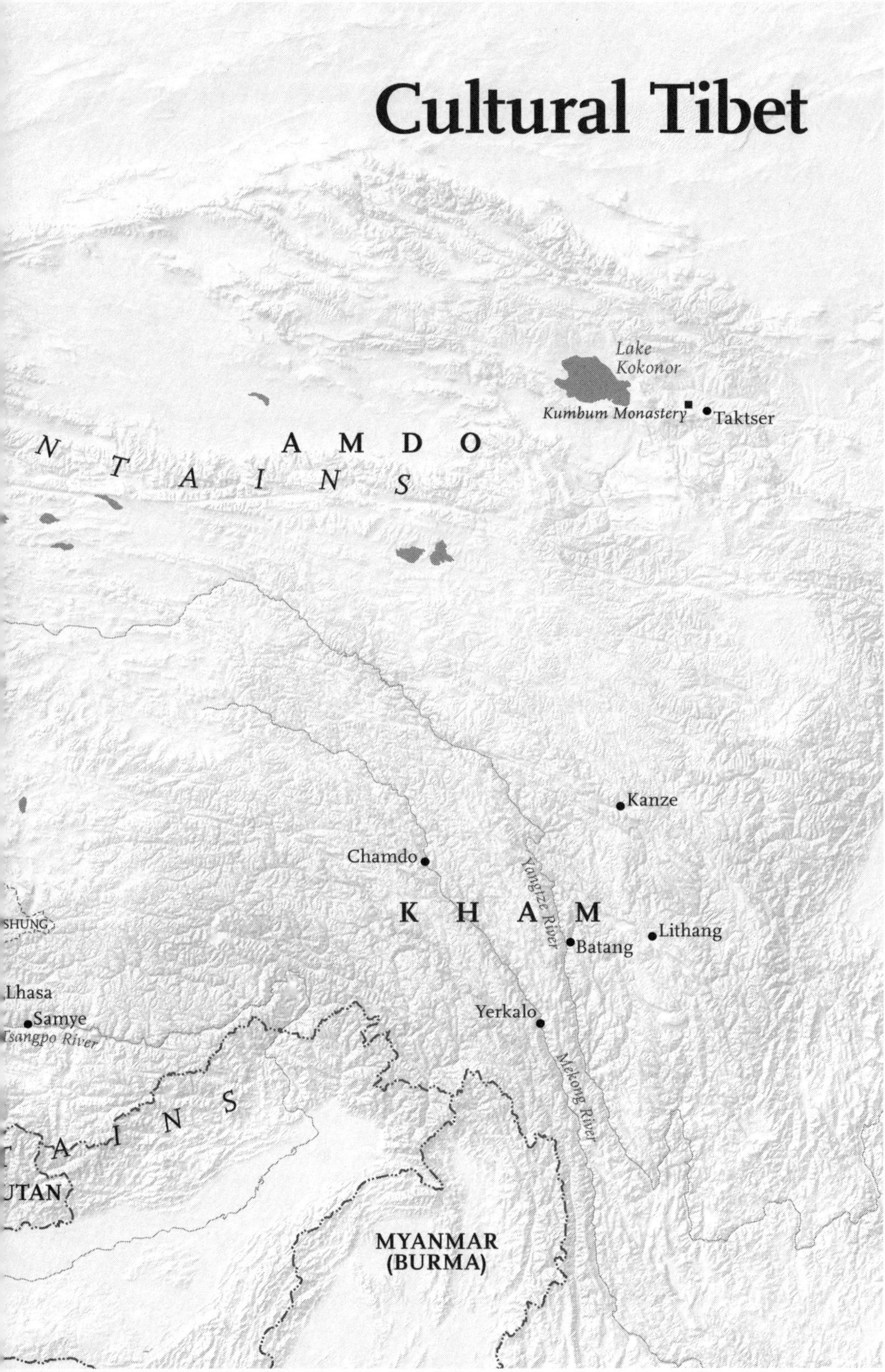

INTRODUCTION

Waldorf Astoria Hotel, New York, August 1989

Striding up to Reception, I announce my purpose.

"I am looking for Mr. Tenzin Tethong, private secretary to His Holiness the Dalai Lama."

Under my arm I am carrying the draft manuscript of the Dalai Lama's autobiography, *Freedom in Exile,* on which I have been working for the past several months.

The receptionist stares at me blankly. Perhaps it is my strong English accent.

"Mr. De Whaaat?" she demands in a slow drawl.

Three decades later, such a response is unimaginable. One of the world's most instantly recognizable people, the Dalai Lama sells out sports stadiums from Sydney to São Paolo, from Oslo to Johannesburg. With around 20 million Twitter followers, the Dalai Lama has more than the pope, and his online presence continues to grow. He is a recipient of the Nobel Peace Prize, the Congressional Gold Medal, and the richest award of them all, the Templeton Prize for spiritual progress. He holds the freedom of cities and honorary degrees too numerous to list. His image adorns wristwatches and screensavers, while his Amazon page gives details of more than two hundred books crediting him as author. Sales of several individual titles run into the millions. Unquestionably, the Dalai Lama is one of the best-known and best-loved public figures of modern times.

Yet for all his latter-day superstardom, few know much about the Dalai Lama or about the culture he embodies. And of what is known, a great deal is misunderstood. For example, many people suppose that the Dalai Lama is a religious leader — a sort of Buddhist pope. But unlike the pope, who claims authority over every priest and prelate in Christendom, the Dalai Lama has no jurisdiction over any other lama or monk. Neither is he the head of his own particular faith tradition, nor is he the leader of any of the subgroups within that tradition. In fact, he is not even abbot of the monastery of which he is a member. So when he says, as he often does, that he is "just a simple Buddhist monk," the Dalai Lama is not just being characteristically modest. He is straightforwardly telling the truth. The Dalai Lamas — of which the present one is the fourteenth — have only ever been simple Buddhist monks, even though the Great Fifth Dalai Lama was one of the most powerful men in Asia, and even though the Dalai Lamas have always been venerated by people far beyond the Land of Snows (as Tibetans often refer to their country).

From a political perspective, however, the Dalai Lamas have been anything but ordinary. Beginning with the Great Fifth, they have been — in theory at least — temporal leaders of a people whose country is the size of western Europe, spanning over fifteen hundred miles from a border with Pakistan in the west to China in the east, and almost a thousand miles from Mongolia in the north to India, Nepal, and Burma in the south. But it is little known that in 2011, the present Dalai Lama renounced his claim to lead his people as head of state in favor of a democratically elected layman. As a result, the office of Dalai Lama is now purely a teaching office. This makes perfect sense, however: the word *lama* is the Tibetan translation of the Sanskrit word *guru* — a spiritual guide.

Together with these misunderstandings, the Dalai Lama's image as smiling saint for all seasons fails to do justice either to the Dalai Lama as a person or to the tradition he represents. It neglects his extraordinary achievements in settling a diaspora community now a quarter of a million strong. It neglects how he has unified a people previously sharply divided along geographical, tribal, and sectarian lines. It neglects how, in so doing, he has opened up the institution of the Dalai Lama to all Tibetans in a way that it never was before. It neglects his political reforms. It neglects his remarkable attainments as a scholar-practitioner: he is unquestionably one of the most accomplished and learned masters of Vajrayana Buddhism to have emerged within the past century. It neglects the astonishing impact the Dalai Lama has had on the shape of the modern world. Above all, it neglects one of the most extraordinary cultures ever to have evolved on the face of the earth and the complex, often turbulent history that brought it into being.

In writing this book, therefore, I have sought above all to set the Dalai Lama's deeds in the context of the history and culture of the Tibetan tradition, and it is for this reason that I have shown in some detail the circumstances of how the regency that governed Tibet until the Dalai Lama was of age both came into being and came to an end. Without some understanding of what and where the Dalai Lama comes from, we are likely both to miss the scale of his accomplishments and to misconstrue the enormity of the challenges he has faced.

I hope particularly to show how the Dalai Lama's motivations have caused him to act in the way he has acted — these motivations being themselves determined by his understanding of the Tibetan tradition. I take as my starting point the fact that what has chiefly inspired him is the bodhisattva vow he took at the age of fifteen. Out of compassion, he committed himself to direct his every thought, word, and deed to the benefit of all sentient beings in their quest to overcome suffering. The Dalai Lama's life story can thus be understood as a teaching that shows, from the perspective of the tradition, what compassion really is and how this construal of compassion plays out in the everyday world.

Here, though, I should say something about the words "tradition" and, especially, "Tibetan tradition" as I use them in this book. When I claim that the Dalai Lama exemplifies the Tibetan tradition, I take the term to denote that which is handed down, or handed over, from one generation to another — not just the habitual practices of many Tibetans over time but also the body of ideas and beliefs that attach to these practices. When, for example, I say that, according to Tibetan tradition, there are many hells, some hot, some frozen, I am saying that according to the understanding of most orthodox believers within the tradition, this is the case. I don't mean to claim that all Tibetans everywhere have always believed this, only that most have and do.

At the same time as making this point about tradition, I should also emphasize that, so far as the Tibetan *religious* tradition is concerned, there is Buddhism with, so to speak, local accents but no such thing as a specifically

Tibetan Buddhism. From the Tibetan point of view, the Buddhism preserved within this tradition is the highest, most complete form of Buddhism — even if some of its teachings and practices are regarded as heterodox by others.

Because of my interest in setting the Dalai Lama in the context of Tibetan culture and history and presenting his biography as a lived lesson in what, from the perspective of his tradition, it is to be truly compassionate, I have been less interested in recounting what the Dalai Lama says. Both his spiritual teachings and his political views are recorded in the hundreds of books and many thousands of hours of video and voice recordings that have been made over the sixty years since he came into exile. It is to these sources that those interested in the Dalai Lama's spiritual and political philosophy should turn.

As to what the Dalai Lama is actually *like,* I regard this question as secondary to the question of what the Dalai Lama *means* — not merely by what he says but also by what he does. There is something to be said for personal detail, but in my opinion this tells us much less about the man than that, for example, his religious commitments include some that a number of authorities even within his own Gelug school consider to be dangerously mistaken. How the Dalai Lama interprets and shapes the Tibetan tradition, and, especially, where he departs from it, are in my view more telling and, from a historical perspective, more significant than what his favorite television program is or what his hobbies are. For the record, his preferred viewing is nature programs — he is a fan of David Attenborough — while for hobbies, though he is less active than formerly, he has been an enthusiastic amateur horologist, and he continues to take a keen interest in the garden surrounding his residence.

Having said this, given that I have had the enormous privilege of working with the Dalai Lama on three of his most important books, including his (second) autobiography, I should at least attempt an answer to the question of what he is like as a person.* The best way I can think of doing so is by recounting the beginning of a conversation I had with him some years ago. I told him how my wife had recently chided me that it was a disgrace how, after knowing His

* I once calculated that these books alone entailed spending in excess of 250 hours working alone, or in narrowly restricted company, with the Dalai Lama.

Holiness for then more than a quarter century, I still could not hold a proper conversation with him in his own language. I had to admit she was right, I said, and for that, I told him, I ought to apologize.

"Well, if it comes to that," he replied in his familiar heavily accented English, "it is me who should apologize. I have been learning your language since nineteen forty-seven!"

In those few words are summed up the grace, the humility, and the kindness of the man.

I first met the Dalai Lama in Dharamsala, his exile home in India, during March 1988, when I went to interview him on behalf of the London *Spectator*. There was one thing about that first encounter that struck me at the time as slightly strange and has since come to seem prophetic. When I was shown into his audience chamber, I had just enough time to register that the room was empty before I realized the Dalai Lama was standing almost directly in front of me. It was not as if he had been there all along and I suddenly noticed him; rather my impression was that he literally appeared out of nowhere.

Something similar occurred a year or so later — but this is supposed to be a biography, not autobiography. Suffice it instead to say that quite a lot of our work that followed over the years since then was undertaken while the Dalai Lama was away from his exile home and on the road — in the United States, Denmark, Italy, Germany, France, the UK, and elsewhere in India. This has allowed me to see him in a variety of different settings, from which I have gleaned some observations perhaps worth relating.

I know him, for example, to be fastidious — his nails are always neatly trimmed — though he is not the least showy as to dress. His clothing is of good quality but not the finest. His shoes are sturdy and well polished, but of respectable and not high-end provenance. Rupert Murdoch — a media tycoon and not a moralist — once called the Dalai Lama a "canny old monk in Gucci loafers." He was wrong. The Dalai Lama wears Hush Puppies as a rule, never Gucci. At home he wears flip-flops.

It is true that the Dalai Lama has a fondness for good timepieces, but he does not have a collection. He wears an unornamented gold Rolex. Invariably he gives away any he no longer has use for. In fact, I have one of them (gifted by him first to someone else). It is a plain stainless steel Jaeger-LeCoultre

Memovox with a mechanical alarm (which would no doubt have appealed to him) that he wore for a time during the 1960s.

Although quite the opposite of extravagant in terms of possessions, the Dalai Lama has admitted to having a somewhat "free-spending" nature. When he was a child, he would buy as many animals destined for slaughter as he could — to the point where his officials ran out of room to keep them. As an adult, on more than one occasion he visited shopping malls during his first trip to the United States in 1979. His tutor Ling Rinpoché cautioned him against making unnecessary purchases, however, and so far as I know, he has rarely been seen in any sort of retail outlet since. He does not use a computer, so he is not an online shopper. Instead his extravagance — if such it is — is limited nowadays to giving away money, mainly to humanitarian causes. When he won the Templeton Prize in 2012, he immediately donated the great majority of its almost $2 million award to the Save the Children Fund.* This was in honor of the charity's generosity to Tibetan refugees in the early days of exile.

In private, the Dalai Lama is attentive to others' needs and will, for example, ask if you prefer coffee if only tea has been served. He will ensure that there are nuts or cookies available alongside the *dri churra* (a molar-cracking dried cheese from Tibet) of which he is fond. He will adjust the blinds so the sun is not in your eyes. He may ask whether you find it too hot or too cold and have the heating or air-conditioning adjusted. If it seems to him that the room layout for an audience could be improved, he will have his staff move furniture around until he finds it satisfactory. I recall one occasion during the early days of our acquaintance when I came across him moving chairs in his hotel room in preparation for a press conference.

The Dalai Lama is a hearty eater, though this is in part because, as an ordained monk, he may eat only twice a day, and never after noon — though he might choose to do so if he is a guest at a luncheon while abroad, and he may also take a cookie or two during the course of the afternoon if he has had a particularly arduous day. As to diet, he is not fussy. He leans toward vegetarianism in principle but, on account of illness and doctors' advice, he eats meat

* He also gave $200,000 to the Mind and Life Institute and the remainder, approximately $75,000, for science education within the Tibetan monasteries in exile.

without scruple — though one need have no doubt he prays for the postmortem well-being of each creature that he consumes.

As for looking after his own needs, he sometimes jokes that he would not know how to make a cup of tea. Nor does he cook and, aside from helping make *khabse* (New Year's cookies) in the kitchens of the Potala Palace when very young, he has rarely seen the inside of a kitchen. At least when younger, however, he would happily build a fire. But he has always been restricted in what he has done for himself, having been surrounded with staff and attendants since very early childhood. Of these he retains a small community. Within his household, there are around ten, including cooks and orderlies. He has four or five personal attendants, all of them monks, as well as a number of retainers who, because of their age, have only the lightest duties and who remain with him simply as friends. It is to this little community that he turns for conversation and respite at the end of the day. In terms of office staff, they are divided into Tibetan and English sections, most, though not all, of whom are laymen. He employs four (up from only two until comparatively recently) principal private secretaries, who are in turn supported by a small number of subordinates. Although the Dalai Lama appoints these men himself (and, out of consideration for his monastic state, they are all men), their names are submitted to him by the Central Tibetan Administration. Together they constitute his eyes and ears beyond the confines of the Ganden Phodrang, as his home headquarters is known (much as the administration in Washington is known as "the White House"). To be sure, he also listens carefully to what visitors tell him, and he has family and friends from whom he gains intelligence.

If he is less well informed than he should be on a given topic, it will be because the people surrounding him have failed, for whatever reason, to brief him as fully as they ought. Perhaps inevitably, given the small pool of people on whom he has to rely, this does sometimes happen.

Besides his permanent staff, there are larger numbers of bodyguards. At home, the Dalai Lama is watched over by a contingent from the Indian army in addition to his Tibetan security. As to his relations with these, he maintains a certain formality except with the most senior of them, but he is considerate of their needs too. He always has a friendly word for those who keep watch at night when he goes for his early morning walk. (He is in the habit of strolling outside, or along hotel corridors, as soon as he has completed his first prayers.) And when traveling, he invariably takes time out to talk to those who serve him.

Much is made of the Dalai Lama's sense of humor. I have often thought that Tibetan humor generally is quite similar to the English: ready, often earthy, and with a love of irony and absurdity. The best success I have had with a joke was a very innocent one about a mouse. I would not tell him a vulgar story, however. He would likely think it odd that anyone other than his closest family or colleagues would do such a thing. But he is no spoilsport. He once asked me about the wedding of a young Tibetan official that I had attended — whether anyone had gotten tipsy? When I said yes, he was not at all disapproving. When I learned that, besides nature programs, he would sometimes watch an episode of the perennial English comedy series *Dad's Army,* I once sent him a box set, but I do not know whether he ever saw it. I also included a *Mr. Bean* film, as I thought this would appeal to him.

Although he does not stand on ceremony — he actively dislikes formality and any sort of pretense — the Dalai Lama is conscious of the dignity of his office. On one occasion when I failed to produce a *kathag,* the silk offering scarf it is customary to present on meeting, he did not hesitate to reprimand me. On another occasion, I committed one of those faux pas that seemed innocuous to me as a foreigner but which must have caused serious offense. Again, he made me aware of my mistake, but kindly. I do not believe he would have done so if he had not known me as well as he does, however. He is sensitive to others' feelings. That said, he does sometimes make an artless remark that takes people aback. I recall hearing that he laughingly scolded a fellow writer for having fingernails "that looked like claws."

The Dalai Lama is also both affectionate by nature and often tactile. He will pretend to give friends a playful slap on the back of the head. He may clasp your hand and hold it, or nuzzle his cheek against yours, or stroke your beard. Being tactile is a characteristic he shares with his predecessor the Great Thirteenth Dalai Lama, who, having evaded a pursuing Chinese army by fleeing over the mountains into neighboring Sikkim, was rapturously received by the people each according to his or her custom. Some bowed, some offered salaams, some prostrated themselves, but there were three little Scottish girls on ponies — their father was a local missionary — who insinuated themselves into the procession right behind behind him. When he slowed to acknowledge the crowd, they jumped down and ran ahead to await the Dalai Lama at the government guesthouse where he would be staying. As he walked up to it, the Great Thirteenth paused unspeaking to run his fingers through Isa Graham's flaxen locks, "feeling it between finger and thumb, as one feels silken threads to test their quality and texture." Disappearing into the building, he came out only a few moments later to feel her hair again while the crowd gasped.

In considering these personal characteristics, it is vital we do not lose sight of the fact that the Dalai Lama is a monk before he is anything else — and a monk with enormous ritual responsibilities. A weakness of a biography like this is that it cannot avoid giving the impression that the subject's life is all about his public deeds. In the case of the Dalai Lama, however, it is actually his interior life that is the more important. It is therefore essential that the reader bear in mind the Dalai Lama's total commitment to his monastic calling. Every day on rising, without fail, he begins with at least three hours of prayer and meditation. Every evening, without fail, he concludes with an hour or more of the same. And during the day, he will pray and study to the extent his schedule allows, very often including when eating. When on retreat, which he undertakes for extended periods of up to three weeks at least once a year, but also for shorter periods of a few days multiple times during the course of the year, he increases his commitment (by rising at 3 a.m. instead of 4:30) and limits his involvement with worldly affairs to an hour or two per day whenever possible.

I have already mentioned my deficiency in spoken Tibetan. Though functionally literate in the language, I am also reliant on a dictionary or the good offices of some kind person save for the shortest and most basic texts. In some ways, though, this has been a blessing. It has meant that I have come closer to a number of Tibetan friends than might have been the case if I were more self-sufficient. It has also been a constant reminder that I write as an outsider, as an observer, looking in.

It is arguably less of a failing that I am not a Buddhist. It has enabled me to ask questions and think thoughts that would otherwise have been more difficult, if not impossible. But for this same reason, I have no doubt that some of what I say here will seem to some impertinent and possibly even disrespectful, even though I mean neither impertinence nor disrespect. It is also possible that some of the material may be painful to some of my readers. With respect to this, I take encouragement from the Dalai Lama himself, who, on many occasions, has spoken of the need for fair and balanced assessment of the facts. I trust that I have succeeded; certainly this has been my aim at all times.

PART I

A Prophecy Fulfilled

I

The Travails of the Great Thirteenth

It is tempting to begin our story with the first Saturday in July 1935, when, by the Gregorian calendar, the present Dalai Lama was born. And yet to do so would be to ignore the context of that birth. In a way, it would be more accurate to begin with the evening of the seventeenth of December 1933, and the circumstances surrounding it, when the Great Thirteenth Dalai Lama "withdrew his spirit to the Tushita paradise" — where dwell all those on the point of Enlightenment — as pious tradition expresses the matter. The death of the previous Dalai Lama is what precipitates the birth of the next — even if, as in this case, it happens that more than nine months elapse between the two events.

Yet there is also a case for beginning with the birth of the First Dalai Lama, since, after all, each incarnation is considered to share the same mental continuum. But besides necessitating a long digression into history, this would be problematic. It turns out that the First Dalai Lama was in fact the Third. What happened was that a lama by the name of Sonam Gyatso was summoned by

Altan Khan (a descendant of Genghis) to Mongolia, where they met in 1578. Altan, the new strongman of Central Asia, was looking for a way to legitimize his rule, and Sonam Gyatso, as one of the most renowned lamas of the day, looked to be just the person to lend him respectability. Accordingly, Altan, in the idiom of that time, conferred on the Tibetan a number of high-flown titles, one of which pronounced him Dalai Lama. The word *dalai* is simply a Tibetanization of the Mongolian word for "ocean," which in turn translates the second half of Sonam Gyatso's name. Yet because Sonam Gyatso was in fact the third incarnation of a lineage connected with Drepung, Tibet's largest monastery, it followed that he must, in fact, be the Third Dalai Lama.

There is an added complication, however. Besides being the third exemplar of the Drepung line, Sonam Gyatso is also considered to have been forty-second in an unbroken lineage going back to the time of the historical Buddha, who lived during the fifth century BCE. It is this lineage that associates the Dalai Lamas with Chenresig, the Bodhisattva of Compassion, whom they are understood to manifest on earth. And yet this lineage is itself antedated by yet another that connects Chenresig with a young prince who lived 990 eons ago. How long is an eon? A disciple is said once to have asked the Buddha the same question. He replied with an analogy: Suppose there were a great mountain of rock, seven miles across and seven miles high, a solid mass without any cracks. At the end of every hundred years, a man might brush it with a fine Benares cloth. That great mountain would be worn away and come to an end sooner than ever an eon. It becomes apparent that, as soon as we start delving into the history of the Dalai Lama, we are faced with the most profound of questions. Indeed, it turns out that, so far as the present Dalai Lama is concerned, we have before us not merely the biography of one man but the story of a being who, from the perspective of his tradition, has been perfected and purified of all defilements through the performance of unnumbered good deeds over countless lifetimes and who manifests here on earth not for his own good but for that of all others. This is, moreover, a story in which the remote past is just the other day and matters supernatural are as real as the natural and as close as right next door.

To understand the Dalai Lama, therefore, we need to try to catch a glimpse of the world as Tibetan tradition sees it: not as one that began with a single moment of Creation, nor as one where everything might ultimately be expressed as a string of mathematical formulae — a world of atoms and electrons, protons and neutrons. We should not even think of it as a world explicable in terms of quanta and probability. The world as it is understood through the lens of Tibetan tradition did not begin with a big bang which sent the Earth spinning among galaxies and solar systems and ever-expanding space. The world according to Tibetan tradition has no beginning at all. Indeed, the world we see around us exists not on account of atomic or subatomic particles but on account of the accumulated karma of numberless sentient beings over eons of time.

So let us begin our story not with the birth of the present Dalai Lama, or Lhamo Thondup (the *h* in Lhamo and in Thondup can both be safely ignored, while the *T* in Thondup is hard, almost a *D*), as the infant Fourteenth was known at birth, nor with the death of his predecessor. Let us ignore convention and begin instead with a homely snapshot of the visit of the Thirteenth Dalai Lama to a village in far eastern Tibet one fine day during the spring of 1907.

Returning from the small monastery of Shartsong, the Precious Protector — this being one of the epithets by which all Dalai Lamas are commonly known by Tibetans — repaired to the grassy summit of a nearby hill together with his companion for the day, Taktser Rinpoché. (Taktser is pronounced roughly *Taksé*. It means, literally, the Place where the Tiger Roared. Rinpoché, an honorific applied to the highest class of monk, but also to certain places and objects, means something like Precious One.) The Rinpoché, who took his name from the village that stood beneath them, was the most important lama of the local area, which lay at the farthest extreme of the northeastern province of their country, known to Tibetans as Amdo.

We have grown used to the idea of nation-states with clearly defined borders, but for most of history the demarcation between peoples — even those of different ethnicity — was never so sharply drawn. From the Chinese perspective, at that time Taktser and its environs lay firmly within Qinghai province. But from the Tibetan perspective, for the best part of a millennium (roughly from the seventh to the seventeenth century), the village had been unambiguously part of Tibet. And although at the time of the Great Thirteenth's visit the Chinese had reasserted their control over the area, the majority of the local population remained Tibetan.

After commenting favorably on the natural beauty of the landscape, the Dalai Lama expressed his desire to visit Taktser village. So it was that, following a picnic lunch, the Great Thirteenth personally visited each homestead. There, we are told, he delighted the householders by engaging them in conversation and asking innumerable questions about their lives. So moved was one villager that she subsequently took a scoop of ashes from the fire on which the Dalai Lama's lunch was cooked and buried them in the courtyard in front of the family home.

At the conclusion of his visit, the Precious Protector announced that he had fallen in love with this pretty little valley and promised one day to return. Alas, he never did. Or at least he did not do so in his guise as Thirteenth Dalai Lama. But it was here that twenty-eight years later the present Dalai Lama was born — into the family in front of whose house those ashes lay buried.

The circumstances of that fateful picnic back in 1907 were hardly propitious. This was a moment of history when the Chinese empire of the Qing dynasty was tottering toward extinction while the British Empire, although at its peak in terms of power and prosperity, was soon to fade after the maelstrom of the First World War, creating a vacuum that would be filled by the twin terrors of fascistic nationalism and communism. At this moment, the Tibetan leader was in exile from Lhasa, his capital. Three years previously, British troops under the command of Colonel Francis Younghusband had Gatling-gunned their way into central Tibet, causing the Dalai Lama to flee north to Mongolia. This invasion, arguably one of the least glorious feats of arms in the long history of the British Empire, had come about ostensibly as a result of the Dalai Lama's government refusing to recognize Britain's protectorate over Sikkim, a small Buddhist kingdom sandwiched between Tibet and India. In fact, it had more to do with British paranoia about the rising power of Russia. That, and the dream one of the Great Thirteenth's closest advisers had of a pan-Buddhist federation in Central Asia uniting Mongolia, Tibet, and other Buddhist lands under the spiritual leadership of the Dalai Lama and the military protection of the Russian Empire.

This adviser was Agvan Dorjieff, whose unfamiliar name must have sounded thrillingly sinister to contemporary British ears. When, around the turn of the century, it became clear to Queen Victoria's ministers that Dorjieff had personal links with the tsar himself, there grew a conviction that Something Must Be Done. Questions were asked in Parliament.* People wrote to newspapers demanding action, while Lord Curzon, viceroy of India, began to plot. For him it was essential that Tibet remain a neutral buffer between the Russian Empire and the northern borders of the British Empire.

The military campaign that ensued was as swift as it was brutal. The first action occurred on March 31, 1904, and resulted in the expenditure by the British of fifty shrapnel shells, fourteen hundred machine-gun rounds, and 14,351 rounds of rifle shot for no loss of life on the British side but 628 Tibetans slain. Among the dead were two generals and two monk-officials. Even Younghusband admitted it was a massacre. He did, however, admire the Tibetans' calmness and tenacity under fire. For their part, the Tibetans were astonished not just by the firepower of the *inji* invaders but also by their code of conduct in war. Never before had they seen their wounded treated in enemy field hospitals and those taken prisoner merely disarmed and given cigarettes and a small sum of money before being set free.

Less than a fortnight later, Younghusband was camped outside the vast fortress of Gyantse, which lay just a few days' march from Lhasa. From there he issued an ultimatum to the Dalai Lama, giving the Tibetan leader until June 12 to send competent negotiators or he would resume his march. While they had no interest in conquest, what the British wanted, aside from favorable trading rights, was to compel the Tibetans to accept a British presence in Tibet so that they could monitor and, if necessary, check developments that might prove harmful to India, the jewel in the crown of their empire.

As for the Dalai Lama, he and his council of ministers, the Kashag, were determined to refuse any contact until the invading army withdrew. Younghusband's letter, sealed and beribboned in best imperial fashion and carried to Lhasa by a newly released prisoner, came back unopened several days later. The Tibetans calculated that, however mighty the British, they would never

---

* Whether by spooky coincidence or as evidence of some strange karmic link, the first of these was put by my great-grandfather Sir Henry Norman, Baronet (then plain Mr.).

be able to take Gyantse fort. The wrathful protectors of the Buddhadharma (the doctrine or Way of the Buddha) would see to that. But Gyantse fell in no time, and Younghusband resumed his march. Hastily appointing a senior monastic official as regent, the Dalai Lama fled north in the direction of Mongolia. He could at least be sure that his co-religionist there, the Jetsundamba Lama, would offer him sanctuary and protection until the British could be got rid of.

The Dalai Lama's welcome by the senior-most religious figure in Mongolia was less than generous, however. The Great Thirteenth's official biography notes a dispute over the relative height of the two men's thrones when they met, but it is also recorded that the Dalai Lama was appalled to discover that the Mongolian, against the rules of monastic tradition, had taken a wife and was both given to drink and addicted to tobacco. He even had the temerity to smoke in the Dalai Lama's presence.* This was a major insult. Nonetheless, the Dalai Lama was compelled to remain at the Mongolian hierarch's headquarters in Urgya (modern-day Ulaanbaatar) for the time being.

When, in September of that year, Younghusband withdrew from Lhasa, the Tibetans were as amazed as they were relieved. It seems they fully expected a wholesale British takeover on the model of previous invasions of Tibet by Mongolians and Manchus in turn.† But relief turned to dismay when it became clear the British were adamant that the Dalai Lama must remain in exile.

The Great Thirteenth therefore stayed in Urgya another year. One of the few Europeans who had an audience with him at this time was a Russian explorer, who gives us a description of the Dalai Lama's demeanor during their conversation. It was, he declares, "one of great calmness." The Dalai Lama "often looked me straight in the eye, and each time our glances met, he smiled slightly and with great dignity." When, however, "the matter of the English and their military expedition was touched upon, his expression changed. His face clouded with sorrow, his gaze fell and his voice broke with emotion."

Meanwhile in China, Cixi, the Dowager Empress, was similarly devastated

---

* From the perspective of the tradition, tobacco is an intoxicant and is therefore prohibited.

† From the Chinese perspective, the Manchus themselves were, like the Tibetans, a "barbarian" race — in contrast to the "civilized" Han over whom they ruled from 1644 to 1912.

by the British seizure of Lhasa. "Tibet," she wrote, "has belonged to our dynasty for two hundred years. This is a vast area, rich in resources, which has always been coveted by foreigners. Recently, British troops entered it and coerced the Tibetans to sign a treaty. This is a most sinister development . . . [W]e must prevent further damage and salvage the present situation." When, a year later, rebellion, led by the monks of Batang Monastery, broke out against the Chinese presence in Kham, the second of Tibet's two eastern provinces, she took this as her cue and dispatched an army under one of her generals, Zhao Erfeng. This was to prove the last major undertaking of the now exhausted Qing dynasty, in power since the mid-seventeenth century.

The Khampa rebellion took place in 1905, two years before the Precious Protector's visit to Shartsong. There was at the time a small Chinese outpost in the township of Batang, which stands amid fertile plains irrigated by the upper Yangtze River. This had been established following the invasion of central Tibet, by Mongol descendants of Genghis Khan, when the Manchu emperor of China was called on for help by the Tibetans. The unintended but inevitable consequence of this was that Tibet fell under the sway of the Qing empire.

From the perspective of the Tibetans, however, the relationship between themselves and the Qing dynasty was to be regarded in terms of the relationship between the Dalai Lama and the reigning emperor. In Tibetan eyes, the arrangement was not a political one. It was, rather, a spiritual relationship whereby the Tibetan hierarch and the Chinese emperor were respectively priest and patron. This was seen in the association between Rolpai Dorje, a high lama close to the Seventh Dalai Lama, and the then emperor, to whom he gave spiritual teachings. (The emperor and the Dalai Lama never met; the relationship was thus enacted by proxy.)

Understanding how this priest-patron relationship works from the Tibetan point of view is crucial to understanding how Tibetans conceive of what at first glance looks like a straightforward surrender of sovereignty to the Chinese, first under the Yuan dynasty and then again under the Qing. To do so, it is important to realize that from its earliest days, Buddhism has been a religion of renunciation. To begin with, its teachings were preserved and propagated by celibate men, and latterly women, living in forest-based communities away from "civilization." The Buddha specified that his followers were to be mendicants, to beg their bread rather than to bake it. This meant they were dependent on others for their survival, a dependency that, as the religion spread and the tradition of communal living in monasteries developed, led to the need for patronage on a large scale. This came to be provided by those princely families that had awakened to the truth of the Buddhist teachings. But while the *sangha,* or monastic community, was materially dependent on this patronage, it was understood that those providing it were similarly dependent on the *sangha* for their spiritual well-being. And since, according to the Buddhist analysis, spiritual well-being takes precedence over material well-being, the *sangha* took at least theoretical precedence over the royal house — even if, of course, the religious community could not survive without its patronage.

When today the Chinese government points to the historic ties between China and Tibet and claims that these show that Tibet is, and has long been, an "inalienable part" of China, it sees only the political arrangement whereby, among other things, the emperor stationed his troops there. It ignores totally the spiritual dimension, which for Tibetans is of far greater importance.

This said, when the monks of Batang Monastery rose up against the Chinese troops in 1905, they could well have been accused of forsaking their own side of the bargain by taking the lead in a ferocious bloodletting. Indeed, so grotesque are the accounts of the atrocities they committed that it seems hard to believe they are not exaggerated. The sources, though varied, are in such agreement, however, that it is clear they are not.

The uprising targeted not only the Chinese but also a small mission operated by two French priests of the Roman Catholic Church. The priests and their converts were all murdered. Subsequently the unrest spread across the neighboring countryside. This included a small Sino-Tibetan trading station where another missionary community had taken root and which was at the time served by two more French priests. Staying with "the hospitable and venerable" chief of the mission at the time was the renowned Scottish botanist and plant hunter George Forrest. On hearing that the Chinese garrison stationed nearby had been "wiped out almost to a man," the three foreigners, together with their small community of converts, fled by moonlight. The next day, one of the priests was shot, "riddled with poisoned arrows . . . the Tibetans immediately rushing up and finishing him off with their huge double-handed swords." The remainder of the "little band, numbering about 80, were picked off one by one, or captured, only 14 escaping." One who almost succeeded in evading their attackers, a band of some thirty monks, was Père Dubernard, the other priest, but he was

> eventually run to ground in a cave . . . His captors broke both arms above and below the elbow, tied his hands behind his back, and in this condition forced him to walk back to the blackened site of [the mission]. There they fastened him to a post and subjected him to the most brutal humiliation; amongst the least of his injuries being the extraction of his tongue and eyes and the cutting off of his ears and nose. In this horrible condition he remained for the space of three days, in the course of which his torturers cut a joint off his fingers and toes each day. When on the point of death, he was treated in the same manner as [his fellow priest], the portions of the bodies being distributed amongst the various lamaseries [monasteries] in the region, whilst the two heads were stuck on spears over the lamaserie of the town.

Those in charge of the Catholic mission believed that the atrocities followed specific instructions by the Dalai Lama himself, but this seems unlikely in the extreme, given what we know of the Great Thirteenth's attitude toward both capital punishment and the practice of mutilation. He accepted that capital punishment was in certain circumstances a regrettable necessity, but in one of his earliest decrees he had reserved it for crimes of treason alone. He also decreed the abolition of mutilation, and while he permitted flogging, he much preferred restorative justice where possible. On one occasion he ordered a disgraced official to plant a thousand willow trees, on another that the guilty party should repair a stretch of road.

What the destruction of the Catholic mission and the attempt to kill Forrest tells us, therefore, is that the monasteries were often a law unto themselves. It also tells us that if our image of pre-Communist Tibet is one of monks serenely meditating in the mystic fastness of their mountain retreats, we must revise it. But the monks' uprising also highlights graphically the intense feeling that Tibetans had toward outside interference, whether it came from missionaries wanting to preach the gospel or from Chinese wanting to "pacify" them. All and any intruders were unwelcome. Their overriding motive was to protect the Buddhadharma, which they feared—rightly as it turned out—would be harmed if outsiders (that is, non-Buddhists) gained admittance to their country. Indeed, when the first Christian missionaries came to Lhasa back in the eighteenth century, they had been warmly welcomed. Their personal morality and keen interest in Buddhism recommended them as worthy spiritual seekers. It was only gradually that the *sangha* came to realize that despite their friendliness, their high culture, and their manifest sympathy for the poor, these foreigners were not merely interested in learning about Buddhism but were in fact intent on destroying it through conversion.

In Batang, the Chinese *amban,* or governor, met a fate similar to the missionaries'. The monks of a nearby monastery succeeded in capturing him and, having flayed his skin, they stuffed it with grass and paraded it around town, subsequently using this disgusting image first in a ritual for banishing evil and then for target practice within the monastery, before finally trampling it underfoot.

When the Dowager Empress's general arrived in the local area, the reprisals began at once. Desiring to make himself feared by the Tibetans, he immediately ordered three prisoners to be placed in a cauldron of "cold water, tied hand and foot, but with their heads propped up." A fire was then "built under the cauldron and slowly the water was brought to a boil." Some prisoners "had oil poured upon them and [were] burned alive. Others had their hands cut off and sent back as a warning to those from whom they came. Others [were] taken and, with a yak hitched to each arm and each leg . . . torn in pieces."

Informing the populace that henceforth they should consider themselves subjects of the Qing emperor, General Zhao ordered not only that they were to wear Chinese dress, but also that the men should adopt the hated Manchu queue (pigtail) and desist from sporting the traditional Khampa topknot. This, often dashingly threaded with strands of red-dyed wool, made them "resemble living demons" according to him. The presence of Butcher Zhao, as he was quickly named, "only made confusion worse confounded," in Forrest's account, and it took almost a year and many more atrocities before Zhao succeeded in forcing a peace. It took him all that time to starve into submission the three thousand monks of Chatreng Sampeling Monastery, who had taken to arms with especial ferocity. But when they finally surrendered, he had no compunction in executing every last one of them.

Unexpectedly, Zhao was not without his allies among the local Tibetan population. According to one witness, "in order to curry favour with the Chinese," members of the local Tibetan population brought numbers of their own countrymen in to be beheaded. "Heads fell every day, and so many bodies lay in the streets of Batang that at times the dogs feasted. No one dared touch or bury them, for fear they would be considered friends of the dead and in turn suffer the death penalty."

By the time Zhao had completed his "pacification" of Kham, the Dalai Lama, much disturbed by the news reaching him from the south, especially the suggestion that the general had soled his soldiers' boots with pages of scripture torn from the monasteries' holy books, had left his unwelcoming host in Urgya and relocated to Kumbum Monastery some five hundred miles to the north of Batang and its environs. Kumbum was especially important to the Precious Protector because of its association with Je Tsongkhapa. It was he who had been the progenitor of the reformed Gelug school of Buddhism to which the Dalai Lamas have all belonged. Kumbum was also, as it remains, Amdo's most important religious center, housing in its heyday several thousand monks.

By remarkable coincidence, John Weston Brooke, an English explorer, and the Reverend Ridley, yet another missionary, were present at Kumbum on the day in late October 1906 when the Dalai Lama arrived there. Describing the occasion, they inform us that the Dalai Lama's entourage was preceded by a Chinese band which made a "shrieking" and "diabolical" noise on the approach to Kumbum, "five or six men . . . shuffling along in a gait that was neither a walk nor a run. They were dressed as they liked, played as they liked, and shuffled as they liked." Behind these musicians came the imperial standard bearers, in the same disorder, followed by Tibetan outriders "dressed in wonderful long yellow coats and curious hats made of gilded wood, riding rough, high-spirited ponies . . . Suddenly," they report, "a distinguished-looking Tibetan galloped out of the crowd and shouted to the onlookers to '*koutou.*'"

The Englishmen dismounted from their ponies but "refused to do more, so [the Tibetan official] left us to harangue the Chinese, who were quite indifferent and only laughed and said rude things."

Ridley and Brooke were subsequently granted an audience with the Precious Protector, though it could hardly be counted a success. They found themselves quite unable to persuade him that the British were, as Ridley claimed, "a kind people," still less that if he "would come to India and meet with them and learn to know them, he would not mind their coming to his country." Instead, Brooke claimed that he had "never seen such a hard, expressionless face as that of the Dalai Lama."

The description seems unfair. It was too much to have expected the Precious Protector to be wholly gracious, given that, as Englishmen, the two visitors stood for the enemy who had deprived the Tibetan hierarch of his throne. Besides, we have it on the authority of several other European visitors that the Great Thirteenth was by no means wholly unbending. Years later he formed an unlikely friendship with the British political officer for Sikkim, Sir Charles Bell, who confirms the Dalai Lama's habitually stern expression but notes also the "welcoming smile that softened his features" whenever they met for talks.

The Dalai Lama remained at Kumbum for more than a year. As if the horrific news of Zhao's scripture-trampling marauders in the south were not enough, the Great Thirteenth also had to contend with the lack of discipline he found among the monastic community at Kumbum itself. "Many monks," we are told, "had taken to drinking, smoking and gambling." He therefore made it his business to renew respect for the *vinaya,* the monastic code that regulates both the spiritual and the administrative life of the *sangha.* The Dalai Lama also reinvigorated the academic side of Kumbum's monastic life, paying particular attention to the monks' proficiency in debate. This might have caused resentment as, typically, the monasteries firmly resisted any interference, no matter from whom. But such was the Tibetan leader's prestige, and such his personal magnetism, that he succeeded without alienating his hosts. Indeed, so deeply venerated was he that, day after day throughout his stay at Kumbum, he received countless pilgrims from far and wide, all seeking audiences with him. He would frequently bestow his blessing on crowds of thousands, while to visiting monks he gave spiritual teachings and initiations, ordaining many hundreds. Though it is true that some of Kumbum's officials grumbled at the expense of maintaining him, for as long as he remained with them, the Great Thirteenth enjoyed the highest esteem of the local people.

To be sure, the Dalai Lama's time at this, the greatest of Amdo's religious foundations, was not all gloom. In any case, it is pleasant to think of him enjoying at least some respite from his many difficulties when he went on pilgrimage that fine spring day to Shartsong Monastery and stopped on his way back to give his blessing to the little village of Taktser.

2

A Mystic and a Seer: The Regency Established

The Great Thirteenth's promise to return one day to Taktser was duly recorded by his officials and then, no doubt, completely forgotten. Something of his relationship with the village was preserved when, in middle age, the Precious Protector was asked to confirm the identity of the new incarnation of his friend Taktser Rinpoché, who had recently died. This he did, and the boy entered the monastery at Shartsong. But the time that elapsed between the Great Thirteenth's visit to Taktser in 1907 and his rebirth there in 1935 was so full of incident it is hardly surprising that it was not until long afterwards that anyone noticed the significance of his promise to return.

It was similarly not until many years later that anyone saw the significance of another seemingly trivial deed of the Great Thirteenth. Sometime during 1920, when repair work to the eastern wing of the Potala Palace — the magnificent thousand-chambered seat of government and principal residence of the Dalai Lamas — was being undertaken, the Great Thirteenth gave instructions for a blue bird to be painted on the wall of a staircase that led to the north side of the West Chamber on the floor above. He also called for a white dragon to be painted on its eastern wall. This, it is said, perplexed everyone because there was neither scriptural nor iconographic warrant for such images in these locations. A strict canon governed all forms of representation and their placement, although of course the authority of the Dalai Lama would certainly trump such considerations. It was not until long after that anyone realized the significance of the images. The blue bird represented the year (that of the Water Bird) during which the Great Thirteenth would depart this life (1933). The white dragon indicated the year of the Iron Dragon (1940), in which his successor would be enthroned.

It is notable that high lamas sometimes furnish explicit details of both their death and their next incarnation, including when and where they will be reborn. Occasionally the most highly evolved masters go so far as to give not only the name of the infant into which their stream of consciousness will pass but also those of its parents. But that level of detail is usually available only after intensive investigation, while here, the choice of imagery at the Potala sounds more spontaneous.

Other than these, the Great Thirteenth gave few indications of his intention to withdraw his mind from earthly existence. Ordinarily, high lamas can be expected to do so. But the only other sign the Great Thirteenth vouchsafed was his recent summoning of a Nepalese photographer operating in Lhasa at that time to come and take his portrait, a gesture in which some saw significance. His passing was therefore as great a shock to his attendants as it was to the general populace. So swift was his decline that there were even whisperings of foul play.*

His portrait was taken at the Norbulingka Palace in November 1933. A few weeks later, the Precious Protector developed a cough, though he continued to work as usual. After about a week without improvement, the Great Thirteenth failed to appear at the public audience scheduled at the Upper Tantric College on the twelfth of December. By now he had developed a high fever. Then,

---

* Remarkably, this allegation found its way onto the front page of the *Daily Illini,* the student newspaper of the University of Illinois, on December 20, 1933. Presumably the story was picked up from a British source.

on the sixteenth, the Precious Protector broke with his usual routine of letter writing in the morning and took first to his chair and then to his couch. That night he refused the two bowls of soup he normally took before going to bed.

Sometime after 10 that night, the Lord Chamberlain sounded the alarm. Summoning the other attendants, he instructed them to call the three seniormost members of the court, including the chief secretary and the treasurer. Not having been informed of the Dalai Lama's illness before this moment, they were surprised to learn that the Precious Protector was suddenly very unwell. On arrival, they immediately prostrated themselves and, as is customary whenever a high lama falls ill, begged the Dalai Lama to remain in his body. It is believed that this is under his control and that how and when he dies is a matter of his choosing.

An hour later, the Nechung oracle was ordered to attend — this being the state oracle and the government's go-to supernatural counsel and support. The medium arrived in such a hurry that one account claims he did not even have time to dress properly. He subsequently went into a trance, during which he administered some medicine. It seems that the Dalai Lama tried to refuse this, but the medium forced it on him.

When Nechung came out of his trance, the Precious Protector's doctor contended that the "Seventeen Heroes for Subduing Colds" that the oracle had administered was far too strong for the Dalai Lama's present condition, which, as if in direct confirmation, worsened immediately. By noon the following day, he was unconscious.

A deputation of high lamas was now admitted to the Presence to entreat him further to remain in the body. But he opened his eyes only briefly, breathing his last sometime around 6:30 p.m.

The first that most people knew of the Dalai Lama's passing was when butter lamps were lit on the roofs of the Potala Palace and of nearby Sera Monastery. It was many more days before the news made its way to the farthest reaches of Tibet. Meanwhile, it became incumbent on the government to appoint a regent who would steer the ship of state on a steady course until the new Dalai Lama could be found and educated to the point where he was able to take over the helm. In light of the degree to which the Great Thirteenth had centralized power into his own hands, and the level of involvement he maintained in all aspects of both spiritual and temporal affairs, it is at first sight remarkable that he seems not to have given much thought to his own succession. One might even argue that such negligence is evidence of a certain megalomania. The devout would simply counter that, foreseeing all things, the Dalai Lama merely withdrew his spirit for a brief period in order that he be young and vigorous when it came to meeting the challenges that lay ahead.

Besides, the Dalai Lama did leave a final testament as a guide to those responsible for selecting the regent and looking after the welfare of the Tibetan people until the moment when his successor would reach his majority. It is remarkable for its prescience. Isolated from the world he might be, but the Great Thirteenth had a firm grasp of the great movements of the day. He understood clearly the danger communism spelled to the free practice of religion. Despite the deep misgivings of the monasteries, which were hostile to the notion of a standing army (when necessary they would supply armed monks), he was adamant that Tibet needed a strong and independent military establishment:

> If we are not able to protect our own country, then everyone . . . will be wiped out so completely that not even their names will remain. The estates and property of the monasteries and monks will be annihilated . . . [and] we will be forced to wander the land as servants of our enemies. Everyone will be subjected to torture, and both day and night will be an unending round of fear and suffering. Such a time as this will come for sure!

His words fell on deaf ears, however, and, within a matter of days, a bitter struggle for power broke out.

Ordinarily the regent was chosen from among the high lamas of four particular monasteries, but the Great Thirteenth had caused one of these to be destroyed for its treachery during the recent occupation of Lhasa by a Chinese army. Furthermore, any one of the three most powerful men in Tibet at the time of the Great Thirteenth's demise was in a strong position to seize power from the monasteries. These were Kumbela, the Lord Chamberlain; Tsarong, the former army commander; and Lungshar, an ambitious aristocrat with modernizing tendencies who was Tsarong's implacable foe. Langduen, the ultraconservative but ineffectual chief minister, was not one of them. There was, however, one entity still more powerful than these three men: the combined influence of the three great monasteries in the Lhasa region — those of Ganden, Drepung, and Sera — also known as the Three Seats. As it happened, Tsarong was absent from Lhasa at this time and, not desiring to join the fray, played no part in the events that followed.

It was thus a straightforward contest between Kumbela and Lungshar, with the Three Seats casting the deciding vote. Lungshar's strongest suit in this regard was his professed hostility to the idea of an independent army. At first, however, Kumbela's position looked impregnable. During the last years of the Dalai Lama's life, his authority had been supreme, and for the few days after the Precious Protector "withdrew his spirit," most seem to have anticipated that Kumbela would assume the regency. Besides being the Great Thirteenth's most trusted servant, to whom was delegated the day-to-day running of the household, Kumbela was de facto commander in chief of the *tongdra,* the Dalai Lama's personal bodyguard, which he had formed just a few years previously.

In recruiting the rank and file of this bodyguard, Kumbela's strategy had been to do so solely from among the gentry. His thinking was that, having a better education than the lower orders, they would make better soldiers. Kumbela saw to it that they were well fed and wore specially tailored uniforms, paying for their gold-embroidered insignia out of his own pocket and personally ordering the officers' uniforms from Calcutta. The officers (themselves all members of the aristocracy) even went for training in machine gunnery at the British garrison still stationed at Gyantse. When the Dalai Lama died, it thus seemed certain that Kumbela would exploit his position. Yet for reasons that are not at all clear, he made no attempt to do so. Perhaps he saw his appointment as regent as a foregone conclusion.

Lungshar was quick to exploit this inaction.

Of all the high officials within the late Dalai Lama's government, Lungshar was the most worldly wise, having traveled widely outside Tibet. When the Great Thirteenth came up with a scheme whereby five boys from the gentry class were sent to England for schooling, it was Lungshar who accompanied them. He subsequently visited several European countries, taking careful note of the political systems of each. What seems particularly to have impressed him was the way in which Britain had managed to avoid the violent revolutions against monarchy that had afflicted Europe during the course of the previous century. On returning to Tibet, he therefore set about gathering support for a constitutional settlement that would see some of the Dalai Lama's temporal power vested in a secular authority organized according to democratic principles.

But if his sympathies were for government elected by popular vote, Lungshar's methods were decidedly Machiavellian. When the National Assembly took up the question of Kumbela's culpability in the Precious Protector's unexpected demise, Lungshar cleverly used the occasion to instigate revolt among the Dalai Lama's bodyguard.

In the end, the erstwhile Lord Chamberlain was charged not with murder but with the lesser crime of failing to keep the National Assembly informed of the Dalai Lama's health. For this he was stripped of office, relieved of all his property, and banished to a remote district far from the capital.

With Kumbela out of the way, Lungshar and his supporters could argue for a regency by a council made up of the existing prime minister and two more officials, one monastic and one lay — the layman in question being Lungshar himself. The National Assembly was, however, dominated by the abbots of the Three Seats. While there was considerable support for Lungshar's idea among the more progressive elements of the aristocracy, the conservative faction was bound to take sides with the religious authorities. The result was a stalemate. This in itself was a victory for the conservatives since the inevitable outcome was recourse to the deities. The matter of who should be appointed regent would be decided by divination, while each of the candidates would be a leading figure within the monastic community.

A grand religious ceremony was duly held, which the entire government of several hundred officials attended. Presiding was the ex-abbot of Ganden Monastery. From a total of three possibilities, the name that emerged was that of the youngest, the twenty-four-year-old Reting Rinpoché.

Of all the candidates for regent, Reting Rinpoché was unquestionably the most charismatic. Born to a humble family in central Tibet, he had quickly displayed signs of exceptional ability. It is held that, when he was around five years of age, the young prodigy became angry with his elder sister, stamping his right foot on the ground with such force that it imprinted itself on the very rock on which he was standing. A second indication of genius came not long afterwards, when his mother left him to watch over a pot of *thukpa* (meat broth with noodles) while she went to milk the family cow. After some time, the little boy came running and announced that it was about to boil over so he had closed up the pot. When she came back, his mother saw that he had taken off one of his bootlaces and used it to tie off the neck of the earthenware vessel. A third sign of the boy's high spiritual attainment came on an occasion when he drove a wooden peg into solid rock. He explained that this was to tie his horse to — even though his family did not then own one. This must therefore be a portent, since only the aristocracy and high lamas had horses. The boy had subsequently been recognized by the Great Thirteenth himself as the authentic reincarnation of one of his foremost teachers.

As to the character of the Rinpoché, as a young man he was — according to the testimony of one of his nieces — kind, playful, and solicitous. She also attests to a characteristic of his that many took to be a sign of the highest spiritual attainment, a "delicate fragrance about his person."

Some of the foreigners who met Reting Rinpoché, a man slightly below average height, with enormous protruding ears and a perpetual frown, were less than favorably impressed. Hugh Richardson, then British political officer for Tibet, described him as "gauche," "self-centred," and "immature," while General Sir Philip Neame, who undertook a military inspection of the Tibetan army (at the request of the Tibetan government itself) in 1936, described him as "a very mediocre personage of little personality, brains, or education, and of no particular family, chosen . . . [for] being a nonentity."

Whatever his true qualities, the new regent had been selected by the gods themselves. It might have seemed to some of Lungshar's supporters, therefore, that nothing was to be done. But Reting was young and Langduen, the chief minister, who continued in office, was weak and indecisive. Commenting on the recent installation of electric light in the capital's more important houses (including his own), Langduen timorously remarked that "new things only bring misfortune." If Lungshar acted fast enough, there remained a good chance that he could seize the initiative and achieve the end he desired.

Today, the more secular-minded remember Lungshar as power-hungry and self-serving. To the more pious, he is simply seen as wicked and to have gotten the fate he deserved. What tends to be overlooked is the fact that he seems genuinely to have taken to heart the late Dalai Lama's concerns for the fate of Tibet. Like the Dalai Lama himself, he had acquired from his travels a sense of the momentous events taking place elsewhere in the world. To the east, the Chinese were attempting to reunify following a disastrous civil war and invasion by the Japanese. To the west, Russia, having overthrown dynastic rule by the tsars, was in the process of a violent collectivization of agriculture and industry. To the south, Indian opposition to British rule was increasingly forthright. To the north, Inner Mongolia, although nominally independent, was effectively under Russian control. It was clear to Lungshar that if Tibet were to survive as an independent state in the modern era, it would need to concern itself with the modern world.

The reforms Lungshar had in mind would see the power of the great landed families redistributed among the more numerous (and more progressive) minor aristocracy. This was revolutionary in itself. But what made his ambition especially dangerous from the point of view of the monasteries was the implicit threat to them implied by his intended greater role for the National Assembly. That of the Kashag, the council of ministers, would thereby be downgraded. This would have, as a further consequence, a diminution of the prospective new Dalai Lama's political power when eventually he reached his majority. While at first the monasteries were reassured by Lungshar's professed anti-military stance, gradually the ramifications of his scheme began to dawn on them.

A month after his selection, Reting Rinpoché was formally installed as regent. Meanwhile, Lungshar worked hard to secure support. By mid-March 1934 he felt confident enough to hold his first open meeting. With roughly a quarter of the National Assembly declaring for him, his position was by no means secure, but it was adequate for his purposes at this stage. For now, Lungshar's aim was simply to put a petition to the Kashag. This was designed to undermine the position of its most powerful member, Trimon Shapé.

Lungshar intended to present this petition on May 10, the timing of his submission known to only a few. One of these, an early ally, had by this time decided that his own career prospects were in fact best served by throwing his support behind Trimon. He therefore sent a warning to Trimon that Lungshar was poised to make a move against him. While Lungshar's intentions were almost certainly peaceful, the warning clearly implied that Trimon's life was in danger. Early on the morning of the tenth, therefore, Trimon left his house with several servants and sought an immediate meeting with the regent and the chief minister. Together they decided that Trimon should flee to Drepung Monastery while orders were issued for Lungshar's arrest.

The petition was duly presented to the remaining three members of the Kashag later that morning. In the afternoon, Lungshar was summoned to a meeting of the government department of which he was a member. At first undecided whether to attend or not, he seems to have determined to go on the grounds that he had done nothing illegal and there was some chance that the officials he was to meet with could be brought into the fold. This was a major miscalculation. He was met at the Potala Palace with an arrest order accusing him of serious crimes, including, disastrously, failure to appreciate the kindness of the late Dalai Lama. While waiting for the official who should at this point have ceremonially removed his topknot and robe of office, Lungshar made a bid to escape. He had left the servant to whom he had entrusted his pistol just outside in the corridor. As ill luck would have it, the servant was at that moment on his way back from the latrines downstairs. Recognizing Lungshar's plight, he held out the weapon toward him as his master ran down the stairs. But just as the two men met, the servant was seized by several janitors while Lungshar was overpowered by a palace guard. He was forcibly escorted back to the regent's office.

Having undone Lungshar's topknot and taken his government robe from his back, the official and his assistants began to remove his footwear. As they did so, Lungshar managed to break free and swallow a piece of paper that had fallen out of the first boot. But he was unable to do so a second time as another piece of paper fell out of his other boot when it was removed. On inspection, this had written on it, next to an occult symbol, the fateful words *Do harm to Minister Trimon.*

This was black magic.

Or so the story goes. The alternative version is that the black magic component was a later invention to justify Lungshar's punishment. Trampling on a person's name would, with the aid of a wrathful deity, bring about the violent demise of the victim. A similar tactic had been employed in an attempt on the life of the Great Thirteenth some four decades previously — not so long ago that the event should have been forgotten. On that occasion, the young Dalai Lama, having suffered several bouts of illness, summoned the oracle in an attempt to discover the cause. It transpired that a pair of boots belonging to one of his teachers was implicated. On questioning, the reverend teacher agreed that there did seem to be something strange about the boots: every time he wore them, he suffered a nosebleed. When they were examined, it was found that the sole of one of them contained a piece of paper on which the Dalai Lama's name was written adjacent to the symbol for *shinje she,* Lord of Death*. Again this was black magic, and in this case it was being employed in the most heinous of crimes — there being none greater than the attempted killing of the Precious Protector. As a result, the ex-regent, who was behind the plot, and three accomplices — including the then chief minister — were arrested, charged with treason, and sentenced to death. The Dalai Lama intervened and the death penalty was rescinded, but the ex-regent nonetheless died in mysterious circumstances, apparently drowned in a vat of water. Meanwhile his co-conspirators all had bamboo driven under their nails and received a hundred lashes before being sent into exile. Even the chief minister's wife was forced to wear for a week the *cangue* (a portable pillory consisting of a wooden collar, worn around the neck, to which the victim's hands were shackled).

In Lungshar's case, his crime seemed to his enemies to warrant the severest penalty. Not only had he tried to undermine the position of the Kashag by introducing reforms that must harm religion itself, but also he had resorted to the dark arts. It was thus decided that he should have his eyes put out.

It is arguably a favorable sign that this punishment had not been handed down for so long that no one could be found who had experience of carrying it out. Members of the butcher caste tasked with the operation were forced to rely on the folk memory of their clan. Involving the application of yak knuckles to each temple and a tourniquet tightened until the eyeballs popped out,

* Also known as Yamantaka.

the technique proved successful on one side only. Eventually, the recalcitrant globe was simply gouged out with a knife and the sockets cauterized with boiling oil.

The humiliation of Lungshar (who, though he survived the experience, unsurprisingly lived only a year longer, incarcerated in a dungeon of the Potala Palace) meant that the government of Tibet during the regency period remained, on the one hand, rigidly conservative and, on the other, indecisive with respect to any serious issue with which it was confronted. But what the incident tells us about the politics of Tibet at the time is of considerably less significance than what it tells us about the Tibetan tradition itself. Lungshar's proposed reforms were both moderate and reasonable. Full democracy and the accountability of government to the Tibetan people were not in question, though his plans were a step in that direction. The mere fact that Lungshar could be accused of black magic suggests that the tradition itself rendered Tibet completely unready to take its place in the modern world.

3

A Child Is Born

While Lungshar was in the process of discovering just how premature was his vision of a new Tibet, the search for the new incarnation of the Dalai Lama began in earnest. Following his enthronement as regent in 1934, Reting Rinpoché's primary task was to sift and assess the various signs and portents brought to his attention. An early event concerned the embalmed body of the lately departed Precious Protector. It had been seated, wrapped in gauze, facing south in its burial chamber. But when after some time the embalmers came to put in fresh salt, they found the head inclined toward the east. This they took to be significant, and when it happened again, there could be no doubting its importance.

The utterances of the various oracles associated with the Dalai Lama were also of the greatest interest at this time, and not just what they said but their actions, too. When three of them all turned to the east and threw offering scarves — again not once but twice — this was of clear significance.

Further help came from signs in nature. Among those noted by the monastic officials charged with collating evidence were some curious cloud formations that appeared on the northeastern horizon. There were also some unusual botanical indications. It came to the attention of the authorities that snapdragons had bloomed unexpectedly underneath the stairs that stood at the eastern end of the public discourse area adjacent to the Jokhang, the most important temple in Lhasa. And then there was the matter of the strange star-shaped fungi that appeared at the base of a wooden pillar standing to the northeast of the shrine where the late Dalai Lama had been entombed.

It was concluded that, taken together, all these signs indicated that the search for the new incarnation should be conducted in the east. What was needed now was greater precision. More than a thousand miles separated Lhasa from what was then considered to be the border with China. It was in hopes of getting a more fine-grained answer that, during the summer of 1935, the regent traveled to the monastery founded and consecrated by the Second Dalai Lama during the first decade of the sixteenth century. This was Chokor Gyal in southern Tibet. Situated at a remarkable fifteen thousand feet, the monastery is overlooked by three mountains, each regarded as the abode of a different tutelary, or guardian, deity.

Of still greater significance, however, is the lake that lay half a day's journey away, Lhamo Lhatso. This is held by tradition to be the dwelling place of Palden Lhamo — the Glorious Goddess — the protector deity most closely associated with the Dalai Lamas. These protector deities (of whom somewhere between fifteen and twenty are fully attested) are central to the Tibetan tradition. They are quite distinct from the tutelary deities; their chief characteristic being to channel the "wrathful," or negative, aspects of particular fully enlightened beings. This wrath is deployed to guard both the doctrine itself and the community of practitioners. It can also be made available to communities and individuals as an aid to overcoming obstacles. In the case of some protectors, for example Yamantaka (Lord of Death), they may also be taken as meditational deities, whereby the form and attributes of the deity are (imaginatively) assumed by individual practitioners as a means to overcome their own negative thoughts and emotions in the quest for Enlightenment. But these are specialist practices; on the whole, the protectors are treated with great caution. It is well understood that, misdirected, their fearsome energy can cause untold harm.

The power of the protectors can be appreciated in their iconography: the Glorious Goddess, Palden Lhamo, is described as having a dark blue body—

> in her right hand she brandishes a club over the brains of those who have broken their promises to her; in her left hand, on a level with her heart, she holds a skull-cup filled with blood and other substances used in exorcism. Her mouth is open and between her sharp teeth she gnaws on a human corpse. As she does so, her joyous yelps resemble roaring thunder. She has three red, round eyes, which gleam like lightning. Her yellowing hair stands on end and her eyelashes and beard blaze like the fire which flames up at the end of cosmic eons. In her right ear she wears a lion, in her left, a snake. On her head she wears a diadem of five skulls, while round her neck is draped a garland of fifteen freshly severed heads, dripping blood.

Small wonder that, faced with depictions of these extraordinary beings for the first time, the Victorian explorers of Tibet were convinced that the Buddhism they found practiced there was a debased form of the religion, which, cut off from its original sources, had degenerated into mere devil worship. (One wonders what the first Buddhists to travel in the West made of Christians praying to a deity disfigured and nailed to a cross.) In any case, what those explorers failed to realize was that, from the Tibetan perspective, the protector deities, for all their gruesome attributes, are ultimately agents of compassion.

Following his retreat at the Second Dalai Lama's monastery, and after conducting the appropriate *sadhanas* (rituals) to propitiate the Glorious Goddess, the young regent did indeed experience a detailed vision in the waters of the lake. First, he saw three letters of the alphabet (actually syllables), *Ah, Ka*, and *Ma.* There followed a vision of a three-storied monastery with three distinguishing features: its second story was painted the color of turquoise, its top story was adorned with a golden roof, and there was a "thread-like" path leading east from the monastery to a hill, on top of which stood a single-story building with a blue roof.

Having noted down the contents of his vision, the Rinpoché took these details as the object of further meditative investigation. On returning to Lhasa, he also consulted with Nechung and other oracles over the course of a full year. At the end of this time, he ordained three search parties. Each headed by a *tulku* (a reincarnate lama) and assisted by three senior monks, these search parties were to conduct investigations in three far eastern districts. One search party was dispatched to the southeast, another went roughly due east, while the third went to the northeast.

Not that Reting Rinpoché's instructions went entirely unopposed. There were those who were skeptical that the Dalai Lama would take rebirth so far from Lhasa: Would there not be a danger that if he was from some remote part of the borderlands, he might fall into Chinese hands? Surely the gods would not take that risk? Furthermore, there was a promising local candidate, a boy born into the family of the Great Thirteenth Dalai Lama. Soon after his birth, a horse from the Dalai Lama's stables had broken loose and run straight to the infant's house, a credible indication that there was a connection between the Precious Protector and the baby boy. But Reting was adamant that the first symbol he had seen in the waters of the lake referred to Amdo, the eastern province. In clear confirmation, the oracle of Samye Monastery took off his breastplate and gave it to Kewtsang Rinpoché, the *tulku* appointed to lead the party that would go to Amdo.

The three teams left Lhasa during the autumn of 1936. As it turned out, the two that went east and southeast found not a single plausible candidate, while even the one that was sent to Amdo did not at first find any that seemed promising. Nevertheless, one significant early event was a meeting between Kewtsang Rinpoché and the Panchen Lama — after the Dalai Lama, the second-most-important and powerful *tulku* in the land — who was then residing at Riwoche.

The Ninth Panchen Lama was at this time living in self-imposed exile. He had fled his monastery at Tashilhunpo in protest at the Great Thirteenth's imposition of new taxes to fund the army. When the Dalai Lama found out, he had been outraged, sending an armed party to apprehend him. It arrived too late, however, and the Panchen made good his departure, first to Mongolia and then to China. "It is not known why you have left your monastery," wrote the Precious Protector subsequently, "in which you should now be sitting in meditation. You seem to have forgotten the sacred history of your predecessors and wandered away to a desert . . . like a moth attracted by lamplight."

Traditionally, the Panchen and Dalai Lamas serve each other as religious teachers in successive incarnations, the older one acting as mentor to the younger. This was most famously the case when the Fourth Panchen Lama tutored both the Fourth and the Great Fifth Dalai Lamas (there have so far been two Dalai Lamas acclaimed as Great, the Fifth and the Thirteenth, though it is whispered already of the present incarnation). It is also true that there are some who point to the fact that — at least according to one way of reckoning — the Panchen Lama lineage is the senior lineage. And it is indisputable that, considered as a spiritual master, the First Panchen was more highly accomplished than the First Dalai Lama. There had thus always been rivalry, not so much between the individuals themselves as between their respective *labrangs,* or estates. In this instance, it is generally believed that the Panchen Lama, a man of "singular sweetness and charm," according to Sir Charles Bell, had been put up to his eastern escapade by the men surrounding him.

That the Panchen Lama's animosity was not personal is attested to by the fact that, when he met with the search party leader, the Panchen Lama gave Kewtsang Rinpoché a list of candidates whose names had been brought to his attention and whom he had investigated by the usual methods of meditative inquiry. It included the name of Lhamo Thondup, the boy who would eventually be proclaimed Dalai Lama.

Thus equipped, the search party made its way to Kumbum Monastery, arriving in the spring of 1937, where it was greeted by a large number of local dignitaries, both monastic and lay.

Not until winter did Kewtsang Rinpoché and his men finally reach the village of Taktser, however. Perhaps one reason for their slowness to investigate the boy there was the fact that the family into which the candidate had been born had already yielded an important incarnation — that of the Taktser Rinpoché, his older brother, and reincarnation of the man with whom the Great Thirteenth had enjoyed a picnic lunch three decades previously. By now, the new Taktser Rinpoché, thirteen years older than Lhamo Thondup, was a novice at Shartsong Monastery. It must have seemed highly unlikely that the same family could harbor one still greater. Besides, it was not as if the parents were particularly distinguished. They didn't even speak proper Tibetan but a kind of hybrid language known as *siling ke,* which necessitated that the team take an interpreter with them.

Yet the search party was startled to realize that the architectural features of the birthplace of the child matched precisely the details provided by Reting Rinpoché on the basis of his vision. And they were immediately impressed with the now two-year-old boy they met. A member of the party later recalled how he went straight up to Kewtsang Rinpoché and "pulled the rosary [he] wore round his neck and said, 'give me this!'

"'Tell me who I am and then I will give it to you,' replied Kewtsang Rinpoché.

"'You are an *Aka** from Sera. *Mani, mani,*'† the boy replied spontaneously.

"'Who is the man [next door]?' asked Kewtsang Rinpoché, and the boy replied, 'Tsedrung Lobsang!'"

Then he pointed to the interpreter and gave his name too. According to the official account, he gave all this information spontaneously and "without any hesitation or doubt." The members of the search party also noted that his mannerisms were "extraordinarily profound for his age."

Such were the first miracles. For his own part, the Dalai Lama himself remembers almost nothing of this first interview, save for the piercing eyes of the man who subsequently became his senior personal assistant. As the search party went to leave Taktser the following day, they did so with heavy hearts; they longed to stay and bask in his presence. When the boy "firmly insisted" they take him with them, it was only by his parents' playing a trick on little Lhamo Thondup that they were able to prevent the boy from following after.

So as not to arouse the suspicions — or, presumably, the hopes — of the

* Probably meaning "uncle" but used by children to refer to any authority figure.

† *Mani* probably refers either to a *mani* stone — a stone with a prayer inscribed on it — or the prayer (mantra) itself.

family, Kewtsang Rinpoché had disguised himself as a servant during this first visit to the boy's house. The search party had portrayed itself as a group of pilgrims en route to nearby Shartsong. After a brief return to Kumbum Monastery, however, in order to confer with his colleagues (and, we may assume, with the deities), and to send a message to the government back in Lhasa, Kewtsang Rinpoché together with his team returned to Taktser a few weeks later.

On this occasion he did so in his official capacity as head of one of the search parties looking for the new Dalai Lama and warranted to thoroughly examine the child. Along the way, the search party met with a number of auspicious signs, faithfully recorded. First, they encountered several people carrying barrels of curd, milk, and water. Second, they met with a young Chinese close to the house who suggested a route that took them to the front door of the boy's house rather than the more usual direct route which led to the back door. Third, just as they reached the door, they heard the sound of a conch shell being blown from the top of Kumbum Monastery, calling the monks to assembly. Finally, on entering the house, they heard a cuckoo — the first, they noted, of spring.

It was teatime when they arrived, and while refreshments were being served, the boy appeared. Wearing a kind of "jump-suit," he had a "look of joy on his face."

With the usual courtesies discharged, now came the moment of truth. Could the child recognize what had belonged to him in his former life from among other objects that did not? Kewtsang Rinpoché began by holding up two dark-colored rosaries and asking which one the little boy wanted. The right one, as it turned out. The same happened with a pair of yellow rosaries: the boy correctly chose the one that had belonged to the Great Thirteenth. There followed a near disaster. On being shown two canes and pausing for a while, the little boy picked out the wrong one. But after a moment, he picked them both up again and examined "the handle and the tip of each with concentration." They were both of the same design, the only difference being in the tip, one of which was made of bronze, the other of plain iron. This time, he held on to the correct one, "holding it straight with its tip to the floor." In itself, this near mistake was a most auspicious sign: it was later recalled that the Great Thirteenth had in fact given away the first cane to a colleague. That must be why the child had picked it up and then put it down.

There followed a test involving three lengths of fabric which the boy had to identify from among others before he was presented with the final two objects. These were a small hand drum made of ivory, and another, larger *damaru,* a drum with two faces. The first the Great Thirteenth had used for summoning his attendants; the second was a more elaborate instrument furnished with a "golden belt and [a] brocade handle." Most children would no doubt have selected the larger, gaudier of the two instruments, but without hesitation, the small boy chose correctly and, "holding it in his right hand, he played it with a big smile on his face; moving around so that his eyes could look at each of us from close up. Thus, the boy displayed his occult powers." The four members of the search party were left spellbound.

That night, staying with the family, Kewtsang Rinpoché made further inquiries. The test had been highly persuasive but was by no means the end of the matter. It must therefore have been somewhat disconcerting when he asked the child's parents whether any auspicious signs had accompanied the birth of their son. "No," they replied, "nothing of that kind." From some of the local people, however, they learned that there had been, among other indications, a rainbow directly over the house at around the time of the birth. Also, the boy's father had been seriously ill and in fact had nearly died. But when the child was born, the father had enjoyed a miraculous recovery. And it was remembered that in the past, whenever a great lama had been reborn in the locality, it had been presaged by a series of natural calamities. In this case, there had been four years of successive crop failures, and the boy's family had themselves lost some of their most valuable livestock. Five of their best horses bolted one day and leaped over a cliff to their deaths below. Then seven of their mules sickened and died, one by one. Thus encouraged, when they finally turned in that night, the members of the search party were so excited that none of them could sleep, "even for a moment."

The skeptical reader will doubtless see this whole account as a classic example of myth-making. There is even some support for this view from within the tradition itself. The Great Fifth Dalai Lama — whose birth is said to have been accompanied by a rain of flower-shaped snowflakes — wrote disparagingly in his autobiography about the selection procedure he himself underwent. In his case it was less formal, with only his teacher present. When he was shown the "images and rosaries," he could, by his own account, "utter no words" of recognition. Nonetheless, when his teacher went out of the room, the Dalai Lama heard him say, "'I am absolutely convinced he recognised the objects.'" To be fair, the present Dalai Lama disputes a straightforward reading of this passage, cautioning that the Great Fifth had a "very sarcastic" style of writing which ought not to be taken at face value.

We should remember, however, that the word "myth" has come to denote something that "didn't really happen" and has thus become a generally pejorative term. Yet this development rests on the assumption that the only events that can be securely known to be true are those that can be verified empirically. The point to be borne in mind is that from the Buddhist perspective, the way things *really* are is quite different from the way science tells us they are. Science leaves out karma (the fruit, or consequences to us and to our future selves, of our actions), and it leaves out the supernatural. What looks, from a modern perspective, to be "mythological" and therefore not actually or even possibly true is considered by the tradition to be both possibly and in many cases actually true.*

---

* It is also worth remembering that the dominance of this impoverished view of what is possibly true is a very recent development in the history of thought. Most people, most of the time, have taken the larger view that our senses are not the only source of reliable evidence — even if the contrary idea has been around as far back as we can see. In the West, the ancient Greek philosopher Democritus, a contemporary of Gautama Buddha, is associated with this position.

4

The View from the Place of the Roaring Tiger: Tibet's Nameless Religion

It is often said that the present Dalai Lama comes from a humble peasant background, but this is not strictly accurate. According to family legend, his ancestors served as soldiers in the army of Tibet's greatest monarch, the seventh-century King Songtsen Gampo. Subsequently, they lived for many generations as nomads, herding their flocks from place to place before eventually settling in the region of Taktser. By the time of the Manchu conquest of China and the Tibetan borderlands in the mid-seventeenth century, the family had become relatively prosperous, and for the next two hundred years that remained the case. But then, toward the end of the nineteenth century, disaster struck. The village was destroyed during a rebellion against Manchu rule, and the family, made destitute, was reduced to living in "grinding poverty" in the caves of the surrounding hills.

It was not until one of its members was recognized as the reincarnation of a famous lama that the family's fortunes revived. This was Taktser Rinpoché, the man with whom the Great Thirteenth shared the picnic. (He was also the great-uncle of the present Dalai Lama.) Because of the continued danger, the young prodigy was taken as a child to Mongolia to be educated. There he gained a reputation as a great teacher and, returning home in middle age, is said to have brought with him a vast fortune, including ten thousand camels. This is surely an exaggeration, but as a result of their now famous scion's generosity, the lama's relatives were able to buy back the land they had lost and to build a house that, in the words of one of the Dalai Lama's older brothers, was "one of the best in the village . . . a new Chinese style home that was large and spacious." The family into which the present Dalai Lama was born was thus one of petty landowners. They were not aristocrats to be sure, but neither were they members of the very large class of people that was directly dependent on the monastic or aristocratic estates. Employing three servants (one of them Chinese, another a Hui Muslim), they owned "over fifty sheep, a number of yaks, and several *dzomo*" (a female cross between a yak and a cow).

Entered from the lee side, the new Dalai Lama's family home was a miniature fortress built around all four sides of its internal courtyards, at the center of which stood a pole hung with prayer flags bleached by the sun and torn by the constant breeze blowing in off the nearby mountain range. There were no windows in the outer walls, however, and the few internal openings were covered with rice paper, not glass. The southern wing of the house included a dog kennel and a sheep pen, while the northern wing contained the family chapel next to the best room — the room in which visitors were received — and the main bedroom. The east wing was taken up by the kitchen, which was divided into two equal halves, and included the main living space. There was a large stove and a tub for water; one side of the space had a wooden floor while the other was of compacted earth. The west wing served as a cow barn and stable, with a storeroom and a guest room adjacent. Yet it was not in the guest room but in the stable, alongside the cattle, that the children were brought into the world. The first to survive was Tsering Dolma, a daughter born in 1917. She was followed by three sons — Taktser Rinpoché (1922), Gyalo Thondup (1928), and Lobsang Samten (1933) — before the Precious Protector, who was born, according to the Tibetan (lunar) calendar, on the fifth day of the fifth month in the (female) Wood Pig year of the sixteenth Rabjung calendrical cycle — or July 6, 1935, according to the Western calendar.

Up at cockcrow in the dark hour before dawn, mother to light the fire, father to take the horses to water, the family lived, until they moved to Lhasa when Lhamo Thondup was officially acclaimed, the rugged but satisfying life of pastoralists everywhere. At the time of the boy's birth, the village comprised some thirty homesteads and so, we can assume, had a population approaching two hundred. Because children in such communities were seen as a boon, not a burden, families tended to be large — while there was no question of grandparents moving out. Yet childhood was something of a contest with nature, and life tended not to be long. With no doctors within many days' walk, still less a hospital, it is little wonder that of the sixteen children the Dalai Lama's mother bore, only seven survived into adulthood. Nonetheless, the eldest recalled in his autobiography that he and his siblings lived a "happy and contented life in our remote village," adding that they "found it strange when the occasional travellers passing through found it necessary to express sympathy with us on account of what they perceived to be our hard lot."

For food, the main staple was *tsampa,* roasted barley flour made edible by adding either tea, milk, or *chang* (barley beer) and kneaded into small balls in a bowl. Another staple was potato, which featured at most meals, but legumes were scarce except in their brief season. There was fresh meat, though in the autumn months only, this being the time when the animals were ready for slaughter. For the rest of the year, dried meat had to suffice. The only exception to this rule was if a beast died unexpectedly. When an animal was brought to the table, it was honored by being consumed in its entirety. Everything that could be eaten was eaten; anything not edible was put to use. The intestines, carefully drawn, were used as casings for sausage and stuffed with congealed blood and gobbets of fat, and *tsampa* flour. Brains and brawn, tripe, liver, and lights (or lungs) were all washed, seasoned, and roasted. The lights were considered a special delicacy, while some of the tripe was set aside and used for storing butter. The kidneys, nestled in sheaths of fat, were cooked in the glowing embers of the hearth. The trotters too made good eating, while the horn was used for making glue.

In the summer, raspberries and strawberries and bilberries could be picked wild in the woods nearby, while from the family vegetable plot came radishes and other salad foods and wheat for milling. Peas were grown for fodder, and there was dairy produce aplenty. But above all, in this household there were baked goods in abundance: deep-fried *khabse* cookies and plump loaves of bread, rolls fat with butter and sugar and raisins, and sticky dumplings soft as pillows, all made in the Amdo style. Even today, family members recall with wistful pride the delicious confections of the *gyalyum chenmo* (literally, the Great Royal Mother).

Because the household economy depended for its health on the produce grown and the livestock reared, with the occasional sale or purchase of a horse, every storm rolling in from Kyeri, the mountain in the shadow of which the village stood, was watched with apprehension. A single hailstorm could destroy the labor of many weeks, and the house had to be battened down every time. Yet in spite of the frequent violence of the climate, sheep and goats, pigs, yaks, *dri* (the female counterpart of a yak), and *dzo* lived alongside the horses and the human folk in symbiotic kinship. Apart from the weather (the winters were bitter, and snow came often), the only natural enemies universally acknowledged were the wolf and the *hu-hu* — bands of marauding men of the local Hui population.

Though wolves rarely attacked people, a wolf pack could easily carry off a flock of sheep or, on occasion, bring down cattle and sometimes even horses. No surprise, then, that the man who came home with a wolf carcass was considered a hero, and wolf hunting was an important activity, though other predators — mainly foxes and lynx — were hunted as well.

But the *hu-hu* were more to be feared than any wolf pack. Descendants of Central Asian traders who had settled in China during the Middle Ages, the Hui constituted the principal ethnic group, other than the Tibetans, settled in the region. Every so often they would conduct raids among the Tibetan community, scouring the countryside for plunder. Then as now, the Tibetans lived mostly in the more remote areas, while the Hui — still for the most part traders — were found in and around the larger settlements, notably Siling, where there was a large mosque. And while on the whole the Tibetans lived quietly off the land, the Hui, who were more directly exposed to the greater Chinese economy, were more restive. Especially during the declining years of the Qing dynasty and then, more recently, during the Chinese civil war which broke out during the late 1920s, conditions were harsh, and from time to time unrest led to looting. The situation was complicated by the fact that, following the fall of the Qing, the Hui elite had joined forces with the Chinese Nationalist Guomindang party. The Hui leader Ma Bufang was one of their number, and it was his soldiers who, not long before the birth of the Dalai Lama, had fought a battle with the Tibetans and slaughtered not only the combatants but their children too. Joseph Rock, the Austro-American explorer, writing in *National Geographic,* described how their little heads were "strung about the walls of the Moslem [Hui] garrison like a garland of flowers."

Yet if wolves and marauding gangs were a perennial threat to the family's security, a threat in many ways still more serious was that posed by entities of quite a different order. This threat was described by the Dalai Lama's mother in her autobiography, where she speaks of the visits of a *kyirong,* a type of ghost that can change its form at will. The first haunting the Great Mother recalls occurred when she lay gravely ill. On this occasion, the *kyirong* manifested as a young girl who appeared in a dream, but who remained visible after the Great Mother awoke. The dream girl held out a bowl of what at first sight seemed to be Chinese tea, but which turned out to be blood. As the patient tried to sit up in bed, the ghost "slipped to the door, laughing all the while, and disappeared."

On another occasion, the Dalai Lama's mother was sitting beside her ailing newborn. All of a sudden, she heard first the heavy footsteps of the *kyirong* on the roof of the house, then the sound of it descending to the door and unlatching it. The *kyirong,* she wrote, came in "and stood beside me." Thinking that the ghost — the appearance of which is not described — could not harm her child, the *gyalyum chenmo* took the baby up in her arms. But then the lamps, which she had just lit, flickered and went out. The next thing she knew, the child was crying on the floor ten feet away, though the "lamps were once more lit, and I was still sitting upright. I was not aware how my child had got to the floor." For the next fourteen days, the baby was severely ill, "his eyes swollen out of all proportion. He cried constantly, and nothing I could do would comfort him. In the mornings I would notice bloody scratch marks in and around his eyes, and there were bloodstains on his cheeks. Three weeks later his crying ceased, but he seemed lifeless. When he could finally open his eyes, to my horror [they] had turned from brown to blue. He had become blind."

The *kyirong* was not finished with the family yet, however, and appeared some time later in the form of an old man. After this visit, her baby's eyes became swollen again while an older daughter's eyes also became infected. This time, the son's illness was fatal; he died just past his first birthday.

These stories are worth relating, as they give a clear picture of the world into which the Dalai Lama was born. It was a world enchanted. Not enchanted in the optimistic Disney sense of frolicking fairy princes and princesses, but in the darker sense of the visible world possessed by a realm of beings only rarely seen. In this conception of nature, humans are largely unwelcome intruders on earth, who must contend with a hidden host, the jealous guardians of territory considered by these entities as theirs by right. It was a world that would have been familiar to countless millions of people elsewhere at this time. Among the country dwellers of Ireland, for example, the *aes sidhe,* the "Fair Folk," were still well attested, and even today we hear of Laplanders sure that their farms are guarded by trolls.

If there is a major difference between the folk beliefs of Tibetans and those of other peoples, it is only the strength of the hold they had — and to some extent continue to have — over the popular imagination. Many scholars speak of these folk beliefs in terms of Tibet's "nameless religion." It is not just that houses are haunted by shape-shifting ghosts. Every feature of the landscape and every creature dwelling within it falls under the aegis of some sprite or spirit or deity. Even the bolts of lightning in a storm were said to issue from the mouths of celestial dragons. Every mountain, every lake, every river, every stream and waterfall, the forests, the wildernesses, even each individual tree and shrub belongs in some sense to one or more god or godling. So too does every valley, field, and pathway, not to mention every town, village, and even monastery. If that were not enough, the very stars and planets above have their attendant deity. Father Desideri, an eighteenth-century Jesuit missionary to Tibet, wrote of the "dreadful and tedious solitude" of the territory he crossed on his way to Lhasa. He was quite wrong. For Tibetans, their country, so barren and empty to the European eye, positively brims with life unseen. There are minor deities (known as *lha*) in every strange rock formation, every cave, and every cavern. Even the tools of agriculture, the implements of the kitchen, the saddles and tack of horses, the harness of yak, *dri,* and mule have their presiding spirits. And woe betide anyone who neglects to appease the hearth gods. For the nomadic population of Tibet (much smaller in size today than it used to be, but perhaps great enough to account for half the country's total population* during the period in question), these hearth gods are of particular importance. They are "strange jealous creatures [that] swarm at the rising of the smoke in a new tent, and take proprietary though at times perverse interest in the new hearth. Because of their displeasure, children die or are born dead. Their frightful blows bring blindness, strange swellings and the swift rotting of anthrax . . . What tent can hope for peace if the hearthstone spirits are angry?"

There is, then, no place or object that does not fall within the purview of some unseen being which, like the *kyirong,* may take on outward form from time to time and as occasion demands — with which human beings must contend: entities like the *shi dre,* the *gson dre,* and the *rollang.* The *shi dre* is the form most often assumed by victims of calamity such as violent death — whether by rockfall or by murder. In the latter case, the deceased may pursue the perpetrator of the crime relentlessly until he too comes to a hideous end. The *gson dre* are, by contrast, a kind of spirit whose interest is restricted to women, mainly at night, whose bodies they inhabit and whose actions they control. This demon's hapless victims become its plaything, bringing misfortune and lingering disease — no doubt often venereal — to those women it possesses. The *rollang* are similar to the zombies and undead familiar to the Western imagination. These take possession of a corpse at the very moment when the spirit animating it departs and, having done so, wreak havoc among the living.

Some of these unseen beings are more powerful than others. The mountain gods, for example, are of great importance in that they command the loyalty of many, while the influence of the hearth gods extends only to those who come into contact with the hearth's fire. The influence of the *lu,* or *naga,* is restricted to bodies of water. Nonetheless, in every case, because of their nature, anyone wishing to live in peace must perforce enter into relationship

* It is impossible to give an accurate number for the total population of Tibet. Even today, no reliable numbers exist. Suffice it to say that Tibetans have traditionally claimed around 6 million, while the Chinese offer a figure around half this.

with these beings. Similarly, anyone wishing to embark on some enterprise, whether it be a journey by land or a river crossing or the building of a house or the pitching of a tent, must take care to identify on whose territory they will be encroaching and take appropriate measures to appease and propitiate them.

In most cases, offerings are made—whether of food, money, or prayer. For propitiation of the mountain gods, it is usual to build cairns—sometimes made of animal horns and generally adorned with prayer flags—and, one day in the year, to offer weapons. To the hearth deities are made daily offerings of *tsampa* flour. In the past, some of the more powerful deities would demand blood sacrifice, though since the advent of the Buddhadharma, superior methods using only symbolic sacrifice are now employed—and to better effect. A highly trained adept may call on the gods to produce rain or to avert hailstorms. But some of the more troublesome minor beings, such as the *kyirong,* can be extremely difficult to deal with. Certain kinds of wood smoke can be helpful, especially that of the juniper tree or of particular types of rhododendron. In some circumstances, the performance of meritorious deeds, such as redeeming animals destined for slaughter, may prove effective. In others, a scapegoat may be required. Tibet's first Western-trained physician, Dr. T. Y. Pemba, describes in his autobiography how, when he fell sick with a mysterious illness at the age of around thirteen, his family called on the services of some monks from their local monastery. For several days they recited prayers and chanted, but when the boy's condition continued to deteriorate, his parents resorted to more drastic measures. They bought a sheep that was destined for slaughter—the choice of animal being determined by the fact that the boy had been born in a Sheep year, reckoned according to the Tibetan lunar calendar. It was then painted and kept "almost as a pet." When this, too, failed to bring about any improvement, a ritual using a human scapegoat was performed. This entailed finding another youth to participate, since, Dr. Pemba explains, "it was believed that in this ritual, my disease would be transferred to the other boy." For this reason, "only a very poor family was likely to allow one of its children to take part."

Unfortunately for Dr. Pemba (but presumably to the relief of the scapegoat), the ritual did not work. At first, everyone was perplexed. But when Dr. Pemba's family "found out that, the day before [I fell sick], I had been awful enough to urinate in the stream where a fierce deity was believed to live, they were sure this had brought on my illness." They began to leave offerings of food at the water's edge and begged the deity to relent. "I suppose he forgave me because in a few days I became much better," he wrote, though he later concluded that the illness was meningitis.

Dr. Pemba takes a thoroughly modern view of his illness. What this viewpoint lacks from the traditional perspective is a plausible account of *why* these events occurred in the first place. Why did Dr. Pemba fall ill? Why did the Great Mother find her infant suddenly on the floor? To say simply that the one acquired an infection and that the other merely imagined that she had not fallen asleep lacks the explanatory power of a supernatural cause. And for all the Dalai Lama's interest in contemporary scientific endeavor, this world in which human beings must contend with supernatural beings was the one into which he was born and the existence of which, to this day, he does not disavow.

5

"Lonely and somewhat unhappy": A Hostage in All but Name

Although Kewtsang Rinpoché was certain he had found the authentic reincarnation of the Great Thirteenth, there remained two other candidates on the Panchen Lama's list to examine. The first child the search party interviewed after returning from Taktser turned out to be more promising than any other they had seen so far, apart from Lhamo Thondup. But this one was too shy even to touch any of the objects that had belonged to the Great Thirteenth. He was subsequently identified as the reincarnation of a lesser figure. The other child unfortunately discounted himself in the most comprehensive manner by dying before he could be examined. This brought to an end the Rinpoché's work, and he submitted his report to the government in a coded telegram as well as by messenger traveling on horseback. It was now left to the regent to look at the evidence supplied by all three search parties and to consult with the oracles. Why it took several months for his reply to come back is not clear, but among the reasons must have been the fraught political situation prevailing in the Amdo area at that time.

Following the fall of the Manchu dynasty, the Nationalist government, now under the leadership of Chiang Kai-shek, had come to power in China. But already its authority was being seriously challenged by Mao Zedong's Communists, and civil war had broken out. Crucial to the Nationalists' campaign to hold off a Communist army that crossed the Yellow River in 1936 was the Hui Muslim warlord Ma Bufang. By annihilating the Communists in a fierce battle, he succeeded in establishing himself as governor of Qinghai, the western Chinese province that claimed much of Amdo as its own territory. This he ruled with little regard for the central government.

Kewtsang Rinpoché realized correctly that if Ma came to know of the strong likelihood that the infant Dalai Lama was under his jurisdiction, there was every chance that not only would he seek to extort large sums of money from the Tibetans, but also that he might try to send a military escort with the boy to Lhasa. If this happened, it would give the Chinese government the opportunity to claim a presence in the Tibetan capital. The search party leader thus determined to keep the child's identity secret and announce only that he was one of several promising candidates.

In the meantime, the infant prodigy was taken by his parents in the fall of 1937 to Kumbum Monastery, where he would reside until his final confirmation by the authorities in Lhasa. There was nothing unusual in this: boys would be "given" to a monastery, often at an early age — though it was rare for one quite so young. In the case of the Dalai Lama, his parents decided that Lobsang Samten, his next elder brother, should also enter the *sangha* at this time so that at least little Lhamo Thondup would have a companion close to his own age. That their eldest son, the sixteen-year-old Taktser Rinpoché, was already studying at the monastery must have given them further comfort at the thought of leaving their youngest child there. Yet despite the fact that the three brothers would be together, the little boy was distraught when he realized that his mother meant to leave him at the monastery, and he begged to be taken home. In his autobiography, Taktser Rinpoché wrote how Lhamo Thondup was soon joined in his lamentation by Lobsang Samten, and recalled how, "a last attempt to distract my little brother by getting him to look at the dancing snowflakes outside the window . . . failed, and then we were all three in floods of tears."

Thus began what, as the Dalai Lama later wrote — with how much understatement we can only guess — was "a lonely" and "somewhat unhappy period of my life." Having two brothers as companions hardly made up for the separation from his mother, from whom he was barely weaned. By way of compensation, he quickly formed a close attachment to the man he called Ponpo, the monk attendant who was his principal caregiver. The memory of time spent enfolded in the warmth of this monk's robes never left him, and he has spoken of how, for comfort, he would sometimes suck a mole on the man's face "until it became red." Indeed, he became so attached to Ponpo that he could not bear to lose sight of his robe. Even when his attendant was in the kitchen, the little boy would watch the hem of his garment through the curtain that separated the cooking area from his living quarters, lying on the floor to do so. Yet although the outsider is horrified at the thought of a child barely out of infancy being torn from its mother's breast and handed over to unknown male caretakers, the Dalai Lama himself feels no animosity either toward his parents or toward the system that dealt the blow.

Kumbum turned out to be a decidedly bracing environment. While his brother Lobsang Samten was having lessons, the Dalai Lama "had no one to play with," and he remembers "peering round the curtain in the doorway to try to attract his attention without letting his tutor see me." On one occasion, the four-year-old Dalai Lama watched horrified as a young monk was beaten for some failure in his studies, though he also remembered that the teacher who beat the boy "was very nice to me, and . . . would give me peaches as I sat inside his robe." And yet while it might look as though there were advantages in being a candidate for the highest office in the land, these were unevenly granted. The future Dalai Lama and his two brothers also had an uncle — a brother of their father — at the monastery, to whom the younger ones took "a childish dislike," partly on account of the mustache of which he was unbecomingly proud, and partly on account of the fact that he was often cross with them. On one never-to-be-forgotten occasion, the little boy muddled the pages of scripture his uncle was reading, at which he "picked me up and slapped me hard. He was extremely angry and I was terrified. For literally years afterwards I was haunted by his very dark pockmarked face and fierce moustache. Thereafter, whenever I caught sight of him, I became very frightened."

As the Dalai Lama confessed later, "for the most part" he was "quite unhappy" during his time at Kumbum. The fact that he was considered possibly to be the earthly manifestation of Chenresig counted for little. "As far as I knew, I was just one small boy among many."

While waiting for word to come back from the regent, and hoping to fool the governor, Ma Bufang, Kewtsang Rinpoché requested permission to test an additional ten boys at Kumbum Monastery. The governor objected to the venue and proposed another, which the Tibetans were compelled to accept. When Ma Bufang was informed that the boy from Taktser had performed more successfully than the other candidates and that the search party was requesting permission to take him to Lhasa for further tests, the governor's interest was aroused and he ordered that all the candidates be brought to his headquarters in Xining so he could conduct his own examination. More dangerous still, the child who had so impressed the search party also made the greatest impression on the governor. Ma Bufang advised the Tibetans that this was undoubtedly the one they were looking for. It was now inevitable that he would use the child as a bargaining chip.

Several months after this event, the Lhasa authorities delivered the momentous news that the boy from Taktser was indeed the authentic rebirth of the Great Thirteenth. Reting Rinpoché, having deliberated with the utmost care and consulted with all the relevant supernatural authorities, was entirely confident in the matter. The child should be brought to Lhasa as soon as possible. Predictably enough, as soon as word got out, and despite the fact that, officially, the Tibetans continued to insist that the boy from Taktser was but one of several candidates, no one was taken in.

Finding the reincarnation of the Great Thirteenth was something to be shouted from the rooftops. This brought more than mere honor to Taktser and its environs. This was more even than a blessing. This was the earthly manifestation of Chenresig, Bodhisattva of Compassion, erupting into the human realm right here on this piece of now-and-always-to-be-hallowed ground. This was a theogony — the coming of a god.

There followed what proved to be a lengthy wrangle, which escalated from a straightforward demand from the governor for payment of 100,000 silver dollars (equivalent to somewhere between $15,000 and $20,000 at the time, an enormous sum in those days) to negotiations that involved not only Ma Bufang's administration but also the Chinese central government, the (British) government of India, and the Tibetan government.

Furthermore, as soon as Reting Rinpoché's confirmation was received from Lhasa, the monastic authorities at Kumbum announced that every monastery in the area and all the local people must be given the opportunity to receive the Precious One's blessing. It was inconceivable that he should be among them and that for mere reasons of worldly affairs people should be prevented from enjoying his benediction. When Kewtsang Rinpoché demurred, there was even a moment when some of the younger monks at Kumbum threatened the search party with violence.

Ma Bufang's demand for an initial payment of 100,000 silver dollars was soon followed by one for a further 300,000 in cash to be paid to the governor's office. In addition, the authorities at Kumbum themselves put in a demand for a full set of the late Dalai Lama's ceremonial robes and a throne plus a set of the Great Thirteenth's two-hundred-volume edition of the scriptures, all to be written in gold. This, they argued, was fair recompense for the costs associated with looking after the child and his family, which had by now moved nearby, and in any case an appropriate acknowledgment of the monastery's role in his discovery.

Not having the funds available, the Tibetans turned in desperation to the Chinese Nationalist (Guomindang) government for help — with predictable results. The Chinese set their own — unacceptable — conditions, the most troubling of which was their insistence that an escort of the Nationalist army go with the boy to Lhasa. They also wanted the Tibetan government to declare publicly whether or not the boy from Taktser was in fact the new Dalai Lama. The Tibetans prevaricated but in the end agreed to a representative of the Guomindang traveling to Lhasa — though he had to do so via India. Still, however, the Tibetans insisted that the child was only one of two candidates. An official announcement would not be made before the boy could be examined alongside the Lhasa candidate — the boy whose connection with the Great Thirteenth had been indicated by the horse escaping its stable (but who, in reality, had already been ruled out).

By this time, Lhamo Thondup was almost four years old and had been at

Kumbum for over a year and a half. It was clear to all that he was an exceptional child, whatever Lhasa might finally decide. Some photographs taken by an American journalist* who visited Kumbum in early 1939 show the alert, curious, self-assured features still recognizable more than eighty years later. We glimpse, too, a trace of authority in his bearing. This is a child who looks more than equal to the task that lay in front of him. Though his time at Kumbum may not have been a happy one, it is clear from these images that it had not defeated him.

It was a matter of great satisfaction to the child Dalai Lama when, finally, word came that he was to leave for Lhasa. As he later put it, he "began to look to the future with more enthusiasm." Although he realized he would not be returned to his mother, at least he had the prospect of seeing her every day: his parents, now elevated to the rank of the highest nobility in the land, were to join him on the journey. The family party also comprised his maternal grandmother; the terrifying monk uncle; his older sister, Tsering Dolma, and her husband; his second-eldest brother, Gyalo Thondup, together with — though he was only eleven years old — the boy's fiancée, a "strikingly pretty girl" in the estimation of one European who saw her in Lhasa soon after their arrival; Lobsang Samten; and their younger sister, just born, Jetsun Pema.

Traveling in a caravan that took almost three months to cover the distance — there were at the time no roads and, apart from three cars, since abandoned, which the Great Thirteenth had imported to Lhasa, and a bicycle belonging to the British mission, no wheeled vehicles of any sort in Tibet — the Precious Protector was conveyed, together with Lobsang Samten, in a sort of palanquin carried on the backs of a pair of mules. According to the Dalai Lama himself, the journey was by no means an entirely serene progress through the vastness of the Tibetan landscape: "We spent a great deal of the time squabbling and arguing, as small children do, and often came to blows. This put our conveyance in danger of overbalancing. At that point our driver would stop the animals and summon my mother . . . When she looked inside, she always found the same thing: Lobsang Samten in tears and me sitting there with a look of triumph on my face. For despite his greater age, I was the more forthright."

---

*This was Archibald Steele, a reporter for the *Chicago Daily News.*

For two months the caravan made its way slowly from east to west without passing a single settlement. Typically, each day's journey covered no more than ten miles, and at the end of each stage a tented encampment would accommodate the travelers. What most impressed little Lhamo Thondup was the wildlife, which in those days remained in great abundance, among them "the vast herds of *drong* [wild yaks] ranging across the plains, the smaller groups of *kyang* [wild asses] and occasionally a shimmer of *gowa* and *nawa,* small deer which were so light and fast they might have been ghosts." Gyalo Thondup, the second-eldest brother, recalled how, when they reached the shores of the Kokonor, the huge (2,600 square mile) lake that divides historic Tibet from Mongolia, they saw "thousands of red tufted cranes and wild geese," which they all chased but could never catch.

What the Dalai Lama does not mention, because for him as a Tibetan it is unremarkable, is the vividness of the landscape through which they traveled: the sharp clarity of outline afforded by the atmosphere at high altitude. By day, the eye can see mountains on the horizon more than a hundred miles away; at night, the intensity of light when the sky is cloudless is scarcely to be imagined. You have never truly seen the stars nor had any inkling of their number until you have seen them in the pristine night skies of Tibet. Yet when there is cloud cover, and there is only the struggling flame of candles, the black of night takes on new meaning. And both by day and by night, the traveler must at all times be alert to sudden changes in the weather and the hazards they bring: the storms appearing as if by malevolent miracle from an empty sky, every cloud presaging torrential rain that turns placid mountain streams into raging torrents in a matter of minutes, or hailstones the size of golf balls that destroy crops in an instant, or blankets of snow that scar the retina when the sun shines on it. So too with the wind: one moment the breeze is soft as the caress of gossamer, a moment later someone descries a huddle of black hurtling forward like a posse of wild horsemen, and before there is time to take cover, a choking dust blizzard is upon you and a marrow-freezing wind tears at your clothing. This was an environment in which merely to stay alive was, for many, an ordeal — an ordeal that had to be confronted on a poor diet and was fraught with the ever present danger of brigandage on the one hand and, on the other, the onset of disease against which there was no remedy save the chanting of prayers and the casting out of spirits. And in spite of the extraordinary abundance of wildlife, here too there was serious danger. From the wolf packs that would carry off livestock to the cobras that infested the lower-lying regions, from the rabid dogs roaming village and countryside alike to the delicate but deadly monkshood, a species of wildflower that can kill without leaving a trace in a matter of hours, hidden menace lurked everywhere. As for the terrain itself, beyond the plains stood the looming mountains with their giddying ravines, plunging waterfalls, and the breathless passes between them, while to the north lay the upland desert where all was barren and desolate, save perhaps for a huddle of black horsehair tents far in the distance betokening a lonely nomad settlement.

At last, three months after setting out and ten days' journey from Lhasa, the caravan was met by a government official bringing the formal proclamation that the boy from Taktser had indeed been declared the authentic incarnation of the Great Thirteenth.

It was here that, a few days later, the regent came to prostrate himself before the Dalai Lama as the child presided over the first of many religious ceremonies that would culminate in his ascension to the Lion Throne early the following year. Recalling the days spent at the encampment, the Dalai Lama's second eldest brother, Gyalo Thondup, speaks in his autobiography of the comings and goings of "the officials, secretaries and monks" who made up the senior echelons of government and the "processions going on for hours; the food; the tea; the incense; the drums; the horns; the cymbals; the huge masks; the colourful costumes; the dancing and dramatic re-enactments" of historical events. It was at once a celebration, a pageant, a medieval fair, and a religious festival.

After several days of ceremonies, what had begun as a caravan and was now a cavalcade many thousands strong moved off. The next stop was Reting Monastery, from which the regent hailed. Dating from the tenth century, the foundation boasted a cedar forest said to have sprung from the hairs on the head of Atisha, the great Indian scholar saint to whose memory the monastery was dedicated. Here, the regent and the Dalai Lama's father discovered their common love of horses. Already there was magnificent stabling for dozens of splendid animals. It would not be long before these horses were joined by many more from the trading caravans brought from Amdo to Lhasa by the *yabshi kung,* as the Dalai Lama's father was now known. As was his right, the regent was invariably offered the pick of the crop among the horses the *yabshi kung* subsequently imported from the eastern breeding grounds, while the *kung* was often invited to elaborate picnic parties and horse gymkhanas arranged for the mutual gratification of the two enthusiasts.

It was also at Reting Monastery that the regent briefed the Dalai Lama's parents as to what they could expect in Lhasa. They would find many flatterers, and some people would certainly try to harm them. In particular, he warned the *gyalyum chenmo* never to accept food that had not been cooked in her own kitchen, "as it might be poisoned."

Leaving Reting Monastery for Lhasa, a week's journey distant, the caravan made its way to the environs of the small monastery of Rigya just outside the city. Here, on the plain below, a huge tented encampment had been erected. At its center stood the Macha Chenmo — the Great Peacock — a splendid blue-and-white construction that was only ever used to welcome the new Dalai Lama back to his temporal home. A poetic description of the return of the Sixth Dalai Lama gives some idea of the splendor of the occasion. At night it was said to have seemed that all "the stars of heaven [had] come down to earth." Then when the newly recognized Dalai Lama resumed his journey for the short distance to Lhasa, it caused "such a thunder of hooves as had never before been heard."

No film of the event — which took place on October 8, 1939 — survives, though there are still photographs, and we know enough about Tibetan ceremony to have a good sense of what it must have been like: the sumptuous silk brocade of the lay officials, the ladies' magnificent jewelry of silver and turquoise and coral, the impossible headdress of even humble womenfolk — strange lattices of wood, adorned with precious stones, beneath which the hair was braided and strung like so much wash hung out to dry. And alongside them, the grave countenances of the solemn but inwardly exultant clergy, the eager bustling of the crowd seeking a place to stand, the longing expressed in the torrent of mantras recited, the smoke of incense burning, the reverent hush and humble obeisance of the common people as the procession drew close. But one has to think past these outer manifestations of gladness to recognize the true — the inner — and spiritual significance of the occasion. The profundity of the emotional connection Tibetans have with the Dalai Lama is beyond anything others can easily imagine. It was with a mixture of awe, reverence, and yearning, coupled with the tenderest feelings of possession, blessedness, and good fortune, that the whole population turned out to greet their beloved. That he was a somewhat unruly child who pulled away from the regent to get back to his mother and, to his terror, had to be manhandled back to his place by a bodyguard "with big bulging eyes" was nothing to them. The one in whom the *bodhi* — the awakened mind of the Buddha — resides is not merely a monarch. He is someone who connects, in himself, the seen world with that unseen.

PART II

The Lion Throne

6

Homecoming: Lhasa, 1940

To those for whom the city represented what its etymology suggests — *lha,* "gods," *sa,* "earth," and hence "the gods' dwelling place on earth" — we can suppose that what occurred on that day when the Fourteenth Dalai Lama came home to Lhasa must have seemed a glimpse into the very mysteries of existence. To Tibetans generally, a visit to the holy city was the fulfillment of a lifelong ambition. It had then, as it still does, the same draw as Jerusalem, Rome, and Mecca have for followers of the Abrahamic religions. Merely to visit its shrines and holy places is to acquire spiritual merit. To such people, the mystical aura of this, the place to which the earthly manifestation of Chenresig, Bodhisattva of Compassion, was now returning, would render invisible the squalor and deprivation that might be the first thing to have struck a time traveler from the modern age.

According to Alexandra David-Néel, the fearless and indefatigable French explorer who reached the capital during the 1920s, Lhasa was "a town full of animation, inhabited by jolly people whose greatest pleasure is to loiter and chat out-of-doors." A less flattering picture is presented by the Japanese pilgrim Ekai Kawaguchi, who visited some years earlier. Describing the city as a "metropolis of filth," he recoiled in horror at the puddles of water into which people would openly defecate. In contrast to the broad squares where the great dramas of the liturgical year were enacted, there lay alleyways "narrow and devious," crowded, and "obscured by tumbledown buildings whose mud and stone walls were forever disintegrating and collapsing," the paths between them potholed with "pools of sludge." William Stanley Morgan, the Welsh-born doctor attached to the 1936–37 British mission to Lhasa, was appalled by the beggars he encountered "squatting or lying in the dust by the roadside." They were, he wrote, "mainly old and infirm — some blind and others lame or deformed. Many had huge goiters [from] long standing thyroid deficiency. Clad in sheepskin chubas [the traditional Tibetan gown] or bundled up in a mass of rags, they hung with dirt." He blanched, too, at the sight of the city's communal garbage dump, consisting of "great piles of offal eight and ten feet high" and surrounded "with a black and slimy ooze." His traveling companion, Freddy Spencer Chapman, a future jungle war hero, was particularly distraught over the dogs swarming around the refuse. "They were at once a revolting and pathetic sight — bodies bared with skin disease, huge suppurating sores covered with flies, lamed, often dragging a . . . useless leg, eyes gouged out, ears torn off . . . Nothing I had ever seen could compare with them."

To a Tibetan out-of-town visitor such as T. Y. Pemba, however, Lhasa was a place of wonder and delight. "The ordinary residents," he wrote, "were gay, witty, sharp and flamboyant . . . [and] Lhasa prided itself on having the gayest, prettiest and perhaps the 'loosest' women in Tibet." The city was divided into several different communities: there was a Muslim quarter, a small Nepalese quarter, and a quarter where the *ragyabas* lived — the butcher caste who also took the dead to the places of sky-burial, where the corpse was dismembered and fed to the ever-hovering vultures. The houses of these *ragyabas* were made almost entirely of animal horn. There were particular places where criminals would gather, too, some yoked together in pairs and shackled at the feet, others handless, having been mutilated for their misdeeds, the stumps "immersed . . . in boiling oil to arrest the bleeding." Although the Great Thirteenth had not approved of the practice, there is reason to suppose that it was carried out at least until the end of the regency period, and it remains a familiar trope of propaganda put out by the Chinese that it was they who outlawed such barbarism.

Owing to the absence of roads, let alone modern methods of communication (save for the telegraph line up from India that the British had installed for their own benefit), the city was one where rumor and counter-rumor were a continuous feature of life. Once, at around this time, the people were struck with terror when a story began to circulate that an army of Kazakhs was approaching, led by "an Amazon with breasts that hung to her waist." Her army was reputed to be so huge that it took a whole day to review it, while it was said to be "armed with strange secret weapons of immense power." It turned out the "army" was a ragged band of starving men, women, and children who had fled Sinkiang province and were on their way to seek asylum in India.

Lhasa was at this time a city with a settled population of probably no more than ten thousand. This might double or even triple during the most important annual festivals or, as in this case, at the Dalai Lama's homecoming. Within a few hours' walk stood the three largest monasteries in Tibet: Sera, with seven thousand monks, at around five miles distant; Drepung, with perhaps as many as ten thousand, around seven miles away; and Ganden, the third-largest monastery with a population of around three thousand monks, which was just under twenty miles from the capital. Almost every able-bodied monk would decamp and make his way to the city on great occasions such as this, crowding the streets "from sunrise to sunset," while at night, visitors slept crammed in stables and camped in courtyards.

In marked contrast to the squalor of large parts of the city stood the Dalai Lama's two palaces, the Potala and the Norbulingka, and the mansions of the aristocracy. It was the Norbulingka to which, with his next-elder brother, Lobsang Samten, the Dalai Lama was taken on this joyous occasion. Built as a summer retreat for the Seventh Dalai Lama at around a mile and a half to the southwest of Lhasa, the palace was topped with a golden roof and fronted with pillars, its windows glazed and protected from the sun by awnings decorated with auspicious symbols rendered in appliqué. Altogether more homelike than the Potala, it was surrounded by leafy parkland and several well-tended gardens that provided sanctuary to a menagerie of animals, including variously "a herd of tame musk deer; at least six enormous Tibetan mastiffs which acted as guard dogs . . . a few mountain goats; a monkey; a handful of camels; two leopards and a very old and rather sad tiger," and a large number of birds, including "several parrots; half a dozen peacocks; some cranes; a pair of golden geese and about thirty very unhappy Canada geese whose wings had been clipped."

It was at the Norbulingka that the Precious Protector had his first presentiment that he might indeed have some special connection with the Great Thirteenth. Up until that moment he had merely accepted what he had been told. But on this occasion, or so his mother informed him later, he announced that he would like to go to the Chensalingka. This was a building erected in the grounds of the Norbulingka by the Great Thirteenth. "She told me that we entered one room and I pointed to [a] box and said to open it. My teeth would be there." Sure enough, it was found to contain teeth that had belonged to his predecessor.

The Dalai Lama's parents had, in the meantime, taken up residence in a mansion situated beneath the northern wall of the Potala. This was to be their home until a new, more modern dwelling could be built for them. Although family photographs of this time show happy faces, the installation of the newcomers from Taktser was not entirely to the satisfaction of Lhasa's leading families. Some clearly still felt that the relative of the Great Thirteenth was a more suitable candidate, given his better connections.* Not only were the new Dalai Lama's family uneducated commoners (his mother was illiterate), but also they spoke a dialect that marked them as being from a part of Tibet hardly known in Lhasa.

Himself of lowly birth, the regent was attuned to the difficulties the family faced and arranged for the government to grant several landed estates to them, to ensure their independence. Even so, it takes little imagination to see what an ordeal those first few months must have been for the new arrivals, plunged into the round of formal entertaining that is the lot of the families of high officials everywhere. The fact that they needed an interpreter to begin with (the

---

*This was Ditru Rinpoché, still alive at the time of writing and a respected lama in his own right.

Amdo dialect they spoke was sufficiently different from the high-flown locutions of Lhasa as to need translating) was no doubt difficulty enough.* The records of the British officials who knew them well show the Lhasa aristocracy to have been little different from aristocracies anywhere else — fond of flummery and elaborate etiquette. The leading ladies were no doubt quick to share their opinions of the manners and comportment of the *gyalyum chenmo,* while the men (a lot of them idly rich and not a few of them habitual opium smokers) would have been eager to take the measure of the *yabshi kung.* Many aristocrats had by now been exposed to polite British society in places like Kalimpong and Darjeeling, and the disparity between their level of sophistication and that of the new Dalai Lama's family would have been immediately apparent. But while the *yabshi kung* received mixed reviews, the *gyalyum chenmo* captivated the hearts of prince and pauper alike with her simple, unaffected charm. Legendarily generous, she was humble, kindly, and warmly affectionate.

The new Dalai Lama's first public engagement after his homecoming was the tonsuring ceremony at which both he and the now eight-year-old Lobsang Samten were inducted as novice monks. As was his right, and only fitting, the regent himself performed the ritual haircutting that marked the Dalai Lama's entry into the monastic novitiate and gave the young hierarch his new name: Jamphel Ngawang Lobsang Yeshe Tenzin Gyatso.

When at last the proceedings were over, the child returned to the small building within the grounds of the Norbulingka which was to be his home for the first year in Lhasa. To begin with, the Dalai Lama's mother had right of access to him, and they saw each other regularly, if not every day. And though life promised to be lonely for one so young, the following days were enlivened by the New Year festival which began shortly afterwards, commencing with the ceremony of the Priest's New Year and ending on the twenty-seventh day with the "Sky Archery" ceremony. Strolling minstrels and wandering friars frequented every street, while the more pious, clad in leather knee and elbow

* Still in common use today, honorific Tibetan is almost an entirely different language from colloquial Tibetan.

pads, circumambulated the Jokhang Temple, measuring their body length on the ground. "One saw many of these people, their faces dusty and bruised, their eyes tight with pain and [their] mouths set hard," noted an observer. Above all, though, this was a time of rejoicing, a time for families to come together, for old friendships to be rekindled and new ones formed. There was street theater and music and dance. Two perennial favorites were the lion and peacock dances, the former featuring an imp who tries to tame the beast, succeeding at last, to the delight of the crowd.

Unfortunately for the young Dalai Lama, he was forbidden to participate in the celebrations. From his point of view, the most important element of the proceedings was the Monlam Chenmo, the Great Prayer Festival, which began on the sixth day of the New Year. A central feature of Monlam, the Brilliant Invocation of the Glorious Goddess, necessitated that he move to a suite of rooms at the top of the Jokhang Temple, where he would reside until the final day of the festival. Preceded by ranks of soldiers with bayonets fixed, the boy was carried in a palanquin whose bearers marched with a peculiar gait so as to minimize its swaying. Once the Precious One was safely within the temple, the carousing could resume once more, whereupon "the crowd really let themselves go . . . [T]here was great merrymaking that night."

Dating back to the eighth century, the Jokhang is considered the most important temple in all Tibet and is a place of pilgrimage sacred to each of the different traditions within Tibetan Buddhism. There are four principal schools, or sects, within the Tibetan tradition: the Nyingma (literally the "Old Ones," who are associated with the seventh-century sage Padmasambhava, the Lotus-Born One), the Sakya (dating from the eleventh century and associated with the Kon clan of central Tibet), the Kargyu (dating from the twelfth century and associated chiefly with Karma Pakshi and Milarepa), and the Gelug (founded by Tsongkhapa in the fifteenth century and the only one to require celibacy of its monks). Here, despite his tender years, the boy was to preside over a ceremony at which incense was offered to Palden Lhamo, the Glorious Goddess and protector deity (the one invoked by the regent at the lake called Lhamo Lhatso), in whose spiritual care the Dalai Lamas subsist.

Several days later followed the most spectacular of all the New Year public ceremonies. This was the Casting-Out of the Votive Offering, and it was only on the eve of this event that the young Precious Protector was permitted to come down and walk among the crowds. It was, as he recalled in his autobiography, "one of the best moments in the Dalai Lama's year." This was the one day, he wrote, when "I was allowed outside to walk round the streets so that I could see the *torma,* the huge, gaily coloured butter sculptures traditionally offered to the Buddhas on this day. There were also puppet shows and music played by military bands and an atmosphere of tremendous happiness amongst the people."

With its strong military character, the ceremony that followed was notable for its displays of martial prowess. Soldiers sang war songs in honor of the Glorious Goddess as they brandished their bows and arrows and fenced with swords. Part of the proceedings enacted a standoff where men armed with guns would aim at an opposing rank and shout abuse at them, taunting them in an episode known as "the Incitement." This culminated in a series of flashes and bangs as firecrackers exploded. The foot soldiers departing, a detachment of cavalry then appeared, riding slowly beneath the Dalai Lama's window while he remained sequestered inside. On reaching the entrance to the temple forecourt, the riders would dismount and prostrate themselves before him, though to his intense frustration, the Dalai Lama could only peep through a yellow curtain. It was then the turn of the monks of Namgyal Monastery, who appeared in their finest vestments, carrying on their heads the tall, curved yellow felt hat characteristic of the Gelug order, some censing the air with sweet-smelling herbs, others carrying musical instruments. There was also a contingent carrying the *shinyen* cymbals, the purpose of which was to drive out evil.

After preliminary invocations, the assembled religious began a ceremony to welcome the *torma,* which were now brought forward, accompanied by a phalanx of monks. Consisting of "wooden frames bound with leather on which stood various images and decorations, all made of butter" brightly dyed, the sculptures were a most impressive sight, standing up to thirty feet tall. The images having earlier been ritually infused with the evil of the past year, the Namgyal choir now began chanting the liturgy of exorcism. When this was complete, the sculptures were taken out of the courtyard and carried in procession to an open space on the southern side of the city while the monastic orchestra continued to play. This, though, was but the prelude to the grand finale of the day's proceedings, the arrival of the Nechung oracle, possessed already by the spirit of Dorje Drakden.

Some silent film shot by an aristocratic cineaste at the 1959 Monlam Chenmo gives us a glimpse of the oracle in action. Bursting forth from within the temple itself, the medium — his trance fully developed — rushes out clasping a sword in one hand and a bow and arrow in the other. The crowd visibly gasps. Golden and shot through with flaming color, the oracle's tunic is adorned with a breastplate of polished silver that radiates light at his every move. On his head he wears a vast crown — said to have weighed more than eighty pounds — decked with peacock feathers, studded with precious stones, and trailing plumes of white horsehair. As the musicians urge him on with a giddy rhythm that mounts faster and faster, the oracle, holding his weapons aloft, begins to dance. Lifting his legs high, he whirls around and around in a crescendo of color, the sunlight flashing off his breastplate as if it were on fire. After several breathtaking gyrations, Nechung* leaves the courtyard and, now supported by two attendants and accompanied by the monastic orchestra, heads off down the road in the direction taken by the party bearing the *torma.*

When at last the oracle reaches the place where the *torma* now lie on a mass of brushwood, he fires an arrow toward them and, to the intense satisfaction of all present, the pyre erupts in butter-fueled flames to the screams and yells of the crowd, heard above the still chanting monks. This signifies the destruction of the old year's evil, wiping the slate clean at the dawn of the new. Finally, three ancient cannon — known respectively as the Idiot, the Old She-Demon, and the Young She-Demon — are fired. Their reports could be heard by the Dalai Lama, who, to his continued frustration, remained in his apartment in the Jokhang. There he had to await the final procession, which would wend its way slowly back from the site of immolation, so all those participating could abase themselves beneath his window.

The next day was the last of the Great Prayer Festival. A procession of monks, including the Ganden Throne Holder — technically the most senior religious authority in the land — followed an image of Maitreya, the Buddha

---

* Although, strictly speaking, one should say "the medium of the Nechung oracle," it is simpler to refer to him as Nechung or "the oracle."

to come, around a circuit which brought them to a halt in front of the chamber where the Dalai Lama remained hidden behind his gauze curtain. Again, the Nechung oracle appeared in a trance, and, following his ritual dance and presentation of an offering scarf to the image, all would prostrate themselves beneath the youngster's window.

But what of the little boy himself? While we might prefer to imagine the holy child rewarding these supplications with inward grace and outward benediction, by his own account he behaved no better — and possibly even a little worse — than the majority of small boys might in his position. "The sight of all those people down there was too much for me," he wrote. "I boldly poked my head through the curtain. But, as if this were not bad enough, I remember blowing bubbles of spit which fell on people's heads as they threw themselves down to the ground far below!"

During the time of the Great Thirteenth, Maitreya's procession was followed by an appearance of the Dalai Lama's elephant. After forcing its way through the crush of maroon-clad monastics, it would kneel at the foot of the building and trumpet its salute before leading the procession out of the courtyard. This was the moment for the cannon to be fired once more, at which the religious ceremony would conclude and the secular entertainments begin. Its report signaled the start of a horse race. Surprisingly for a people who made so much use of the animal, these horses were riderless. Urged on by the crowds of spectators that lined the route from Drepung Monastery to the center of town, they were joined at the halfway mark by human athletes, who, at the sound of a second gunshot, would take off, competitors of both species occupying the same space on the road. As the Dalai Lama put the matter, "This tended to result in enjoyable confusion as both arrived simultaneously."

Shortly after the conclusion of the New Year festivities, the young leader's formal enthronement ceremony was held in the Potala.* According to witnesses, the child could not have conducted himself more perfectly. A "solid, solemn but very wide-awake boy, red-cheeked and closely shorn," he "sat quietly and with great dignity, completely at ease in these strange surroundings, giving the proper blessing to each person."

---

* On February 22, 1940, to be precise.

But if the people were thus reassured, the ceremony was of little consequence to the boy himself. He was more eager to get his hands on the gifts the British delegation had brought for him. These included a Meccano construction set, a pedal car, a tricycle, a "nightingale clock," and, most exciting of all, a pair of parakeets. Of the two brothers, however, only Lobsang Samten was permitted to attend the children's party given at the Dekyi Lingka—literally, the Garden of Happiness—which housed the British mission. The Dalai Lama's monk caretakers deemed it unsuitable for him to go. This was cruelty enough, but when the head of the British mission, Sir Basil Gould, explained to Lobsang Samten that it would be better if the birds could remain at the Dekyi Lingka until they had acclimatized properly following their journey over the mountains, the Dalai Lama was distraught. Unable to bear the wait, the young hierarch sent a messenger to the British two days later requesting that the birds be sent at once. They were duly dispatched, together with detailed instructions for their care. Another two days followed before, to their surprise, the British received the birds back. It transpired that the Precious Protector was persuaded that perhaps the sahibs should after all be responsible for the creatures until they had adjusted to the Lhasa climate.

The parakeets were doubtless the source of many moments of welcome distraction during that first year. When, however, the New Year festival inaugurating the subsequent (Iron Snake) year—1941—came to an end, what had amounted to a honeymoon period for the young Dalai Lama also came to a close. During the past year, his duties had been minimal, but from now on he would have to participate in the daily tea ceremony in the Great Hall—a magnificent, somewhat low-ceilinged chamber, its walls covered with frescoes topped with gilded stucco. This was a formal gathering of senior government figures over which the boy Dalai Lama presided while affairs of state were discussed, but in which he played no part. More onerously, it was at this moment that he, together with Lobsang Samten, now began their formal education as novice monks. This entailed shifting his quarters from the Norbulingka Palace to his new residence in the penthouse on the top floor of the Potala, again with Lobsang Samten for company, where he occupied the same suite of rooms that both the Great Fifth and the Great Thirteenth had occupied. Besides a bedroom, this comprised a small private chapel and several large anterooms, though, unlike accommodations in one or two of the aristocratic mansions, it did not have a bathroom.*

Rising miraculously from the Marpo Ri, the Red Hill, the Potala is unquestionably one of the architectural wonders of the world, wholly dominating the Lhasa townscape even today. (In 1994 it was added to the UNESCO World Heritage list.) And as anyone who has set eyes on it will testify, it is an extraordinary feat of human ingenuity. "The contrasts and rhythms of different materials, of solids and voids, of heavy and light, of monochrome and intense colour, are startling, subtle and pleasing at the same time," according to one guide to Tibetan architecture, while the "seemingly floating golden roofs are ethereal forms in contrast to their solid substructure." In all, the building covers around 1.3 million square feet (more than half again as large as Buckingham Palace) and stands nearly four hundred feet high. It has, moreover, fully a thousand rooms, the largest of which, the West Main Hall, has a floor area covering some 7,250 square feet.

Dating back to the mid-seventeenth century, though the site was originally built on much earlier — certainly no later than the seventh century and very likely long before that — the building consists of two separate but connected palaces, the White and the Red. Inaugurated by the Great Fifth Dalai Lama's teacher of the magical arts, who drew a sacred mandala at its heart, the Potala took half a century to complete — though even this seems too short a time when one considers not just the size of the structure but also its incredible complexity. Stonemasons, carpenters, woodcarvers, and artists came from all over Tibet as well as from among Nepal's Buddhist community.

Besides quartering the Dalai Lamas — year round before the Norbulingka was built — the Potala was home both to a large community of monks and to a small number of laymen. Namgyal Monastery, the foundation to which the Dalai Lama himself belonged, and which existed primarily to serve him through its prayer and liturgy, was situated within its precincts and numbered up to two hundred monastics. The Potala was, furthermore, the seat of Tibet's religio-political government.† This was the institution, inaugurated by the

* The Tsarong mansion already had two.

† I use this term to translate *chos srid zung 'brel.*

Great Fifth, that united the spiritual and temporal realms under the leadership of the Dalai Lama. For this reason, besides the monks of Namgyal, thirty or so highborn monastic officials who composed the upper echelons of the civil service were also in residence, plus another large contingent of monk clerks, not to mention serving staff, kitchen staff, and the guardians of the various storerooms, as well as resident tailors, prison guards, and inmates of the palace dungeons. In addition there was a garrison of soldiers, together with a contingent of grooms for the Dalai Lama's and government officials' horses stabled within the Potala's many-storied splendor.

Yet for all its magnificence, few would deny that the Potala is also somber in the extreme. Outside it looks more like a military fortress than the palace of the Bodhisattva of Compassion, while inside it feels more like a giant sepulcher than anyone's home.

The military character of the building is by no means as inappropriate as it might at first seem, however. It was built with an eye both to withstanding a lengthy siege such as the Mongols might have undertaken and to the often overlooked martial aspect of the Dalai Lama institution. It is hardly surprising, then, that, like his predecessor, the present Dalai Lama came to prefer the Norbulingka as a place to live.

With respect to these military overtones, it is vital to recognize that quite as important as the Dalai Lama's authority over the temporal realm is his authority over the unseen forces of the Tibetan Buddhist pantheon — not just the minor deities of home and hearth but also the protector deities of the Buddhadharma. Many of these protectors are conceived of as warriors, masters of their own fortresses with retinues of armored minions. Besides being an impregnable redoubt to protect the Dalai Lama and his government against their earthly enemies, the Potala is thus also a visible symbol of his role as one whose power extends to the realm of the gods. Not merely an earthly protector of his people, he is their supernatural protector as well. He guards his country and his subjects against the unseen hosts in thrall to the cravings of untamed desire and the karmic consequences of unexpiated sin.

The funerary aspect of the Potala's interior has much to do with the fact that it also functions partly as a giant mausoleum. The reliquary stupas, or tombs, of the Fifth, Seventh, Eighth, Ninth, and Thirteenth Dalai Lamas are all contained within its walls. Those of the Great Fifth and the Great Thirteenth are particularly splendid, as befits the achievements of those two incarnations. Indeed, the tomb of the Great Thirteenth stands three stories high and necessitated considerable structural alteration to the palace to accommodate it. Smothered in gold and set with thousands of precious stones, it faces an altar on which stands an offering mandala composed, it is said, of 200,000 pearls. But for all the magnificence of the carvings, the statuary, the mural paintings, the *thangkas,** and other products of the Tibetan artistic genius, as the Dalai Lama himself would be the first to admit, the place was hardly suited to the five-year-old boy whose home it now was.

Placed under the care of three principal attendants, the Master of the Ritual (*choepon khenpo*), the Master of the Kitchen (*soelpon khenpo*), and the Master of the Wardrobe (*simpon khenpo*), the Dalai Lama was looked after with, according to one British official, a "devotion and love, almost surpassing the love of women." But this can hardly have been adequate recompense for the lack of a mother's love from the point of view of one so young. Moreover, the rooms he occupied were as dismal as they were disastrously ill-kept. "Everything ... was ancient and decrepit," he later recalled, "and behind the drapes that hung across each of the four walls lay deposits of centuries-old dust." The rooms were also pitifully cold and dimly lit, and so badly infested with mice that the curtains surrounding the little boy's bed ran with urine.

The environment in which the young Dalai Lama began his academic career was decidedly austere. Yet, in the Tibetan tradition, the emphasis placed on learning is such that, for the Gelugpas at least, scholarship and sanctity are almost synonymous. The boy's education was thus of crucial importance for, unless he could command the respect of the monastic community, he could not hope to govern effectively. To understand why this is so, we need to have some idea of the way in which the monasteries functioned — and to

---

* A *thangka* is a religious painting executed on a scroll that is generally bordered with silk brocade. The most important contain paint infused with the powdered relics of one or more high masters.

a large extent continue to function — within Tibetan society. The main purpose of the monasteries is twofold. They exist, first, to furnish their members with an environment conducive to private spiritual practice and to provide a superlative education such that the more able of them can become teachers of the dharma. The Three Seats of Ganden, Drepung, and Sera (the Harvard, Yale, and Princeton of Tibet) are in this respect very much like the medieval universities of Europe, which grew out of the teaching faculties of the various Christian religious orders. While the different halls or colleges of the Christian universities, like the Tibetan monasteries, fulfilled the liturgical practices — the masses and devotions — of their particular order, there are important differences between the ancient European universities and their Tibetan counterparts. This was reflected in the other principal function of the monasteries, which was to mediate between the seen world and the unseen.

It is in this second function that the major differences lie. For Christians, God is transcendent. That is to say, God exists independently of the world, even if He pervades it. In Buddhism, there is no such transcendent realm; the world is unbounded, so although there are levels of being that start with the gross and ascend through different strata to the most refined state, the realms of the Buddhas, these realms are not considered to exist "outside" or "beyond" the totality of all that there is. The monasteries are thus deeply concerned with "this-worldly" matters, even though this concern is principally focused on the gods and godlings of the supernatural realm. They are not only seats of learning, then, but also fortresses from which spiritual armies are mustered through ceremonies — lasting sometimes whole days and nights, during which millions of mantras may be recited, tens or even hundreds of thousands of liturgical texts chanted, and thousands of pages of scripture read — which are then sent forth to do battle with the enemies of the Buddhadharma.

Of course, as is the case with every institution, even in their heyday there were few really excellent monks and many who were "lazy, stupid and mere parasites." For those whose intellectual gifts did not mark them out as future scholars (the majority), the daily ceremonies were largely what monastic life consisted of. As to their other duties, some were designated as traders and bankers, undertaking business on behalf of the monasteries, chiefly through selling and bartering the produce of the landed estates that supported them. But monastic officials would also make loans and collect taxes on lands the monastery owned. Others would work in the monastery administration, while still others, because of their artistic skill, would be employed in the workshops as painters and sculptors. Those suited to more menial tasks might work in the kitchens or perhaps as tailors. Up until 1959, there also existed a distinct subclass of monks known as the *dob dob*. These were fraternities of monks whose principal concerns were sport, fighting, and to some extent sexual adventure. These, according to one observer, were "tough looking characters, with dirty greasy clothes[,] their faces painted with black streaks." With regard to their sporting activities, these were generally conducted off-site and might include running or weightlifting, while their fighting often involved wielding the heavy keys that were typically worn on a chain around the waist. Latterly they had taken to practicing with firearms as well. As for their sexual exploits, they would sometimes lie in wait around Lhasa in the evening in the hope of capturing young aristocratic boys, on whom they would take their pleasure. Yet if the *dob dob* were feared by both layman and monastic alike, they were also very often the ones who would nurse the sick and dying. The *dob dob* should not, however, be confused with the monastic proctors and disciplinarians, who would keep order with whip and staves during the great liturgical ceremonies, prodding those who fell asleep and lashing those who were unruly. These were monks of good reputation who, together with the abbot and chant master (the *umze*), comprised the leadership of the monasteries. The more physically imposing of their number made up the monastery police force. Padding their shoulders to look still more fearsome, they would patrol the monastic precincts carrying an elaborately decorated mace as a sign of office.

Although there was a sharp division between the different activities of the monks, the larger monasteries were made up of two or more colleges, or *dra tsang*. These were further subdivided into *khang tsen*, or "houses" (rather like Griffindor and other houses in the Harry Potter novels). These *khang tsen* had strong local affiliations, so that monks from Kham were likely to join one, monks from Amdo another, those from Mongolia still another, and monks from central or western Tibet another again. Similarly, each college was generally home to one or more incarnation lineages. But although some colleges were inevitably wealthier than others, and although the monasteries themselves had their own landed estates, almost without exception, anyone joining had to have at least some independent source of income. This would usually come from the individual monk's own family or from a wealthy patron, but in any case, lack of funds could be a major source of difficulty for even the most able scholars. It was only when such individuals graduated and were able to teach in their own right that they could hope to become self-sufficient.

In the case of the Three Seats, besides the heads of each college, there were also various senior monastic appointments. Yet while these senior lamas, all of whom had come up through the ranks, were acclaimed teachers, the system of recognizing reincarnate lamas (or *tulkus*) meant that immense prestige also attached to this other class of monks — whether or not they were themselves notable scholars. And it was these *tulkus,* a sort of monastic aristocracy, who played a key role not only in the religious life of Tibet but also in its political life.

The development of the *tulku* system, which finds its apotheosis in the institution of the Dalai Lamas, was in fact unknown until the thirteenth century. Its first instantiation came when a widely admired teacher and thaumaturge gave directions that enabled his reincarnation to be identified.* Here, though, it is important to be clear about what is being claimed when a child is identified as a reincarnation of a high lama.† It is not that the soul, or even the essence, of the deceased passes into the body of his successor. As we shall see, it is a fundamental claim of Buddhist thinkers that there is no substantial self. It is rather the accumulated karma attaching to the stream of consciousness that manifests through one individual which is passed on to, or made manifest in, another sentient being. That said, to the uneducated peasantry of Tibet, reincarnation is understood very much along the lines of a soul entering a new body, even if it is doctrinally incorrect.

It is also important to realize that a clear distinction is drawn between *re-*

* This was Karma Pakshi, ca. 1204–1283.

† All lamas who reincarnate in this way enjoy the highest status: there are no low-status or minor reincarnate lamas.

birth and *reincarnation.* In essence, while rebirth is what befalls all sentient beings, reincarnation is open only to those far advanced along the path to Enlightenment. The difference lies in the ability of those who reincarnate to be able to choose the timing and manner of their rebirth. This reflects the notion that all reincarnates are understood to manifest the boundless compassion of one or more bodhisattvas — beings who stand on the verge of Enlightenment and thus have most of the attributes of one who is fully enlightened, including, for example, omniscience, yet who choose to remain among sentient beings in order to help them on their way to Enlightenment.

No reliable figures exist as to the number of reincarnate lamas scattered throughout the Tibetan Buddhist world at the time of the Dalai Lama's boyhood, but certainly many hundred and very likely more than a thousand seems plausible. It was, in any case, the most important of them who ruled Tibet at this time, alongside the senior-most monastic officials and the aristocracy. How this played out in the years immediately prior to Tibet's "liberation" by Communist China will be seen in the catastrophic clash that broke out between two of the most important *tulkus* after the Dalai Lama himself.

7

Boyhood: Two Cane-Handled Horsewhips

The Dalai Lama is, from the perspective of the Tibetan tradition, both an object of worship and a source of merit. By worshipping him, and even more by giving materially to him, one acquires merit — merit that, one hopes, will contribute to a favorable birth in the next life. From his very first days in Lhasa, therefore, the young Dalai Lama attended ceremonies and functions at which he received not just the occasional foreign delegation but the much more numerous pilgrims, whether lay or monastic, for whom merely to be touched on the head with the red cotton tassel at the end of a short wooden stick, which was the Dalai Lama's means of blessing them, was the crowning moment of their lives. Thereafter, "death held no fears." One young visitor who joined the waiting line at this time noted, however, that, "surrounded by several elderly monks who now and then bent down and whispered to him," the boy himself looked "no different from our urchin friends."

But if his public duties were vital to maintaining a connection with his people, from a personal perspective it was the Dalai Lama's formation as a monk that took precedence over all. We might ask why this was so, why he needed educating at all, given that one of the chief characteristics of bodhisattvas is omniscience. It is true that, from the perspective of Buddhist tradition, learning for the Dalai Lama and other high incarnations is to a large extent a question of relearning. But though Chenresig himself is all-knowing, it does not follow that his earthly manifestations are not subject to the usual constraints of embodied existence. Together with Lobsang Samten, the Precious Protector therefore began his day in just the same way as any other novice monk.

Having risen at dawn, they would set about their first task, which was to prepare the room in which their teacher would join them. Then, while awaiting his arrival, the boys would begin performing the preliminary invocation to Manjushri, Bodhisattva of Wisdom. This prayer ends with the syllable *dhih,* pronunciation of which is thought to sharpen one's faculties. The boys would repeat it as many times as possible in a single breath: *dhih, dhih, dhih, dhih, dhih, dhih, dhih, dhih* . . . This done, they would start reciting the lines they had memorized the previous day, chanting at the top of their voices for maximum impact, and rocking their small bodies rhythmically back and forth. No doubt there was often more laughter than industry, but on hearing the footsteps of the Dalai Lama's tutor, they would fall silent.

Describing these early days, the Dalai Lama recounts how, as the tutor took his seat, one of two cane-handled horsewhips that hung on a pillar in the room would be taken down by an attendant and placed beside his teacher, who sat opposite the little boy's throne on a "raised seat with no supporting cushions or backboard." The teacher in question was Ling Rinpoché. Appointed as assistant tutor alongside the regent, who acted as senior tutor, Ling Rinpoché came to be the single most important person in the Dalai Lama's life. A man with incredible powers of recall and an acknowledged clairvoyant, he also had a reputation for being a stern disciplinarian. In the biography he later wrote in homage to his tutor, the Dalai Lama tells, approvingly, the story of how, as deputy abbot of Gyuto Monastery, Ling Rinpoché punished some monks for not knowing the words to a particular series of chants. Ordering them to collect sand in sacks, he paraded them for inspection in the monastery courtyard. For reasons that are unclear, he further ordered that one of them be flogged. This caused a number of monks to grumble about Ling Rinpoché. Yet the

Dalai Lama commends the punishment as a good deed, noting that when a smallpox epidemic struck soon after, "it is said that those monks who had to ferry bags of sand, apart from one or two, recovered from the disease," this at a time when the fatality rate following infection was somewhere between a third and half of all cases.

According to the Dalai Lama, Ling Rinpoché was one of those rare beings who could manifest the *siddhi* — the magical powers — of the most advanced yogins. On one occasion during a divination ritual he threw a stick that landed upright, an event that "everyone present regarded . . . with astonishment." The Dalai Lama also notes uncritically the story that a particular statue in his tutor's monastery would change its appearance according to whether Ling Rinpoché was in good health or not. When he was, it would turn its face to the sky. When not, it would be downcast.

If the fact of corporal punishment was very much present, even for one so exalted as the Dalai Lama, so too was that other staple of a traditional education: learning by rote. Even today, the novice studying in a Tibetan Buddhist monastery dedicates much of his first ten years as a monk to memorizing the most important texts and rituals of his craft. This he does by chanting out loud — itself held to be a meritorious act because it benefits the many supernatural beings that surround humans at all times, who may not have had the opportunity to study the dharma for themselves. Although rote learning has become unfashionable in modern schools, one reason for the high value placed on memorization of texts in the Buddhist tradition is that, in order to understand a text, it is considered essential to have the words available for instant recall. What is known darkly becomes illumined when the meaning is expounded by the teacher.

Helpfully, the majority of texts that the novice is required to commit to memory are written in verse form. Pass by a monastery when the youngsters are studying and you might think the whole place is in an uproar as they fight to make their voices heard. This is encouraged as, in so doing, they learn to concentrate to the point where nothing can distract them — for which reason a teacher will sometimes deliberately try to throw them off. A relatively recent story is told of how one of the novices at Namgyal Monastery was reciting a text when the Dalai Lama himself entered the room and proceeded to scratch him on the back. It was bad enough that anyone should do this, but that it was the Dalai Lama himself must have produced extraordinary emotion on the part of the young monk. It is to his great credit that history relates a successful outcome: he got to the end of the piece without fault or stumble.

The first text the Dalai Lama learned was one known as the Ganden Lha Gya Ma: the Hundred Deities of Ganden. Composed in honor of the fourteenth-century Gelug master Je (Lord) Tsongkhapa, this is a short devotional practice that calls on the master and his two chief disciples:

> From your place at the heart of the One Who Is to Come —
> Guardian of those hundreds of the blessed in the Joyful Land —
> Come! Reposing on a cloud white as the freshest curd,
> Come! All-knowing Lobsang Drakpa,
> Come! And bring your two heart disciples:
> Take your places before me,
> And seat yourselves on lion throne, lotus, and moon

Although the Dalai Lama often says he was a poor student, he is widely acknowledged as having the ability not just to quote verbatim from all the root texts but also, in his teachings, to be able to quote lengthy passages from the prose commentaries. It is evident he did not waste all his time.

The Dalai Lama also has a fine hand. Within the tradition, penmanship is regarded as an art in itself, and he was taught calligraphy from the beginning. This was in marked contrast to the education of most other novices, among whom the ability to write was rare. Remarkably, it was not uncommon for even the most proficient scholars to be unable to write even their own names. There were several reasons for this. Writing was regarded as the province of monastery administrators and, as such, a less important occupation than the study and mastery of the sacred texts. Partly, too, the denigration of writing reflected the innate conservatism of the monasteries. Writing was the source of innovation and therefore should be taught only to those who could be trusted. It was also regarded as unnecessary: there was little if anything that had been left unsaid. Above all, however, at least within the major monastic institutions of Ganden, Drepung, and Sera, skill in debate was regarded as a greater accomplishment.

For those who did learn to write, the task was complicated by the fact that there were three major scripts to master: one (*u chen*) is used for the printed word; a second (*u me*), a more cursive script, is used for everyday correspondence, note taking, essay writing, and so forth; and a third (*chu yig*) is a highly stylized cursive script used in formal correspondence and legal documents. Possibly in a dissenting move on the part of his writing tutor, for practice in the third, and most demanding, script, the boy Dalai Lama was given the text of the Great Thirteenth's final testament, with its dire warnings of ruin if the Tibetan government did not set aside its habitual infighting. As a result, not only did the Dalai Lama develop an elegant hand, but also, from an early age, he was aware of the disastrous extent to which his predecessor's recommendations were being neglected.

By the time of the Precious Protector's homecoming, many influential Lhasans had grown to dislike the regent, Reting Rinpoché, intensely. Personally, he was known to be fond of soccer and marksmanship; he was in fact something of a crack shot. It is said he once persuaded a young associate to allow him to shoot an egg from his outstretched hand. When, afterwards, Reting asked what had given him the confidence to do so, the monk replied that he had taken the view that if the shot had killed him, he would have died at the hand of a high lama and would therefore be assured of a favorable rebirth. But if these eccentricities could perhaps be overlooked, the venality of the Reting *labrang* (or household) could not.*

As was customary, following the new Dalai Lama's arrival in Lhasa, the National Assembly met to discuss an appropriate reward to be bestowed on the regent for successfully identifying and repatriating the rightful occupant of the Lion Throne. While there was general agreement that a reward of sev-

---

* Roughly equivalent to a modern-day personal trust, the *labrang* is the legal owner of the estates and other property attaching to the *tulku* who becomes its life tenant. When he "manifests the act of passing away," the assets of the *labrang* pass to his successor. Much like a modern-day trust, the *labrang* may well have a trading arm, and it will also have a household which it maintains. At that time, the *labrang* manager of Reting was a notably grasping character, a man completely unable to resist an opportunity to make money, whether by extortion, taxation, or pushing the boundaries of trade agreements entered into innocently by others.

eral landed estates would be suitable, one of the regent's placemen announced that fifty or even sixty estates would be inadequate to express the gratitude the government should properly feel toward him. This prompted an argument in the course of which one of the more outspoken ministers repeated a proverb:

> After eating the mountain, hunger is not satisfied,
> After drinking the ocean, thirst is not slaked.

This was interpreted by the regent's party as an open insult, and the minister in question was forced to resign. Shortly afterwards, Reting moved to reward the monk who had spoken in his favor by making him abbot of an important college. This incensed the college members, all of whom remained loyal to the present incumbent. A standoff ensued and resulted in the regent's finally having to back down. But before he did so, his support within government circles had largely evaporated. Not long afterwards, rumors began to circulate about the regent's sexual indiscretions.

It seems inescapable that these rumors were grounded in fact and that not only did Reting have a male lover but also he had also fathered a child by a relative's wife. And whereas a blind eye could be turned to the one (indeed, homosexual relationships were nothing unusual within the monasteries and were condemned only if the parties engaged in penetrative sex), to the other no leniency could be shown. A monk who had broken one of his root precepts* was no longer a monk. It was for this reason that posters began to appear in Lhasa asserting Reting's unfitness to administer vows to the young Dalai Lama. Within the Tibetan tradition, vows are not sworn by the one who will keep them but are "administered," or "conferred," by someone who already maintains the precepts the novice vows to keep. In this case, the regent was due to confer the thirty-six preliminary monastic precepts on the Dalai Lama as part of the *getsul* ceremony, at which the boy would formally embark on the path to full ordination as a *bikshu* (the title given to one who is so ordained) in the

* Besides chastity, these included vows not to kill, not to steal, and not to boast about one's spiritual attainments.

Mahayana* tradition — the Mahayana being the more recent of the two great schools within Buddhism taken as a whole.

This was a scandal of the most serious import. Of course, the Regent could simply deny the rumors — as many advised that he should. But for all his faults, it is clear that Reting Rinpoché took his vocation seriously. He had offended against the precepts of his calling, and he could not and would not try to pretend otherwise. He therefore announced that various spiritual and oracular sources had given strong presentiments of danger to his life if he did not at once resign his position and undertake a lengthy retreat.

Who, then, should take his place as regent? It is clear that Reting saw resignation as only a temporary measure. He would indeed undertake a lengthy retreat, but once the *getsul* ceremony was out of the way, and when the scandal had died down, he would reassume his position until the Dalai Lama came of age. With this in mind, he would ask his own teacher, the elderly Taktra (pronounced, roughly, "Ta-tag") Rinpoché, to stand in for him.

Many of those closest to Reting urged him to reconsider. He could avoid the *getsul* ceremony by claiming illness. But Reting refused. In that case, at least one of his advisers urged, he should make sure not actually to relinquish power. Taktra should act only in matters of minor importance. Reting must not make the mistake of letting go of "the orphan's box of brick tea."

The story of the orphan's box of brick tea (the tea that Tibetans generally drink is made from leaves compressed into bricks for ease of transport) perfectly illustrates the thought processes of a traditionally educated Tibetan. Once there was a child who became orphaned. Being in need, he went at once in search of his uncles and aunts. On asking succor of them, he was serially rebuffed. "I'm not your uncle." "I'm not your aunt." Alone and distraught, the orphan went on his way, when, as great good luck would have it, he came across an abandoned box of brick tea. These were riches indeed! It was a time

* Mahayana means literally the Great Vehicle, in contrast to Hinayana, meaning, pejoratively, the Lesser Vehicle, though this usage is less usual today. Instead, Theravada is preferred. This — earlier — tradition rejects (generally speaking) as spurious the Mahayana scriptures, which only began to emerge at the beginning of the first millennium, some five hundred years after the death of the historical Buddha.

when tea was in great scarcity. All of a sudden, he found himself besieged by people claiming to be his relatives. At this he bowed down before the box: "Because of you, I have found uncles. Because of you, I have found aunts." It is, of course, a version of the story of the goose that laid the golden egg.

Reting is said to have laughed on being reminded of the story, knowing full well that in his case the box of brick tea symbolized his power as regent. But still he would not budge.

The first the now seven-year-old Dalai Lama knew of the matter was when asked who he thought should replace Reting as his senior tutor. It is likely that the question was posed in such a way that the only answer was Taktra. In any case, the appointment suited the boy, who considered the elderly Taktra "a very gentle man." But though Taktra may have been gentle in person, and apt to fall asleep on those occasions when he came to conduct a lesson with the Precious Protector, it turned out that in his dealings with others, he was as stern and unyielding as his politics were dictatorial and his religion was reactionary.

Right away the new regent, installed in early 1941, determined that Reting should have nothing further to do with the young Dalai Lama. Partly this was due to Reting's behavior. But one thing that seems particularly to have concerned the new regent was his former student's dabbling in Nyingma teachings and practice.

Since the demise of the Great Thirteenth, a major development within Gelug circles was the increased popularity of devotion to the protector deity Dorje Shugden, claimed guardian of the legacy of Tsongkhapa. It was held that Shugden took severe exception to anyone belonging to the Gelug school who took Nyingma teachings, and Reting had done just that. In 1937 he had sought out a reclusive Nyingma hermit* to initiate him into the mysteries of *dzogchen,* a set of esoteric practices said to have been brought to Tibet by Padmasambhava, the eighth-century wonder-worker and saint known as the Lotus-Born. The new regent was, by contrast, determined that the young Dalai

* This was Chatral Rinpoché (1913–2015). Note that it is not enough merely to read and accept the validity of a body of scripture. The seeker must receive them in a transmission from a suitably qualified master.

Lama should not be exposed to heresy of this sort. He therefore appointed as assistant tutor, alongside himself as senior tutor and Ling Rinpoché as junior tutor, the charismatic young Trijang Rinpoché, an aristocrat with fine manners and a large following among the upper echelons of Lhasan society. In common with both regents and with Ling Rinpoché, the new assistant tutor was a student of the most renowned lama of the early twentieth century, Phabongka Rinpoché, and of them all, none guarded his legacy so zealously. The reason this was so significant is that Phabongka Rinpoché was the deity's chief advocate and cheerleader.

Whereas Ling Rinpoché, who came from a humble background, was distinctly otherworldly, Trijang Rinpoché was more outgoing, with a much-admired talent for his ability simultaneously to compose and recite religious verse — a kind of spiritual rap, if that is not too profane an analogy. And he too was an accomplished mystic. A somewhat alarming example of his powers is seen in his foreknowledge of the death of those with "perverted intentions": whenever he dreamed of yaks, sheep, or some other living creature being killed in connection with a given individual, it was a sure sign of that person's imminent demise. This he attributed to "the wrathful assistance of the protector," Dorje Shugden, to whom he was especially close. In another dream, he "saw a platter with many frogs on it." Two of these jumped out from under the cloth covering the platter, and, he recalled, "I could see fresh red sores on their backs," while the rest of the frogs became "soft and mushy." This he understood as a sure sign that he would soon recover from a severe illness. But an even more remarkable sign of Trijang's spiritual attainments was his ability to influence the weather. In his autobiography he records how on one occasion, after he had given a short teaching while traveling, a black cloud suddenly formed, and his party was caught in a hailstorm that hurled down particles of ice "the size of dried apricots." The thunder and lightning were so violent that it felt as if the sky and earth were being rent asunder. Inside the tents, sparks of fire and a smell like gunpowder seemed to presage a thunderbolt. At once the Rinpoché made an offering to the local spirits and sought the aid of the protector deities by making a tea offering to them. But though he recited the prescribed mantras and undertook the requisite visualizations as best he could, nothing had any effect. It was only when he burned some fresh excrement (presumably his own) that the gods relented. "Immediately the sky above became clear, like the opening of a skylight."

Unfortunately for the young Dalai Lama, this new appointment served only to increase the burdens he faced. As Trijang Rinpoché recalled in his autobiography, "His Holiness seemed a bit shy on my first visit, as his personal attendants had apparently mentioned that Trijang Tulku had a short temper." It seems indeed that Taktra Rinpoché was concerned at the boy's tendency to misbehave. "On the advice of the precious regent . . . I maintained a serious expression and did not smile." Yet he was even colder toward Lobsang Samten, whom he would scold "with a grave countenance, chiding him for distracting his younger brother."

This was evidently the beginning of a somewhat irksome period in the young boys' lives, though from his autobiography, *Freedom in Exile,* we gather that the Precious Protector's natural ebullience prevented him from ever falling into despondency. Clearly one who enjoyed the rough-and-tumble of boyhood play, the Dalai Lama relates a forbidden game that involved placing a wooden board at an angle and running at it as fast as possible to see how far he and Lobsang Samten could jump. He was also fond of soccer, despite this too being forbidden out of religious scruple. When the British mission had introduced the sport to Lhasa some years previously, the monasteries, seeing the enthusiasm that Tibetans quickly developed for the game, were appalled. Correctly seeing it as an agent of foreign influence and change, they likened it to "kicking the Buddha's head," and soon after, the civil authorities instituted a public ban.

If the Precious Protector was at times a somewhat unruly student, he could, as we have seen, conduct himself with becoming gravity. In December 1942, a pair of American spies from the Office of Strategic Services (one of the organizations out of which the CIA was subsequently created) paid the Dalai Lama a visit in the Potala. Disappointingly for them, the protocol of the day demanded that the Precious Protector receive them in silence and that they leave him in silence — though this was clearly not the case when Thomas Manning met the six-year-old Ninth Dalai Lama in 1811. As Captain Ilya Tolstoy (a grandson of the great Leo) wrote, he and his companion were "immediately impressed by his young but stern face and not at all frail constitution."

Tolstoy and his companion, a Captain Dolan, had come to Tibet in the hope of surveying an overland route between India and China that could be used to supply the Chinese Nationalists against the Japanese, who had recently invaded large parts of China. The usual route across Burma had been cut when the Japanese ousted the British from that country. The Tibetan route was never used, but the connection thereby established with the United States came soon enough to have important consequences for the Dalai Lama. In the meantime, however, it was the gifts the Americans brought that were of most interest to the boy. Alongside a signed photograph of President Truman, a model of a nineteenth-century sailing ship executed in silver, and several pieces of glass, it was the multi-movement Patek Philippe pocket watch that pleased him the most. (By chance he had sent it for repair in Switzerland at the time of his flight into exile in 1959 and still has it in his possession.)

In fact, the two OSS men were not the only Americans in Lhasa during this period. The photographer Archibald Steele, who had happened to be in Kumbum at the time of the Dalai Lama's discovery, visited in 1944 on assignment for the *Chicago Daily News.* From his reports it is clear that, outwardly at least, an atmosphere of calm prevailed in the Tibetan capital while the Second World War raged far away. Noting that when an enterprising trader brought a consignment of motorcycles to Lhasa, it took only one incident of a government minister's horse being frightened for a ban to be proclaimed, Steele had no reason to doubt the senior government minister's claim that, really, "nothing ever happens here." Events such as the Dalai Lama's removal from the Potala to the Norbulingka Palace on the eighth day of the third month, the Festival of Mahakala, were in any case of far greater import to Tibetans than what was going on in the world on the other side of the Himalayas. For the Dalai Lama, too, the weeks that followed were most enjoyable. It was during this time that he had the pleasure of watching the theatricals that were held outside the palace grounds. Besides operas and *cham,* the religious dances famed for the acrobatic whirling and leaping of the performers, there were also satires in which the players dressed up as members of the aristocracy and lampooned them. "It was," as the Dalai Lama recalled in his autobiography, "such a happy time!"

Yet beneath Lhasa's calm exterior, an explosive confrontation was brewing. At the beginning of the Dalai Lama's ninth year (1944), the Nechung oracle had warned of looming obstacles that could harm the Precious Protector. In the Buddhist view, an "obstacle" is a spiritual circumstance likely to produce a negative impact on one or more individuals if not cleared by means of appropriate action. In the case of a high lama, this would normally take the form of a long-life ceremony, during the course of which the protector deities are besought to intervene on his behalf to clear away accretions of negative karma. It might be thought that as a manifestation of a bodhisattva, the Dalai Lama would be impervious to such hindrances, but that is not the case. Because of his exalted position, he is in fact especially vulnerable. Moreover, the greater the perceived danger, the greater the spiritual firepower that needs to be deployed in his defense. It was at this moment that, sensing an opportunity, the self-exiled Reting made a move. Given the nature of their deep spiritual connection, he could plausibly advance himself as the right person to intercede on the Dalai Lama's behalf. It was now three years since he had given up the regency, and this being the standard length of time for an important retreat, his reappearance in Lhasa should cause no surprise. Taktra, however, suspecting correctly that Reting was hoping to reassume the regency, did not respond to his overtures.

The reason for Taktra's silence is not hard to determine. Not only was he intent on keeping his position for personal reasons, but also Reting had further alienated himself from the government by maintaining independent contact with Shen Zonglian, the suave Harvard-educated representative of the Chinese Nationalists who had been stationed in Lhasa since 1937. Reting's continued closeness to the Dalai Lama's family was a further source of dismay. The *yabshi kung* had by this time also become deeply unpopular. Keenly aware of his status, the Dalai Lama's father never failed to exercise the privilege of having people on horseback dismount when they encountered him in the street. On one occasion when someone failed to do so, he had the man flogged. On another, he confiscated the rider's horse (even though the man was sick and unable to walk). He had, as a result, recently been publicly censured by the National Assembly for bad manners.

Most concerning of all was the confluence of these two associations. Following private discussions between Reting and the Chinese representative, arrangements had been made for Gyalo Thondup, the Dalai Lama's second-eldest brother, now seventeen years of age, to be sent to China to be educated. And not only that, but also he would be enrolled in Nanking University as a special student under the direct sponsorship of Generalissimo Chiang Kai-shek himself. Astonishingly, this meant that the Dalai Lama's brother would become the houseguest of the president of China.

Gyalo Thondup first met the Generalissimo and his American-educated wife soon after arriving in Nanking. Thereafter he was a frequent guest at their house. "They came to treat me as a son," he wrote many years later. Finding them "unfailingly warm and gracious hosts," he "visited their home frequently and often dined with them on the weekends." What especially impressed him about the couple was how well they treated their staff and how austerely they lived. "Dinner at the home of President and Madam Chiang was," he recounted, "invariably simple."

Given this level of intimacy, it is clear that the Generalissimo had marked Gyalo Thondup as an important future ally. No doubt when the Dalai Lama attained his majority, Gyalo Thondup would have been put forward as the Chinese president's personal representative in Tibet, responsible for seeing to the implementation of the Nationalists' five-races policy, *zhonghua minzu,* whereby the Han, Manchu, Tibetan, Hui, and Mongol peoples would unite to form the Chinese nation.

Taktra could do nothing about Reting's arrangement with the Chinese on Gyalo Thondup's behalf, but he could continue to ignore Reting's pleas for a meeting, while the ex-regent himself fretted and began to plot.

Meanwhile, the young Dalai Lama continued his education and attended the daily tea ceremony. Then at night, he and Lobsang Samten would listen in gleeful terror to the ghost stories told by the "sweepers" — the serving staff — in the Potala. And he would count down the days to his mother's next visit.

8

Trouble in Shangri-La: Devilry and Intrigue on the Roof of the World

When Reting resigned the regency, Taktra had wasted no time in eliminating his predecessor's allies in government. Nonetheless, Reting still had powerful supporters. In the eyes of the people, nothing could detract from the fact of his childhood miracles, nor from his gift of the return of the Dalai Lama. When he finally reappeared in Lhasa in December 1944 in the company of a large and splendid retinue, it was only a matter of time before open confrontation would break out between the present regent and his predecessor. For his part, Taktra Rinpoché had no intention of relinquishing his position.

As for any opinion the Dalai Lama might have had, he was not consulted. Although he was required to attend the morning tea ceremony that brought together all the government's senior members, his role in affairs of state at this stage was minimal and purely formal. All that was demanded of him was that he be a good pupil and study hard. And this, indeed, was a matter of some concern to Taktra. The reports reaching him from the Dalai Lama's tutors were far from encouraging. It was therefore decided that the boy must be separated from his brother, Lobsang Samten, who was instead enrolled in one of Lhasa's few (private) schools.

This was a serious blow. Now the two brothers saw each other only once a month. "When he left after each visit," the Dalai Lama wrote in adulthood, "I remember standing at the window watching, my heart full of sorrow, as he disappeared into the distance." In place of his brother, his serving staff — the monk "sweepers" who cleaned the rooms and served as waiters — became the Dalai Lama's playmates. These uneducated men from lowly backgrounds were his constant companions, and it is largely thanks to them that the Dalai Lama can look back fondly on this period of his childhood. "They were full of fun and joy . . . always joking," he declared. Somewhat unexpectedly, the games they played mostly involved pretending to be soldiers. It turns out that many of the men had been recruits in their youth and had trained in British army drill. They taught the Precious Protector how to stand to attention and present arms using pieces of wood for guns. Then "we would march [around] the gardens." They would also fight mock battles in the Norbulingka park, while back at the Potala, where to go outside meant only to go out onto the roof, the young Dalai Lama would spend hours engrossed in copies of *Life* magazine, with their dramatic pictures of the world war just concluded, and fashioning squadrons of tanks out of *tsampa* dough.

The sweepers were also an inexhaustible source of stories and folktales, of which Tibet has a generous supply. Popular motifs include shape shifters and talking animals, wicked stepmothers and benevolent strangers, scurrilous monks and beautiful goddesses, hermits in caves and wandering minstrels, foolish girls and fortune-tellers, not to mention the ghosts and demons whose capricious nature is the bane of Everyman's life. There were also stories concerning the Potala itself — about the great birds that would come and carry off small boys, and about Arko Lhamo, the merest mention of which occasioned terror in the boy's innermost being. This was a demon spirit said to occupy a storeroom in the dungeons below.

The looming dispute between the Taktra government and the former regent came a step closer when Reting called on the government to drop charges against some monks from his alma mater, Sera Che, one of the colleges at Sera

Monastery.* They had been accused of beating a government debt collector — with, among other weapons, a leg of dried mutton — so badly that he died of his wounds.

Here it is important to say something about loyalty in traditional Tibetan culture. As in medieval Europe, ties between individuals as well as with the institutions that gave them a home were sacrosanct. Not only were ex-students morally obliged later in life to contribute materially to their monastery, but also they had an obligation to defend its honor as staunchly as if it were their own family. In the traditional view, this extended to the shedding of blood where necessary.

Even though the Sera monks were charged with manslaughter, Reting Rinpoché was determined that Sera Che should not lose face and be forced to hand the accused over for questioning. Had he been successful in reclaiming the regency, this would have been a relatively easy matter to arrange. But the fact that he had failed to do so did not lessen the obligation he felt, and he continued to support the Sera authorities in what became a trial of strength with the government.

The standoff continued throughout the whole of 1945, coming to a head only as the Great Prayer Festival of the following year approached. This was to be the first in which the young Dalai Lama would act in an official capacity. It was therefore essential that there be no disruption or break with protocol. Knowing this, the abbots of Sera announced that the monastery would not participate in the forthcoming ceremonies unless the charges against their monks were dropped. At the same time, weapons were distributed throughout the monastery in case the government should decide to try to apprehend the presumed culprits by brute force. The monastery leadership was convinced that the case did not lie within the government's jurisdiction and was a matter for themselves alone. In other words, what lay at the heart of the dispute was the question of the central government's right, and indeed its ability, to impose its authority on individual monasteries.

---

* Che was one of the two *khang tsen,* or colleges, that made up Sera Monastery, the other being Sera Mey.

The government, for its part, refused to budge. As a result, none of Sera's monks were present at the opening ceremonies of the New Year festival. When the government subsequently announced that the case could be postponed if the monks attended as usual, the Sera abbots interpreted this move to mean that the case would now be settled in their favor. The monks duly came to Lhasa and were present at all the remaining New Year ceremonies.

Ultimately the disastrous standoff between Sera Che and the government had no impact on ensuing events, and it is doubtful whether the Dalai Lama was even informed. For him, the most important aspect of this New Year festival was his induction at Drepung Monastery, which marked his formal entry into the course of learning that would culminate in the award of the *geshe* degree. Something like a doctorate in the modern Western university curriculum, it is this that qualifies a monk to take students and to be a teacher of the Buddhadharma.

The Dalai Lama's junior tutor, Trijang Rinpoché, records a lighthearted moment during a rehearsal for his young student's debut at Drepung when all those present had a fit of the giggles as the preliminary prayers were being chanted. First Ling Rinpoché burst out laughing, then the boy, then the abbot of Namgyal Monastery, the Lord Chamberlain, the chief attendant, and, finally, the junior tutor all "laughed uncontrollably." Everyone, that is except Taktra Rinpoché, the regent, who looked on sternly.

In the event, the Dalai Lama gave an impressive demonstration of his abilities, to the great satisfaction of his tutors. But with the 1946 New Year festival concluded, events in Lhasa took a turn for the worse. The agreement to postpone the case against the Sera monks turned out to be nothing more than that. The regent had no intention of dropping the charges. Instead he planned to arrest the abbot of Sera Che when he came to the Norbulingka later in the year for the traditional reception of the monastery leadership by the Dalai Lama. Perhaps warned, the abbot avoided the ceremony, claiming ill health. He then called on his monks to join him in open revolt against the government. But in another twist, part of the college refused to support him. Realizing that without their full backing there was no chance of facing down the government, the abbot resigned on the spot and, together with his closest supporters, fled in the direction of his native place.

The government, alerted to what had happened, immediately sent troops to apprehend the abbot, dead or alive. But while he himself escaped, disguised as a beggar, his brother, who was with him, was mortally wounded in an engagement to the east of Lhasa. Because of their strong family resemblance, the soldiers mistakenly assumed that they had killed the abbot. Only when his head and hands arrived back in Lhasa, sent as proof of mission accomplished, was it realized that the intended target had escaped. He, meanwhile, sought refuge with the Chinese, who gave him a warm welcome. At last, however, the government was able to prosecute the monks it had sought for so long. They were all duly flogged.

Reting Rinpoché, now returned to his own monastery and following events from afar, was incensed. At first he wanted to go to Sera Che and lead a rebellion against the government in person, lamenting that it was he himself who had given Taktra his position first as assistant tutor to the Dalai Lama, then as senior tutor, and finally as regent. And although he was eventually dissuaded from taking so drastic a course of action, Reting's next move could only be interpreted by the government as a staggering betrayal. Writing directly to Chiang Kai-shek, he asked for Chinese support against the Tibetan government on the grounds that the regent was pro-British. If the Nationalists would send troops to enable him to take back the regency, he, Reting, would cooperate fully with the Chinese.

As if this were not enough, the ex-regent's closest advisers urged immediate action. Reting Rinpoché argued that his people should wait until the Chinese responded. But those surrounding him were desperate men, and while he might be a Buddhist practitioner gifted with extraordinary insight, Reting's judgment in temporal matters was decidedly poor. To their continued entreaties, he replied that he would support them in whatever they decided was necessary, adding only that they should be careful. Rashly, they decided that what was needed was Taktra's liberation from earthly existence. The problem they now faced was that the regent rarely ventured out in public. Two possibilities were considered. One was to ambush him as he returned to Lhasa from his hermitage later in the year. This would enable the attack to take place at night, far from the city. Ultimately this plan was abandoned. Instead he was to be hit with hand grenades during his inspection of the butter sculptures at the conclusion of the next Great Prayer Festival.

As it happened, Taktra did not venture out on the evening to inspect the *torma.* At this time another political faction, the Tibet Improvement Party, had begun recruiting members. Founded by a group of dissident monks—which included Kumbela, Lord Chamberlain to the Great Thirteenth, exiled following the latter's death—and supported by a wealthy trader from the eastern province of Kham, the group was allied to the Chinese Nationalists and committed to the overthrow of the government, by revolutionary means if necessary. Aware of its existence, and recognizing his own unpopularity with many who felt that, when it came to graft, he was no better than his predecessor, Taktra remained out of sight. He did, however, move to ensure that the Dalai Lama himself was further isolated from the looming crisis by curtailing his mother's access to him. His concern was that she was "misinforming" her son. As a result, not only did she have to arrange her visits in advance, but also she needed to be accompanied by an official.

Whether or not Taktra Rinpoché had anything to do with the death of the Dalai Lama's father shortly after the Great Prayer Festival of 1947 is a matter for conjecture. What is known is that the *yabshi kung* became ill soon after eating a large amount of a pork, a meat of which he was particularly fond. It is plausible that trichinosis was the cause of death, given that he was ill for almost three weeks. But many say that he was poisoned. He was, after all, deeply unpopular with large numbers of the aristocracy and, from the regent's point of view, immensely dangerous: he remained close to Reting, his eldest son was being touted as the next abbot of Kumbum Monastery, and his second son was a personal guest of President Chiang Kai-shek in China, not to mention that his fourth son was Dalai Lama. A family legend contends that the poisoner was the manager of the *yabshi kung*'s country estate outside Lhasa. But whether or not the accusation is true—and the Dalai Lama himself retains an open mind on the matter—it was certainly to the regent's advantage for this increasingly well-connected ally of Reting's to be taken out of the picture at this time.

One might expect the death of his father to have had a considerable impact on the Dalai Lama, but in fact they rarely saw each other, and in contrast to his reaction to the deaths of others close to him, the Dalai Lama has never made much of this loss.

Meanwhile, given that the regent had no scheduled public appearance before mid-April, the Reting plotters, impatient to act, turned to still more desperate measures. They devised a package bomb consisting of a wooden box concealing a standard Mills bomb of British manufacture. Once the firing pin was withdrawn, a sliding lid held the trigger in place. The device was delivered to the regent's secretary with a message identifying the contents as a secret report from the governor of Kham. Since it was usual for important missives to contain a gift, the size and weight of the box would not have aroused suspicion.

Unfortunately for the plotters, their plans fell victim to the traditional Tibetan habit of interpreting the word "urgent" to mean something other than a requirement for immediate action. The package was placed in a drawer, where it sat for several weeks. After some time, one of Reting's associates threw an anonymous note through the window of Taktra's residence suggesting that important information was being withheld from him. This, however, was seen as nothing more than a crude attempt to sow discord and was ignored by Taktra's household. A servant of the regent's secretary became curious about the package, however, thinking it might contain something valuable, and decided to see for himself. Carefully opening the box, he heard a hissing sound and, judging it possessed, ran from the room, narrowly escaping injury when it exploded.

News of the assassination attempt was passed back from the British mission to London, where the story found its way into the newspapers. The *Daily Mail* published a report under the headline "Trouble in Shangri La." But although the regent's office was unable to trace the individual who had delivered either the bomb or the later message, the regent was now alert to the serious danger in which he stood.

Two weeks passed before Taktra hit back. When he did so, it was on the basis of a top-secret telegraph message received in Lhasa from the Tibetan representative in Nanjing (the Nationalists' capital, also known as Nanking). His contacts had obtained direct proof of Reting Rinpoché's request for urgent military assistance from the Chinese. This was incontrovertible evidence of the ex-regent's treachery. Taktra moved with unusual haste. That very night he dispatched two ministers and a detachment of two hundred troops to Reting

Monastery. Meanwhile, orders were given for Reting Rinpoché's Lhasa residence to be sealed and searched. As Taktra hoped, this yielded plenty of incriminating evidence, including at least one grenade wrapped in silk brocade. But some of Reting's men, apprised of the impending raid, escaped in the direction of Reting Monastery, hoping to alert the ex-regent to the danger he faced.

When, the following week, soldiers arrived at his monastery, they discovered Reting Rinpoché innocently feeding birds on the roof of his house. Although this was an arrest, it was conducted with the full formality that was the ex-regent's due; the officers all prostrated themselves three times and offered a *kathag.* He gave them his blessing in return. They then "invited" him to go with them back to Lhasa. But of course it was on their terms, not his. He was compelled to ride a mule rather than his usual mount, a horse called Yudrug, which they dared not let him ride, as it was well known to possess supernatural powers.

As soon as news of Reting's arrest reached the monks of Sera Che, an angry mob demanded that the senior monk scholars compel the abbot to intercede with the government. But although they tried, the abbot was an appointee of Taktra's and not inclined to act. On realizing that the scholars had been rebuffed, the mob immediately stormed the abbot's house. They were met by his chief steward, who, fearing for his master's life, pulled out a revolver and shot the ringleader and wounded another of the rebels. Unluckily for him, his revolver then jammed and he was in turn cut down with a sword, along with two of his servants. Meanwhile, the abbot, who lived upstairs, ran onto the roof and tried to make good his escape. But coming to a gap between buildings, he hesitated to jump and was slain by the monks pursuing him.

Sera Che was now in open rebellion against the government in support of their beloved brother, the ex-regent. One of the college's incarnate lamas declared himself "war leader" and set about organizing troop dispositions. A plea to negotiate with the government was swiftly rejected; instead, a group hastened to Lhasa with the intention of breaking into Reting's house to retrieve the weapons locked inside. They were prevented from carrying out their plans, though they did inflict a number of casualties in the attempt.

Undaunted, the Sera monks, correctly assuming that the party escorting Reting back to Lhasa would pass in front of the monastery, lay in wait. When the posse appeared, the monks unleashed what fire they could muster from their depleted armory. The government's forces fully anticipated this, however, and, as soon as the monks appeared, began to shoot. One eyewitness described how a stream of monks burst from the monastery precincts, only to be driven back by the weight of fire. Many died that day, while Reting himself was duly incarcerated.

Another eyewitness to this dreadful scene was the young Dalai Lama, watching events unfold from the roof of the Potala. With his telescope he had a good view of Sera Monastery a mile distant. For him, the spectacle was first and foremost a matter of wonder and excitement. "At last," he recalled, "this was some proper work for my telescope to do." But we do not get any sense that he was alert to the danger he himself was now in. With Reting out of the way, the only limit to the regent's power would be the person of the Dalai Lama, who, as a twelve-year-old boy cut off from his family, would be in no position to fight his own battle, should that prove necessary.

Next day, the Sera monks launched another attack on Lhasa to try to seize some weapons kept in a house belonging to a trading partner of the Reting estate. Fearing just such an attempt, the government had already sealed the house, but this time the monks were successful. With the loss of only three of their number, they managed to make off with a large consignment of matériel. In response, the army was ordered to deploy the artillery. The first attempts to shell the rebel monastery later in the day were unsuccessful, however. To the jeering of the monks, the army commander sent urgently for J. T. Taring, one of the officers who had trained with the British in India. Describing how he was summoned during the night, Taring subsequently recalled how, as if in presentiment of what was to follow, he and many others heard a loud moaning sound "like the call of the guardian deity of the cremation ground."

Re-sighting the guns, Taring scored a direct hit on one of the buildings where the monks were suspected of hiding. But even though it was by now clear to the rebels that the government was prepared for all-out war, they refused negotiations. They would back down only if the government released the ex-regent, fully restored his rights and property, and dropped all charges against the bomb plotters. Short of that, they announced, they would have no regrets even if Sera Che were reduced to rubble.

By the time the crisis had fully played out, at least two hundred monks would die, though some estimates put the eventual death toll at nearer three hundred. Around thirty government soldiers were also killed.

When the monks finally gave in, they put down their weapons, returned to their cells, and resumed their prayers as if nothing had happened. The five ringleaders were immediately seized and thrown in jail, there to spend the rest of their lives. A minority continued to defy the government, and it would be several more weeks before they were captured. They were all flogged, with between one and two hundred lashes apiece, before being put in irons and having the cangue fastened around their necks.

While the siege of Reting Rinpoché's alma mater was moving toward its bloody conclusion, the ex-regent himself remained in custody. Because the government now had in its possession not only copies of the letters he had sent to the Chinese but also a clear instruction to kill Taktra, he had no room to maneuver. His only real hope was to appeal personally to Taktra Rinpoché in his capacity as the regent's *chela,* or spiritual son. This bond is regarded as sacred and therefore impossible to abrogate. But his captors ensured that the appeal was not heard. In the meantime, Reting faced calls for various torments, including that his eyes be put out, as Lungshar's had been, or that he be sewn inside an animal hide and thrown off a high cliff in accordance with a seventh-century edict of King Songtsen Gampo.

For more than a week the government ministers deliberated over what punishment should be meted out to the ex-regent. At one point, the Precious Protector was approached (it is not clear by whom) to intervene on Reting's behalf while the ex-regent lay incarcerated in the dungeons below the Potala. But as he explained later, "my position was hopeless." With his father dead and himself isolated not just from Lobsang Samten but also, lately, from his mother, the future ruler was given no opportunity to express any opinion he might have, let alone influence proceedings at this critical moment. Then, on May 8, Reting suddenly died. He had recently complained of a headache and asked that he be moved to a brighter, less cramped cell. This request was refused, but he was permitted a visit by a doctor, who prescribed medicine. It is said that around midnight, piercing screams could be heard coming from the area of the Potala where Reting was imprisoned.

Immediately rumors began to spread. According to one, the ex-regent had died from having his testicles crushed, supposedly in punishment for having broken his vow of celibacy. Another, more plausible, held that the medicine he had been given was in fact poison. Still another charged that he had been strangled. But whatever the cause, all Lhasa was in shock. In spite of his many faults, Reting Rinpoché was held in highest regard for his spiritual accomplishments, and his popularity among the laity was immense. Loud were the shouts of sorrow that went up when mourners came to view his body, displayed in the temple at his Lhasa residence.

No sooner was Reting out of the way than the regent took the opportunity to revisit the question of the identity of the Dalai Lama himself. Support for Ditru Rinpoché, the nephew of the Great Thirteenth, still remained strong in certain circles. It would be hugely advantageous to Taktra if he could show that Reting had made a mistake in the selection process. The prestige Reting had enjoyed as the one who had found the Dalai Lama would then be his. Accordingly, with the connivance of the National Assembly, it was agreed to put the question to the deities once more, and Nechung was publicly invoked in a trance.

This was a startling development. It amounted to an attempted coup d'état, though in the face of Taktra's disloyalty to the young Dalai Lama, the deities made it resoundingly clear that the current occupant of the Lion Throne had been correctly identified. Yet this was still not enough for the Dalai Lama's detractors, and, astonishingly, the matter was put to the deities one more time. And even when this additional investigation came down clearly in favor of Tenzin Gyatso, there was a move — unsuccessful — to question them yet again.

Humiliatingly, Taktra had been publicly rebuked by the deities. It is hardly surprising, therefore, that from this point on, though he had defeated his opponent, the regent found himself completely isolated. His plan to keep the Dalai Lama in a similar state of isolation became increasingly ineffective. Showing considerable initiative, the Precious Protector used his close relations with the sweepers to maximum effect. From them he learned not only about the petty injustices they had to face on a daily basis but also about the inequity of the taxes imposed on the lower classes. On one occasion, with their help, he eavesdropped outside the door when the regent and other high officials were hearing a complaint brought by a peasant. "The officials started bullying him, and they just would not allow him to talk," he recalled. Gradually, the young Dalai Lama began to get a sense that social and political reform was urgently needed.

The Dalai Lama was also keenly aware of Tibet's backwardness with respect to modern technology. By this time he had discovered the Great Thirteenth's cars lying neglected at the Norbulingka and was eager to see them running again. Together with the Great Thirteenth's driver, he started working on them, cannibalizing parts from one for the benefit of the other. Meeting eventually with success, he made his first attempt at driving, which ended in an embarrassing shunt, the effects of which he did his best to disguise. Seeking as much information about the outside world as possible, he also began taking his first English lessons from one of the four young men who had been sent to England for education by the Great Thirteenth.* But it was not until 1949, when he was fourteen, that he was finally able to free himself completely from the regent's control.

* This was Chang Ngopa Rinzin Dorje, also known as Kusho Ringang.

9

The Perfection of Wisdom: The Higher Education of a Tibetan Buddhist Monk

Without question, the person who had the greatest impact on the Dalai Lama as he grew to maturity was Ling Rinpoché. Although his senior tutor was a strict disciplinarian, the Tibetan hierarch feels only gratitude for the way he "did his best to instil good qualities in me" and continues to hold him in the highest regard. The growing awareness of his responsibilities not just to the Tibetan people but to all sentient beings was evidently almost overwhelming at times. The Dalai Lama speaks of having felt like a boat cut adrift, imperiled on the one hand by whirlpools and waterfalls, and running aground on the other, but it was Ling Rinpoché who helped stabilize the craft. By others, the Precious Protector's senior tutor is remembered as a man with little in the way of small talk, reserved — though not without a keen sense of humor — and a monk whose conduct was in every way exemplary. Later, the two men developed a firm friendship, marked by deep respect on both sides.

It was Ling Rinpoché who first introduced the young Dalai Lama to the discipline of *tsoe pa* (generally translated as debate but more accurately as dialectics). This was, as it remains, the cornerstone of the education of a novice monk in the Tibetan tradition.

As anyone who has witnessed a monastery courtyard during a debating session will be aware, it is also one of its chief glories. Observing the shouting, the laughter, the jeering, the foot-stamping, and the flourishing of rosary with which the challenger belabors his adversary, you could be forgiven for thinking you were watching a prizefight. It is only the figure of the defender sitting rock-like and imperturbable that reminds you this is a scholarly rather than a pugilistic contest. It was this practice that lay at the heart of the young Dalai Lama's education: his prowess as a debater would determine his reputation as a scholar.

We would have to go back to the Middle Ages in Europe to find anything close to what remains a vital element of Tibetan culture. But while debate in the Tibetan tradition strongly resembles the Western Socratic method, it differs from it in one crucial respect. Whereas the Socratic method is a free inquiry into the truth or falsity of a given proposition, Tibetan debate is principally concerned with clarifying that which is already known: *the way things really are.* If this sounds like a travesty of what dialectics ought to be, that is to miss the point. Although debate in the Tibetan tradition may approach its subject matter with forensic precision, it is not an inquiry. It is, first, a method of sharpening the logical reasoning skills of the practitioner and, second, a discipline that aims to reinforce what the Buddha* revealed when he proclaimed the Four Noble Truths, namely:

1. The truth of suffering
2. The truth of the cause of suffering
3. The truth of the cessation of suffering
4. The truth of the Path to the cessation of suffering

We might paraphrase this by saying, first, that, contrary to what the Christian Bible tells us, the world is not "good." It is unsatisfactory. When we are in it, we suffer. Moreover, all those things of the world that we think will make

* The word "Buddha" may be translated as "one who is awakened."

us happy or bring us satisfaction are in fact only causes of further suffering. To put the matter in Judeo-Christian terms, the world itself is, in a sense, the Fall. Second, suffering is not gratuitous; it is caused — by our karma coming to fruition.* This includes not only moral suffering (the suffering attendant on negative acts, whether done by us or against us) but also natural suffering, like illness, old age, and death. Third, there is, fortunately, a way to overcome suffering (this could be called the gospel — the "good news" of Buddhism) through eliminating the causes of suffering. Fourth, the way to eliminate the causes of suffering is to follow the Path, indicated by the Buddha, to its final end, which is liberation from suffering, or nirvana.†

The basic handbooks of debate, the *Collected Topics,* were, for the Dalai Lama, as for every student entering a Gelug monastery, the principal object of study from the moment he was introduced to them. It was these that set out what it was that must be learned, while debate was the means by which the young scholar learned first to internalize and then to defend, through logical argument, what he had learned.

Because the principles around which Tibetan debate is structured are universal, anyone familiar with the basics of Aristotelian logic will have no trouble following those of the Indo-Tibetan tradition. Both trade on the inadmissibility of contradiction, and both recognize argument as requiring one or more premises to reach a conclusion. Like Aristotelian logic, Indo-Tibetan logic is essentially syllogistic and thus does not attain the mathematical precision of modern predicate logic. Yet adherents of both systems uphold their ultimate superiority even in the face of modern advances.

---

* It is important to realize that the doctrine of karma is by no means deterministic. The most highly realized practitioners may in certain circumstances be immune to its effects. Moreover, the present moment is precisely an opportunity to effect a transformation of one's accumulated karma. For example, when a negative memory (itself a karmic residue) is correctly contextualized, it may go from being a negative to a positive imprint. My memory of an accident or mishap may continue to distress me until I understand it as a timely warning to change my behavior.

† Such liberation is often termed "Enlightenment," but this can be misleading. It suggests a moment of epiphany. From the Buddhist perspective, one who is enlightened is straightforwardly one who has passed beyond suffering into nirvana.

Where the Indo-Tibetan philosophical tradition differs from the classical Western philosophical tradition is in its assumptions about the way the world really is. For Aristotle and his successors, the world is on its way to its final consummation in perfection. In the Indo-Tibetan system, the basic premise is that the world is chiefly characterized by suffering and that the cause of suffering is ignorance. Ignorance of what? Ignorance of the way things really are. The purpose of logical analysis is thus, in the Buddhist view, to dispel ignorance. As we come truly to understand the nature of things, so we will understand the need to become truly and limitlessly compassionate as a means to final liberation. What is it to be truly and limitlessly compassionate? Above all, being compassionate entails desiring that others cease to suffer and thus doing all we can to aid them in their quest to overcome suffering. Since the path elaborated by the Buddha is the sole means of overcoming suffering, the best help we can give others is guidance along that path. The better qualified we are, through our mastery of the teachings and practices that lead to liberation, the better equipped we will be to exercise compassion. And such mastery, it is held by the Gelug school, is best achieved through proficiency in debate, by means of which the practitioner develops his or her understanding of the great classics of Buddhist literature.

It was essential that the young Dalai Lama be accomplished in the art not just because of this, however. At the end of his formal education as a monk there would be no final written examinations, just keenly observed public debates. Although, as Dalai Lama, the Precious Protector was spared the rough-and-tumble of the courtyard (though one suspects he would have relished it) and instead had the advantage of being assigned a number of sparring partners (or *tsenshab*) with whom he would debate under the direction of his tutors, his eventual graduation was not a mere formality. He would have to earn the monastic community's respect just like any other prospective teacher.*

* Not all the Dalai Lamas have been great scholars. The Fourth, a Mongolian descendant of Genghis Khan, never learned Tibetan to an adequate degree and was likened, somewhat uncharitably, to an "empty box" (by Desi Sangye Gyatso in his biography of the Great Fifth); the Sixth refused to take holy orders, preferring instead to write love poetry and go on adventures with the more louche among the aristocratic youth of his day; the Eighth, a sickly young man,

But there was another — vital — element in the education of the Dalai Lama. His inner development as a meditator was of equal if not greater importance, and here too Ling Rinpoché's influence was paramount.

At the beginning of the meditator's training, the mind is likened to a rampaging elephant which it is his business to subdue, just as the mahout subdues the elephant. This is done in thirty-three carefully programmed stages. To begin, the elephant runs away from the mahout. But with persistence and gentleness, the beast is brought to the point where it will accept a rope. In the diagrams used in Buddhist textbooks to depict the process, the elephant is shown at the beginning as black in color and led by a black monkey. The monkey symbolizes distraction, while black symbolizes lethargy — the two great obstacles to taming the mind. When, at around the halfway mark, the mahout at last takes charge of the elephant, he finds it reluctant to move. But gradually, with persistence and kindness, the elephant is persuaded to follow its master. Eventually, trust is built up and the elephant does its tamer's bidding until eventually it no longer needs the rope. First it follows, then it allows itself to be mounted. The monkey is similarly tamed before being sent on its way. Finally, at the thirty-third stage, the mahout and the elephant become friends and the animal does whatever it is bidden.

Many today are somewhat familiar with Buddhist meditation thanks to the popularity of mindfulness. But within the Tibetan tradition, mindfulness is only one of a wide range of techniques. Moreover, it is almost invariably practiced alongside "insight," or single-pointed meditation — and always within the ethical and spiritual framework of Buddhism. Insight meditation aims at increasing the practitioner's ability to concentrate, single-pointedly, and with the mind fully alert, on a given object, whether this object be physical, such as a statue or a *thangka,* or visualized, such as a meditation deity — for hours on end in the case of the most accomplished practitioners. But there are many other techniques as well, some involving breathing and others physical exercises, while still others involve practitioners visualizing themselves as

---

showed little aptitude for philosophy and spent most of his time sunning himself on the veranda.

deities. All aim at the eventual goal of complete mastery of the practitioner's mental states.

It is also important to understand that these practices are, from the point of view of the tradition, in no sense a turning away, or a tuning out, from the world. The Tibetan word for meditation, *gom,* means, literally, familiarization. Thus, for example, in "exchanging self for other," the meditator becomes familiar with the emotional states attendant on visualizing a friend, a random individual toward whom one has no particular feelings, and an enemy. Having identified the positive, neutral, and negative emotional states that these different visualizations arouse, the meditator becomes thoroughly acquainted with the first emotion — with the intention of developing the very same feeling toward the enemy as the yoga progresses.

The Buddhist theory of mind expounded in the *Collected Topics* entails that each of the senses constitutes a distinct consciousness. Something seen is thus an object of eye-consciousness, something heard is an object of ear-consciousness, something smelled is an object of olfactory consciousness. And yet, most important of all, and most radical, is the further understanding that ultimately there is no substantive self that bears these different aspects of consciousness, or in which mind itself may be said to reside. Buddhism teaches that what we mistakenly suppose to be our "self" is precisely the cause of the suffering we endure.

But if the self is ultimately illusory, what of physical objects? According to some thinkers, matter is a karmic effect of beings existing (where karma is the imprint on the individual mental continuum, or stream of consciousness, of a being's actions, whether positive, negative, or neutral). Physical objects (including rocks, rivers, and oceans) are held to be the fruit of the deeds of sentient beings over limitless time. Furthermore, the universe we see around us is not made up of vanishingly small non-physical particles out of which first matter, then life, then consciousness emerge. Other Buddhist thinkers are agnostic as to the origins of matter, saying only that the existence of physical objects is just an aspect of the way things are. Generally speaking, however, in Buddhism mind precedes matter. Does this then mean that consciousness itself is what reality ultimately consists in? In fact, although there is a Buddhist school of thought that holds this to be the case, the Gelug tradition, following Nagarjuna's Middle Way approach, speaks of two truths, "conventional" and "ultimate."* Traditionally taught only to those deemed capable of hearing it without misunderstanding, the doctrine maintains that what we take to be real is illusory: no more substantial than the foam that appears on a fast-flowing stream, or the reflection of the moon in a pool of water, or a flash of lightning in the dark of night. The ultimate nature of reality is empty—indeed, it is emptiness itself.

Here is not the place for a discussion of the merits of this claim. Suffice it to say that it has found support among contemporary anti-realist philosophers worldwide. It is also important to understand that, at least for Tsongkhapa (founder of the Dalai Lamas' Gelugpa sect and Tibet's most subtle philosopher), the doctrine is not, as is sometimes maintained, the nihilistic claim that ultimately nothing at all exists. It is instead a claim about how things exist: they exist, but only dependently—hence the further claim that all phenomena are interdependent. There is no first cause, and nothing that exists does so essentially. This should not be taken to mean that the Buddhist tradition as handed on to the Dalai Lama was without a clear picture of how the world we inhabit came into being. On the contrary, Buddhism has a detailed theory of both the natural and the supernatural realms, and cosmology was a major component of the curriculum set out in the *Collected Topics.*

In brief, the traditional scheme envisages a great four-sided world mountain, Meru, which rises out of a vast ocean.† To north, south, east, and west are grouped a number of islands. One of these islands, Dzambu Ling, the Rose Garden, is the one we humans inhabit. In other words, our world is flat. Why do we not see Mount Meru? Because the side toward which we face is composed of lapis lazuli—the color of the sky. And what of the sun and the moon? These are held aloft by cosmic winds which carry them in an orbit around the mountain. Beneath the earth lies, first, the realm of the *yidag,* the hungry ghosts, then the hell regions, eight of them cold and eight of them hot.

* Nagarjuna (ca. 150–250 CE), arguably the greatest Buddhist philosopher, is most widely known for his Mulamadhyamakarika, or *Verses on the Fundamental Wisdom of the Middle Way.*
† Saint Isidore of Seville, the late-antique encyclopedist, also places a great mountain at the center of the world.

Altogether there are six realms that together make up samsara, the always unsatisfactory state in which all sentient beings subsist until they attain Enlightenment. At the top there is the realm of the blissful gods; beneath this comes that of the demigods. Third comes the human realm. Beneath the human realm is the animal realm. Next comes the realm of hungry ghosts and finally the realm of the various hells. Yet, although the human realm is not at the top of this hierarchy, it is only as a human that a being has the opportunity to become enlightened during this very life.

The blissful gods are held to reside on the summit of Mount Meru, while the demigods live at different levels, according to status and spiritual development. The human and animal realms need no explanation, but that of the hungry ghosts demands one. A being (whether god, demigod, human, or animal) who in this life is gluttonous and driven by the desire for food is in danger of being reborn as a "hungry ghost," or *yidag.* These piteous creatures have enormous bellies, absurdly long and thin necks, eyes that emit pestiferous and fiery gases that dry up everything their gaze alights on, and mouths the size of the eye of a needle. Subsisting in the underworld, not far below the surface of the earth, they are perpetually tormented by their inability to satisfy their hunger.

As for the hell realms, as one might expect, these increase in severity the further down one goes; by the time we reach the sixth hell, the custodians of this realm seize the damned, throw them into large cauldrons, and boil them like fish before impaling them on red-hot iron stakes until their intestines obtrude and flames burst forth from every orifice.

With respect to the realm of the demigods, although their conditions are far superior to those on earth (there are no food shortages or natural disasters to worry about), the inhabitants are not to be envied. They spend their time fighting and are almost invariably reborn in the lower realms. Even those who attain the highest heavens and experience bliss to a degree we humans cannot imagine are not immune to suffering and death, nor from the possibility of sliding back into one of the other realms through the accumulation of negative karma. They remain within samsara.

Although today the Dalai Lama rejects a literal reading of this cosmology, nonetheless, in just the same way that the Genesis story lies behind Big Bang theory and continues to haunt the Western imagination, the traditional picture of the world elaborated in the scriptures grounds the Mahayana worldview and continues to haunt the Tibetan imagination. It is also true that, by the time of the Dalai Lama's boyhood, this traditional Tibetan view of the universe was under pressure. Children of the aristocracy and merchant classes educated by the British in India already had a very different picture of the world — which is undoubtedly part of the reason why the English language school in Lhasa that opened in 1947 was shut down after only one term. The monasteries were opposed on the grounds that its presence would harm the Buddhadharma.

It was for similar reasons that the young Dalai Lama was forbidden to speak to Lowell Thomas, the legendary American journalist and broadcaster, who visited Lhasa in 1949. During his audience, the fourteen-year-old Dalai Lama "smiled when asked and agreeably changed position for our cameras," Thomas noted. But that was all. It was not until late in 1949 that the teenager at last contrived a meeting at which he could actually speak with a foreigner. This was the thirty-three-year-old Austrian mountaineer and, notoriously, former SS Oberscharführer and Nazi Party member Heinrich Harrer, one of Lhasa's six resident Westerners.* There might have been one more — a Catholic missionary based at Yerkalo. But soon after setting out for Lhasa, where he intended to implore the Dalai Lama's protection, he was shot by monks from a nearby monastery.

Much has been made of Harrer's dubious past (which forced a re-edit of the film based on his travelogue of the same name, *Seven Years in Tibet*). That he was not a dedicated Nazi (he claimed to have worn his uniform only once, on the day he married his first wife) is attested to by the fact that, having escaped from a British internment camp at Dehra Dun in northern India together with fellow Austrian Peter Aufschnaiter, he decided to try for Lhasa rather than proceed to Japan (Germany's ally at the time). He was an adventurer, not an ideologue. A stronger case can be made for a link between the

* Apart from Harrer and his fellow Austrian Peter Aufschnaiter, the others were Hugh Richardson, the British political officer; Reginald Fox and Robert Ford, both of them British radio operators; and a White Russian refugee by the name of Nedbailof who helped electrify the capital.

Nazis and Reting Rinpoché, at least when he was regent. During the 1930s, the Ahnenerbe, the institute founded by Heinrich Himmler to give academic respectability to the party's racial ideology, sent a total of three expeditions to Tibet, the last of them attending the 1939 New Year celebrations in Lhasa. The purpose of their visit was to determine the truth of a claim that the Tibetans were in fact descendants of a lost Aryan tribe. Reting Rinpoché was on good terms with the expedition leader, Ernst Schaefer, who was well liked by Himmler. All five members of his team were Nazi ideologues, and one was subsequently convicted of being an accessory to the murder of eighty-six Jews at Auschwitz. A famous photograph shows Schaefer and his men posing with senior Tibetan officials in front of a swastika flag and two SS pennants they had put on display at a dinner party in Lhasa. Some see in this evidence of an unambiguous link between esoteric Vajrayana Buddhism and Nazism.

After several unsuccessful attempts, Harrer, together with Aufschnaiter, had reached Lhasa during the middle of January 1946 following two years of grueling travel.* Given that the prohibition against foreigners entering Tibet without government permission was rigorously enforced, this was a very considerable feat.

En route, the two of them had passed themselves off variously as itinerant dentists, as traders, and as the advance party of an important foreign dignitary. Having survived more than one serious attempt on their lives, they were given a cordial welcome in Lhasa by the aristocratic family whose house they chanced to enter on their arrival in the capital. Eight days later, by which time they had been visited by many of the highest-ranking laity — including an army general eager to learn all he could about the German tank commander Erwin Rommel — they received word that the Dalai Lama's family wished to meet them. But it was to be more than three years before Harrer's first meeting with the Dalai Lama himself. In the meantime, he and Aufschnaiter had to apply for asylum. At first their application was refused, and it was only thanks to Aufschnaiter's engineering skills that they were eventually allowed to stay. Subsequently Auf-

* In fact, they had four other companions to start with, of whom two made it into Tibet, but they split into separate parties. The others turned back before reaching Lhasa.

schnaiter worked on a hydroelectric power project and helped plan the city's first sewage works, while Harrer, who had good English and was an accomplished lensman, soon found himself in demand as a translator and occasional court photographer.

Eventually, Harrer was approached by Lobsang Samten — by this time serving as Lord Chamberlain — with a request to build a movie theater for the Dalai Lama in the grounds of the Norbulingka Palace. As the Dalai Lama recounts in his autobiography, one of the things he had found among the belongings of the Great Thirteenth was an old film projector, which, astonishingly, by taking it apart and carefully reassembling it, he had returned to working order. He was now eager to put it to use.

When Harrer and the Dalai Lama did finally make each other's acquaintance in the second half of 1949, it was clearly only after a carefully orchestrated campaign. Harrer reports of their first meeting that the hurried blessing the Dalai Lama bestowed on him "seemed less like the ceremonial laying-on of hands than an impetuous expression of feeling on the part of a boy who had at last got his way." This enthusiasm was in marked contrast to the coldness with which the monastic officials surrounding the Precious Protector acknowledged Harrer's greeting.

In his travelogue *Seven Years in Tibet,* Harrer includes a chapter portentously titled "Tutor to the Dalai Lama." This is an overstatement of their relationship. Although Harrer and the teenaged Dalai Lama met more or less weekly over a period of a little more than six months, their time together was entirely informal. It was a friendly, sometimes joshing relationship — the Dalai Lama nicknamed Harrer *gopse,* or "straw head" — albeit one they both took seriously. They remained friends until the end of Harrer's long life.

It was helpful that Harrer was as down-to-earth as his protégé. The Dalai Lama, impatient with the protocol that surrounded him, and already conscious that the religious education he was getting was inadequate to the political role he must soon undertake, was eager to learn as much as he could from his new friend. "He seemed to me like a person who for years brooded in solitude over different problems," Harrer recalled, "and now that he at last had someone to talk to, wanted to know all the answers at once."

Harrer quickly found that, besides being boundlessly curious, the youngster was also intensely serious. The Dalai Lama soon sorted the eighty films in his collection into those that were educational in some way and those that were mere entertainment. The former he watched more than once — a documentary about Mahatma Gandhi being a favorite — while the others he set aside. And when he asked a question, he expected a full and reasoned answer, such that Harrer had to take "the utmost trouble to treat every [one of them] seriously and scientifically." Yet it was always clear where the Dalai Lama's true priorities lay. He would invariably break off their conversations in plenty of time for his official studies, as he did not like to keep his real tutors waiting — any more than he liked to be kept waiting himself. On one occasion Harrer was ten minutes late for an appointment and was scolded for his temerity.

The picture of the young Dalai Lama that emerges from Harrer's account is one of a highly intelligent, inquisitive, studious, serious-minded yet good-humored young man with a keen sense of his responsibilities and a nature as affectionate as his mind was open and eager. "Sometimes," recounts Harrer, "he came running across the garden to meet me, beaming with happiness and holding out his hand." Regarding Harrer himself, despite the strange irony that the incarnation of the Bodhisattva of Compassion was tutored by a former SS man, we have no reason to suppose that Hugh Richardson spoke in bad faith when giving his assessment of Harrer, even if it does seem somewhat extravagant. He once said* that, if there was only one other person left on earth, he would have wanted that person to be Harrer. As for the thought that Harrer must have known about the Holocaust, we have similarly no reason to suppose he had any inkling of it until after the war. He left Germany in 1939, while the Wannsee Conference that inaugurated the Final Solution did not take place until January 1942. This does not touch the question of whether the Dalai Lama's friend was an anti-Semite, surely a precondition of membership in the SS. It seems that, at the very least, he must have been when he joined, even if fellow

* He said this to me, in a (filmed) interview at his home in St. Andrews, Scotland, in 1994. Richardson, having been the British political officer resident in Lhasa, subsequently worked — in an identical role — for the Nehru government until 1950.

mountaineer Reinhold Messner is right in believing that Harrer's experiences in Tibet caused him to change his mind. It is also undeniable that Tibet's esoteric Buddhism speaks loudly to the romantic strain in fascist ideology. And if what chiefly motivated Harrer was curiosity and love of adventure, it is difficult to imagine that his dream of reaching Lhasa was not partly inspired by fantasies about what he would find there.

When, at the Dalai Lama's request, Harrer began to teach him English, the Austrian was surprised to discover that the youngster had already taught himself the Roman alphabet and would transcribe the pronunciation of words "in elegant Tibetan characters." Harrer was duly impressed. "What versatility!" exclaimed the Austrian. "Strenuous religious studies, tinkering with complicated mechanical appliances, and now modern languages!" Together they would "listen to the English news on a portable radio and [take] advantage of the passages that were spoken at dictation speed."

As well as wanting to learn English from him, the Dalai Lama tasked Harrer with teaching him the rudiments of arithmetic and geography (his favorite subject, though even more than classroom study, he enjoyed working on mechanical devices). Math he did not take to, but he was astonished, Harrer tells us — just as many Westerners today are astonished — to hear that Tibet was as large as it is. And he was delighted to discover that the highest mountain in all the world rose on its southern extremity. Besides instruction in these subjects, the young man was also eager to learn about current affairs and modern developments like the jet engine and the atom bomb. It turned out that the Dalai Lama was familiar with all the different types of aircraft and armored vehicles used by the various powers in the recently concluded war. He was also familiar with the names of the great men of the day — Churchill, Eisenhower, Molotov. Yet it was apparent that he often "did not know how persons and events were connected with each other." As to any concerns the Austrian may have had about his young friend's capacity to absorb all this new information, "he continually astonished me," Harrer recalled, "by his powers of comprehension, his pertinacity and his industry."

If Harrer's picture of the young Dalai Lama shows him not to have been so very different from any other highly intelligent teenager of his time — or indeed of any time — there was one thing that might at first strike us as unusual: the Precious Protector had not a trace of skepticism with respect to the religion he was being brought up in. Not for him the wrestling with faith of Saint Augustine. According to Harrer, the Dalai Lama was, for example, "convinced that by virtue of his faith and by performing the prescribed rites he would be able to make things happen in faraway places." Moreover, "when he had made sufficient progress, he would send me there and direct me from Lhasa" by means of telepathy. As we shall see, the Dalai Lama's conviction that the supernatural realm is not imaginary is one that he maintains to this day.

10

"Shit on their picnic!": China Invades, 1949–50

While the young Dalai Lama was learning all he could about the modern world from Harrer, following the end of the world war, events within it were reaching a climax. In China, the Communists were moving ever closer to victory. When Ma Bufang, the Muslim warlord who had demanded ransom for the Dalai Lama's release, lost his headquarters to the Reds during the summer of 1949, it was clear to Tibetans that China's capital must soon fall. It remained only for Chiang Kai-shek to withdraw to Taiwan before, on October 1, Chairman Mao declared the founding of the People's Republic of China. This brought to an end more than twenty years of strife, during the course of which countless millions had died. But while the Communists' victory caused deep uneasiness on the part of the Tibetan government, the regent, Taktra Rinpoché, offered no response beyond ordering the Three Seats to begin the ritual chanting of the scriptures.

For his part, the young Dalai Lama still played no active role in government affairs. During the winter of that year, he did, however, instruct his junior tutor,

Trijang Rinpoché, to renew the protector support substances in the Potala. This entailed reconsecrating various ritual objects so as to ensure the constant presence and protection of the wrathful protector deities. According to Trijang, the substances used included such items as "double-edged steel swords with scorpion hilts tempered in blood and poison . . . [a] bow made from the horn of an uncastrated ox . . . [b]lack banners with mantras and figures drawn on them with weapon-spilled blood . . . the skull of an illegitimate child filled with charmed substances . . . a corpse shroud around which the long mantras of calling, expelling and slaying . . . had been written," and an image of Palden Lhamo on which "were smeared the juices of sexual union."

Meanwhile, Tibetan government officials did eventually dispatch a letter to their Chinese counterparts acknowledging the Communists' victory. Addressed to "the honourable Mr. Mao Tse Tung," it began by explaining that "Tibet is a peculiar country where the Buddhist religion is widely flourishing and which is predestined to be ruled by the Living Buddha of Mercy or Chenrezig. As such, Tibet has from the earliest times up to now, been an Independent Country whose Political administration had never been taken over by any Foreign Country." The letter ended, one short paragraph later, with the demand that "those Tibetan territories annexed as part of Chinese territories some years back should now be returned to their rightful jurisdiction."

To the Chinese, who had a lively sense of history, the claim that Tibet had "always been independent" can only have seemed nonsensical. What was the office of Imperial Preceptor, created in the thirteenth century by the Yuan emperor Kublai Khan, if it was not an office for the governance of Tibet? And had not the Qiangxi emperor sent troops to aid Tibet in expelling the Nepalese incursion in the seventeenth century? Indeed, had not the Dalai Lamas' very recognition been subject to ratification by the Qing throne? What was this if not subjection? And as to foreign interference, China was no foreign country — though Britain was, and so was India.

In fact, Tibetans do not deny any of these claims. But they interpret them very differently. Furthermore, Tibetans cannot forget that, for almost three hundred years from the middle of the seventh century, Tibet was the center of a great trading empire, controlling what came to be known as the Silk Road linking Rome in the west with China in the east. Tibet was at the time also the major military power of Central and Southeast Asia. Frequent were the defeats dealt China by Tibetan armies in the Tarim Basin and elsewhere. There was even a thrilling moment — in 763 CE — when Tibetan forces deposed the T'ang emperor and, if only for three weeks, set up their own in his place. This was an extraordinary feat of arms: Chang'an, seat of the T'ang empire, was at the time a city of a million people, one of the greatest the world had ever seen — rivaled only by ancient Rome in terms of size and sophistication. By the end of the eighth century, the Tibetan emperor controlled territory stretching as far as Persia in the west, to the Bay of Bengal in the south, to within striking distance of Chang'an in the east, and up to the Pamirs (in modern-day Tajikistan) in the north.

In 821 the two emperors entered into a treaty, the terms of which were inscribed on three stone stele, or pillars, in both Chinese and Tibetan script, and erected one on the border itself and one each in the respective capitals, "in order that it may never be changed [and] so that it may be celebrated in every age and every generation." The one in Lhasa still exists for all to see. It stands near the base of the Potala, albeit partially shielded from view by its "protective" covering, still proclaiming that "both Tibet and China shall keep the country and frontiers of which they are now in possession," and that

> the whole region to the east of that being the country of Great China, and all to the west is, without question Great Tibet ... from either side of that frontier there shall be no warfare, no hostile invasions, and no seizure of territory. There shall be no sudden alarms and the word "enemy" shall not be spoken ... Between the two countries no smoke or dust shall appear ... Tibetans shall be happy in Tibet and Chinese shall be happy in China.

From the Tibetan perspective, the treaty between the emperor and his Chinese counterpart has never been abrogated.

What happened when the thirteenth-century Yuan emperor Kublai Khan summoned Phagpa, head of the Sakya sect, which was then the most prominent in Tibet, to the imperial court was not, for Tibetans, the political subjugation of one country by another but rather the establishment of a spiritual relationship between two individuals. In exchange for religious instruction granted by Phagpa at Kublai's request, the Khan entered into a priest-patron (*cho yon*) relationship, whereby the Khan gained spiritual merit through taking religious teachings and the lama gained the emperor's material support. And whatever the political ramifications of such a relationship, they did not change the terms of the earlier treaty. The same applies with respect to the relationship between the Dalai Lamas and the Qing emperors of the eighteenth to the twentieth centuries. Again, theirs was a personal, spiritual relationship that conferred obligations on both parties. Crudely put, the priest prayed for the emperor and the emperor paid for the priest — and paid not just in terms of treasure but in blood, too. It became a royal duty for the emperor to protect his guru.

From the Chinese perspective, the spiritual teachings of the priest were an offering of tribute to the emperor. Once tribute had been paid, the emperor would graciously provide his protection on the grounds that the tribute payer had rendered himself a vassal. So whereas the ancient treaty spoke of an alliance between the two thrones, the new dispensation understood the relationship as one in which the one summoned was subordinate to the will of the one summoning.

In January 1950, Mao announced the return of Tibet to the Chinese Motherland as one of the Communist Party's top priorities for the year. Soon after, he called on the Tibetan government to send representatives to Beijing to discuss how they wished to facilitate this "liberation." For many weeks, his communiqué went unanswered.

Eventually the Tibetan government stirred itself to appeal to the British and American governments and, in spite of its tardy recognition of Indian independence, to the nonaligned Indian government as well. But although the Indians (albeit with American and British connivance) did agree to supply arms (including mortar bombs but not antiaircraft shells as requested), it was far too little to make a difference and at least ten years too late, given the training that would be required. Although, on the back of this gesture, the bodyguard regiment, which had disbanded itself on the demise of the Great Thirteenth, was hastily revived, there was never a realistic chance that it could be made battle-ready in time. One thing the Tibetan government did do was to send Robert Ford, a British radio operator it had employed to instruct a small cadre of officials in the use of telecommunications, together with two radio sets, out to Chamdo in the east. Understanding that, if the Communists were to take Lhasa, they must first take Chamdo, the Tibetans reckoned that posting Ford there with his radios would at least give the government some warning in the event of disaster.

The new technology brought with it a number of problems, however. When Lhalu, the outgoing governor of Chamdo, had occasion to speak with Trijang Rinpoché over the air, he was nearly undone by the novelty of the experience. Before beginning the call, he "approached the microphone reverently and placed a ceremonial white scarf . . . in front of it [and] bowed his head as if to receive a blessing." Although his replacement, Ngabo (the *g* can safely be ignored), a young reform-minded aristocrat, was less troubled by etiquette, the new governor was so afraid of its breaking down that he refused to allow the second set out of his sight. Any chance he had of early warning about hostile troop movements from sending it out closer to where the Chinese were likely to approach from was thereby lost.

The spring and summer months of 1949 passed with a heightening sense that something immense was about to happen. One day a comet appeared in the dawn sky to the south of Lhasa, followed on August 15 by a massive earthquake (measuring 8.6 on the Richter scale) in the southeast, technically just inside India, though in an area settled by Tibetans. This, Harrer reports, was accompanied by "thirty or forty" dull explosions and a strange glow visible in the sky to the east. Though Harrer assured the Dalai Lama these were nothing more than physical events, for the Dalai Lama — to this day — they were clearly more than that. When the capital of a stone pillar at the Potala was found lying on the ground and a gargoyle on the roof of the Jokhang started gushing water, despite the "blazing summer weather," it was taken as conclusive proof, if further evidence were needed, that the deities were mightily perturbed.

Not long afterwards, a series of posters appeared on the walls along the street leading to the Norbulingka Palace bearing the slogan "Give the Dalai Lama the Power," and rumors began to sweep Lhasa that the oracles were urging the regent to step down. There was by this time a general feeling that only the Precious Protector could save his people from looming catastrophe. For the time being, however, he remained sequestered within the Norbulingka, his only real contact with events in the outside world coming from Harrer's weekly visits.

The Chinese government meanwhile stepped up pressure on the regency, calling on it to send competent negotiators at once. Initially the proposed talks were to have taken place in Hong Kong, but the British, who administered the territory at the time, not wishing to become involved, demurred. The venue was then shifted to New Delhi. At the same time, the Chinese sent an emissary (actually a monk volunteer) to Chamdo with a series of demands. Conveniently for the Tibetans, he died soon after his arrival—of poison, according to the Chinese, who were furious. Finally, the Communist leadership announced in September that if it wanted to avoid war, the Tibetan government should immediately acknowledge that Tibet was part of China, that the People's Liberation Army (PLA) now be deployed on Tibet's international borders, and that Tibet immediately cut all ties with the "imperialist powers."

For the Tibetans, this was completely unacceptable. Yet the prospect of war was equally untenable. Unable to see a way out of the conundrum, the government did what it always did when faced with a dilemma. It stalled. Accordingly, on October 5, 1950, Mao, his patience spent, ordered the PLA to attack multiple Tibetan positions in the eastern province of Kham.

Ngabo's defense plan amounted to little more than hoping that the mere presence of his troops, together with reinforcements on their way from Lhasa, would be sufficient to give the PLA pause. Then, if the negotiations taking place in Delhi could just be put off a little longer, winter would intervene, and the gods would have more time to work a miracle.

This was hopelessly optimistic. The Chinese were perfectly capable of launching an attack in winter. As for the thought that the battle-hardened PLA would be put off by the arrival of a few hundred reinforcements from Lhasa, that too was a vain hope. It is true that the PLA was far from home, with a long and vulnerable supply chain. But the Chinese army command was well aware that the Khampas, in whose province Chamdo lay, were hardly less hostile to the Lhasa government than they were to the Chinese themselves. As recently as 1934, a Khampa warlord had made a serious bid to wrest control of the region from Lhasa. Ngabo could not count on anything more than minimal support from the local tribespeople.

On October 7 the Chinese struck again, this time cutting off Chamdo's southern escape route. The local army commander responded by surrendering his entire force without a fight, leaving the town at the mercy of the PLA. Because of his refusal to deploy the second radio set, news of this catastrophe did not reach Ngabo for several days, however. It has been argued that Ngabo willfully betrayed Chamdo into the hands of the Chinese, a charge that his subsequent collaboration with the Communists supports. But the fact is, even if he had been able to stall the PLA's advance, the outcome was inevitable. Nonetheless, he did not wish to surrender without being ordered to do so. He therefore contacted his opposite number in Lhasa in order to ascertain the instructions of the Kashag, the regent's four-man cabinet. There was no reply. On the third attempt, Lhasa was finally goaded into responding.

"Right now," Ngabo was told, "it is the period of the Kashag's picnic and they are all participating in this. Your telegrams are being decoded and then we will send you a reply."

At this he exploded.

"Shit on their picnic! Though we are blocked here, and the nation is threatened and every minute may make a difference to our fate, you talk about that shit picnic!"

There was no further contact with Lhasa that day. This was the time of year when almost the entirety of the populace took themselves off to the parkland outside the city for a week of relaxation (not to say drinking and gambling), the wealthy in their tents, the poor camped al fresco. Ngabo thus had no orders as to whether he should try to hold Chamdo or whether he should withdraw. Already convinced that resistance to the Chinese would be futile, the governor determined that, in the absence of clear directions from Lhasa, he would simply await the arrival of the Chinese and hope to effect an escape at the last moment.

The next day, news of the loss of another town to the south of Chamdo came in, followed that evening by a message from Riwoche in the southeast that the PLA were now in occupation of that town as well. Chamdo was surrounded. Without telling anyone, Ngabo abandoned his post that night.

At seven o'clock the following morning, Ford, the British radio operator, realized something was amiss. Having woken to the sound of bells ringing and horses' hooves on the street outside, he looked out to see "people . . . running in all directions." His immediate concern was the reaction of the local Khampa population. Realizing that the government forces were in full retreat, they wasted no time in looting what possessions and weaponry the Lhasans had left behind. And beyond that, it was clear that they were intent on killing any remaining government officials they could lay their hands on.

Showing rather greater initiative than Ngabo, Ford made his way to the radio station and disabled the transmitters before heading south in the hope of reaching the Indian border. Unfortunately for him, the earthquake two months earlier had rendered this impossible and he was forced to follow the retreating governor in the direction of Lhasa. Managing to evade hostile Khampas, he caught up with Ngabo later that same day. But they could go no farther and were both taken into Chinese custody. While Ngabo and his entourage were treated to a hearty meal and his soldiers each given a silver coin and told to return home, Ford was taken back to Chamdo, where he was interrogated and charged with being a British spy.*

With Kham now lost, it could be only a matter of time before Lhasa followed. Having no other option, Taktra therefore instructed the government's

* For the next five months, Ford was held in solitary confinement in a rat-infested cell, forced on many occasions to sit motionless for sixteen hours at a time. "I was never struck a single blow," he later recalled, "but mentally it was no holds barred." Over the subsequent three years, he was subject to relentless interrogation and "re-education" before finally signing a false confession in May 1954. He was sentenced to ten years in prison. No sooner had this sentence been pronounced than he was told that he was to be deported. Whether this was true or another attempt to break him he did not know for another six months until, eventually, he was taken across China to one of the railway bridges that led into Hong Kong and told to walk across, not knowing "whether I would get a bullet in my back." Phodo, as he was affectionately known by Tibetans, subsequently became a vocal supporter of the Tibetan cause and was invariably called on by the Dalai Lama whenever the Precious Protector visited Britain. In 2011 he was honored by the Tibetan community in exile, who symbolically handed over a one-hundred-sang note by way of back pay, together with an apology for the delay "due to extenuating circumstances." He died in 2013 at the age of ninety. I had the privilege of meeting him twice. He was as courteous and self-effacing an individual as ever to have been the partial cause of an invasion of one country by another.

chief negotiator to inform the Chinese ambassador that the Tibetan government was now willing to accept Chairman Mao's terms. The Dalai Lama, following events as best he could, was devastated. Instinctively he knew that he must act. While the news that Chamdo had fallen was grave, the regent's decision to surrender seemed to him utter folly. Surely, he argued, the correct thing to do was to consult with the deities before taking such a large step as to surrender sovereignty. That the regent did not face down the fifteen-year-old Dalai Lama shows how uncertain of his own position he now was. He agreed to a divination at which the Dalai Lama and the highest-ranking members of the government would be present. This would take place in the Mahakala chapel at the Norbulingka, where the protectors Mahakala and the Glorious Goddess would both be invoked to give their opinion.

With respect to the Dalai Lamas personally, after the Glorious Goddess, Mahakala is the second-most important of the protectors. Recognized within the Hindu tradition as a consort of Kali, the Destroyer, Mahakala is held to have shown his care for the Dalai Lama institution when the first Dalai Lama (Gendun Drub, 1391–1474) was an infant. One night, bandits attacked the encampment where his family was settled. Fearing for her baby's life, the future Dalai Lama's mother took the child and hid him in the cleft of a rock before fleeing. When she returned the next morning, trembling for his safety, she found a raven protecting the little boy. This, it was later understood, was Mahakala in earthly form. To commemorate the episode, the protector is often shown in *thangkas* and sculpture with a raven's head.

The result of the divination showed that the protectors were of the firm opinion that no such concession should be made to the Chinese, and an order countermanding the original directive was immediately sent to the government's negotiators in Delhi. It came too late, however. The Chinese were already pressing for a date for formal negotiations to begin in Beijing. Chairman Mao was determined that Tibet should come into the fold, and to be seen to come into the fold voluntarily rather than be forced to accept terms. But he had made it abundantly clear that if Tibet did not come willingly, he was prepared to order the PLA to move on Lhasa.

The Tibetan negotiators understood that the only hope for Tibet was full-throated support from any one of either the Republic of India, Great Britain, or the United States — and preferably from all three. But the Indian government of Jawaharlal Nehru was determined not to be drawn into a conflict which it had neither the resources nor the will to prosecute. Rather, Nehru dreamed of a new world order in which both China and India could participate on an equal footing with Britain, America, Russia, and the great powers of Europe.

The British, for their part, made clear that they did not wish to become involved and merely reiterated their policy of recognizing Chinese "suzerainty" over Tibet — though without ever defining precisely what they meant by the term.

As for the United States, it had begun to take an interest in Tibet, seeing there an opportunity for opposing the spread of communism in the East. Overt support was not in question, however, and even America said that it would not back the appeal that the Tibetans, acting on the secret advice of the Indian political officer resident in Lhasa (no longer Richardson), now sought to have heard by the United Nations.

In the meantime, following the divination in the Mahakala chapel, the Tibetan government held a further audience with the deities, this time consulting the Nechung and Gadong oracles for their advice on what action should now be taken. At first the deities were less than forthcoming. Nechung said only, "If you don't make good offerings, I cannot protect religion and the welfare of the people." The Gadong oracle likewise said nothing of consequence. Exasperated, one of the ministers in attendance pleaded with Nechung: "While we [humans] are dull and stupid, you are the one who has brilliant wisdom and knowledge of things. You also have the special responsibility for Buddhism in general and Tibet in particular. You should not be behaving like an ordinary human being, so give us a proper prophecy."

At this, the medium (still in a trance) began dancing. When he came directly in front of the Dalai Lama, he prostrated himself three times and, with tears streaming down his face, proclaimed that power should at once be transferred to the Dalai Lama. Taktra Rinpoché now had no option other than to resign. All that remained was for an auspicious day for the formal handover ceremony to be chosen. The date settled on was November 17, 1950 — a scant four months after the Precious Protector's fifteenth birthday.* From now on, all important decisions would be referred to him.

Yet if this was a moment of immense significance both to the Dalai Lama personally and to the history of these times, it was the Dalai Lama's adoption of the sacred bodhisattva vow at just this moment that was, from his own point of view, still more important. With this he pledged to serve others with every fiber of his being unceasingly until such time as they should all become enlightened. It is a commitment that he has often commemorated since by quoting the prayer of the revered eighth-century monk Shantideva:

For as long as space endures
And for as long as living beings remain,
Until then, may I too abide
To dispel the misery of the world.

A week after the Dalai Lama's assumption of temporal power, Tibet's appeal to the United Nations was heard. But given India's desire not to antagonize the Chinese, and given that both Britain and the United States were content to follow India's lead, it was inevitable that this would not amount to anything. For the Tibetans, there was nothing to do but accept the Chinese demand and send a delegation to Beijing, no matter what the Dalai Lama's or the deities' feelings on the matter might be.

The most pressing question to be answered now was whether the Dalai Lama should remain in Lhasa or leave. When the British invaded in 1904, the Great Thirteenth had fled north to Urgya. This time, however, the only plausible destination outside Tibet was Sikkim to the south, and perhaps from there into India. In 1950 Sikkim was still an independent state, ruled by a Tibetan prince, or Chögyal, with a predominantly Tibetan population. Again this question was not one that could be decided by earthly opinion alone, so the deities were consulted. Their verdict was that, for safety's sake, the Dalai

* The Dalai Lama thought of himself as sixteen, however. According to the Tibetan way of reckoning, sentience begins at conception and a child is a year old at birth.

Lama should quit the capital. It was decided, however, that rather than head straight into exile, he should take refuge in the village of Dromo (known locally as Yatung) on the Tibetan side of the border. There he could be in close proximity to Dungkhar, a monastery with which Taktra Rinpoché and the Dalai Lama's two tutors all had close connections. This was an early-sixteenth-century Gelugpa foundation and seat of a famous oracle. It was also home to a large number of hermits. These hermits would in some cases withdraw from the world until the end of their natural life and have themselves immured in their cells in the hills surrounding the monastery with only a small aperture, closed up by a brick, through which to receive food once daily.

The plan was for the Dalai Lama to quit Lhasa in secret, accompanied by his court and senior members of the government, while two *tsit tsab,* or chief ministers, appointed by the Precious Protector would remain behind in Lhasa to deal with the Chinese as and when they arrived. It was, however, clear to the local populace that something significant was afoot because of the number of heavily laden mules seen leaving the Potala. These carried the contents of the Dalai Lama's treasury, which the Chögyal had kindly agreed to keep in his strong rooms until the crisis was resolved.

According to Harrer, outwardly life in Lhasa "followed its normal course." But inwardly people were terrified. Despite the stories that had begun to circulate of heroic actions by individual soldiers, it was well understood that the army at Chamdo had been routed. And people had a keen memory of the plunder and arson of the last Chinese army to descend on the holy city when it had chased the Great Thirteenth out four decades earlier.

It was therefore a considerable surprise when it became apparent that the People's Liberation Army was showing exemplary restraint in Chamdo. Prisoners were well treated, rations were paid for, and, crucially, respect was being shown to the *sangha.* Not only had there been no looting, but also the soldiers were treating the local population in Chamdo with courtesy. Clearly they were obeying their orders to the letter: "You are not allowed to propagandize against superstition . . . [W]hen visiting monasteries, you should make contact first. And when you go on a visit, you are not allowed to touch the images. Also you should not spit or fart in the vicinity of the monastery."

It is often forgotten that in its early days, the leadership of the Chinese Communist Party genuinely believed it possible to bring about a more just and equitable society for all peoples by putting into practice Karl Marx's political philosophy. Liberation was not just about China securing its borders but about sharing the benefits of revolution. This entailed the abolition of feudalism and, with this, the implementation of true justice. As in China, so it would be in Tibet: the land would be taken from the hands of the aristocracy, the monasteries, and the gentry and distributed among the people. No longer would one small group of individuals lord it over a vastly larger group purely on account of an accident of birth.

Of course, Tibetans saw matters quite differently. They understood well enough that theirs was a backward country. Doubtless there was a minority that would have welcomed the overthrow of the feudal system. But for the majority, what Marxist theory understood to be a socioeconomic system was simply the Tibetan way of life. Whether your position in life was high or low, it reflected the karma accumulated during former lives. If you were treated harshly by your landlord, you could at least be certain that he would suffer in a future life. The way to mitigate your own suffering was through spiritual practice and the accumulation of merit. For the majority, therefore, all talk of reform was met with outright hostility. For now, however, Mao let it be known that there was no question of actually implementing change before the Tibetans were ready for it.

The sincerity of this reassuring pledge was sharply contradicted by the Dalai Lama's eldest brother, who made a sudden appearance in the capital just before the Precious Protector left for the south. Following his election as abbot of Kumbum Monastery a year earlier, Taktser Rinpoché had observed at first hand the behavior of the Communists in Amdo. It had quickly become apparent that, whatever the Communists might say about leaving people free to practice their faith, the reality was quite different. He had found himself dogged by a pair of party officials delegated to accompany him everywhere and harangue him at every turn: the monks of Kumbum must be integrated into the labor force; the practice of using butter to fuel the thousands of lamps should cease at once. Why were the monasteries' resources frittered away on incense and silk offering scarves? And when had prayer "ever filled a man's belly"? Did he not have to admit that religion stood in the way of progress?

It did not take the Rinpoché long to conclude that he could better serve his people by resigning the abbacy and using his position as brother of the Dalai Lama to try to win support for Tibet among the countries of the free world. In the meantime, he advised the Precious Protector to go into exile without delay. The Communists would show their true colors before long, and it was essential that the Dalai Lama be out of harm's way. They had even suggested that he, Taktser Rinpoché, should kill the Dalai Lama if he showed signs of resisting Tibet's liberation! With these shocking words, the Dalai Lama's eldest brother left Lhasa for Dromo accompanied by their mother.

Following a few days later, the newly enthroned leader made it his business to talk to as many ordinary people as he could. Passing himself off as a young official, the Dalai Lama succeeded in having a number of eye-opening conversations. Because he was a member of a large caravan, there was no danger to his person, but for ordinary people, traveling in Tibet was fraught with danger, not just from the elements, which might at any moment unleash their fury, but from bandits who would often attack smaller parties. These conversations, he noted later, gave him further insight into the "petty injustices of life suffered by my people," and he "resolved as soon as [he] could to set about making changes to help them."

If the Dalai Lama himself found reasons to be grateful for this unsought departure from his capital, many of those whom his traveling party encountered en route were distraught. On one occasion they passed by a large group of young monks. The Dalai Lama, dressed in layman's clothes, went unnoticed, but his tutors following behind were besieged. As Trijang Rinpoché recalled: "It was heartbreaking... The monks surrounded us on all sides, throwing scarves and money left and right. Openly weeping, they held onto the reins of our horses and would not let us go."

The Precious Protector arrived at Dungkar Monastery on January 2, 1951. Dromo, lying some three hundred miles southwest of Lhasa and situated in the valley said by locals to be the most beautiful in all Tibet, was famous for its wildflowers and gurgling mountain streams—and for the bears that roamed its forests; many of the region's woodcutters were horribly disfigured from encounters with them. The Dalai Lama's stay there offered welcome respite from the tense atmosphere prevailing in Lhasa, and he quickly resumed his "usual routine of prayers, meditation, retreats and study." This included "retreats on single-deity Vajrabhairava, Eleven-Face Avalokiteśvara, and the inner practice of protector Kālarūpa," all of them meditation yogas* associated with the Diamond Path of Anuttara tantra, into which the Dalai Lama had recently been initiated.

According to its proponents, the Diamond Path originates with what is known as the Third Turning of the Wheel, which the Buddha is said to have enacted when he preached to an audience of bodhisattvas. Some say this occurred during his earthly ministry, others that it took place in one of the Buddha realms. It was not, however, until the eighth century that any historical evidence for the tradition begins to emerge. This takes the form of a body of esoteric literature emphasizing the individual practitioner's inward Buddha nature. Crudely put, the path to Enlightenment becomes primarily a matter of clearing away the accretions and obstructions of accumulated karma to reveal the already enlightened state in which, in fact, all sentient beings subsist.

With their emphasis on elaborate ritual and on highly structured meditative practices, the tantras are considered the most powerful weapons in the spiritual practitioner's armory. They are also the most controversial. Many—including the majority who follow the Theravada tradition—do not accept the tantras at all, arguing that they are pseudepigrapha: writings that falsely claim authority. Nonetheless, they are central to Buddhism in the Tibetan tradition and were by now part of the Dalai Lama's daily practice. They are held by their proponents to be a method of transmuting the mind in such a way as to realize the innate (already enlightened) Buddha mind that all beings have seeded within them—though it is also well understood that they should be taught only by appropriately qualified teachers, and then only to a minority of students. It is often said that tantra is akin to the kiss of a beautiful woman with teeth like the fangs of a snake.

* The word *yoga* means discipline. A *yogi* or *yogin* is one who engages in a given discipline or practice.

If the tantras are controversial within some Buddhist circles, another matter of controversy among Tibetans more generally also dates from this time at Dromo. It was here that the Dalai Lama formed a close connection with Dorje Shugden, the deity popularized by Phabongka Rinpoché during the time of the Great Thirteenth. At the deity's request (speaking through an oracle), the Precious Protector composed a prayer in his honor titled "Melody of the Unceasing Vajra." Structured as a classical "seven-limbed" invocation, the "Melody" pays homage, makes verbal offerings, confesses the supplicant's faults, rejoices, requests the deity to turn the wheel of the dharma, requests that the upholders of the dharma not pass into nirvana before all sentient beings pass beyond suffering, and ends, finally, with a dedication. As it turned out, in forming this connection with Dorje Shugden, the young Dalai Lama unwittingly implicated himself in a contest that was to explode violently more than four decades later.

In the meantime, the Dalai Lama's most pressing task was to respond to the Chinese demand that he send negotiators to Beijing to ratify an agreement for the "peaceful liberation of Tibet." It was finally decided that Ngabo, the former governor of Chamdo, together with a small delegation that included the Dalai Lama's brother-in-law, should proceed to the Chinese capital.

Arriving toward the end of April 1951, the Tibetans were met at the railway station by Zhou Enlai, Mao's second in command, amid great fanfare. The result of the ensuing negotiations over the future status of Tibet was, of course, a foregone conclusion. The Communists had already prepared the document they wanted the Tibetans to accept. In response, the Tibetans presented a list of points they wished to discuss with their counterparts. The first point they took issue with, against the Communists' claim, was the suggestion that the Dalai Lama was under the heel of foreign imperialists. Whatever the Chinese might suppose, there was no imperialist influence or power in Tibet. Harrer and Aufschnaiter were by now gone; Richardson was back in Scotland; Ford was a prisoner of the PLA; and Reginald Fox, also a radio operator, had gone with his Sikkimese wife to India.

The Chinese stood firm. It was made clear to the Tibetans, as one delegate expressed the matter, "that if they were so arrogant as to refuse to accept that Tibet was part of China, then they could all go back home any time they pleased." In that case, a single wireless message would be sent to the PLA and it would advance immediately on Lhasa. Responsibility for any loss of life that occurred would be on the Tibetans' shoulders and theirs alone.

Could the Tibetans have called the Communists' bluff? Perhaps. On the one hand, had they done so, there could have been no pretense that what followed was a "peaceful liberation." On the other hand, Mao had made clear that Tibet must be taken whatever the price in diplomatic terms, and Ngabo and the other members of the delegation were well aware of the fact. They concluded that they had no option but to accept. The Seventeen Point Agreement for the Peaceful Liberation of Tibet was signed and sealed* in the Great Hall of the People in Beijing on May 23, 1951.

Throughout the discussions leading up to the signing of the agreement (which many Tibetans maintain is no such thing because it was signed under duress), the Tibetan delegation was in radio contact with the Dalai Lama's court in Dromo, so the outcome cannot have come as a surprise to them. Yet in his autobiography the Dalai Lama recounts that the first he knew of the provisions of the seventeen points was when he listened to the Tibetan-language news broadcast on Chinese radio that evening. From this it is obvious that, as still only a fifteen-year-old boy, he was not informed of every detail of what was being said and done in his name. It is also a reminder that even in those most difficult days, the Dalai Lama's spiritual life took priority over his worldly responsibilities.†

The question that faced the Dalai Lama and his court now was whether they should return to Lhasa or cross over the border into Sikkim and from there to India. It was a relatively easy journey, a matter of a few days only. For the time being, there was no way the Chinese could prevent such a move. But

---

* When Ngabo objected that he had not brought the official government seal with him, the Chinese provided him with one of their own devising.

† I recall being astounded when, during one of our first meetings, the Dalai Lama told me that, as a rule, he devoted more than 80 percent of his time to spiritual matters, and less than a fifth to worldly matters. He confirmed this during an interview on April 2, 2019.

although the government of India had begun by saying that it would grant the Dalai Lama asylum if requested, by this time it was much less clear that he would be welcome on Indian soil.

To add to the young leader's dilemma, a meeting between his minister for foreign affairs and an American government official had yielded the information that if the Dalai Lama would publicly repudiate the Seventeen Point Agreement, the United States would be sympathetic to the idea of supplying armaments to oppose by force the Chinese occupation of Tibet.

While the representatives of the Three Seats present in Dromo were united in their wish to see the Dalai Lama return to Lhasa, many of the government's lay officials were of the view that he should seek exile, if not in India, then elsewhere. Both Sri Lanka (then Ceylon), because it was a Buddhist country, and America, because the Dalai Lama seemed likely to be welcome there, were discussed as possibilities. In his absence, once a suitable place in exile could be determined, a military campaign would be fought with such assistance as might be forthcoming from the United States and from the Chinese Nationalists in Taiwan, who had also indicated their interest.

Among supporters of this view were the recently laicized Taktser Rinpoché (known henceforth as Jigme Norbu) and the Dalai Lama's second-eldest brother, Gyalo Thondup, who had just returned from China to Tibet. Perhaps the most surprising advocate of armed struggle was, however, the Lord Chamberlain, Phala, recently appointed after Lobsang Samten's retirement on health grounds following a stress-induced breakdown.*

On the one hand, the Dalai Lama believed what his eldest brother told him about the Chinese in Amdo and could see the imminent fulfillment of his predecessor the Great Thirteenth's prophecy. On the other hand, he was mindful of China's proximity and vast superiority in terms of numbers and military might, no matter that, as Gyalo Thondup later wrote, "the US [seemed] so great and powerful that it could make almost anything happen." Without firmer assurances of help from outside, the Precious Protector concluded that he had better return to Lhasa. The deities concurred, though to the consternation of many who felt certain that for the Dalai Lama to return

* According to Harrer, he suffered a heart attack.

to Lhasa would be to walk straight into a trap. Appalled, one minister even demanded to see inside the second dough ball used in the divination to ensure that it didn't have the same answer written inside.

It remained only for the Precious Protector to meet with General Zhang Zhinwu, Mao's personal emissary, who arrived in Dromo shortly afterward. In his autobiography the Dalai Lama describes watching the general and two aides-de-camp approach the monastery through his binoculars: "three men in drab grey suits." Their meeting was, he notes, "coldly civil."

11

Into the Dragon's Lair: The Dalai Lama in China, July 1954–July 1955

Just before his departure from Dromo, the Dalai Lama received a secret letter from Heinrich Harrer. The Austrian had been in contact with the American embassy in Delhi. The United States government had confirmed that it wished to assist the Dalai Lama, and Harrer urged his young friend to abscond to India. This, he suggested, might be done by adopting any one of three possible stratagems. The Dalai Lama could choose a small group and leave unannounced at night; Harrer himself could come to Dromo in disguise to escort him; the third alternative was to rendezvous at a designated spot where a light aircraft would pick him up. But although they were given due consideration, none of Harrer's proposals was adopted. This assurance of American support was welcome, but too much was uncertain and there was little concrete to go on. The Dalai Lama thus departed Dromo for Lhasa on July 22, 1951.

En route to the capital, the Precious Protector stopped several times to give teachings. When, at one of these, the *vajra* (a ritual hand implement symbolizing the irresistible force of a thunderbolt) that he was holding slipped from his fingers and fell into the folds of Ling Rinpoché's robes, "many present remarked that this was an extraordinary thing to happen and were convinced that it was a very auspicious sign," he later recalled. It demonstrated clearly the depth of the link between *guru* and *chela,* between teacher and pupil. And in the light of this happy event, there can be little doubt that all were convinced the decision not to go into exile had been the right one.

The Dalai Lama returned home to an emotional welcome. Only the presence of the PLA's General Zhang and his staff marred the occasion. When, however, an advance guard of six hundred Chinese troops arrived two weeks later, people began to grow seriously alarmed. A rumor flew around that the soldiers wearing gauze face masks, of which there were a number, were human flesh eaters. The subsequent arrival of the main body of troops — more than seven thousand — precipitated a complete collapse of morale. There could no longer be any doubt that Tibet was lost. Almost overnight the population of the capital increased by 50 percent, though no provision had been made for them. Also, while the soldiers camped outside the city, many of the senior ranks, together with party officials, demanded rooms and offices within Lhasa itself. At once the price of both food and accommodation rocketed, to the grievous discomfort of the poor — though to the private satisfaction of the aristocracy, who were quick to seize the opportunity for profit. By releasing small quantities of grain at a time, local landowners, who had ample supplies (grain kept for many years in the Tibetan climate), were able to ensure that prices remained high. The Chinese were nonetheless "incredibly over-generous," according to the resident Indian mission officer, and, paying in silver with dayan (the old Nationalist currency), "in a short time . . . spent prodigal sums."

To be fair to them, the Chinese were well aware of the need not to overburden the populace and immediately began planting underutilized land outside Lhasa. But if this was in itself objectionable to Lhasans, what made it vastly more so was the use of "nightsoil" — human feces — to fertilize the crop. To the Tibetans, this was an abomination.

The first concern of the Chinese was to build a garrison for their army and, at the same time, to establish a supply chain that would enable it to be provisioned with men and matériel from army headquarters in southwestern China. This required a road link to Chengdu, work on which began at once.

As for governance, Tibet's new masters were content to allow the Tibetan National Assembly to continue to function. With regard to the Dalai Lama, he would continue to be recognized as head of state. But, understanding that his chief responsibility was to continue his education and deepen his spiritual practice, the Precious Protector himself played little direct part in the drama unfolding beneath the steep walls of the Potala.

Another communication addressed to the Dalai Lama personally and sent indirectly from the US embassy in India declared that America was "willing to help Tibet now" and would welcome a public repudiation of the Seventeen Point Agreement, in which case it would support an appeal to the United Nations and both assist with any application for asylum and help arm a resistance movement. But while this was taken as evidence of America's continued goodwill, the offer was not acted on. From his own perspective, if he was to lead his people, the Dalai Lama must first earn their respect in his capacity as a lama, and the best place for him to do that was in Tibet. To this end, rather than immersing himself in any kind of political resistance to the Chinese, he requested instead that his senior tutor initiate him into the mysteries of the Kalachakra, considered by many to be the most powerful of all the tantras. This required that Ling Rinpoché undertake a qualifying retreat during the winter in preparation for conferral during the forthcoming New Year of the Water Dragon (1952).

The Dalai Lama's political role was in the meantime delegated to the two *tsit tsab* he had appointed the previous year. This did not prove a very satisfactory arrangement. As one aristocrat recalled many years later, the two chief ministers "refused to respond positively to the Chinese" no matter what the circumstances and instead invariably "challenged and confronted them in an angry and adversarial manner." For several months, General Zhang put up with this, mindful that his main responsibility was to "make harmonious relations and eliminate hatred between nationalities." But the formation of a grassroots opposition movement, the Tibetan People's Association (TPA), which began to demonstrate publicly against the Chinese presence, meant it was only a matter of time before the general lost patience. When he finally did so, it was for the surprising reason that the two *tsit tsab* had taken the side of the TPA against the Tibetan government. If there was one thing still less pleasing than the presence of the Chinese to most of the aristocracy, it was expressions of dissent against themselves by the masses. The TPA's demonstrations amounted to a repudiation of the government's policy of appeasement and (profitable) collaboration with the Chinese. Moreover, to the aristocracy, the TPA's agitation seemed guaranteed to provoke the Chinese, to say nothing of the danger of harm to their own interests. For its part, the main concern of the TPA itself was the likely injury to religion if the Chinese remained. Yet paradoxically, it did not have the support of the monasteries, which were also nervous about antagonizing the Chinese. When, therefore, an angry General Zhang demanded that the *tsit tsab* be dismissed and the TPA proscribed, the two chief ministers had no one to speak for them.

In this, the first decisive moment of his career as political leader, the Dalai Lama chose not to back his two ministers, even though he had appointed them, and even though they stood clearly on the side of the people. Instead, he reluctantly accepted their resignation. Although Tibetan history has its share of warrior leaders, the tradition expects the Dalai Lama to be a spiritual, not an earthly, hero, and his acquiescence in the Chinese demand is early evidence of the Dalai Lama's understanding that his political vocation was to be a keeper of the peace and a seeker of dialogue rather than one who confronts and faces down an overwhelmingly superior foe. One consequence of this acquiescence was, however, that the hundred or so members of the Tibetan People's Association were sent for "reeducation."

Another difficulty the young leader faced at this time was how to manage relations with Tashilhunpo Monastery and the young Panchen Lama. Following the death in 1937 of the Ninth Panchen Lama, still in exile from his headquarters at Tashilhunpo, two rival candidates had emerged. Just as was the case when the Panchen Lama was consulted during the search for the Dalai Lama, so tradition held that the Dalai Lama be consulted during the selection of the new Panchen Lama. In this instance the Dalai Lama was too young to play a meaningful role in the procedure, so it was the regent who had taken it on. Given residual tensions between the two sees (in the original sense of the word "see," meaning a seat of authority), it was perhaps inevitable that they should opt for different candidates. One consequence of this was to bind Tashilhunpo more firmly first to the Chinese Nationalists, to whom it turned for support against the Ganden Phodrang (the Dalai Lama's government), and then to the Communists. When Mao came to power, the young Tashilhunpo-approved candidate sent a congratulatory telegram praising the Communists for completing the "grand salvation of the country and the people" — or, rather, his closest advisers did. He himself was only eleven years old at the time. When the Chinese came to Lhasa, they thus had a powerful ally whose own followers could be relied on to support them against the Dalai Lama. It was therefore incumbent on the Dalai Lama to forge a new relationship with Tashilhunpo. But when the young Panchen Lama was brought to Lhasa in 1952, it was clear that whatever good personal qualities he may have had, the Chinese were unwilling to allow him to develop any sort of friendship with the Dalai Lama.

Meanwhile, the inflation that had beset the Lhasa economy eased later that year when the PLA's first crop was harvested, and an atmosphere of uneasy peace took hold. This was helped by the fact that, although some in the Communist Party leadership were impatient to begin implementing socialism in Tibet, Chairman Mao continued to insist on gradual integration. He was encouraged in this by General Zhang's early assessment of the Tibetan religious hierarchy. Zhang believed that the Panchen Lama definitely remained favorable to Beijing, while the "Dalai Lama belongs to the middle but may possibly turn left."

One of the things that may have encouraged Zhang in this view was the creation by the Dalai Lama of a Reform Bureau within the nominally still functioning Tibetan government. This office called for a series of reforms that sought, on the one hand, to bring about genuine improvement in the lives of ordinary people and, on the other, to preempt the Communists' program. Among other initiatives, these reforms required that all civil servants, whether lay or monastic, become paid employees of the government. This was intended to put a stop to the graft — the bribery, extortion, and selling of favors — by means of which those in public office had, in place of any salary, traditionally looked after their own interests. Another initiative of the bureau was a program of land reform, which called for the voluntary distribution among the landless of some of the aristocracy's manorial possessions. If the introduction of salaries was not universally welcomed, this proposal was even more unpopular. The aristocrats protested that "if you take away the pastures, you lose the flowers too" — the flowers being the taxes and interest that the government itself received from these holdings. Events soon overtook the work of the bureau, but its very existence shows that from the beginning, the Dalai Lama saw no contradiction between his religious faith and social and economic reform.

In the meantime, the Precious Protector's eldest brother, Jigme Norbu (formerly Taktser Rinpoché, abbot of Kumbum), had arrived in the United States and made contact with officials from the State Department. The Dalai Lama, communicating with him via letter carried by trusted intermediaries to India, and from there to America, instructed him to hold off on requesting direct support for the time being. From the Precious Protector's point of view, following his initiation into the Kalachakra tantra earlier in the year, the most important thing for him to do was to master it.

In the decades since, the Dalai Lama has made the rites of the Kalachakra tantra a central feature of his public ministry and, at the time of writing, has conferred it thirty-four times, many in the West. As he explains it, the tantra is a powerful support to the cause of world peace. Involving the creation of an astonishingly intricate mandala using individual grains of colored sand (a mandala is a two-dimensional symbolic representation of some aspect of the world, in this case the palace of Kalachakra, Lord of Time), the tantra includes elaborate rituals, accompanied by complex hand movements known as *mudras,* during which initiates visualize themselves in a variety of different settings, culminating in entry to the palace. By way of preliminaries, participants meditate on the miseries of samsara — the otherwise endless series of births and deaths to which all beings are bound until they become enlightened — recognizing it for what it is: "an ocean fraught with frightful sea monsters . . . the crocodiles of birth, ageing and death."

With regard to the visualizations, these are, again, directed toward familiarizing the mind with particular mental states. One of them involves imagining oneself being born as a child and entering the body of Kalachakra through his mouth. Once inside, the practitioner melts in a single drop of *bodhichitta* (the aspiration to seek liberation for all sentient beings) and descends through the deity's body via its energy centers, before exiting via the tip of his erect penis and entering, through the "lotus" of her vagina, the womb of Kalachakra's sexual consort, Vishvamata. If this were not startling enough, we discover that the Kalachakra texts also give detailed information about building trebuchets — a kind of oversized catapult, used as a siege engine in medieval times — and flamethrowers. It turns out that an important aspect of the tantra is that it is held to have been taught initially to the king of Shambala, a hidden land from which, at the end of our present era, he will lead an invincible army in airborne ships to defeat the barbarians who have taken over the world.

As the Dalai Lama is now at pains to stress, these martial aspects of the tantra are to be understood symbolically, not literally. The real enemy is not the barbarian horde but the ignorance that gives rise to the afflictive emotions of anger, greed, strife, and so forth.* It is nevertheless clearly more than a coincidence that the Dalai Lama's focus at this time was on a set of practices the character of which is both apocalyptic and concerned with deliverance from evil.

Likewise, it cannot be mere coincidence that, during the winter of 1952, Trijang Rinpoché was to be found again restoring a number of *thangkas* depicting the protectors. It might be that the collective karma of Tibetans was such that the protector deities had been unable to keep the Chinese at bay, but it did not follow that the deities should be abandoned. On the contrary, they must be encouraged to redouble their efforts on behalf of the people.

The Chinese, having by this time completed the garrisoning of their troops in a new barrack complex in Lhasa, turned their attention to building the infrastructure for their future administration of Tibet. This included a new hospital and a school open to all. There were also party initiatives aimed at recruiting cadres to work for the implementation of socialism. Not everything the Chinese did in this regard was unpopular. As Lobsang Samten's future wife recalled: "When we passed fourteen, we became members of the Youth Organisation. Actually although our parents were not very keen, many of us were really enthusiastic for this new order of things . . . [W]e did a lot of good work,

* Remarkably, although the texts do not specify precisely who these symbolic barbarians are, it is clear from the fact that their religion is founded in a place called Mecca, their men circumcised, and their women veiled that it is Islam that the tantra has in mind. The first textual evidence of the Kalachakra tantra dates from the tenth century — a time when Buddhist northern India was being invaded by Muslims.

social work, planting trees, cleaning the main street outside our school. It was fun too, there were lots of social gatherings and dances. We enjoyed the freedom . . . a freedom we'd never had before the Chinese came." It was, however, mainly the aristocrats, and particularly the children of the aristocracy, who benefited from these innovations. They were the ones who could afford to patronize the teashops and restaurants that sprang up to cater to the Chinese. And they were the ones who had previously been most constrained by social convention. The Precious Protector was, of course, removed from all such activities. In effect, he was now little more than a figurehead whose official role in government was occasionally to dignify meetings with his presence. This does not mean that he was not keenly interested in every development, but his primary focus remained his education.

An important milestone in the Dalai Lama's life occurred during the New Year festival of 1954, when, now eighteen, he received full ordination as a priest, or *bikshu,* at which point he accepted the full 253 precepts of monkhood.* His ordination was itself preliminary to the Dalai Lama's first conferral of the Kalachakra initiation, to an audience said to have been a hundred thousand strong, in the grounds of the Norbulingka. Such a figure sounds implausibly high, but we can be confident that it would have been in the tens of thousands. The initiation, with its evocation of a world on the brink of destruction, was a dramatic event on many levels, not least that it occurred in the context of discussions over whether or not he should accept an invitation to travel to Beijing. Chairman Mao wanted the Dalai Lama to attend the inaugural meeting of the National People's Congress that autumn. This was to mark the formal adoption of China's new constitution. The Three Seats and the majority of senior government officials were vehemently opposed, while only a few — including Ngabo — were in favor. There were many concerns, not least the proposed methods of transport. The plan was to go via road, rail, and air, none of which appealed to his advisers — least of all the flying component. As one official explained to his Chinese counterpart: "The aeroplane is linked neither to the heavens, nor does it touch the earth . . . [W]e cannot risk it."

---

* In contrast, nuns maintain a whopping 364.

There was also serious concern that, having gone to China, the Precious Protector might not be permitted to return. This had happened to an earlier incarnation of Chenresig, who was more or less held hostage by Kublai Khan.* More pressing still was the perceived risk that the Dalai Lama, being young and impressionable, might have his head turned. Given his enthusiasm both for the Reform Bureau and for all things mechanical, this seemed eminently possible. In the event, however, the Dalai Lama, having consulted the great protector Mahakala, declared that he would go in spite of the objections expressed not only by Tibetan officialdom but also by a resurgent Tibetan People's Association.

It turned out that the airplane journey should have been the least of anyone's worries. Much more dangerous was the section where the road ran out and the travelers were forced to walk. Trijang Rinpoché wrote in his autobiography: "We were terrified of the possibility of boulders hurtling down on us in landslides, or of [ourselves] falling thousands of feet into deep gorges [as we made] our way falteringly across makeshift wooden bridges built over torrents swollen by the heavy rains, their spray filling the air."

With the Chinese in charge of the arrangements, the Tibetans were compelled to accept a very different alternative to the elaborate manner of traveling to which they were accustomed. In between settlements, they slept in "shabby tents" and were required to share the PLA's mess arrangements. The Dalai Lama was somewhat aghast at being offered a spittle-smeared mug of tea by a soldier, though, being thirsty, he noticed its condition only after drinking from it. The whole experience was humbling, and yet, as Trijang Rinpoché remarked in connection with a tantric practice that speaks of "Brahmins, outcasts and pigs all sharing without division," they treated the experience as "an observance of pious practice."

On his arrival in Chamdo, on August 19, the Dalai Lama was welcomed by

* This was Phagpa Lodro Gyaltsen (1235–1280), who became Imperial Preceptor for Tibet in the court of the Yuan emperor Kublai Khan, a fact that supplies one of the arguments the Chinese government makes in connection with Tibet's claimed status as a vassal state since the thirteenth century.

a large crowd of local Tibetans and two Czech nationals,* one a photographer, the other a journalist. Having been carefully briefed by their Chinese minders — not to wear anything made of metal, not to cross his shadow, not to get too close — they were surprised by the Dalai Lama's informality and approachability. When they began taking photographs of him, the Precious Protector instructed his own photographer to take photographs of them. Subsequently, he suspended a prayer ceremony in order that the Westerner might be able to take up the optimum position for his shot.

When the Dalai Lama finally took to the skies for one leg of the journey, in the Chinese premier's private aircraft, he was not much impressed, remarking, "The craft in which we flew was very old and even I could tell it had seen better days."

Completing the last leg by train in the company of the Panchen Lama and his entourage, the Dalai Lama was met on arrival in Beijing by Zhou Enlai, second in the Communist Party hierarchy after Mao Zedong, and Zhu De, head of the PLA. The Tibetans were then taken to a house previously owned by the Japanese mission, a sizable three-story mansion, the top floor of which was given over to the Dalai Lama and his two tutors, while his family occupied the remainder. Among these were his mother, his eldest sister and her husband (who was head of the Precious Protector's bodyguard), Lobsang Samten, their younger sister, and their six-year-old youngest brother, Ngari Rinpoché.

Almost at once the Tibetans were plunged into a program that was to occupy them often from early morning until late at night. The very next day there was a welcoming banquet in Zhongnanhai's great Pavilion of Purple Light; then, according to the Dalai Lama's mother, the day after that, "with no rest," they were "required to attend" a political meeting.

Presumably because he wanted to create a sense of anticipation, Mao did not schedule a meeting with the Dalai Lama until the following week. In the meantime, everything was done to reassure the young leader that China was the future and that future was bright. A major role in this was played by a

* These were Josef Kolmas and Jan Vanis. The story is from Vanis, via his nephew, also Jan, who kindly shared with me the transcript of his uncle's recollection.

young Khampa by the name of Phuntsog (pronounced something like "Punsock," where the *u* is as in "put") Wangyal, but generally referred to as Phunwang (similarly pronounced "Punwang").* Originally from Batang, where the Catholic missionaries were murdered, Phunwang had attended a Chinese school, which by that time was one of several foreign establishments in the town, including a revived Catholic mission school and an American mission school and orphanage (each of which continued in existence right up until the Communists came to power). His best friend was a student at the American mission school, and through him, Phunwang came under the influence of the missionaries, whose ideals of brotherly love made a lasting impression on him.

While still a teenager, Phunwang began reading works by Lenin and Mao and became a founding member of the Tibetan Communist Revolutionary Group. As with many revolutionaries, a major spur to Phunwang's political zeal was the hypocrisy he witnessed around him. He once saw a young woman being viciously beaten by a monk. Her crime was to have brewed beer for the monastery. Seizing the whip, Phunwang demanded to know why the monks who drank the beer were not being punished instead. On another occasion, he was disgusted to see a number of freshly severed human ears nailed to the gates of a local magistrate's headquarters.

Phunwang also deplored the burden on the common people of the corvée system. This was the rule that officials on government duty could commandeer transport, fodder, food, and accommodation. While some aristocrats were open to the idea of change, most were, he wrote later, "elegantly dressed, sophisticated socially, completely out of touch with the ordinary people, ripe for revolution."

A major component of Phunwang's thinking was the notion that Khampas must set aside their traditional hostility to central Tibet and recognize that, ethnically, they were the same. But while many were sympathetic to the

* It is common practice for family and friends to abbreviate names to the first syllable (though in fact any combination of syllables can be used) of the two given names. Aside from aristocratic or otherwise well-known families and some lamas, it is unusual for Tibetans to have or to use surnames, or family names.

idea of throwing off the Chinese yoke, and some even saw the need for social reform, the thought of making common cause with the central Tibetan government was anathema to most, who took the view that the Chinese were better masters than their own central government. As he recalled in his autobiography, the Tibetan government exerted high taxes and flogged "anyone who couldn't pay." while, although "the Chinese acted as our lords . . . they didn't steal things from the people." He did not confine his hostility to the ruling class of his own government, however. He was even more horrified at the treatment inflicted by the Chinese Nationalist soldiery, recounting with distaste one occasion when they "tied a prisoner to a wooden post in the centre of their garrison's courtyard and systematically began to stab him with their bayonets. When their victim's screams became too distressing, they gagged him. They stabbed him everywhere, but not too deeply, because the idea was to allow each of the hundreds of Chinese soldiers to wet his bayonet with the blood of a living enemy. This, they believed, would bring them luck."

By the time of the Dalai Lama's visit, Phunwang was a trusted member of the Communist Party and self-evidently the ideal liaison officer. It was he who accompanied the Precious Protector to each of his meetings with Mao and he who interpreted between them. As events would prove, Phunwang was disastrously naïve about the Communists, yet it is important to acknowledge the genuineness of his idealism—which appealed enormously to his young charge.

When the Dalai Lama finally met the Great Helmsman, as Mao was also known, the Chinese leader "did not," in the estimation of Phunwang, "act like the great leader he was, but spoke informally, [as if to] a friend." For his part, the Dalai Lama "spoke well, without any nervousness." The conversation lasted around an hour, with Mao doing much of the talking. When it was over, the Chinese leader escorted the Dalai Lama to his car and opened the door for him. "Your coming to Beijing was like coming back to your own home," said Mao, shaking the Dalai Lama's hand. "Whenever you come to Beijing, you can call me. You can come to my place whenever you want to. Don't be shy." The meeting was a splendid success. The Dalai Lama, thrilled to meet the man he had heard so much about, could hardly contain his delight. "He was so excited," Phunwang recalled, that "he hugged me," exclaiming: "Phunwang-la,* today things went very well. Mao is a great person who is unlike others."

The party leadership could hardly have dared hope for such an outcome, and when the Dalai Lama applied to join the Communist Party, it must have seemed that the ultimate prize was within its grasp. (In the end, though, nothing came of his request.)

A week later, the Chinese were given further encouragement in their thinking that the Dalai Lama might become an ally. At a speech to the first National People's Congress, on September 16, 1954, the Precious Protector announced that "one of the main fabrications of the enemy for sowing discord is that the Communist Party and the People's Government destroy religion . . . But these pernicious rumours . . . have been utterly exploded. The Tibetan people have learned from their own experience that they have freedom of religious belief." This is a startling statement. It is true that freedom of religious belief was enshrined in the new constitution. It is also certain that Phunwang would have had a hand in writing this speech. But did it represent the Dalai Lama's honest opinion?

It was now four years since his elder brother had resigned the abbacy of Kumbum Monastery, yet the Tibetan leader could hardly have forgotten Jigme Norbu's account of Chinese heavy-handedness. He had by this time also heard reports of similar behavior elsewhere in Kham and Amdo. In a speech made during the 1990s, the Dalai Lama admitted that "when dealing with the Chinese, you have no choice but to be conciliatory . . . On those occasions when I met Mao Zedong, I flattered him a little." It seems possible, therefore, that the Dalai Lama was calculating that his best hope of keeping religion safe was to amplify Mao's words, and so hold him to them. It seems that both men had similar opinions of each other as key players in their respective domains. Mao saw the Dalai Lama as crucial to winning over the Tibetans. The Dalai Lama, having seen how Mao was regarded by his deputies, understood that his strategy should be to develop a strong personal relationship with the Chinese leader.

---

* The suffix *–la* (correctly *lags*) denotes an honorific. It is used as a mark of respect: the Dalai Lama does not place himself above such considerations.

In the days following, the Tibetan leader, though not accepted as a full member of the party, was appointed a deputy chairman of the Standing Committee of the National People's Congress. This was a wordy title for a position that carried neither weight nor responsibility, but it did show that the Dalai Lama had won approval from the party leadership. A week later, Chairman Mao made an unexpected announcement. In place of the planned Military-Administrative Committee that was intended to manage the transition between the "liberation" of Tibet and the full implementation of socialism, the party would create a new Tibet Autonomous Region (TAR) with the Dalai Lama as its chairman and the Panchen Lama as his deputy. This was a pleasant surprise to the Tibetans. The word "autonomous" was extremely heartening, even though it soon became clear that the proposed TAR would not include Kham or Amdo. Nevertheless, with strong support from the Dalai Lama, the proposal was officially accepted by the Tibetan delegation.

In between the formal engagements at which affairs of state were discussed, the Dalai Lama and his entourage were frequently invited to evening entertainments. On one occasion he attended a performance of the Chinese state opera. There were also dance parties in the evening, which occasionally he and the Panchen Lama attended. At these it was common for girls from the state dance troupe to go up to guests and invite them to dance. Though Mao himself was an avid consumer of lissome females, and though Zhou is known also to have taken mistresses from among the dancers, the Chinese premier gave strict instructions "not to let the lamas dance even if they wanted to."

These parties were not wholly wasted on the Precious Protector. He was, wrote Phunwang, "extremely alert, and he liked to observe people and size them up. He noticed right away that Zhou was a very good dancer and told me that the way Zhou danced made him appear youthful . . . By contrast when Mao and Zhu De danced, they showed their age."

Phunwang was similarly observant. "Meeting often with the Dalai Lama made me realise that he was not in good physical condition. In fact," he wrote, "it worried me enough that I suggested he start doing exercises to radio music every morning." Phunwang was also surprised to learn from the Dalai Lama of the spartan nature of his life and concluded that the food he ate was considerably inferior to that enjoyed by most aristocrats in Lhasa.

Another of Phunwang's observations was that the Precious Protector was not an enthusiastic small talker. Such conversation he declared to be "silly. Wasteful." Yet on the subject of socialism for Tibet, he was "extremely interested, and asked many questions." Tibet was, "he openly agreed, backward and had to be reformed. Without reforms, he said, there was no hope for Tibetans to progress."

Early the following year, the new arrangements regarding the administration of Tibet were signed into law and the political component of the visit was concluded. The remainder of the Dalai Lama's sojourn in China was to be spent on the road, as both he and the Panchen Lama were taken on (largely separate) tours of the country. Some remarkable film footage survives. There are vignettes of the Precious Protector, well wrapped up in a smart overcoat, visiting a steelworks. We see him waving to crowds from a jeep. There is a moment when, saying good-bye at a train station, the Panchen Lama suddenly remembers his manners and, removing his hat to touch foreheads, gives his senior a cheeky grin. The two had been kept largely apart by their respective (Tibetan) courts, and while officially relations between them were cordial at best, a glimpse of warmth is evident.

The tour itself was a partial success. The Dalai Lama showed himself "eager to learn about all aspects of Communism," wrote Phunwang. But his friends and family were less so. The tour was highly regimented. "From morning till evening there was some programme," his mother recalled. "On some days we had to get up at four in the morning, and we would not return until seven in the evening." At the beginning of every meal a bell would sound, and when it was over, the bell would ring again. In the industrial centers, they found the cities "clogged with pollution and smoke," while, apart from in Shanghai, where "traces of the old gaiety" could still be seen, "the uniformity" of the blue shirts and trousers and blue serge hats of the people they met depressed the Tibetans. They themselves still wore the dazzling silks that were now made only for the export market. But more than anything else, they were struck by the poverty of the peasantry in the countryside, where, for lack of livestock, ploughs were yoked to human beings.

According to one young Tibetan official, it was clear that the Dalai Lama and his party were "never taken to any place that would give us adverse opinions." Furthermore, the Communists habitually claimed more than was their due for the improvements they showed to their guests. "Our guides [said] that all the machinery in the plants had been manufactured by the Chinese themselves," and since most of the Tibetans present could not read English, they didn't doubt it. "However," as the British-educated official wrote later, "I could plainly read the words, 'made in U.K.' or 'made in U.S.A.' on most of the machinery . . . We had a good laugh about Chinese attempts to fool us."

None of this is to say that the Tibetans were wholly unimpressed by what they saw in China. Many of the lay contingent could recognize the advantages of modern transport. Nor were they unappreciative of the efforts to ensure their material comfort. Most were delighted with the food — though not Ling Rinpoché, who preferred to rely on the bag of *tsampa* he carried with him everywhere. Nonetheless, all were mightily relieved when it was announced that they would be returning to Tibet following a modest celebration of Losar, the Tibetan New Year, in Beijing.

At a banquet the Dalai Lama hosted to mark the event, the Chinese leader again impressed the Precious Protector with his charm. Picking up morsels with his own chopsticks, Mao even shared food from his plate — to the horror of the Dalai Lama, who was all too aware of the Great Helmsman's stinking breath and rotten teeth. A slightly sour note was struck when the Dalai Lama explained to Mao that it was customary to toss a pinch of *tsampa* in the air as an offering to the gods. The Communist leader did so, but then threw a second pinch to the ground, "with a mischievous expression" on his face. This bad impression was drastically reinforced when Mao escorted the Dalai Lama to his car. Having asked the Tibetan leader whether there was anyone in Lhasa who could send a telegram, and having spoken of the need for continual direct contact with him, he praised the Dalai Lama for his scientific cast of mind, adding conspiratorially that, really, "religion is poison." It was at that moment when the young leader realized that Mao had completely misjudged him. He had mistaken the Dalai Lama's scientific turn of mind for skepticism about spiritual matters. For his part, the Dalai Lama had wanted to believe Mao when he said that religion had nothing to fear from communism. Now he saw that the Chinese leader was "the destroyer of the Dharma after all."

12

The Land of the Gods: India, November 1956–March 1957

The Dalai Lama's first important stopover on returning to Tibet was Kumbum Monastery, his temporary home in infancy. Having presided over several great ceremonies, albeit with a reduction in the number of monks in attendance, he traveled with his entourage from there to Taktser, his birthplace. To his mother's dismay, as she recalled in later life, the place "had become wretched. We saw signs of poverty everywhere; peasants wore tattered clothes and lived in a scene of total destitution." Worse, the local population was prevented from even seeing the Dalai Lama.

Matters improved somewhat as the Dalai Lama traveled west, making a slow and prayerful progress from shrine to shrine and from monastery to monastery. But many people had shocking stories of Chinese brutality to tell. In the end these were so numerous, and so clearly evidence of bad faith on the part of the self-styled liberators, that what little of the Dalai Lama's optimism had survived his final encounter with Chairman Mao had all but evaporated by the time he reached Lhasa on June 30, 1955, just one day short of a year since he'd left and a week before his twentieth birthday.

And there were not only temporal but also spiritual portents of impending disaster. The Dalai Lama's junior tutor, Trijang Rinpoché, who for the first part of the return journey had traveled separately via Kham, recounts how the contents of a magical box he encountered en route which had hitherto provided an inexhaustible supply of "miraculous iron pills" had recently dwindled to nothing. Then on the last leg from Chamdo, an event occurred that could only be interpreted as highly inauspicious. Hardly had the Dalai Lama and his two tutors crossed a bridge on foot — damaged by a wild torrent, it was deemed too dangerous to drive on — than it split in half and went crashing into the ravine, leaving all their luggage on the other side. Heavy rain also affected the Dalai Lama's procession into the Norbulingka, forcing all who took part to wear protective clothing over their ceremonial attire, and "it occurred to many," Trijang Rinpoché recalled, "that this was not a good omen."

Yet at a religious teaching he gave soon after, the Dalai Lama articulated a positive view of Sino-Tibetan relations. China had not come to be "lord" over Tibet, he explained, but had instead come as an equal partner to assist the Tibetans in the secular development of their country. Recognizing that the Communists' claims to friendship and fraternal concern were the only weapons that could be used against them, he began — as he had clearly intended following his first meeting with Mao — pursuing a strategy of taking the word of the Chinese leader at face value. The autonomy for Tibet promised at the party conference and the religious freedom guaranteed in the constitution were both plainly stated. It was therefore a matter of holding the Chinese to their commitments.

Almost no sooner had the Dalai Lama given his speech than news started to circulate of the arrest not only of several Khampa chieftains but also of a number of lamas in Kham for resisting Chinese interference. This was shocking. Even so, when he met Alan Winnington, the British communist writer and Beijing correspondent for the *Daily Worker,* the Dalai Lama was in an extremely cautious mood. When asked what had happened in Tibet since the signing of the Seventeen Point Agreement, the Dalai Lama replied dutifully that before "liberation, Tibet could see no way ahead. Since [then], Tibet has left the old way that led to darkness and has taken a new way leading to a bright future of development." Here was a young man evidently resigned to economies of truth because he dared not tell the whole.

In fact, on the way back from Beijing, the Dalai Lama had confided in Trijang Rinpoché his belief that, from his way of speaking, Mao "harboured a low opinion of Tibetans," as well as "many other things that [Trijang Rinpoché] must keep secret within the innermost core of [his] heart." The reality was that the Dalai Lama was keenly aware of the disastrous position he was in.

An early test of how genuine the Chinese commitment was to true autonomy for Tibet came with the formation of a new Tibetan People's Association. Ostensibly a charitable organization founded to distribute alms for the poor of Lhasa (whose condition communism had manifestly not succeeded in abolishing), its first thought was to submit a petition to the Chinese requesting the withdrawal of all their troops from Tibet. On the advice of the Nechung oracle, this petition was put to the cabinet in advance of the first meeting of the Preparatory Committee of the Tibet Autonomous Region. Of course, no petition was ever going to make a positive impression on the Chinese, and the petitioners understood this. But at the time they hoped that submitting it would encourage the Kashag to cease appeasing the Chinese and take a firmer stand. Instead, the petition's main effect was to give the Communists the opportunity to test the Dalai Lama's loyalty to the Motherland.

It took two months for the Kashag to respond. In the meantime, the Tibetan government was caught in an agony of indecision. The Chinese were adamant that the "fake Tibetan People's Association" must be disbanded. The ministers, however, feared that if they went head-to-head with the TPA, there would be trouble.

The outcome was inevitable. The Dalai Lama himself would have to step into the breach. Only he, not the Kashag, had the authority to take on the TPA. An edict, signed by the Precious Protector, was drawn up and published by tacking up a poster in several public places. It began by referring to the unhappiness of the people on account of the Five Poisons — ignorance, attachment, aversion, pride, and envy — as a result of which "even the insects living under the earth have not been happy." It went on to remind the reader that in Tibet, "there is no custom of a few people from the masses calling a people's meeting and interfering in the work of the government." Such meetings were "a very serious error." Research, it said, had shown how "most of the people in this Association had sincere thoughts," but they "had been deceived by bad leaders" who "wanted to uproot the good laws of old Tibet" and "wanted to do bad deeds." The TPA must be disbanded at once, and the leaders were to "confess their errors." Concluding on a threatening note, it warned that "if there are some thoughtless people who don't listen and continue to do this, we will apply strong punishments."

The Tibetan People's Association duly disbanded, and its leader subsequently went into exile in India with a view to making contact with the Dalai Lama's brother, Gyalo Thondup. For his part, GT, as he was known, had formed a small group of émigrés determined to do whatever they could from outside Tibet to resist the Chinese. This included renewing contact with the American embassy in Delhi and cultivating those members of the Indian government who were sympathetic to the plight of Tibet and nervous about China's designs both on the disputed Northeast and on large swaths of territory in Kashmir to which the Communists laid claim. Despite the recent 1954 Panchsheel (Five Principles of Coexistence) Accord between India and China, there was still a significant number of Indian politicians who fell into this category.

Among them was Apa Pant, the Oxford-educated prince turned Gandhian freedom fighter, by whom Gyalo Thondup was approached on behalf of the government about a possible invitation to the Dalai Lama to visit India. Jawaharlal Nehru, the Indian prime minister (who had briefly met the Tibetan leader in Beijing), sought the Dalai Lama's attendance at the Buddhajyanti celebrations scheduled for the end of 1956 to commemorate the 2,500th anniversary of the birth of the Buddha. Nehru's purpose in this seems to have been mainly to test China's commitment to the Sino-Indian accord. The Dalai Lama's appearance would also lend prestige to the event and show India's Buddhists that the government was mindful of their interests.

News of the invitation was hugely exciting to the Precious Protector. Not only would it be the fulfillment of a religious aspiration — for Tibetans, India is *arya bhumi,* the land of the gods — but also it would give him the opportunity to speak with the heirs of Mahatma Gandhi, whose successful campaign to rid India of the all-powerful British was such an inspiration to him.

The Dalai Lama was also clearly aware of the mounting opposition to the Chinese occupation in Kham and Amdo. Although Mao had promised gradual reform, and although he had agreed to autonomy for central Tibet, in the eastern provinces feudalism was being brought to an abrupt and bewildering end with the collectivization of farmland. This ought, perhaps, to have been expected, given Mao's recent remark: "On this matter Marxism is indeed cruel and has little mercy."

Although the Chinese understood that the imposition of reform was likely to provoke revolt, especially in Kham, the initial response on the part of the peasantry, the *mi ser* (literally, and for no clear reason, the golden-headed ones), was in fact sullen acceptance. No doubt it was a boon to them, on the one hand, to be relieved of their debts and the obligations of the old system. On the other hand, the psychological impact was immense: a whole layer of meaning had been torn from the world. Despite the hardship, there had been a sense of worth in the fulfillment of one's obligations and the promise of recompense in future lives. Nonetheless, there was little direct resistance and no uprising until the PLA demanded that the Khampa people hand in their guns. It was this, and not the land reforms, that initially precipitated open rebellion.

Matters came to a head when the Chinese demanded that the monks of Lithang Monastery in Kham, together with the local nomad population, surrender their weapons. At this time the monastery held around six thousand monks, most of whom were armed, as was the entirety of the surrounding population, said to have constituted a hundred thousand households. Both the nomad chieftain and the monks agreed that under no circumstance were they prepared to do so. It was indeed the monks who were foremost among the volunteers when the decision was subsequently made to attack the Chinese administrative office adjacent to the monastery. On a snowy day in March 1956, the assault began with the Khampas charging the Communist Party headquarters and setting it on fire. Somewhere between two and three hundred party workers, including a number of local recruits, were killed in the ensuing battle.

Many similar outbreaks of violence occurred elsewhere in the district, with hundreds killed and wounded and terrible revenge exacted against collaborators. According to a Chinese report (doubtless somewhat exaggerated but nonetheless not wholly implausible, given the fate of the Christian missionaries): "If someone supported the CCP [the Chinese Communist Party] . . . with their heart, they would cut out his heart. If someone read materials distributed by the CCP, they would cut out his eyes. If someone listened to the CCP, they would cut off his ears. If someone raised his hand to support the CCP, they would cut off his hand." With surprising ease the Khampas took control not just of Lithang but of a large number of Chinese outposts in the region. It could not be long before the Chinese counterattacked, but, being more familiar with banditry than with conventional warfare, the Khampas in the meanwhile confined themselves to looting whatever arms and armaments they could lay their hands on. When the counteroffensive came twelve days later, the insurgents were quickly driven back. Most made straight for the monastery, which, with its high defensive wall, did at least offer some protection.

Rather than engage in a lengthy siege, the Chinese began tunneling underneath the monastery. Unfortunately for them, the tunnel was discovered. As the Chinese emerged from it, they were "stabbed to death before they even had time to take out their guns."

How the Buddhist tradition, as it developed in Tibet, regards warfare and other forms of violence is not widely understood. It is a given that all intentional killing is wrong, and there is no Buddhist just war theory as such. But one of the Jataka Tales, a compendium of stories about the previous lives of the Buddha, tells how once he was traveling in a boat when he discovered that a crew member intended to kill all five hundred passengers. Because the passengers were all holy men on the verge of Enlightenment, the Buddha foresaw that the killer, if successful, would incur the penalty of 100,000 eons in hell. He therefore killed the man to spare him this fate, at the same time facilitating the Enlightenment of the five hundred. The moral here is that in extreme circumstances, violence may be justifiable in defense of the Buddhadharma. The proviso is that the one engaging in violence must do so out of correct motivation. As the Dalai Lama has said, where this obtains, and "where the motive is good and there are no other possibilities, then seen most deeply it [violence] is non-violence, because the aim is to help others." Remarkably, in certain circumstances, killing, from the Buddhist perspective, can be seen as an act of compassion.

From this, it becomes clearer why the Dalai Lama was taught not to oppose physical force actively in all circumstances. It also goes some way toward contextualizing the fact that, within the monasteries, breaking the vow of celibacy was considered a graver sin than killing a Chinese.

Following the Lithang uprising, the Chinese army command made known that it was nonetheless prepared to offer a negotiated settlement. If the rebels surrendered and handed over their weapons, there would be no reprisals. While discussions over this proposal were taking place, two aircraft dropped bombs on the mountainside adjacent to the monastery. This was to alert the rebels to what would happen if they rejected the offer. Though determined not to surrender, the Khampas could see that holding out against aerial bombardment was out of the question. They decided therefore to take their chances and flee during the night. The first few parties of escapees were successful in breaking out undetected, but it was not long before the Chinese realized what was happening. According to one Tibetan survivor, by this time "the Tibetans were going out like sheep and goats; and the Chinese had automatic weapons, so they killed a large number of people." Even so, a few, including the young Khampa chieftain, held out to the bitter end. Carrying his weapon above his head, he finally surrendered to the Chinese commander, only to draw a pistol from his *chuba* and shoot the man dead before being killed himself.

When news of the carnage reached Lhasa, the Dalai Lama was appalled beyond words. What upset him most was a photograph of the damage to Lithang Monastery. That anyone would resort to aerial bombardment against people who could not defend themselves defied belief. Aside from harming the combatants, what about the collateral damage to innocent people — to elderly monks, to animals and other sentient beings, and to precious religious artifacts? The very idea was beyond comprehension. Realizing what had happened, he later wrote, "I cried."

The Dalai Lama's immediate response to the catastrophe of Lithang was to demand a meeting with the senior Chinese general resident in Lhasa at the time, telling him, "How are Tibetans supposed to trust the Chinese if this is how you behave?" At the same time, he sent first one, then another personal letter to Chairman Mao. That these went unanswered told him all he needed to know about the reality of the assurances Mao had given in Beijing. The letters do not survive, and it is not clear that they were even delivered. In desperation, he entrusted yet another letter to Phunwang, who was to deliver it by his own hand. This too was similarly unacknowledged.

A second offering of the Kalachakra tantra, timed to coincide with the opening sessions of the Preparatory Committee, may have relieved the gloom to some extent. It certainly provided a morale boost for the audience, whose faces were "filled with awe" and "shone with happiness," as one official recalled half a century later. But it was the unexpected news, brought by the maharajah of Sikkim, that Nehru himself had followed up on his plan and written to the Chinese government on behalf of the Dalai Lama to invite him to attend the forthcoming Buddhjyanti celebrations, which really lifted his spirits. The maharajah found the Dalai Lama "anxious to leave," while the invitation had put the Chinese in a quandary. The danger on one side was that the Dalai Lama would become a powerful spokesman for Tibet abroad. On the other, preventing him from going might endanger the nonaggression pact assuring "cooperation for mutual benefit" into which China and India had entered in 1954. In the end, they responded by saying that he was too busy to accept.

Deeply disappointed, the Dalai Lama left Lhasa to pay a visit to Reting Monastery, where, accompanied by his two tutors, he conferred novice vows on the young reincarnation of his former senior tutor, Reting Rinpoché. At the time, Reting Monastery was the repository for some famous relics, including its founder's robes and the Indian texts he had used over nine hundred years ago. There were also some letters written in the great Tsongkhapa's own hand. As the founder of the Gelug school, Tsongkhapa had a special place in the Dalai Lama's heart. Yet while the visitors were delighted to find these relics still intact, they were dismayed to discover that the monastery was in large part ruined. Atisha's reliquary stupa had been robbed of its gilding and precious stones, there were bullet holes in many of the statues, and piles of rubble lay all around. Evidently no attempt had been made to clear up the debris from the destruction wrought during an attack on government troops following the ex-regent's arrest ten years earlier.

On returning to Lhasa from Reting, the Dalai Lama learned of an unexpected development. Following Nehru's intervention, Mao had executed a U-turn on the proposed trip to India, and the Dalai Lama was informed that he would be permitted to go after all. Although Mao took the precaution of scheduling two consecutive visits to India by Zhou Enlai during the time the Dalai Lama was to be in the country, the Chinese made the further decision not to send a large delegation to accompany the Precious Protector. As Deng Xiaoping—later to emerge as Mao's successor—wrote, this was to be "a test" for the Dalai Lama. Mao meanwhile spoke candidly of the risks this entailed at a meeting of the Communist Party Central Committee: "It must be anticipated that the Dalai Lama may not come back, and that in addition, he may abuse us every day, making allegations such as 'the Communists have invaded Tibet,' and that he may go so far as to declare the 'independence of Tibet.'" Yet the prospect held no terror for Mao: "Shall I feel aggrieved at the desertion of one Dalai? Not at all... What harm will his departure do to us? None whatsoever. He can't do more than curse us."

Traveling overland by car via Shigatse, where he joined up with the Panchen Lama, the Precious Protector spent a short time at Dromo, the border town he had last seen in 1951, before continuing the journey on horseback, up the steep track that led to the Nathu Pass, before it plunged down into Sikkim on the other side. The carcasses of mules that had "probably perished from exhaustion" and "clusters of sinister-looking vultures" hopping among them that were a perennial feature of the Tibetan trade routes might have served as a prophetic warning of the fate that was to befall Tibet.

India was a revelation, however. "People," the Dalai Lama immediately saw, "expressed their real feelings and did not just say what they thought they ought to say." The arrangements were, from his perspective, rather chaotic compared with the regimentation in China, but the enthusiasm of the people won him over. Everywhere he went, he was greeted by huge crowds of well-wishers, many of whom had traveled long distances just to get a glimpse of him.

From the Indian point of view, the Tibetan delegation was something of a revelation too. The task of hosting them "was not made easier by the fact that the Lamas' followers were explosively sensitive to the smallest niceties of protocol and were ready to draw daggers at the merest suspicion of a slight," according to one Indian official. Another challenge was the Indians' awareness that any "accident" that might befall the Dalai Lama would be hugely advantageous to the Chinese — a mishap that would be relatively easy to arrange and then to lay at the door of the Indian government. His security was thus a constant source of anxiety, exacerbated by the tumultuous enthusiasm shown for the Tibetan leader whenever he appeared in public. A glimpse of this can be seen in the newsreels shot during his visit and in the recollections of some of those delegated to look after him.

Describing an occasion when he escorted the Panchen Lama to his quarters in Gangtok, Nari Rustomji* wrote:

> We had hardly passed the Palace gates before a crowd that seemed like the entire population of Sikkim lunged madly forward, man, woman and child, with arms vainly outstretched, for a touch of the vehicle we were travelling in. I seriously feared our station wagon would be overturned, but there was no remedy as the police, themselves devout Buddhists, were too overawed by the Presence [a common epithet used by Tibetans both for the Dalai and the Panchen Lamas] to dream of controlling the crowds. Coins, currency notes, ceremonial scarves, amulets came whirring through the windows . . . until at last we were compelled to close them in self-defence. Our security arrangements might have served well enough for common or garden mortals, but certainly not for the Living God, whose only protection now was his own divinity.

With respect to the two lamas' personalities, Rustomji, himself a Parsi (an adherent of Zoroastrianism), recalled his impressions in his autobiography: "I have often been asked whether I was ever aware of supernatural forces emanating from the Lamas' presence. I have to confess that, for all the eager and excited anticipation of their divine immanence, they remained, for me, two very

* Rustomji was the epitome of an official from the latter days of the British Raj: a Cambridge-educated classicist, violin player, and prizewinning gymnast.

charming and sensible young men, of gentle and considerate manner, inquiring and vigorous mind and irresistibly attractive personality."

This attractiveness was, he also noted, not lost on some of their young female devotees, perhaps inspired by folk memories of the dissolute Sixth Dalai Lama. "It was," he wrote, "evident from the homely talk" of some of his Sikkimese friends that

> there were many in Lhasa who were as carried away by the youthful charm of the Lamas as by their divinity, and they told us tales of some of their more passionate young friends whose secret purpose in seeking the Dalai Lama's blessing was that they might be nearer the object of desire . . . Could it really be, wondered the belles of Lhasa, that the Dalai Lama could be utterly immune to feminine allure? It was a challenge to Venus which provoked them to higher endeavours. The Panchen, too, was not without his admirers. And wicked gossip whispered that the chinks in his armour were already showing through.

But while the Panchen Lama's susceptibility to female charms struck Rustomji, he noted that, though the Dalai Lama "had a delightful sense of fun . . . there was something not of this world, ethereal and ageless, in [his] expression that moved me the more deeply."

From the moment he set foot in the country until the day he left, eleven weeks later, the question at the forefront of the Dalai Lama's mind was whether to return to Tibet, or was now the moment to seek asylum abroad? There were strong feelings in both directions among those closest to him. In favor of staying in India were his older brothers Gyalo Thondup and Jigme Norbu — the first already based in India, the second having flown in specially from America. Sitting up with them until midnight, the Dalai Lama recalled, "Their views really shook me." Phala, too, the Lord Chamberlain, together with one of the former *tsit tsab,* took a similar line. On the other side were the four members of the Kashag and, less vociferously, the two tutors, while the representatives of the Three Seats were firmly in favor of returning to Tibet. Also of importance was the opinion of the people of Tibet, who could be assumed to favor his return. For them to be without the Dalai Lama was to be bereaved.

From Sikkim, the Precious Protector flew to Delhi, where his first engagement was to lay flowers and a *kathag* at Rajghat, in honor of Mahatma Gandhi, whose memorial stands there. The experience affected him profoundly. "It was a calm and beautiful spot," he later wrote, "and I felt very grateful to be there, the guest of a people like mine who had endured foreign domination."

The next few days in Delhi were occupied with official receptions at which he was greeted by almost every dignitary in the capital. Not only was the Dalai Lama still nominally a head of state, but also the Tibetan leader was something more than a mere political figure. For many Indians he was an avatar, a holy man without compare. Though they did not share his religion, they nonetheless eagerly sought *darshan* of him: a blessing and a glimpse of the divine.

While he was in Delhi, the Dalai Lama met with Zhou Enlai, the Chinese premier, who was en route to a number of other Asian countries. As the Dalai Lama wrote in his autobiography, he found Zhou "as full of charm, smiles and deceit as ever." Besides telling the Tibetan leader of Mao's recent decision to delay reforms indefinitely in the Tibet Autonomous Region, Zhou assured him that if the Dalai Lama would care to accompany him back to Beijing, Chairman Mao would be glad to see the Precious Protector again and to allay in person any fears he might have. As for Gyalo Thondup and Jigme Norbu (both of whom Zhou clearly suspected of agitating for the Dalai Lama to seek asylum abroad), should they happen to be short of funds, the Chinese embassy would be happy to supply the Dalai Lama with money to give them — though it would be better if he did not disclose its source. This last was a strange remark. For all his guile, it is clear that Zhou was a less astute judge of character than his adversary.

Notwithstanding Zhou's assurance that there would be no reforms in the Tibet Autonomous Region, it left untouched the question of what was to happen in Kham and Amdo. The violent struggle now firmly under way there was certain to continue.

From Delhi, the Precious Protector traveled to Bodh Gaya, where, to his delight, he was able to spend several days conducting ceremonies at this, the most sacred of all Buddhist pilgrimage sites. A speech he made at this time is remarkable for its prescience. Noting that in one of the sutras, or scriptures, there is a prophecy made by the Buddha that 2,500 years after his *parinirvana*

— or passing beyond suffering — the dharma would flourish in the land of the red-faced people, he explained that some held this to refer to its spread in Tibet, "but one scholar has interpreted otherwise. According to him the prediction refers to Europe." What the Dalai Lama could not have imagined at the time was that it would be he, more than anyone else, who would bring this about. Instead, his attention was focused when, on the last day of his stay at Bodh Gaya, unexpected news came that Zhou would be returning to Delhi the following day and sought an urgent meeting with the Tibetan leader.

At once the Dalai Lama sent a message to one of the young Tibetan government officials who had remained behind in Delhi. He was to leave immediately for the northeastern hill town of Kalimpong, where he was to discharge the medium of the Nechung oracle from his Scottish mission hospital bed, where he was being treated for arthritis, and bring him to Delhi the very next day. This was a tall order, given the distances involved and the as yet underdeveloped state of regional air links. Nonetheless, in spite of delays necessitating some frantic negotiation with airline officials and a frosty reception from the other passengers when they finally took their seats two hours after the scheduled departure, the Nechung medium and his two attendants successfully made it back to Delhi on time. It subsequently emerged that his advice was that the Precious Protector should now seek asylum.

Meanwhile, the Dalai Lama himself had fared less well. Arriving in Delhi by train earlier that evening, he had been hijacked by the Chinese ambassador. Without informing his Indian counterparts, the ambassador met the Dalai Lama at the train station and escorted him to his own car, which drove directly to the Chinese embassy. Meanwhile the rest of the Tibetan entourage took their seats in cars provided by the Indian government. The Tibetans arrived back at Hyderabad House, where they were quartered, aghast to find that they had mislaid their precious cargo. Only after frantic telephoning was the Dalai Lama finally located and retrieved from the Chinese embassy, where he had already had the first of what was to be several meetings with Zhou Enlai. It was a stunning diplomatic coup on the part of the Chinese.

These encounters with Zhou surrounded a critical meeting with Nehru at which the Precious Protector sought to determine the prime minister's attitude toward a formal request for asylum. The Indian leader made clear his determination not to make any commitments that would harm India's relationship with China. Indeed, so fully was his mind made up that he barely attended to what the Precious Protector had to say: "At first he listened and nodded politely. But . . . after a while he appeared to lose concentration as if he were about to [fall asleep]." The Dalai Lama explained that he had done all in his power to make the relationship with China work, but that he was now beginning to think it might be better to remain in India rather than return to Tibet. This evidently brought Nehru to his senses. He understood what the Tibetan was saying, he assured him, "but you must realise . . . that India cannot support you." His advice was rather that the Dalai Lama should hold the Chinese to the terms of the Seventeen Point Agreement and speak out forcefully when they failed to do so.

At his subsequent meetings with Zhou, the Dalai Lama gave no indication that he was considering applying for political asylum. Indeed, the (Chinese) transcripts of the meetings have him dutifully speaking in the first-person plural when referring to Chinese government policy in Tibet. Yet it is clear also that the Chinese premier was well aware that the Tibetan leader had been making inquiries. He cautioned the Dalai Lama that, if he stayed in India, he would be in political exile. "At first when you say something bad against us as strongly as possible, you will get some money. The second and third time, when you do not have much to say against us, you will get small sums of money, and in the end they will not have money to give you."

The opposing voices of the Nechung oracle and the Chinese premier were deeply unsettling, and when he left Delhi a few days later in the company of the Panchen Lama for a month-long tour of the country, the Dalai Lama was still in a quandary.

His schedule over the next few weeks consisted of visits to various important Buddhist pilgrimage sites, interspersed with sightseeing trips to several cities including Bombay, Calcutta, Bangalore, and Mysore. These visits to places connected with the founder of Buddhism had a profound impact on the Dalai Lama — none more so than at Vulture Peak in northeastern India, where the Buddha is believed to have preached the Mahayana, or Great Vehicle, for the first time. Here — possibly in prophetic anticipation of the thousands of monks he was himself to ordain over subsequent decades — the Dalai Lama enjoyed a vision during meditation of hosts of monks reciting the Wisdom Mantra: "*Om Ga-te Ga-te, Paraga-te, Bodhi Svaha.*"

The visits to India's industrial centers were of less interest. In news footage shot during this part of the visit, we see the Dalai Lama being shown around an industrial engineering project. He adjusts repeatedly an obviously uncomfortable workman's safety helmet, and it is clear he is not enjoying the experience. Trijang Rinpoché, too, was completely underwhelmed. The factories with their swirling rivers of molten lead reminded him only of the "hell realms."

Doubtless the Indians' intentions were to show the Tibetans that China had nothing on them in terms of material progress, but what impressed the Dalai Lama most was the enthusiasm of the people for their young democracy. The viewer of the contemporary footage is struck by the self-confidence of the crowds that attended the Precious Protector's every public appearance. (Pilgrims could travel at half price on the railways.) On each arrival, the Dalai Lama is garlanded and presented with bouquets of flowers as the press fight for photographs and crowds cheer. In contrast, faithful Tibetans stand meekly patient in hope of catching a glimpse of the Precious One. Yet it is also instructive to look at the demeanor of the Dalai Lama himself. The pressure he felt himself under is palpable. At the Dehra Dun Military Academy he sits, evidently somewhat reluctantly, next to a copiously beribboned general, doubtless comparing the military might on display with what he had seen in China. As the presidential steam train lent to him for his journey draws slowly away from the station, he can be seen smiling and waving somewhat awkwardly in unfamiliar Western style. Following a visit to the Taj Mahal, he takes his place uncertainly behind Nehru on an elephant's back. At the Air Force Academy he follows a more obviously eager Panchen Lama in taking a turn sitting in a training aircraft. In Calcutta he is taken to watch — without very much enthusiasm — the horseracing at the anachronistically named Royal Calcutta Turf Club. It is a relief to see him riding a miniature train with a delight exceeded only by that of the Panchen Lama, who altogether forgets the dignity of his office, veritably whooping with joy. One has a sense that here is a young man embattled, overburdened even, yet also someone determined to do his best whatever the circumstances.

The India trip ended, as it had begun, in Kalimpong. The Dalai Lama took up residence in the very same house as that occupied by the Great Thirteenth in 1911, following his own flight to exile in India when the Chinese sent an army into Lhasa. As it had long been, the town was a nest of spies (to use Nehru's own words). To add to its febrile atmosphere was the presence of hundreds of refugees, mainly from Kham, desperate for the Dalai Lama to call them to arms. Prominent among these refugees was Gyalo Thondup, who had by now come to terms with John Hoskins, the twenty-nine-year-old head of the CIA's Far East Division. America was by now very interested in Tibet as a way to cause trouble for the Chinese Communists. Hoskins, who was based at America's Calcutta consulate, did not have a very favorable first impression of GT. "There was a lot of submissiveness rather than dynamism," he noted. Yet in spite of this poor initial impression, Washington decided the CIA should support the training, equipping, and insertion of an initial eight (later reduced to six) Tibetan agents. Hoskins gave Gyalo Thondup the task of recruiting the men, and he in turn involved his elder brother, Jigme Norbu. The six recruits were all Khampas, of whom four were ex-monks, one of these former ecclesiastics an especially fiery character by the name of Wangdu, who in his youth had shot a man dead for that age-old crime of "disrespect." The agency's estimation of GT changed over time. When eventually the CIA program came to an end, its then operations director requested that Gyalo Thondup "please arrange for your next incarnation to be Prime Minister of a country where we can do more to help you!," noting that he had been extraordinarily successful in obtaining both material and political support from the United States.

It is certain that by now the Dalai Lama knew something of the CIA's interest in supporting a resistance movement in Tibet. But Washington had not been unequivocal in championing the Tibetan cause, having failed in recent communications to make clear that it would back a resolution at the United Nations calling for Tibetan independence. Nor was it certain that the United States would recognize a Tibetan government in exile. Had Washington's assurances been more explicit, it seems possible the Dalai Lama would have ignored the majority of his advisers, who favored returning, risked Nehru's ire, and formally requested asylum. But in the absence of such assurances, the Tibetan leader remained uncertain.

While still considering his options, the Dalai Lama met with several senior government officials who had come from Lhasa ostensibly to escort him on the last leg of his journey back home. In fact, their purpose in coming was to brief the Precious Protector on the continuing deterioration of relations with the Chinese and to implore him to seek asylum.

Inevitably the matter was put, once more, to the oracles — this time not only that of Nechung but also that of Gadong, another highly regarded source of spiritual counsel. When both declared in favor of a return to Tibet, those opposed were appalled. It was well known that Nechung's earlier advice had been to stay in India. Many were doubtful of the new result. Yet when questioned on this very point, Nechung replied that he knew that he would not have been believed if he had spoken in favor of return any earlier. He had therefore adopted "skillful" means. This is the practice whereby a teacher adapts his discourse to the capacity of his audience.

In order to verify that the deities had been interpreted correctly, their pronouncements were also made the subject of a *mo** — a dough ball divination — in front of the *thangka* of the Glorious Goddess by the Dalai Lama himself, but with the same result. This caused further dismay among those pressing for him to remain. "When men become desperate they consult the gods," declared one minister. "When the gods become desperate, they tell lies."

This divination finally decided the matter. Yet although the Dalai Lama was now committed to returning, it was, he announced, with several important provisos. One was that, from now on, taking Nehru's advice, he and the Kashag would vigorously protest any Chinese measures they deemed unacceptable. Another was that, henceforth, the people — that is, the represen-

* Among many other forms of divination practiced by Tibetans, that of *mo* is widely used. Preceded by a period of meditation and accompanied by appropriate prayers and invocations, this is performed by placing in a vessel two or more balls, traditionally of barley dough, distinguished from one another sometimes with dye, but more usually by pieces of paper with possible answers written on them and concealed inside. The balls are then rotated ever more swiftly until one flies out, propelled by centrifugal force. Though simple enough in operation, conducting a *mo* is a grave and serious business. The correct spiritual outlook and motivation are essential if it is to be accurate. And the more spiritually advanced the questioner, the more reliable will be the answer.

tatives of the Tibetan People's Association — would be consulted. But most important, some officials would remain behind in India with responsibility for maintaining links with the Indian State Department as well as the American officials with whom the Dalai Lama's brothers were in contact. And in order to facilitate this, a secret codebook was drawn up and distributed among select members of both the government and the stay-behind party.

But while the Dalai Lama had made up his mind to return, those wishing him to remain had other ideas and immediately set about formulating audacious plans to prevent him from going.

Despite the Precious Protector trying to persuade the Panchen Lama to accompany him to Sikkim, the younger man elected to return directly to Tibet from Calcutta. On his return, he was greeted effusively by the PLA's General Fan Ming. Instead of staying in the capital as planned, however, the Panchen Lama left suddenly for his headquarters at Shigatse. It seems that he had become aware of credible evidence of a scheme to assassinate him. And the putative assassins were not Chinese but Tibetan.

This is astonishing. Most Tibetans could not conceive of such an idea. But given lingering doubts as to the Pachen Lama's authenticity — for a long time, it will be recalled, there were two official candidates — and the serious ill-feeling toward him for his staunchly pro-Chinese stance, the existence of such a plot seems not implausible. Presumably the thought was that if the Panchen Lama was killed, the Dalai Lama would be forced to change his mind and stay in India out of fear for his own safety.

Another scheme called for simultaneous attacks on the Chinese to be carried out in Lhasa and Dromo. Orders were dispatched to the leadership of Tibet's burgeoning resistance movement to foment rebellion in alliance with the recently revived bodyguard regiment. Unfortunately for the plotters, the bodyguard resisted, and the plan came to nothing. Meanwhile, heavy snowfall blocked the Nathu Pass. For two more weeks the Dalai Lama remained in Sikkim. When eventually his party was able to cross the pass, it felt, as Trijang Rinpoché put it, like "being returned to prison."

13

"Don't sell the Dalai Lama for silver dollars!": Lhasa, 1957–1959

The Dalai Lama's first stop on his return to Tibet was Dromo. There, taking Nehru's advice to be more assertive, he told Chinese officials that, rather than focus on any good that had been done, it was important now to discuss openly the failings of the Communist Party's intervention in Tibet. For their part, the Chinese convened a meeting of the Tibet Work Committee. This was the organization that actually implemented Chinese government policy in Tibet. Remarkably, it was decreed that the majority of party cadres then working the country should be returned to China, with only a small percentage remaining. Similarly, many locally recruited (that is, Tibetan) cadres were to lose their positions while the various offices of the Preparatory Committee were either to close or to be greatly reduced in size. It seemed that Chairman Mao was determined to make good on Zhou Enlai's promises to the Dalai Lama. But while the directives were plain, the reality on the ground was very different. The numbers of Chinese actually withdrawn were far fewer than the central government called for. And though reform in central Tibet could wait, there was to be no letup in Kham and Amdo.

There was further bad news for the Dalai Lama when, moving on from Dromo, he went to pay a visit to the Panchen Lama at the junior man's headquarters at Tashilhunpo. It quickly became clear that the Panchen Lama's circle had a message for him. Instead of offering the Dalai Lama accommodation within the monastery itself, they had made arrangements for him to stay within the great fort. But then rumors of a far greater insult reached the Dalai Lama's ears: that the Tashilhunpo monks were performing the ritual for dispersing evil spirits, the implication being that he himself was the evil spirit. Credence was lent to this rumor when news came that an important Rinpoché close to the Dalai Lama had died suddenly — suggesting that the ritual had only narrowly missed its target.

Insult piling on insult, when he went to teach within Tashilhunpo itself, he found that only "torn and inferior" furnishings had been put out for his use, and the throne he was seated on was old and shabby and set up "in a dilapidated room" that was filled not with the Tashilhunpo monastic community but only with monks from neighboring monasteries. Arrangements had been made for the Tashilhunpo monks to receive their grain ration that same day, so that any who sought an audience with the Dalai Lama would miss out. It was, in the Dalai Lama's view, "a very bad show." Taken in isolation, this deliberate snubbing of the Dalai Lama would seem gratuitous. In the context of the rumored attempt on the life of the Panchen Lama, it becomes more understandable. As a result, relations between the two sees fell to a low unknown since the time of their predecessors.

Returning to Lhasa, the Dalai Lama reassumed his position as chairman of the Preparatory Committee for the Autonomous Region of Tibet, but thanks to Mao delaying the implementation of reform, his duties were not onerous. He could thus turn his attention to what was, from his perspective, the most important matter at hand, the Geshe Lharampa examinations marking the end of his formal education. These were now scheduled to take place during the Monlam celebrations two years hence.

A moment of respite that occurred in the meantime was his visit to Ling Rinpoché's hermitage at Gerpa. So thoroughly destroyed in the 1960s that today it is scarcely possible to discern where the building stood, then it was large enough to accommodate a sizable community of monks. At a long-life *puja** performed for the Dalai Lama's benefit, the Precious Tutor spoke movingly of how Chenresig, Boddhisattva of Compassion, had worked tirelessly to help sentient beings free themselves from the wretchedness of samsara. Years later, the Dalai Lama recalled how, "with tears filling my eyes, I prayed that I would indeed, as my root [principal] lama was so fervently wishing, live a long life and accomplish great things for living beings and the Buddha's teachings."

During the summer of that year, 1957, two major events occurred that would have far-reaching consequences. The first concerned the dedication of a "golden throne" to the Dalai Lama. The second, related event was the infiltration of the first CIA-trained agents back into Tibet.

The "golden throne" was an initiative of a wealthy Khampa trader named Gonpo Tashi Andrugtsang, who, at the time of the previous year's Kalachakra initiation, had thrown his weight behind a project to make a symbolic offering to the Dalai Lama of a jewel-studded golden throne as a gift from the people of eastern Tibet. The work of forty-nine goldsmiths, nineteen engravers, five silversmiths, six painters, eight tailors (who worked the brocade), six carpenters, three blacksmiths, and three welders, and containing more than 1,500 ounces of gold — worth something like $2 million in today's money, to say nothing of the value of the lapis, coral, turquoise, and other precious stones — it was almost certainly the most valuable single gift to any Dalai Lama from the laity. Yet while the throne, unprecedented in its extravagance, was an important expression of (mainly) Khampa devotion, its deeper significance lay in the network of communities and individuals the project drew together: it was, in fact, a cover for the recruitment of a rebel army, the Volunteer Force for the Protection of the Dharma, known as Chushi Gangdruk. To begin with, the majority of those it recruited were Khampas, with Amdowas making up the second-largest grouping; it was these who had so far borne the brunt of Chinese "reform." And though the Khampas in particular were traditionally hostile to the Lhasa government, there was not a man among them who would not sooner die than see the Dalai Lama harmed. Of the relationships established between the rebels and Lhasa officialdom at this time, none were more momentous than those

* An act of worship, a ceremony.

with the Lord Chamberlain and with Trijang Rinpoché (whose monastery was in Kham). It was he who became the army's de facto spiritual mentor.

This extraordinary development meant that two of the individuals closest to the Dalai Lama were complicit in what, in the Chinese view, was the establishment of a treasonous organization that went against the Tibetan leader's publicly proclaimed policy of cooperation with China. It also meant that the Lord Chamberlain had a link, via the rebels who were in regular contact with Gyalo Thondup in Kalimpong, to the CIA itself.

By early summer, the agency had taken charge of the six Tibetans recruited by Gyalo Thondup. Following a suitably cloak-and-dagger journey via Bangladesh (then East Pakistan), the six men were delivered to the Japanese island of Saipan. There, to their collective astonishment, they were met by the Dalai Lama's eldest brother, Jigme Norbu, and a Kalmyk lama by the name of Geshe Wangyal, together with a small team of CIA instructors.*

Their leader was Roger McCarthy, a gregarious thirty-year-old whose previous assignment had been to train Lao intelligence service personnel for operations in North Vietnam. He was delighted to be able to report to his seniors that, whereas the Lao had a disturbing tendency to hold hands when frightened, the Tibetans were "brave, honest and strong . . . Basically, everything we respect in a man." Fearless of heights, the trainees quickly gained proficiency as parachutists. It was mastering the complexities of Morse code that was to prove the more challenging component of the training program. They would have to transmit using a script devised by Geshe Wangyal. Since none of the trainees were strong writers even in their native language, the results were never very satisfactory.

By late autumn, the six men were judged ready for infiltration. They would operate as three two-man teams, dropped in different locations, each team equipped with a cache of weapons and supplies. The air drops were successful (though one of the Khampas was unable to jump and had to enter overland), and by December, two of the agents had reached Lhasa, where they obtained an audience with the Lord Chamberlain. He took a close interest in the two

* Geshe Ngawang Wangyal (1901–1983) was a protégé of Agvan Dorjieff, the Tibeto-Buryat confidant of the Great Thirteenth.

men's stories, but when they asked for a message from the Dalai Lama formally requesting assistance from America, he demurred in the idiom characteristic of Tibetan protocol and was "completely non-committal."

It seems not unlikely that the Dalai Lama was informed of the CIA's direct involvement in Tibet toward the end of that year but, for fear of implicating him, only in the most general terms. We might nonetheless ask whether, if a workable military solution had been available, the Dalai Lama would have supported it. Yet even had the United States decided to intervene on a massive scale, as it had in Korea and would in Vietnam, it is hard to see him being more than a bystander in any event.

Following successful insertion of its first batch of agents, whose chief task was to establish communications with Chushi Gangdruk, the CIA elected to step up its support. This was in spite of an inauspicious start. When some subordinates went to brief John Foster Dulles, the agency director, he began by asking where Tibet was, "gesturing in the direction of Hungary" on his wall map. It was decided, nonetheless, that the agency would no longer train agents — of whom there were to be more than 250 by the time the program was closed down a decade later — in Japan. Instead, there was to be a dedicated facility in the United States, close to the unprepossessingly named town of Leadville, Colorado. Formerly a prisoner of war camp for German soldiers captured in Africa, Camp Hale was chosen both for its remoteness and for its harsh climate. It was snow-covered for much of the year, while its mountainous terrain and its altitude, at over nine thousand feet, was ideally suited to the Tibetan training program, code-named "ST CIRCUS."

At this point, the Dalai Lama's eldest brother left the program and took up a teaching post at Columbia University, while Geshe Wangyal returned to his home in New Jersey, where he set up America's first Tibetan Buddhist center in a converted garage. But while Jigme Norbu no longer played an active role in the program, the venerable prelate remained on the books, taking a weekly train to Washington. There, in an agency safe house, its refrigerator well stocked with beer (which Geshe-la, as he was known, drank "to ward off colds"), he would attempt to decipher the often garbled Morse code messages received, via a rebroadcast station on Okinawa, from the teams on the ground in Tibet.

By 1958, while the Precious Protector redoubled his efforts to master the scholastic curriculum, and while the Chinese kept as low a profile in Lhasa as was consistent with having around ten thousand troops in the vicinity, Kham was in open revolt. How bad things were can be seen in what came to be known as the Xunhua Incident of spring 1958, when seventeen PLA soldiers were killed and, in reprisal, 435 rebels, with a further 2,499 taken prisoner. In the crackdown that followed, many "monastery religious personnel" were targeted for especially harsh treatment and "paraded before the masses as living teaching materials." This was just one incident among hundreds that occurred throughout Kham and Amdo during this period.

To make matters worse for the Khampas and Amdowas, the collectivization of farming was so ineptly handled that food shortages became increasingly serious. Recently released records give some indication of the severity of the situation, in which, for instance, fully a third of the population of Namthang township died of starvation at this time, while another third fled. The party officials responsible for implementing reform made sure not to reveal the severity either of the famine or of local resistance, instead sending reports that grossly distorted the picture of what was actually happening. Thus, one local party secretary could report to Beijing that, during 1958, "we took a great leap forward in all aspects of socialist construction" even while many herdsmen were reduced to scavenging for edible plants.

The Chinese were beginning to be alarmed at the levels of local resistance. Already there had been a (staggering, considering the small size of the population) total of 235,000 troop deployments across the three provinces since the PLA's arrival in Lhasa in 1951. The realization, from captured matériel, that the rebels had foreign backing was further disquieting. And while the Chinese could be confident in their overwhelming numerical superiority, Mao was concerned that if control of the eastern provinces was lost, even temporarily, his policy of gradual reform in central Tibet would become unworkable. He therefore hailed the opportunity that rebellion afforded, declaring the news of its outbreak "excellent . . . the greater the disturbance the better." This was all that was needed to justify a merciless campaign against the resistance movement.

Following the CIA's supply drops, Chushi Gangdruk began to show its potential, producing a significant number of small tactical wins over the PLA — an outpost overrun here, a convoy attacked and halted there. But when Gompo Tashi, the Chushi Gangdruk leader, took his men into central Tibet on an ambitious raid against Damshung Airport to the north of Lhasa, they were forced back when the Chinese deployed spotter planes and field artillery against them. Besides lack of arms — there were more volunteers than rifles to go around, and many were armed with nothing more than knives, swords, and ancient flintlocks — the rebels suffered from poor communications and ineffective leadership. At least half of their number had been recruited from the monasteries, and few had any concept of military discipline. Moreover, here in central Tibet the terrain was against them. Forced onto the open plains, they were easy targets from the air.

With rebellion now spreading out of Kham and into the so-called Tibet Autonomous Region, the National Assembly looked on in growing dismay. So long as their collaboration with the Chinese continued, they were secure. What little support they had from the people depended on being able to claim that, without their protection, things would be worse. Yet many, especially the junior members, felt that the Khampas were showing the way.

It was precisely at this moment of escalating violence that, at the end of the year, the Dalai Lama quit the Norbulingka for a tour of the Three Seats. At each of them in turn he would be publicly examined by way of preliminary to the final debates for the award of his *geshe* degree. These final debates were scheduled to take place at the Jokhang during the forthcoming Monlam Great Prayer Festival. His first stop was at Drepung, where the Precious Protector led a prayer assembly to which the monastery responded by offering him a long-life *puja.* Just as this was about to begin, a monk fell into a spontaneous trance, channeling one of the protector deities, and made an offering of *mendel trensum*, a most auspicious occurrence.* Having debated with Drepung's most able scholars and satisfied the community as to his proficiency, the Dalai Lama progressed to Sera, where he was challenged on Nagarjuna's famously difficult text *Verses on the Fundamental Wisdom of the Middle Way.*

* A symbolic offering of the world and all that is in it.

The final stop was Ganden. Remarkably, a short film showing highlights of the Dalai Lama's performance there may be found on the Internet. In crackling black and white, the footage can only gesture toward the magnificence and solemnity of the occasion. Notice the entrance of the Dalai Lama into the monastery, flanked by two men, one lay, the other monastic. See how, in holding their hands, he holds also one end of the offering scarves draped around their necks. In being supported by them, he also leads them: they are bound to him as if by a silken yoke. We do not need to know the precise meaning of this to understand that something of great profundity is being enacted here.

From Ganden, the Precious Protector moved to Tsal Gungthang, a small monastery built in the twelfth century which lay on his way back to Lhasa. Though it would be completely destroyed within a few years, his stop there provided an opportunity for the Dalai Lama to take a few days' rest before returning to the pressure cooker that the capital had become. No sooner had he settled in than word came from the Chinese that Chushi Gangdruk had struck again. Many PLA soldiers had been killed. If the Dalai Lama and his government did not accept responsibility for ensuring that the attacks ceased forthwith, the Chinese would take forceful action. As Trijang Rinpoché noted in his autobiography, the news disturbed the Dalai Lama greatly and he returned to the Norbulingka in a "troubled state of mind." It is testimony to the efficacy of the young leader's meditation practice that, in spite of the mounting pressure on him to act, he was able nonetheless to concentrate on preparing for the final element of his *geshe* exams. The Panchen Lama meanwhile cabled a message to Chairman Mao assuring the Great Helmsman of his own best endeavors to suppress the rebels.

The Dalai Lama's final examination was to take place during early March 1959. As usual, the monks of Drepung assumed responsibility for civil obedience, and the entirety of the local population was involved in the great liturgical events that would culminate on March 10 by the Western calendar. More than ever before, the Lhasa valley was full of tents, with tens of thousands of visitors coming from near and far. News of the rebels' successes contributed to the febrile atmosphere, with the crowds partly festive and partly terrified of what might happen next.

The Dalai Lama's chief of security concluded that with tensions running at such a level, it would take little to spark a riot. Accordingly, it was announced that the Dalai Lama was feeling a little unwell and the public talk that, by tradition, he gave on the first day of the festival had been canceled, along with the customary evening procession to view the butter sculptures. This had an electrifying effect — precisely the opposite of what was intended. People began to fear for the Dalai Lama's safety. It was at this time, during the Gutor festival marking the close of the year, that the Chinese issued him an invitation to attend a performance of a visiting dance troupe as soon as his examinations were over. Without giving the matter much thought, he accepted.

The Precious Protector had something very different on his mind than entertainment. He had performed well at the Three Seats, but what lay before him was an event at which he would contend with more than a dozen specially chosen scholars representing different monasteries throughout Tibet for almost ten hours in four different locations within the Jokhang Temple precincts. This was no mere formality. His reputation as an academic would depend on his performance that day.

When it came, he defended his understanding of Pramana in the morning, of Madhyamaka and Prajnaparamita in the afternoon, and of Vinaya and Abhidharma in the evening. There is no record of the exact questions put to him, but they would have covered all the basics — colors, definitions, comparisons, existents versus nonexistents, and the like — as well as more abstruse subjects pertaining to dependent origination and the two truths. What is on record, though, is that the Dalai Lama did not merely acquit himself well; he established himself — magnificently — as one of the finest debaters of his generation, a reputation that underpins his authority in monastic circles to this day.

Recalling the event years later, the Dalai Lama noted, in splendidly ornate prose, how the "cream of scholars" debated with him on "the difficult points in the vast and profound classical texts," while Ling Rinpoché, to whose credit the Dalai Lama's performance would redound, watched "with close attention." Subsequently, recalled the Dalai Lama, "the nectar of [the Precious Tutor's] words in expressing his pleasure . . . developed in me a great youthful fountain of joy." Similarly, Trijang Rinpoché noted his deep satisfaction at watching the Precious Protector "wither the creeping vine of audacity of those who were so arrogantly proud of their learning." It was, all agreed, a most praiseworthy performance.

The Dalai Lama was now free to enjoy the remainder of the Great Prayer Festival. Yet it was becoming increasingly obvious that something momentous was in the offing. The Chinese thought so too. They were convinced the government was "hatching a plot."

The festival concluded on March 4, and the next day the Dalai Lama left his rooms at the Jokhang to return to the Norbulingka. Back home, there were two immediate items on his agenda. The more important was a proposed visit to Beijing in the spring. It was rumored (correctly as it turned out) that Mao was planning to step down as president, and the Precious Protector was concerned about what the implications for Tibet might be. More immediately, there was the matter of his promised attendance at the performance of the Chinese dance troupe. When two Chinese officials came to offer congratulations to the Dalai Lama on attaining his Geshe Lharampa degree, they asked him to confirm a date. He suggested that either the tenth or eleventh of March would suit.

In the meantime, in an outburst that further heightened the tension, a furious General Tan Guansen (temporarily in command of the PLA in Lhasa) addressed the Tibetan Women's Association, shaking his fist and declaring that unless the Khampas ceased their rebellion, the PLA would "make short work of smashing all their monasteries to smithereens," adding, threateningly: "There's a piece of rotten meat here in Lhasa, and flies have been swarming in. We'll have to dispose of the meat to get rid of the flies."

On the ninth, a Chinese official presented himself at the Norbulingka with a draft protocol for the events of the following day. Unusually, it did not mention arrangements for the entourage that invariably attended the Dalai Lama. Instead, those who were invited (including members of the Dalai Lama's family) received individual invitations. But if this was arguably an excusable departure from established procedure, what followed was not. The Chinese declared that, since the venue was within the Lhasa garrison, there would be no need for the Precious Protector to be accompanied by his bodyguards. If the Dalai Lama must be accompanied, the Tibetans could send two or three personnel. They were to be unarmed, however. The choice, therefore, was whether the Precious Protector would travel from the Norbulingka by car, which the PLA would supply, along a route protected all the way into the headquarters by the PLA, or whether he would bring his own vehicle along a route protected by Tibetan security as far as the river crossing, at the other side of which lay the garrison, where the PLA would take over responsibility for the Dalai Lama's security.

Neither suggestion was acceptable. It was well known that the Chinese had abducted a number of high lamas and government officials in Kham following their attendance at some high-level event. Even if there was no intention to do so on the Chinese side — and there is no credible evidence of such a plan — there was no way that the people would let the Tibetan government run such a risk.

The chief of security returned to the Norbulingka, where he put the dilemma to the Lord Chamberlain and another official. Unable to decide what to do, they sought an audience with the Dalai Lama himself. In his autobiography, the Lord Chamberlain recounted how the Precious Protector responded. "Maybe this isn't as serious as it sounds," he said pensively. "Everything's set for tomorrow, and it seems like a bad idea to cancel."

The three officials demurred. But the Dalai Lama insisted that it would be all right.

There was nothing to be done now except carry out the Precious Protector's wishes. In the first instance, orders were given for a hundred plainclothes security to mingle with the crowd the following day. Yet when word of the impending visit became more generally known, there was resistance from all quarters. Had not the Nechung oracle recently advised that the "all-knowing Guru" be told not to venture outside?

The Lord Chamberlain sought another audience, this time to try to dissuade him from going; but the Dalai Lama insisted. It was too late, he said, to back out now.

Faced with the Dalai Lama's determination, a number of officials decided that it was their responsibility to stop him. When they left the Norbulingka that evening, they began spreading word that the Chinese intended to kidnap the Precious Protector. To this rumor was added the news that there had recently been increased activity at Damshung Airport. Also, a convoy of trucks was reported to have arrived recently at the Chinese garrison. It was obvious that these were going to be used to transport the Dalai Lama to the airport, and he would then be taken captive to Beijing—led off in chains, just as the Sixth Dalai Lama had been.*

The following morning, crowds of people began streaming out of Lhasa in the direction of the Norbulingka. Government officials arriving for work found the road blocked and their way barred. By mid-morning thousands had gathered, and still they kept coming. It was believed by some that the Precious Protector had already been abducted, and rumor and counter-rumor only served to fuel the people's passion. Whenever a minister's vehicle left the compound, it was searched lest the Dalai Lama should be hidden inside by some traitor abducting him. Though clearly the crowd's intention at the outset was simply to protect the Dalai Lama, as the day wore on, its mood turned to anger and bitterness. Cries of "Don't sell the Dalai Lama for *da yuan*" (Chinese silver dollars) filled the air.

Inside the palace grounds, government officials began to fear that the people would attack the Chinese. Yet it was not so much the Chinese who were the object of the crowd's wrath as it was themselves: the ruling class.

No one remembers at what point violence erupted, or what tipped the people over the edge, but the first sign of serious trouble came when a Tibetan official wearing a PLA uniform arrived in a Chinese jeep and sought entry to the palace compound. Knocked unconscious by a flying projectile, he escaped being stoned to death only by the reaction of his driver, who swung the vehicle around and took him straight to the Indian medical mission for treatment. But then, when a group recognized a junior monastic official who, having arrived that morning wearing his monk's robes, was now observing the crowd dressed in white shirt, slacks, a Chinese hat, and a white face mask of the sort often worn by the enemy, they lost all restraint. Some said that he was carrying a pistol, others a hand grenade. He probably wasn't, but they beat him to death all the same.

---

* Back in 1706.

Just as Mao had predicted, the masses were at last revolting violently against the reactionary upper strata, albeit not for oppressing them. It was because they were seen to have betrayed the Dalai Lama.

Even as the crowd exploded with bloodlust, many of the highest-ranking members of the government were at that very moment being sumptuously entertained within the Chinese barracks. As planned, they had gone independently in the expectation of the Dalai Lama's joining them later. After a splendid meal, those present, including the two tutors, were entertained with a film while the laymen played mahjong and the youngsters took to the dance floor.

The Kashag meanwhile, realizing that they had lost control, were concerned above all that the Chinese should not become involved. As soon as it became clear that the Dalai Lama could not safely leave the palace, it was agreed that three senior ministers would present themselves to the Chinese leadership and explain the situation. On arrival, they were met by children lined up along the path into the camp holding greeting scarves and flowers. Clearly the Chinese were unaware of the gravity of the situation and were still expecting the Dalai Lama. On hearing the news, the general exploded with rage, accusing the ministers of orchestrating the uprising themselves. He then warned them that there was no point in pinning their hopes on the Khampa rebels: "Don't forget that we beat the Guomindang, who had an army eight million strong! The Party is showing forbearance. Think it over carefully!" He finished by telling them they must keep the Dalai Lama safe, track down the conspirators, compensate the dead official's family, and bring the murderers to justice.

In the meantime, a group of representatives of the crowd was admitted to the Ceremonial Hall of the Norbulingka. Some called noisily for independence; others wanted to negotiate a new agreement with the Chinese; all were concerned for the Dalai Lama's safety. No clear leaders came forward, and the meeting broke up in disarray.

By 4 p.m., most of the demonstrators had left the precincts of the Norbulingka and were now marching through the Barkor, the pilgrim's route that circumambulates the Jokhang Temple, chanting and shouting variously:

Tibet has always been free!
Chinese Communists out of Tibet!
Down with the Seventeen Point Agreement!
Tibet for Tibetans!

That evening, General Tan sent the Precious Protector a personal letter advising him to stay where he was — presumably so that he could claim that the PLA had been in charge of the situation all along. When the messenger arrived with the letter, he found the Dalai Lama "sitting anguished, with his head in his hands." The Tibetan leader replied apologetically the following day to the effect that he would have liked to have attended the show but had been prevented by "reactionary, evil elements" who were "carrying out activities endangering me under the pretext of ensuring my safety," adding that he was "taking measures to calm things down."

But if the Dalai Lama was genuinely hopeful that these "reactionary, evil elements" were going to return to their homes and continue life as normal, it was a forlorn hope. The next day, armed militia began to build barricades along the road leading to the palace. Machine-gun posts were erected and manned not just by the Khampa militiamen but also by members of the Tibetan army who had taken off their PLA uniforms and insignia. In addition, armed volunteers congregated at the main gate of the Norbulingka to augment the official guard. The Chinese, meanwhile, deployed extra troops along the main road.

Though the crowd outside the Norbulingka on the eleventh was not so large as it had been the previous day, inside there was turmoil, with the people's representatives again gathering. Like them, most of the younger government officials were in favor of repudiating the Seventeen Point Agreement and demanding the restoration of Tibetan independence. At this point, however, the Dalai Lama himself intervened, summoning the entire group of about seventy. The Chinese general had not, he explained, compelled him to accept the invitation to the dance performance. Moreover, he was "not in any fear of personal danger from the Chinese." They should, therefore, "stop holding these meaningless gatherings, which would only bring trouble." In view of this unexpected intervention, it was agreed that the protests should from now on be conducted not outside the Norbulingka but at Shol, the settlement at the foot of the Potala.

A second, more threatening letter from General Tan reached the Dalai Lama later that day. "The reactionaries have now become so audacious that they have openly and arrogantly engaged in military provocations," he declared. "The Tibet Military Command has sent letters, therefore," to the Kashag, "telling them to remove all the fortifications . . . immediately. Otherwise they will have to take full responsibility themselves for the evil consequences." The Dalai Lama duly ordered his ministers to ensure that the fortifications were removed, with the — perhaps predictable — result that they were instead strengthened. In his reply to General Tan on the twelfth, the Dalai Lama could nonetheless claim that he had ordered "the immediate dissolution of the illegal people's conference and the immediate withdrawal of the reactionaries, who arrogantly moved into the Norbulingka under the pretext of protecting me."

Meanwhile, the Tibetan Work Committee cabled Beijing to say that "the Tibetan people had formally arisen and severed ties with our Party leadership and would henceforth strive for 'Tibetan Independence.'" It went on to claim that a "reactionary plot" was afoot to abduct the Dalai Lama. Although Mao himself was out of the capital on a visit to Wuhan, Beijing replied immediately to the effect that it was "a very good thing" that "the Tibetan elite has revealed its treasonous, reactionary nature. Our policy should be to let them run rampant, encouraging them to expose themselves even further. This will justify our subsequent pacification." Accordingly, the committee should "gather every available scrap of evidence of our adversaries' reactionary, treasonous activities" while continuing to court the Dalai Lama himself. Mao was clearly aware of a plan whereby the Precious Protector might withdraw from Lhasa. Nonetheless, he took the view that his departure would do "no harm."

Following this directive, the PLA began to reinforce their positions in and around the city and to obtain accurate ranges for their artillery — all this against the moment when orders came from Beijing to suppress the rebellion. But no special preventive measures were put in place to thwart any possible withdrawal of the Dalai Lama.

On the twelfth, the protesters duly moved to Shol, where, in an event that has been commemorated annually ever since, the women of Lhasa—under the leadership of an aristocratic mother of six who, for her crime, was subsequently executed by firing squad—had already gathered in the thousands to stage their own demonstration in favor of independence. Several ministers attended the people's representatives meeting that also took place that day, cautioning them that the Dalai Lama was suffering from the turmoil: "He looked haggard and was refusing to eat or speak, and kept sighing to himself." Again, no consensus was reached. The crowds of armed militia remained in place outside the Norbulingka, while inside, in fulfillment of Mao's suspicion, a plan to "snatch the egg without frightening the hen" (that is, to extract the Dalai Lama without alerting either the protesters or the Chinese) began to be put together by Phala, the Lord Chamberlain. This had long been contemplated as a possibility but, following the advice of the oracles, now became a reality. As a first step, Phala dispatched messengers to the two CIA operatives whom he had spurned earlier, calling them urgently to Lhasa.

On March 14, the Kashag issued an order for businesses to reopen and for the people to lay down their arms and to desist from drinking alcohol and from quarreling with the Chinese. Although this edict was ignored, it does seem to have contributed to a slight easing of tension in the city. The situation down at the Norbulingka remained chaotic, however, with large numbers of Khampa militia still in place, though they remained without any clear leadership.

Later that day the Dalai Lama again consulted Nechung. The deity counseled him to try to "keep open the dialogue with the Chinese." Presumably this was what lay behind the Precious Protector's careful reply to General Tan's third letter, received on the fifteenth. The general (actually the letter was drafted by Deng Xiaoping in Beijing) suggested, "If you think it necessary and possible to extract yourself from your present dangerous position of being held by traitors, we cordially welcome you and your entourage to come and stay for a short time in the Military Area Command." The Dalai Lama responded by thanking him for his concern and accepting the offer: "In a few days from now when there are enough forces I can trust I shall make my way in secret to the Military Area Command. When that time comes, I shall first send you a letter."

It could easily be argued that the Dalai Lama was being disingenuous here, but the truth is that, even now, he had not yet fully made up his mind what to do. One might also argue that this was the moment for the young Dalai Lama to exercise true leadership, to set aside his own safety and take charge of the situation himself. Yet this would be to misconstrue the whole Tibetan tradition. As we have seen already, the celebrated figures of Tibetan history are not those who renounce their own safety and take on the external enemy. Rather, they are spiritual heroes who renounce the world in order to take on the internal enemy: ignorance. Those who look within the Tibetan tradition for a Saint Louis of France or a Richard Coeur de Lion will do so in vain. Caught between the Scylla of taking the rebel side and facing down the might of the Chinese and the Charybdis of taking the Chinese side and facing down the ire of his own people, the Dalai Lama did precisely what the tradition expected of him. He did nothing. Instead, he continued his practice as usual. He had to wait until either the situation resolved itself or the deities instructed him clearly on what he should do.

This they did, perhaps as late as the fifteenth or even the sixteenth when, having consulted with the Kashag, the Dalai Lama again sought their advice. This time, besides Nechung, the oracles of Gadong, Shinjachen, and Shugden were invoked too. Not in person, to be sure: apart from the medium of the Nechung oracle, who had come to the Norbulingka, the others remained in their own residences. A trusted intermediary was sent in each case. The answer was unanimous. The Dalai Lama should leave as soon as possible. In the case of the Shugden oracle, there was, in addition, an explicit instruction as to which route to take out of Lhasa. If the Dalai Lama followed this instruction, he was promised that neither he nor anyone else in his entourage would come to the least harm. The oracle gave one further stipulation: "Someone bearing the name of Dorje must travel at the head of the victor's party, confidently wielding this sword." Having uttered these words, the medium faced in the direction of Ramagang to the southwest, loosed an arrow, and performed a ritual dance, gesturing with the sword. For his own part, the Dalai Lama himself performed a divination in front of the miraculous speaking image of the Glorious Goddess, Palden Lhamo, who duly concurred.

By now all arrangements were in place: horses had been dispatched to the other side of the Kyichu River, which stood a little over a mile away; food had been prepared by a team of monks from Sera working under canvas in the palace grounds; the Khampa militia had been alerted; the CIA agents had been found and briefed. Within the palace itself, the gate security was warned that a truck might at some point need to go out to the Potala in order to collect ammunition from the armory. If that happened, it was to be let straight through; no need to check inside.

When, on the afternoon of the seventeenth, two loud explosions rent the air within the palace grounds, there was a moment of panic. It was too late! The Chinese were already attacking! But when nothing further was heard, and there was no sign of enemy activity, the consensus of the security detail was that these must be ranging shots. An attack might not have begun, but it was surely imminent. There was no time to lose. The Lord Chamberlain sent an official to the Indian consulate to inquire whether Nehru would grant the Dalai Lama asylum should the need arise. Concurrently, a party of officials was dispatched to the treasury, where, we are told, they withdrew a large gold brick, fifty gold elephant coins, forty gold Tibetan coins, two golden crab figurines, a golden goblet, and 141,267 Indian rupees for immediate expenses. The overture to the consulate was less immediately fruitful. By the time the answer from India came back in the affirmative, the Precious Protector had been gone forty-eight hours.

As soon as darkness fell, the Lord Chamberlain's plan was put into action. At approximately eight o'clock that evening, the Dalai Lama's family — that is, his mother, his elder sister, and his younger brother — left the palace by the southern exit and made their way to the rendezvous on the south side of the Kyichu River. (His grandmother, aged over eighty, had to remain behind.) They were followed by the two tutors, who, together with the four members of the Kashag, lay down under a tarpaulin in the truck, which was supposedly on its way to collect ammunition from the Potala armory. The Dalai Lama himself was to leave on foot, accompanied by the Lord Chamberlain.

The Precious Protector in the meantime explained the situation to a group of the people's representatives, assuring them that his withdrawal was a temporary measure. He then wrote a brief letter to the Panchen Lama before making a final visit to the Mahakala chapel. Already the deity's protection was being invoked by a group of chanting monks. As the Dalai Lama recalled later, "no one looked up although I knew my presence must have been noticed." He then went forward and presented a *khatag,* a gesture that implied not just farewell but the intention to return. "Before leaving," he added, "I sat down for a few minutes and read from the Buddha's sutras," stopping at a passage that spoke of the need to "develop confidence and courage . . . A few minutes before ten o'clock, now wearing unfamiliar trousers and a long, black coat, I threw a rifle over my right shoulder and, rolled up, an old *thangka* that had belonged to the second Dalai Lama over my left." This was the image of the Glorious Goddess That Had Spoken. Then, slipping his glasses into his pocket, he stepped into the chill night air. Met by two soldiers, he was escorted to the main gate in the inner wall, where he was met by the head of the bodyguard. By his own admission, he was extremely scared.

PART III

Freedom in Exile

14

On the Back of a Dzo: *The Flight to Freedom*

It turns out that the Dalai Lama need not have been so frightened, at least with respect to the Chinese. Only days earlier, Chairman Mao had decreed that, should the Dalai Lama "and his cohorts" attempt to leave, "we should not attempt to stop them . . . We should just let them go, no matter where they are headed." It is true that, earlier on the very day when he left, the Politburo, several of whose members had just returned from Wuhan, where Mao was quartered at that moment, had taken a different line — presumably on Mao's orders. In an instruction communicated to General Tan, they called on him to "do everything possible to prevent the Dalai Lama from fleeing," though this was qualified with the injunction that "should he succeed in doing so, it doesn't matter." Unfortunately for the Chinese, even if they wanted to fulfill the order to prevent the escape, it is clear that this latter instruction was not immediately acted on and, just as the deity had said, the Precious Protector did not encounter "the least harm."

The first leg of the journey was on foot to the stream that lay a hundred yards or so beyond the Norbulingka's walls. This was crossed by means of steppingstones, which, the Dalai Lama recalled, "I found it extremely difficult to negotiate without my glasses. More than once I almost lost my balance." On the far side, the Precious Protector was met by a contingent of heavily armed soldiers bringing with them a horse, which he mounted for the mile-and-a-bit ride to the Tsangpo River. At one point the Dalai Lama took a wrong turn in the dark, only realizing his mistake when he found himself alone. Thereafter, the Lord Chamberlain personally led his horse and did not let go of its bridle until it was light the next morning.

At the river, the ferry stood waiting, a cumbersome raft with minimal steering which relied chiefly on the current to get across. While the horses and the majority of the militiamen boarded, the Dalai Lama and a smaller number of companions crossed in a yak hide coracle. On the other side, the rest of his party — numbering around eighty in all — were waiting. Fortunately, the night was moonless with low clouds and poor visibility, but even so, the escapees were terrified to see the flash of torchlight from the Chinese garrison only a few hundred yards away. At first sight, it seems remarkable that the Ramagang ferry, by which the Dalai Lama and his entourage made good their escape, was not patrolled by the PLA, even if the Chinese were not intent on preventing the Precious Protector from fleeing Lhasa. Yet, given their policy of allowing the Tibetan rebels free access to the city, the better to target them later, it is not so surprising.

After crossing the river and traversing the plain that lay between it and the mountains, the party faced a steep climb. At about three o'clock the following morning, the Dalai Lama and his companions took a short rest at a small farm, where they drank tea and regrouped. After little more than an hour, they pressed on. Just as dawn broke, they approached the crossing point between the Tsangpo and the next valley. It was at this point that they noticed how, in the confusion of the night, the horses' tack had been mixed up. The finest saddles and bridles were worn by the shaggiest ponies, while the best horses were adorned with the meanest of harnesses. This provided a welcome opportunity for some hearty laughter as they toiled the remainder of the distance to the pass, reaching it at around eight o'clock in the morning. The Dalai Lama recalls how, at the top, he turned around and looked at Lhasa, praying for a few minutes that he would one day return.

Shortly after the Precious Protector and his companions had begun their descent into the next valley, all those government officials who had not left with the Dalai Lama arrived at the Norbulingka for the customary morning tea ceremony. It was only then that the majority learned of the Precious Protector's escape. The news was received with a mixture of shock and relief that the Dalai Lama was out of immediate danger. In the letter he had written, the young leader put four junior ministers in charge of the army, giving them the task of negotiating with the Chinese. Should they refuse to do so, the ministers "must deliberate profoundly amongst [themselves] and come to an agreement about whether to fight or to use other methods of resistance." No immediate decision was reached, however. Some called for war at once. Others, equally overoptimistic, advocated talking with the Chinese while overseas assistance was sought. In any case, it was decided not to release the news of the Dalai Lama's departure for the time being, as the day was astrologically inauspicious.*

The Chinese meanwhile acted on the new orders from Beijing and moved to seal off the Ramagang ferry. But this was their only important military initiative of the day. Even on the morning of the nineteenth, General Tan can be seen cautioning his commanders to maintain a defensive posture. "We should not be the ones to fire the first shot," he declared. It was only in the evening that he decided on battle. Having contacted Beijing to confirm definitively that the Dalai Lama had fled, Tan issued a warning to his troops that a rebel attack was likely to occur at any moment. In fact, what actually happened was, when a PLA patrol ignored a challenge by rebels stationed close to the ferry, the Khampas opened fire. It was this that gave the Chinese the pretext they

* Right up until this time, the government of Tibet published an astrological almanac which identified days that were or were not auspicious for certain types of government business. A late example can be seen in the museum of the Tibetan Medical and Astrological Institute in Dharamsala.

were looking for. At just after three o'clock on the morning of March 20, the "pacification" of Lhasa began.

Among the targets was the Norbulingka, which came under fire from "countless guns and cannons." The devastation was wholesale. As the day dawned, "from left to right one saw nothing but the bodies of animals and people . . . Throughout the city, Tibetans gave their lives — soldiers and civilians alike." The resistance coalesced around the now seventy-one-year-old Tsarong, a war hero during the time of the Great Thirteenth. His headquarters, set up at the base of the Potala, was well defended, but was no match for the heavy guns that the Chinese quickly brought to bear. After bombarding the palace, Chinese troops soon overwhelmed the assortment of militiamen and their leader.*

How severe the bombardment really was is hard to determine. Tibetan eyewitnesses suggest that it was prolonged and indiscriminate, killing many thousands. Inevitably Chinese reports say that the "rebellion" was put down at the cost of very few lives. Two Communist-sympathizing English journalists who visited Lhasa three and a half years later claimed to have seen no evidence of any damage to the Norbulingka.† It was what followed the crushing of the rebellion that was in many ways more significant. And about this, there is much less doubt.

The Dalai Lama was completely unaware of what was happening. For his part, he hoped that, when it became known that he had left, the crowds would disperse and life in Lhasa would return to normal. The Chinese would have no reason to attack. In the meantime, having walked for the better part of twenty-four hours, the Precious Protector and his party had by now spent the night in a small monastery, where he and his senior advisers held the first of what were to become nightly meetings.

Although the evacuation of the Norbulingka had been several days in the planning, the exact route taken — one of dozens possible — was determined

* It was during this bombardment that the college of traditional Tibetan medicine at the top of Chakpori, previously a striking feature of the Lhasa skyline, was destroyed. In its place today stands an array of communications towers.

† These were Stuart and Roma Gelder of the British daily *News Chronicle*.

only at the last minute and on an ad hoc basis. To begin with, rather than head due south, taking the shortest route, they followed the Shugden oracle's injunction to head in a southwesterly direction. Not only did this take the escape party through country that was impassable to motor vehicles, but also it kept them in territory that was entirely under partisan control. The PLA had concentrated its forces at the main strategic settlements and on the roads running between them. Yet although Chushi Gangdruk forces held the countryside, there was concern about possible attacks from the air. It was reassuring, then, that the weather at this time of year made aviation challenging while the mountainous terrain further increased the level of difficulty for aerial pursuit. Mercifully, too, the Chinese had very limited air assets at this time, and it was not until they were almost at the Indian border that the refugees saw an aircraft at all.

The fact that the Precious Protector had left before word came back from the Indian consulate that he and his entourage would be welcome in India meant that the Dalai Lama was uncertain whether Nehru would permit them to enter the country. One alternative they considered was the state of Kachin in northern Burma (today's Myanmar), where a small community of Tibetan villages stood high up in the borderlands. If, however, he was to proceed to India, there was also some doubt as to whether to take the shorter route via Bhutan or to go directly. But for the time being, the priority was to get as far from Lhasa as possible.

According to some accounts, the fighting in the capital continued for a full six days. The Chinese claimed the rebellion, as they characterized it, was suppressed much more quickly, after which it was only a matter of determining who the ringleaders were. All those deemed to have taken part in the uprising were taken prisoner — certainly many thousands of individuals, of whom large numbers were later to die in custody. Of those who survived, those labeled class enemies remained in prison at least until the death of Mao in 1976, while those judged to have committed crimes against the party and the Motherland were transported to the provinces, where they were enrolled in forced-labor gangs. Their task: the construction of the Workers' Paradise that Tibet was destined to become.

For all who were not known to support the Chinese, the next decade and more was a time of unremitting hardship, pitiful rations, hard labor with inadequate clothing and minimal rest, and repeated *thamzing,* or "struggle sessions."

This was a form of public humiliation during which the accused were forced to confess to crimes in front of an audience who would then abuse them verbally, and sometimes physically. This served as a prelude to punishment and "reform." In addition, victims were sometimes dressed in the most ludicrous attire. A famous photograph shows an aristocrat dressed in ceremonial brocades further adorned with women's underwear and topped with a dunce cap on which the various charges against him were written. Typically, too, the accused would have their hands tied behind their back in such a way as to force them to bend double with their arms straight out behind in a position known as "the airplane." By day, teams of prisoners were forced to compete with one another, singing "patriotic" songs extolling the virtues of Chairman Mao and the Communist Party. In the evening there were interminable classes devoted to the exposition of socialist doctrine. For those who showed a lack of enthusiasm, further torments were meted out through either solitary confinement or other struggles. To make matters worse, there was the ever-present danger of other prisoners, intent on improving their own lot, making accusations against their fellows.

Especially harsh treatment was reserved for the *sangha,* whether as members of the government or simply as people who had taken up arms against the Chinese. Though religion was tolerated while the Dalai Lama remained nominal head of the Tibetan administration, now it was held in official derision. Prisoners caught saying prayers were routinely beaten. The dire prophecy given by the Great Thirteenth had begun to be amply fulfilled.

But this was not yet an understood reality for the Dalai Lama. Five days out from Lhasa (though still little more than sixty miles), the Precious Protector was intercepted by the two CIA agents for whom the Lord Chamberlain had sent, bringing with them a radio, a mortar, and a consignment of rifles, handguns, and ammunition; their arrival was a welcome boon. There had been an American airdrop within the last month, and the Khampa fighters could now be equipped with weapons adequate to their determination to protect the Dalai Lama. Most of these were natives of the area surrounding Trijang Rinpoché's monastery. It was the monks of this foundation who had dealt so harshly with the Catholic missionaries earlier in the century. Fiercely loyal to their homeland — which for them was Kham and not Tibet — most would perish in subsequent fighting with the Chinese. But although their natural suspicion of the Lhasa government — intense to the point of hatred, easily aroused — remained intact, it counted for nothing now that the Dalai Lama himself was in danger. Fortified by their belief in the protection of Dorje Shugden, they ate little, slept little, and lived in daily peril not just from the enemy but also from the weather, often with nothing but the rough sheepskin clothes they stood up in as protection against the elements. These were hard men who lived hard lives.

Yet it can also be said that the Dalai Lama and all those traveling with him showed their hardiness. Although the distance from Lhasa to the Indian border where they crossed is only around a hundred miles as the crow flies, the route they ended up taking was a particularly arduous one, with a large number of mountain passes. There were frequent snowfalls, and for most of the time, temperatures were well below zero. Given that the Precious Protector's habitual exercise was little more than the occasional stroll through the park surrounding the Norbulingka, it was a considerable achievement.

At this juncture, the Dalai Lama hoped that he might still be able to establish a headquarters somewhere inside Tibet that was close enough to the border in case of dire need. But when his party was intercepted by a posse of horsemen who brought news of the bombardment of Lhasa, it became obvious that exile was the only plausible option. In direct confirmation of this, a letter from one of the Dalai Lama's secretaries in Lhasa followed soon after. This made plain the full extent of the horror that had befallen the capital. Evidently the hoped-for negotiations were mere wishful thinking. Plans were immediately put in hand for a formal repudiation of the infamous Seventeen Point Agreement. This, it was decided, would take place at Lhuntse Fort several days hence. Accordingly, it was there, on March 26, 1959, and in a grand ceremony attended not only by the governor, the abbots of eight local monasteries, and the Dalai Lama's entire entourage but also by several thousand people from the local area, that the Dalai Lama, having metaphorically torn up the treaty, reestablished his own independent government with the fortress as its temporary capital.

The fact that the fort was actually situated in eastern Bhutan meant that the proclamation of the Dalai Lama's new government here would cause diplomatic difficulties in the future. The Indian border official who later received the Dalai Lama was certainly most surprised to hear of this excursion into Bhutanese territory, for although ethnically Tibetan, Bhutan was, as it remains, an independent sovereign state,* its borders protected by the Indian government.

Diplomatic niceties notwithstanding, on hearing of the Dalai Lama's proclamation from a report sent over the radio by the two CIA operatives that evening, American officialdom sent its congratulations together with the offer of help should the Tibetans have any specific requests. Told this, the Lord Chamberlain instructed the radio operator to ask whether an airplane might be sent in case of difficulty. Also, could the Americans kindly use their good offices to request asylum for His Holiness in India? A possible landing strip had in fact already been identified, as had a drop zone for supplies. As for the possibility of asylum, Nehru had already signaled his approval via the consulate in Lhasa, though neither the Americans nor the Tibetans were aware of this.

After spending a second night in Bhutan, the Dalai Lama and his entourage rose before dawn on March 27 in order to tackle the steep track that would take them to the last Tibetan villages before the border with India. Disastrously, they soon became lost in a snowstorm. Having no goggles, they wasted several hours as they traveled in the wrong direction before they realized their mistake and were forced to retrace their steps. Once they were over the next pass, however, the weather improved, and they reached a small settlement where they halted in the late afternoon.

The next day there was yet another pass to cross, and it was here that the Tibetans received the biggest fright of their journey. Just as they reached the saddle between the two valleys, they spotted a large aircraft flying at (relatively speaking) low altitude nearby. Though it was too far away to be certain of the type, according to subsequent analysis by CIA officers it was indeed "Chicom" — a Chinese Communist airplane. The Dalai Lama's then twelve-year-old brother, Ngari Rinpoché, is, however, convinced that, given it had no markings, it must have been Indian, though there remains a strong possibility that it was in fact American. In any case, after a few fear-inducing seconds it flew off, leaving the Tibetans in enough doubt to ensure that they kept up the pace as they approached the last leg of their journey. Two days later they reached the

* To the envy of every Tibetan, Bhutan became a member of the UN in 1971.

village of Mang Mang, the last Tibetan settlement before the border. There, for the first time on the journey, and for his penultimate night in Tibet, the Dalai Lama slept under canvas, in a tent that leaked copiously from the rain that began to fall almost at once. After a damp and sleepless night, the Precious Protector contracted a fever, and it was decided he should remain in situ for one more day at least. Moving to the upper floor of a small farmhouse, he passed his last night in Tibet with, as he later recalled, cockerels crowing in the rafters above and cattle lowing in the stable below. On the thirty-first, he made the decision to press on. Too ill to ride a horse, the Dalai Lama mounted instead a more placid animal, a *dzo,* a cross between a yak and a cow. And it was on this humble form of transport that the Precious Protector, the Victor, Lion Among Men, Wish-Fulfilling Jewel, Ocean of Wisdom, earthly manifestation of Chenresig, Bodhisattva of Compassion, quit his homeland and crossed the border with India at two o'clock in the afternoon.

15

Opening the Eye of New Awareness: Allen Ginsberg and the Beats

Word of the Precious Protector's escape spread swiftly around the world, but for want of information, the many news agencies taking an interest in the story were compelled to hold their breath. Ten days after the Dalai Lama disappeared from Lhasa, the Indian president sent an urgent letter to Nehru asking for a report. The prime minister replied, saying, "We do not yet know where the Dalai Lama is." He was being decidedly economical with the truth. Thanks to the presence of the American-trained radio operators among the escapees, Washington — with the help of Geshe Wangyal — was able to monitor the party's progress almost the entire way along its route. Nehru, second only to President Eisenhower, was informed the day before writing to the Indian president that the escape party had arrived safely at the border. But it would not do to broadcast the government's intelligence capability owing to its links with the CIA.

As for the press, there were slim pickings for the hundreds of reporters who converged on the remote tea-growing settlement of Tezpur in far northeastern India. It was here, after resting a week in a remote town close to where he crossed the border, that the Dalai Lama was welcomed by the mayor and a large crowd of well-wishers immediately prior to entraining for Mussoorie, a further two days' journey to the west. There were no interviews, not even for old friends like Heinrich Harrer, who had made a special journey. All that was to be granted him and others was a short, moderately worded statement from the Dalai Lama (the text agreed to in advance with the Indian government) explaining briefly the circumstances leading up to his request for political asylum and thanking the people and government of India "for their spontaneous and generous welcome." Following lunch with local dignitaries, the Dalai Lama and his entourage left for the station without further word. Despite the Tibetan leader's temperate language, his words were immediately denounced by the Chinese. "The so-called statement of the Dalai Lama . . . is a crude document, lame in reasoning, full of lies and loopholes," thundered the *People's Daily*.

Two days after leaving Tezpur, the Precious Protector reached Mussoorie, where Nehru had arranged for the Tibetan leader to stay at Birla House, the splendid country retreat of a family of wealthy industrialists close to the prime minister. On arrival, as indeed he had been all along the way, he was given an exuberant welcome by the local people.

Almost the Dalai Lama's first act on arrival was to preside over the requisite rituals "to invoke the commitment of the Dharma Protectors who had vowed to guard the teachings of the Buddha, in order to quickly pacify these troubling times in the world at large and specifically in . . . Tibet." The deities had not been able to save Tibet, but at least they had kept the Dalai Lama safe.

The very next day, Nehru himself arrived. At first, the Indian prime minister had granted asylum only to the Tibetan leader and his immediate entourage, unaware — as was the Dalai Lama at the time — that there would be a mass exodus of refugees from Lhasa and its environs following in the Precious Protector's wake. But when reports reached Nehru of the fighting in Lhasa, he relented. Now all were welcome, provided they gave up their arms. For Nehru, the whole affair was deeply troubling. As he explained to the Dalai Lama, his "being in India [kept] alive the question of Tibet in the world," which for China was "immediately one of irritation and suspicion." On the one hand, he had hoped that with the mutual accord treaty signed in 1954, there might be permanently friendly relations between China and India. The presence of the Dalai Lama and his followers threatened this. On the other hand, he clearly felt some responsibility for having insisted on the Precious Protector's return to Tibet three years earlier. In their four hours of talks, Nehru assured the Tibetan leader of his welcome, but at the same time emphasized that the Indian government would not support his claim to Tibetan independence. The prime minister's plain speaking on the subject caused the Dalai Lama later to recall that Nehru could be something of a bully. For his part, though, it is clear the prime minister found the young Tibetan leader exasperatingly naïve. When the Dalai Lama told him of his determination both to win back independence for Tibet and to avoid any further bloodshed, Nehru exploded, "his lower lip quivering with anger . . . 'That is not possible!'"

The twenty-four-year-old Dalai Lama may have been politically naïve, but he was well aware that he and his fellow refugees faced a decidedly uncertain future. Many Tibetans, including senior members of the Dalai Lama's entourage, assumed it was simply a matter of time before their return would be negotiated. America and the other great powers would surely support Tibet as soon as they understood the reality of the situation. The Dalai Lama himself had no such illusions. Furthermore, it soon became clear that, while Mussoorie was a congenial place to stay, it was remote both physically and psychologically from the political hub of New Delhi. That the resort retained — as it does to this day — an air of colonial gentility with several once grand hotels and a number of prestigious English-style private schools was small recompense.*

There were some advantages to these new circumstances, however. Left entirely to their own devices, and having few demands on their time, to their satisfaction the monastic element within the Dalai Lama's household was able, as Trijang Rinpoché later wrote, to "focus . . . on religious practice" and "observe the discipline of renunciates."

While life in Mussoorie settled soon enough into quiet routine, one of the most trying aspects of exile quickly became apparent. Information about

* Among them was Doon School, where Nehru's grandson and future prime minister Rajiv Gandhi was educated.

what was happening at home, still more so of what had become of individual people, was almost impossible to come by. The Chinese said only what they wanted to say and refused entry to all foreigners. And such news as did reach the Precious Protector's ears was uniformly bad. The refugees who followed in his wake brought with them shocking tales of Chinese brutality. But then as the springtime heat gave way to the summer's monsoon rain, another, more pressing problem made itself felt. Most of those arriving had nothing but the heavy clothing suitable to the Tibetan climate and were completely ignorant of conditions in India. Worse, they had little resistance to the tropical illnesses that quickly broke out among them. During a visit to Delhi in June 1959, the Dalai Lama therefore urged the Indian government to move them to camps on higher ground.*

By this time a number of international relief agencies were working with the refugees, who continued to arrive in large numbers until, by the end of the year, they were estimated to total around eighty thousand, including many children. In the beginning they were placed in camps close to the border, where the agencies, notable among them the Save the Children Fund and the Swiss Agency for Development and Cooperation, first encountered them. Meanwhile, the Dalai Lama's American friends had also not been slow to act. That summer the CIA was instrumental in obtaining for the Dalai Lama both the recently instituted Ramon Magsaysay Award for Community Leadership and, somewhat improbably, the Admiral Richard E. Byrd Memorial Award for International Rescue. The one commemorated a Philippine politician, the other an American explorer. But together these awards went a good way toward meeting the need for funds for the time being. The agency was also responsible for an investigation of the legal status of Tibet, undertaken by the International Commission of Jurists, whose personnel arrived among the refugees during the summer. The commission subsequently published a report, based on interviews and bolstered by historical research, which argued that Tibet had been, de facto, an independent sovereign state from the mo-

* Many of the refugees, children included, were subsequently drafted to build roads in some of India's most remote areas. This was their chief — often dangerous — employment for many years.

ment when the Great Thirteenth expelled the Qing garrison from Lhasa in 1912. This would form the basis of the legal case for subsequent appeals to the United Nations.

It seems certain that the CIA, acting in concert with sympathetic members of the Indian government, also had a hand in the new statement the Dalai Lama released at this time. Speaking of the "tyranny and oppression" of the Chinese authorities, the Precious Protector said that he would welcome "change and progress," but that the Chinese had "put every obstacle in the way of carrying out . . . reform." Instead, "forced labour and compulsory exactions, a systematic persecution of the people, plunder and confiscation of property belonging to individuals and monasteries and execution of leading men" were "the glorious achievements of the Chinese rule in Tibet."

The public repudiation of the Seventeen Point Agreement that followed (and here one might be forgiven for supposing that the twenty-four-year-old leader had been writing political speeches all his life) was precisely the justification the CIA needed for its continued support of the resistance movement. But while the Dalai Lama's clearly ghostwritten speech was enough for Washington, the Tibetan resistance still hoped for something more. To this end, Gonpo Tashi, the rebel leader, paid an early visit to Mussoorie. There he learned that although the Precious Protector supported the aims of the movement — a Tibet free of Chinese interference — and was full of admiration for the bravery and determination of the rebels, and accepted that there were times when the Buddhadharma must be defended by all means, including violence, giving his support was a step he could not in good conscience take. Besides, the government in exile's impending appeal to the United Nations — which the Dalai Lama was determined to lodge in spite of Nehru's stated opposition — would lose much of its force if Tibet could not present itself as a peaceful victim of China's aggression.

This was a huge personal disappointment to Gonpo Tashi, described by his CIA handler, Roger McCarthy, as "one of the most impressive figures I . . . ever met." Nonetheless, the Tibetan rebel leader played a leading role in planning a major operation scheduled for the coming winter.

In September, eighteen men (the first batch from Camp Hale) were parachuted into Pemba, a district approximately two hundred miles northeast of

Lhasa, where the rebels were jointly led by a layman and a young reincarnate lama. The agents were accompanied by an extremely generous supply of war matériel: 126 pallets of arms and armaments, together with first aid and food supplies, dropped in three separate sorties. Altogether this was adequate to equip something like five thousand men.

Though properly armed for the first time, the rebels proved unable to capitalize on the munificence of their backers. While the CIA envisaged a classic, highly mobile guerrilla operation, with the rebel force taking to the hills and coming down in small numbers to attack the Chinese at moments and in places of weakness before disappearing back to the mountain trails they knew so well, the reality was very different. The Tibetans' modus operandi was, as it had always been, to fight in large, loose, mainly mounted formations. This could be effective when they had numerical superiority on open ground but was much less so in the face of even small numbers of a well-armed enemy properly dug in. More significant still was the Tibetan fighters' vulnerability to air strikes. The result was a foregone conclusion.

Recounting the CIA's reaction to the debacle years later, Roger McCarthy, the director of operations, recalled: "At first we didn't believe the reports coming in. We thought it was an exaggeration, an error. But it wasn't." The Chinese attacked the rebel encampment — home not just to the soldiers but also to their wives and children — with aircraft and long-range artillery. "It was genocide, pure and simple."

One might have expected the experience at Pemba to cause the Americans to lose faith in the ability of Tibetans to wage effective war against the Chinese. That it did not suggests the CIA hoped that, with more rigorous training in guerrilla tactics, Chushi Gangdruk could yet become a serious threat to the Chinese. The Tibetans knew their terrain and could survive the harshest conditions; they just needed to learn to fight in small detachments. This now became the focus of their training in the United States.

While the CIA was hopeful of modernizing Tibetan tactics through its training program, the agency also supported a more traditional force that had gathered at Mustang, a remote ethnically Tibetan province in northern Nepal. With arms and funding channeled through India, several thousand men gathered here to form what was intended as a reinvasion force. To keep morale up and to test the force's readiness to fight, the Mustang guerrillas launched periodic raids into southern Tibet—scoring, on occasion, what has been described as "one of the greatest intelligence hauls in the history of the agency." This was the acquisition, following a raid on a transport convoy, of a blue satchel containing detailed information about PLA troop dispositions and intentions, along with the first confirmed reports of famine and unrest in China during the Great Leap Forward. This was at a time when almost nothing was known either about the internal workings of the Chinese military or about conditions in China itself.

It remains open to speculation how fully aware the Dalai Lama was of the enormous scale of the operations both in Pemba and in Mustang, but there is room for supposing that he did indeed have a clear idea of what was going on, even if he did not know every detail. From the memoir of John Kenneth Knaus, the CIA's director of operations in India, who met the Dalai Lama in 1964, it is evident that the Tibetan leader knew exactly who Knaus was. It is also clear that the Dalai Lama was profoundly ambivalent about the whole business. One side of him, the merely human, wished Knaus and his team every success. The other side, the religious, forbade him to do so. Knaus recalled how, as a result, the Precious Protector imposed "a remarkably effective, though invisible, barrier between us" when the American entered the audience chamber.

For the Dalai Lama, perhaps the only positive thing to emerge from the CIA program was its effect on people's thinking. Knaus reports him allowing that "Tibet had been made up of many tribes who would not co-operate with one another. Now our common enemy—the Communists—had united us . . . as never before."

In April 1960 the Dalai Lama and his entourage moved out of their temporary accommodations in Mussoorie. Early on, Nehru had instructed his officials to find a more permanent base for the Tibetan leader. When the village of McLeod Ganj, a small hill station above Dharamsala, was put forward as a possible solution, the Dalai Lama and his advisers were skeptical. Lying 250 miles due north of Delhi, it was even more remote from the capital than their present quarters. It looked to the Tibetans as if their hosts wanted them as far away as possible. Yet when the Tibetan minister dispatched to assess the offered land and accommodations returned proclaiming that "Dharamsala water is better than Mussoorie milk," with no alternative on offer, a decision was made to accept and move.

On their arrival, a question quickly arose over whether the Tibetan official had been offered an inducement. The monsoon in McLeod Ganj is frequently the most severe in the whole of the Indian subcontinent; it is nothing for forty inches of rain to fall in a month and not unheard of for five inches to fall in a single day. As well as remote, the village was run-down and furnished with only the most basic facilities. The road up was scarcely drivable, and the housing was cramped and dilapidated, while the landowner to whom it belonged still lamented the day when "the Britishers" had left. This was Nauzer Nowrojee, whose family had grown prosperous trading with India's late colonial masters.* Their family's general store was by now as much a museum as it was a business, and the faded pictures of British royalty that jostled with advertisements for forgotten luxuries like Pears soap and the *Illustrated London News* only increased the sense of desolation. By the time of the Tibetans' move, apart from the local Gadi tribespeople who farmed the steep hillsides, the population of this once wealthy resort consisted mainly of a handful of retirees from the Indian civil service and a single English family who had stayed on after Indian independence.

Little more than a year after he quit the splendors of the Norbulingka, the Dalai Lama thus found himself sharing the former district commissioner's residence with "his mother, his two sisters, his brother-in-law . . . the Masters of Robes, Ceremonies and Food, his Lord Chamberlain, and an assortment of secretaries and translators," not to mention several personal attendants. This was a considerable population for a house that had been built for a single family and its staff. It was in poor repair, too: the roof leaked, and during the monsoon, rainwater filled several buckets in the Dalai Lama's bedroom most days for two months and more, while in winter, the only heat came from a handful of small fireplaces scattered throughout the building. True, the winters in Lhasa were colder, but in Dharamsala the damp made it feel colder

* Nauzer Nowrojee was subsequently to find fame as the prototype of the uncle in Rohinton Mistry's novel *A Fine Balance.*

still. At least, though, the Dalai Lama was better off than several senior ministers who found themselves sharing an abandoned cowshed — though by all accounts they did so without complaint, their good humor and dignity intact, despite the lost opulence of the life they had known in Tibet.

If his accommodations left something to be desired, and if the situation in which the Tibetans now found themselves was utterly disorienting, the Precious Protector himself wasted no time taking advantage of the leisure he was suddenly able to enjoy. A Ping-Pong table was installed in one of the reception rooms, and that first winter of 1960–61 there were snowmen and snowball fights, while during the succeeding warmer months, and to the dismay of some of those closest to him, the Precious Protector took pleasure in making excursions among the surrounding hills. Climbing as high as the sixteen-thousand-foot pass below Mun Peak, he and a handful of companions would occasionally spend the night in a small trekkers' hut.

While the Dalai Lama was now able to enjoy personal freedom to an extent that would have been impossible in Tibet, there was no denying that he and his court had effectively been released to a backwater. Nonetheless, he was pleased also to have more time for study and for spiritual practice, and he was glad, too, to have the opportunity to set about bringing real reform to the way the Tibetan government functioned. For a start, he decided — against the advice of Hugh Richardson, the last British political officer in Tibet, who had made an early visit to Dharamsala to offer his services — that a minimum of protocol should be observed toward himself, outside the religious sphere. People to whom he gave audiences were not to be required to sit on chairs lower than his, nor would guests be encouraged to prostrate themselves before him. More controversial still, Tibetans themselves would no longer be required to do so. And from the outset he made it clear that he wished to be accessible to all comers, most especially to any from overseas who asked to see him. Tibet had been isolated from the world for far too long.

Visiting Delhi in 1960, the Precious Protector granted his first televised interviews. One of these was with the director of the World Council of Churches. In it the Dalai Lama comes across as a remarkably grounded and clear-sighted young man. Speaking of the prospects for the Tibetan refugee children, he admits, "We are still backward in the field of education, and we suffer for it," adding: "At the same time, we cannot ignore our own, ancient culture. This must be taught side by side with modern education." Asked in the second interview, with Prince Panu of Thailand, whether his resistance to the Chinese could simply be a cover for the "desire for power and riches," he turns the question around adroitly: "How can that be? If I desired power and wealth, I could surely obtain them by forfeiting the right of my people to resist the invaders . . . I did not become Dalai Lama by use of force and power. Why then should I try to gain [these things]?"

This clarity of vision found its most powerful expression in the political field. Toward the end of 1960, barely eighteen months after arriving in India and only twenty-five years of age, the Precious Protector gave the first of a remarkable series of speeches. "We exiled Tibetans living in free India must exert our fullest effort," he declared, "for the benefit of those who remained behind," forced to work like "beasts of burden," with limited food, "like hungry-ghosts," and experiencing "tremendous fear and agony like hell beings." It was the responsibility of the exile community to do all it could to prepare a better society for the future. They could not and should not "retain all the ancient systems of Tibet," he announced to civil servants in November 1960. "We must have change in the future. As the world is changing rapidly, we should also move together with the rest of the world." Yet while some understood the need for reform, others evidently did not. There were those who "genuinely [strove] hard through many challenges," but also "some people who do not take responsibility according to their . . . abilities," for which failing the Dalai Lama was quick to admonish them. "I am greatly disappointed with some officials, especially some senior officials," he declared.

Evidently aware of the Precious Protector's dissatisfaction at the lack of progress, a group of officials called for a "written oath" of allegiance to him. But he was unimpressed. "The 'written oath' was taken repeatedly in Tibet. And it was again taken as soon as we arrived in Mussoorie . . . A 'stronger written oath' was taken at Bodhgaya. What benefit have these 'written oaths' given? Yet again, today you are taking another 'written oath.' I cannot give credit to these attractive documents, empty words and talks. I believe in facts . . . Attractive paperwork and pretentious speeches are useless." Similarly, repeated offerings of "long-life" religious ceremonies for his benefit only exasperated him. For the Dalai Lama, it was abundantly clear how and why Tibet had been lost. What had happened was due primarily to "our many years of negligence in the past."

Although many were still hopeful that the Dalai Lama, by virtue of his relationship with Chenresig and the protectors, could perform miracles, he did not share this view. As Tibetans, they would have to pay the karmic debt themselves. Moreover, he was all too keenly aware that the charity extended by organizations such as the Save the Children Fund, and covertly by the United States, could not be counted on indefinitely. "Our foreign aid and assistance will eventually be terminated," he noted in a speech in March 1961. "We must be very careful." He was equally clear-sighted about putting excessive faith in diplomatic initiatives. "We should not," he warned, "place too much importance on my brother Gyalo Thondup's attendance at the United Nations Organisation's meeting," which was scheduled for the fall. This was a reference to ongoing attempts to have the issue of Tibet's right to independence raised at the highest level within the international community.

The Dalai Lama also understood the vital importance of recruiting new staff from the younger generation. "They are, by nature, physically stronger," he argued, "more [alert], more creative, and more aware of international events." From now on, therefore, all government appointments would be on merit, not on seniority or birth or status. As for monastic appointments in government, whereby in former times many positions were held jointly by both a monk and a layman, these would cease forthwith. He was quick, too, to take advantage of political trends. Reminding his audience that "Buddha, the compassionate one, has given equal right for both *Bikshu* [monks] and *Bikshuni* [nuns]," he argued that it was appropriate to give "equal opportunity to both men and to women to practice religion." The Dalai Lama also called on Tibetan women to participate in all areas of life in exile, including government.

Not all the young leader's innovations met with approval. His plan to raise revenue through taxation was resisted by some influential Khampas, known as the Group of Thirteen, who claimed that the government in exile was ignoring Khampa needs. This provoked immense resentment on behalf of those loyal to the Dalai Lama, and when one of the thirteen was murdered, a close relative of the Dalai Lama's was accused of being responsible. By no means did the Precious Protector have the unwavering support of all his people even in these days of direst need.

Yet notwithstanding the immense difficulties he faced, for the Dalai Lama, the catastrophe of exile was also an opportunity. He had understood from his discussions with Harrer as a teenager eager to learn about the world that Tibet could not afford to remain in psychological isolation. It was, he later said, "our worst mistake, our greatest mistake." For him, the material benefits of the modern world should not be refused simply on the grounds that they were foreign, and certainly not on the grounds that they were somehow "unnecessary," as some of the more conservative members of the establishment thought. In the Dalai Lama's view, it was a question of navigating a middle way between the outright forsaking of tradition and a complete rejection of novelty.

Again and again in his speeches to members of the Tibetan government in exile, we find the Dalai Lama exhorting, cajoling, encouraging, and imploring his fellow exiles to abandon any thoughts of Tibetan superiority and to embrace modern methods. At times it seems as if he alone saw the reality of the situation the refugees now faced. "We still have faults of delaying and being careless in our actions," he exclaimed, evidently exasperated. "Others set specific times and finish their work ahead of schedule. In our case, forget about completing the work ahead of time; we cannot even complete our work in the specified time."

One of the first tasks he set for the civil service was to develop a constitution that could be tested in exile and taken back to Tibet on their presumed return. A newly created Commission of Tibetan People's Deputies was assisted in this by a member of the Indian Supreme Court, Purushottam Trikamdas, also a member of the International Commission of Jurists. Former president of India Rajendra Prasad was enlisted as well, though he died before he was able to produce his comments. A controversial element of the proposed constitution was a clause providing that the Dalai Lama himself could be impeached if a two-thirds majority insisted on it. Most Tibetans were appalled that such an idea could be conceived, let alone committed to print. To their way of thinking, the logic of democracy demanded that still more power be granted to the Dalai Lama, not less. Yet the Dalai Lama himself insisted on the impeachment clause.

If the Dalai Lama's role was pivotal in the reform process, it was no less so in the practical sphere of resettling the eighty thousand refugees who managed to escape Tibet before the Chinese fully sealed the border. The Nehru government made clear that it would not permit large numbers of potentially restive Tibetans anywhere nearby, and instead granted the refugees land far to the south, in the region of the then minor provincial city of Bangalore — its future status as tech powerhouse not even a wild dream. It was here, on virgin ground, that some fifty-eight villages were established. Arriving at the camps, "many of the Tibetans broke down [and wept] on seeing the thick forest filled with wild animals and the work that lay before them." Yet, in a remarkably short time, the majority became flourishing communities. It was among these that, in due course, the Three Seats of Ganden, Drepung, and Sera were eventually refounded. But first, as the Dalai Lama later explained, "we considered setting up schools to be more important." Accordingly, using English as their primary language, several schools, generously staffed and subsidized by the Indian government, were quickly built, while most of the monastic community remained in the north, quartered in an old prison camp that had at different times held both Mahatma Gandhi and Nehru himself.

Besides overseeing establishment of the refugee villages, the Dalai Lama was also instrumental in bringing into being several institutions intended to help safeguard Tibet's cultural heritage. The first of these was an opera company, the Tibetan Institute of Performing Arts. Another was the Library of Tibetan Works and Archives, which, besides housing a considerable collection of *pecha* — printed religious works in loose-leaf format — also began publishing works relating to Tibetan history and culture, the majority of them in English.

It goes without saying that all this enterprise came at a cost, and, especially in the early years, funding was a major difficulty. At his second meeting with Nehru after coming into exile, the Dalai Lama raised the question of taking out a loan from the Indian government. Could the Tibetan government in exile possibly borrow 200 million rupees (just under $4 million) from the Indian exchequer? Presumably this was to be secured against the eventuality of the Dalai Lama's resuming his position in Tibet. In reply, Nehru expostulated that the Indian government itself did not have such a large sum, let alone such a surplus available to loan. When the Tibetan leader, greatly embarrassed, explained that this was what he had been advised to ask for, Nehru warned him "to be cautious about listening to such advice from his ministers." It was a point well taken.

Soon after, the Tibetan leader decided that the treasure still under the care of the maharajah of Sikkim should be sold. First by mule, then by car, and finally by a specially chartered aircraft, it was transported to Calcutta, where it was melted down, graded, and hallmarked before sale, eventually raising approximately $2 million on the bullion market, or around 26 million rupees. It was clear that there should have been quite a bit more, however. To this day, the disbursement of the Dalai Lama's treasure remains a source of controversy among Tibetans. Several people besides Gyalo Thondup, not all of them Tibetan, were involved in the operation, and each, at one time or another, has been accused of malfeasance. The funds that did become available were used to make a number of investments, apparently at the suggestion of Nehru himself. Besides various pieces of real estate, these included holdings in a paper mill in Bhopal and, by way of an unsecured loan, one in the Calcutta-based Gayday Iron and Steel Company. Only four years later, when the investments were transferred into the Dalai Lama Charitable Trust, the total value had fallen to a mere 8.2 million rupees, less than a third of the original sum.

Another early undertaking, and one that in the future provided significant revenue, was publication of the first of the Dalai Lama's two autobiographies. At the suggestion of Hugh Richardson, David Howarth, an English ex–Royal Navy officer turned popular historian, was commissioned to produce a book that drew on a text dictated by the Dalai Lama and subsequently translated into English. Published in London by Weidenfeld and Nicolson in 1962 under the title *My Land and My People,* it was well reviewed though it enjoyed only modest sales. Nonetheless, the book became essential reading for the increasing numbers of foreigners who began to make their way to Dharamsala. The Dalai Lama also authored at this time the only book ever published under his name to have been entirely written by himself, *Opening the Eye of New Awareness,* a basic introduction to Buddhism in the Tibetan tradition.

Apart from Harrer, Richardson, and Howarth, among the Precious Protector's first overseas visitors were four members of America's avant-garde literary scene, poets Allen Ginsberg and his lover Peter Orlovsky, together with Gary Snyder and his wife, Joanne Kyger, who arrived together at Swarg Ashram (the name of the Dalai Lama's residence) in early 1962. A record of the meeting, which arguably says more about the Beats than it does about the Dalai Lama, is given in Kyger's journal:

> We met the Dalai Lama last week right after he had been talking with the King of Sikkim, the one who is going to marry an American college girl. The Dali [*sic*] is 27 and lounged on a velvet couch like a gawky adolescent in red robes. I was trying very hard to say witty things to him, but Allen Ginsberg kept hogging the conversation by describing his experiments on drugs and asking the Dalai Lama if he would like to take some magic mushroom pills and were his drug experiences of a religious nature, until Gary said really Allen the inside of your mind is just as boring and just the same as everyone elses is it necessary to go on; and that little trauma was eased over by Gary and the Dalai talking guru to guru like about which positions to take when doing meditation and how to breathe and what to do with your hands, yes yes that's right says the Dalai Lama. And then Allen Ginsberg says to him how many hours do you meditate a day, and he says me? Why I never meditate, I don't have to. Then Ginsberg is very happy because he wants to get instantly enlightened and can't stand sitting down or discipline of the body.

The suggestion that the Dalai Lama did not meditate because he "did not have to" is certainly a mistake on the author's part. Nonetheless, Kyger's journal entry is valuable as an example of the blithe arrogance of some of the Dalai Lama's Western visitors in the early days of exile.* But if it is evident that the audience was no great success on either side, the Tibetan leader's meeting with the poets was the first of many encounters with exponents of the West's counterculture.

* I cannot entirely exclude at least my younger self from this accusation.

In an unsettling juxtaposition, Ginsberg's visit took place at almost exactly the same time that the Panchen Lama submitted to the Chinese Politburo what became known as his seventy-thousand-character petition, a document that paved the way for his downfall and subsequent imprisonment. When the Dalai Lama fled Lhasa in 1959, the Panchen Lama was quick to assure the Chinese of his own continuing loyalty. For this he was rewarded with leadership of the Preparatory Committee for the Tibet Autonomous Region, of which position the Dalai Lama was summarily stripped.

For the next two years the Panchen Lama was successfully used by the Communists as their chief collaborator. In 1962 he was presented to a visiting English journalist, to whom he dutifully explained how, as "a cadre of the People's Republic of China, [he was] performing [his] duties in accordance with the policies of the Chinese Communist Party." Yet in fact he had by this time undergone a remarkable transformation. Having witnessed the aftermath of the suppression of revolt in Lhasa at first hand in 1959, and then, in 1960, having toured Amdo province and again seen for himself the abuses inflicted on Tibetans in the name of education and reform, he began to voice criticisms of the party. A year later he took the opportunity to visit his home village while returning to Lhasa from Beijing. Seeing with his own eyes the abject poverty to which his kinsmen had been reduced — all their metal cooking utensils had been confiscated in the local commune's drive to make steel — he declared that now, "in the socialist paradise, unlike in feudal times, beggars did not even have a begging bowl."

The experience persuaded him that he should prepare a formal report to the leadership declaring the many "errors" he had witnessed in the party's imposition of reform in Tibet. Over a period of several months during the early part of 1962, he began work on a petition. Written in Tibetan, it was subsequently rendered into Chinese and submitted during the summer of the same year. One of those he asked to work on the translation refused on the grounds that the criticisms voiced were too dangerous. Some of the statements were indeed toned down on the advice of Ngabo, the man who had lost Chamdo and who was now a senior collaborator with the Chinese, who also suggested that the document include a preamble praising the party for the good it had also wrought in Tibet. In spite of these changes, it remained an extraordinarily courageous undertaking. The Panchen Lama's teacher is said to have prostrated himself and, with tears running down his face, begged the Precious One not to go ahead. He had consulted the oracles and they had indicated clearly that inauspicious consequences would follow. But with astonishing determination, the twenty-four-year-old Panchen Lama ignored all advice.

Although at first the petition was received with little comment, Mao denounced it soon enough as a "poisoned arrow aimed at the Party by reactionary feudal overlords." For his remarkable bravery, the Panchen Lama was arrested and "struggled against" for fifty consecutive days. He was then thrown into prison. From time to time he would be dragged from his cell and subjected to further *thamzing* in front of large crowds. One infamous event that occurred during the Cultural Revolution is said to have "wounded him more than any other." At a public meeting, his sister-in-law was persuaded to accuse him from the podium of having raped her, following which his younger brother beat him on stage for the alleged crime. Afterwards he was put in solitary confinement, and for the next decade, it was unknown whether he was alive or dead.

The Dalai Lama's meeting with Ginsberg thus stands in stark contrast to the reality of life in Tibet, even if it gave an indication of how things presently stood in the West. Indeed, from the Dalai Lama's own perspective, a much more important encounter than his meeting with the Beats was his meeting with the lineage holder of Shantideva's *tong len* practice. Kunu Lama, a Tibetan layman living anonymously in Varanasi, was the recipient of the actual teaching that Shantideva himself had conferred on one of his students and which had subsequently been passed down, teacher to student, in an unbroken stream from generation to generation. To receive a teaching in this way is to hear the very words of the Master as if from his own lips.

Shantideva himself, author of the *Guide to the Bodhisattva's Way of Life,* is one of the Dalai Lama's favorite authors and a great spiritual hero of the Tibetan tradition, while the practice of *tong len,* today popular with many advanced mindfulness enthusiasts and even taught as part of social and emotional learning programs in increasing numbers of schools in the West, entails the meditative exchange of "self for other." The meditator calls to mind someone toward whom he or she feels negatively and imagines exchanging his or her own good qualities for the other's negative qualities. Of course, most who adopt the practice do not have the privilege of direct transmission.

In order to track down the lama, the young aspirant ordered his chauffeur to drive around Varanasi in monsoon rains until, by good luck, he saw the reclusive yogin in the street. To the consternation of those with him, he ordered the car to stop, jumped out, and humbly offered a *kathag* to the teacher, beseeching him for initiation into the practice. At first the lama tried to refuse, saying he was not worthy to teach it to the Dalai Lama. When, however, the Precious Protector followed him into his own home, despite his protestations, he finally consented.

Meanwhile, the fact that Nehru had made it clear to the Dalai Lama that the Indian government would not support any request for him to travel abroad was at the time a source of frustration to the Dalai Lama. The Indian leader did not wish to antagonize the Chinese further than he already had in granting the Dalai Lama asylum. Yet in later years, the Dalai Lama credited his enforced grounding with giving him the opportunity to further his spiritual practice in a way that might not otherwise have been possible — even if it is true that his temporal duties have to this day prevented him from undertaking the three-year, three-month, three-day retreat that every serious practitioner aspires to make at least once in his or her lifetime. When he was finally granted leave to travel, eight years after arriving in exile, his first overseas visit was to Japan, followed three months later by a trip to Thailand, in both cases to participate in Buddhist conferences.

The restrictions Nehru's government continued to place on the Dalai Lama did not prevent Mao from administering a sudden and completely unanticipated reminder of China's territorial ambitions when, following a number of skirmishes with Indian troops, the PLA mounted an incursion across the so-called McMahon line, the border with Tibet bequeathed by the British which the Dalai Lama had crossed two years earlier. Striking precisely at the moment when the world's attention was diverted by the Cuban Missile Crisis (in the fall of 1962), the Chinese outgunned, outmaneuvered, and quickly outfought the Indians, who were ill-prepared and ill-led. Remarkably, the PLA withdrew after barely a month. But the episode left Nehru humiliated and utterly demoralized, his dream of uniting India and China in fraternal cooperation against the old world colonial powers turned to nightmare.

There was, however, an important development in the Indian government's relationship with the Tibetan government in exile that came as a direct outcome of the debacle. In its wake, at the suggestion of hawks in the Foreign Ministry, Nehru consented to the founding of a secret military unit, Establishment 22. Under command of the Intelligence Bureau, and as such directly controlled by his own office, the Special Frontier Force (SFF), as it was also known, would be a specialist mountain warfare unit recruited, except for its seniormost officers, entirely from among the Tibetan refugee community. Though it was originally planned to have a strength of six thousand men under arms, its immediate success saw its numbers double within a short time. The chance to join what Gyalo Thondup, the unit's chief recruiting officer, advertised as an army that would one day retake Tibet was irresistible to many young Tibetan men. Once more the Dalai Lama found himself in the invidious position of feeling admiration at the enthusiasm of the recruits, gratitude to the Indians (and, of course, the Americans) for supporting the venture, and dismay at the violation of the Gandhian commitment to nonviolence with which increasingly he identified. This did not prevent him from presiding over a ceremony at which protective talismans for the troops were consecrated. But it certainly did fuel Chinese mistrust of the Precious Protector's subsequent identification as a leading figure in the world peace movement.

16

"We cannot compel you": Cultural Revolution in Tibet, Harsh Realities in India

The trickle of news coming out of Tibet during this period was, for the Dalai Lama, saddening in the extreme. As for himself, having been stripped of his position as head of the Preparatory Committee for the Autonomous Region of Tibet, he was now officially an outcast, a "villain," a "liar," a "murderer," a "wolf in monk's robes." The worst of criminals, he had pretended loyalty to the Motherland while seeking its destruction all along. His duplicitous letters to General Tan Guansen were all the proof needed. It was pointless therefore to pray to him. More troubling still, the dharma itself was portrayed as nothing more than an elaborate system of exploitation created for the sole purpose of maintaining the power and status of an unproductive elite. If the protectors were real, would they not have protected? They were nothing more than idols made of clay. The reincarnation system was a hoax connived in by the powerful to enslave the ignorant poor. Such was the relentless message of the propaganda sessions to which the populace was subjected on a daily basis. In addition, thousands of monks and nuns were forcibly laicized. Paraded in front of large gatherings of the masses, they were issued with raffle tickets and deemed to have married the person found to have the corresponding ticket.

As for prison life, the cruelty Tibetans encountered can scarcely be imagined. One former inmate explained how

> as the disparity between labour and sustenance widened, our physical strength weakened day by day, the quality of the materials worsened, the hardship increased, and by midday two or three members of each group would be laid out with exhaustion . . . But in spite of such grave hardship, at the nightly group or general meetings, many of the weaker workers were said to be "resisting about reform" and subjected to struggle. There were those who passed away the same night after undergoing the torture of struggle.

Even for those not held prisoner, because of food shortages and lack of money, many of the better-off families were reduced to bartering their treasures for a minute fraction of their true value: priceless jewelry exchanged for a few pounds of butter or sacks of grain. As for the monasteries, their lands were requisitioned without compensation. By the time Stuart and Roma Gelder, two communist-sympathizing British journalists, visited Lhasa in late 1962, the Three Seats were near-empty shells, their populations reduced by 90 percent or more — a fact of which husband and wife wrote approvingly. These were "the last priests of the last and strangest theocracy in human history . . . In a few years, when they would all be dead, none would come here to take their places."

For anyone fortunate enough to have grown up in a genuinely democratic country, the treatment meted out to the Tibetans in the weeks, months, and years following the Dalai Lama's flight seems scarcely imaginable. Merely expressing doubt as to the efficacy of communist methods was enough to endanger one's life. As for religion, any teaching was, of course, forbidden, and any perceived sympathy for the Dalai Lama was severely punished. But what made the Tibetan experience so pernicious was the vindictiveness with which "reform" was forced upon the people, to say nothing of the systematized attacks on their most deeply held convictions. Yet it must be remembered that what took place in Tibet during the early sixties was to a large degree simply a reflection of what was happening in China itself. The "Hundred Flowers" campaign of 1957, when, over the course of several weeks, Mao invited criticism of the party, was followed swiftly by the "Anti-Rightist" movement, when those "snakes" (Mao's word) who had taken the bait were charged with crimes against the party. Soon anyone who was deemed merely to hold "rightist" opinions became a legitimate target. As a result, at least half a million people — many of them from minority groups — were imprisoned, transported to labor camps, or liquidated over the next three years. Among those imprisoned and brutally treated was Phunwang, the Dalai Lama's Communist Party mentor during his 1954 trip to Beijing, convicted of politically incorrect thought. Held for two years in detention with frequent interrogations and humiliations during which, "because they knew I worried about my children, they sometimes let a baby cry outside my cell late at night," he was eventually sentenced to solitary confinement for nine years, by the end of which he had lost the power of speech. This was succeeded by another nine years in the mental patients' wing of Beijing's notorious Qincheng Prison for political prisoners before he was finally released and rehabilitated in 1978.* It took him another two years before he could speak properly again.

To make matters even worse, the Anti-Rightist movement coincided with Mao's Great Leap Forward, an economic campaign designed to transform China from an agrarian society to an industrial society. This initiated a period of extreme hardship for the entire population of the Chinese empire during which tens of millions died through starvation. The inability, already manifest, of agricultural collectivism to deliver reliable food supplies was tragically underscored by three successive years of crop failure, exacerbating an already

* Astonishingly he lived another thirty-six years until his death in 2014, aged ninety-two, having fully recovered and authored several books, one of them a remarkable exercise in Hegelian dialectics intended to demonstrate that, of necessity, *Liquid Water Does Exist on the Moon* (the book's title).

dire situation. The Great Leap was not, of course, a leap forward but a leap into darkness and despair.

Inevitably, those who felt the effects of famine the most acutely were the inmates of the gulags. "During [those] three years [1960–1963]," recalls a Tibetan who lived through the ordeal, "thousands quickly starved to death. In every prison camp horse carts were constantly pulling out loads of dead bodies." One former Tibetan government official recounted how, during those years,

> we began to look for . . . nourishment wherever we could find it. If we saw a worm all the prisoners would run for it and if you got it you immediately popped it in your mouth, otherwise it would be taken away . . . The livestock was also fed on grain, and in their excrement undigested grains of wheat would come out. We would pick these grains out of the manure pile and eat them . . . Sometimes, digging away in the fields, we would find bones. Human bones or animal bones. We would eat this too . . . Even if we knew it was human bone, still we would eat it.

The failure of the Great Leap Forward greatly diminished Mao's authority within the Communist Party, and for a time it looked as if he would lose control altogether. In what must surely rank as one of the most brazen acts of cynicism in history, the Great Helmsman responded in 1966 by unleashing the Cultural Revolution. This was characterized by a vicious hostility to the "Four Olds": old customs, old culture, old habits, old ideas. By attacking tradition itself and going over the heads of the political establishment to appeal directly to the country's youth, Mao, promoting a cult of himself, succeeded in bringing about a destructive furor that for almost a decade teetered on the verge of anarchy. Significantly, though, it secured his position as paramount leader. It is not clear how many died as a consequence of this tactic, but the toll is widely believed to be in the tens of millions. Yet, although it is sometimes alleged that the destruction of Tibet occurred as a result of the "excesses" of the Cultural Revolution, in fact its true destruction had occurred during the years immediately following the Dalai Lama's exile. The main effect of the Cultural Revolution in Tibet was to make the lives of the people even less bearable.

Compelled to work sixteen-hour days, anyone caught merely cooking at home would be severely punished. And now, not only was the Dalai Lama not to be prayed to; he was to be ritually denounced by the masses.

As for the Dalai Lama himself, if, in the wake of Allen Ginsberg's visit, there was a steady trickle of Beats and hippies who sought him out in Dharamsala throughout the 1960s, there were also increasing numbers of more serious seekers. One of these was Robert Thurman, then a student of the CIA's translator monk Geshe Wangyal, but today doubtless most famous for being the father of the actress Uma Thurman. At the time, Thurman, recently divorced, was a young Harvard BA on a spiritual quest. Meeting the Dalai Lama at Sarnath in eastern India when both were attending a conference of the World Fellowship of Buddhists in November 1964, Thurman recalled how he sensed a certain "guardedness" about the Tibetan, while the speech the Dalai Lama gave "sounded strained and formal." There was "a sense of him being from far away and high above and not quite relaxed in his surroundings." Nonetheless, when Thurman expressed interest in monkhood, the Dalai Lama invited him to visit Dharamsala, where he assigned him to the care of Ling Rinpoché.

The two young men (the Dalai Lama was not quite thirty, while the American was still in his early twenties) subsequently met on a regular basis at the Precious Protector's house. It turned out that the Dalai Lama was as keen as ever to learn about the outside world. After discussing the dharma, "he would invariably begin asking me questions about the many things he was wondering about," wrote Thurman, "Freud, Einstein and Thomas Jefferson, life in the Americas and Europe . . . the subconscious, relativity and natural selection." Yet for all the evident pleasure the Dalai Lama took in their meetings, "though basically energetic and cheery . . . [h]e seemed slightly stressed, lonely, a little sad."

Thurman was subsequently ordained by the Dalai Lama, the first Westerner to attain that dignity, though to the Precious Protector's "strong" disappointment ("which lasted quite a while"), the American went barely a year before disrobing and marrying model-turned-psychotherapist Nena von Schlebrügge, the ex-wife of countercultural luminary Timothy Leary, in 1967.

Another important visitor at this time was Thomas Merton. The (by adoption) American Roman Catholic monk of the Cistercian Order of Strict Observance came to Dharamsala in November 1968, en route to Thailand, where he was to die, electrocuted as he stepped out of the shower, just a few weeks later.* His appearance among the Tibetan community seems almost providential, given the recent embassy of Trijang Rinpoché to the Vatican, where he obtained an audience with Pope Paul VI. This was evidently more of a diplomatic success than it was a meeting of minds, however. Neither thought it worthwhile to leave a written record of the event, although Trijang Rinpoché subsequently reported to the Dalai Lama his dismay at the lack of "spiritual depth" of the Europeans: "They are concerned with this life only and have a strong sense of grasping after permanence in all things . . . [T]hey are preoccupied with indulging the mere illusion of joy and happiness."

The Dalai Lama's meeting with Merton took place at a moment remarkable both in the history of Buddhism in Tibet and in that of the Roman Catholic Church. The one faced the catastrophe of invasion by an external enemy committed to the ideology of modern materialism. The other was itself fighting a spiritual war with the same enemy. In a way, therefore, both the Dalai Lama and the pope faced a similar dilemma.

Because so many of the Tibetan rites were specific to particular shrines and temples in Tibet, and because most of the important festivals — especially those pertaining to the New Year — were peculiar to particular buildings and locations within Lhasa, rupture was unavoidable for the Tibetans. No longer would the cavalry assemble in their ancient chain mail in the courtyard of the Jokhang; no longer would the sound of the Old She-Demon, the Young She-Demon, and the Idiot boom to signal the immolation of the evils of the year past; no longer would the ministers in all their medieval finery prostrate themselves beneath the main temple at the close of the last day. All that would have to be let go. But what else could be safely consigned to the past, and what must be preserved at all costs? Together with his two tutors and other high ecclesiastics, the Dalai Lama was compelled to make many hard decisions. "We divided our culture into two types," he explained. "In the first category, we placed that which, we determined, needed to be retained only in books as past

* The last of his three meetings with the Dalai Lama took place on November 8, 1968. Merton died on December 10.

history. The second category included whatever could bring actual benefit in the present . . . Therefore many of our old ceremonial traditions I discarded — no matter, I decided. Let them go." Yet there was no attempt to modernize the liturgy itself. The wording and procedures of all the rituals went untouched, nor was there any move to bring the language or indeed the ceremonial — the vestments, the gestures, or the objects employed — up to date, no thought of *aggiornamento,* of making the faith less mysterious or more readily comprehensible.

The pope jumped the other way. Retaining most of the ceremony and outer trappings of the church, he radically attenuated the liturgy through the adoption of a new Mass, dropping Latin and many other elements of tradition.* Only in their commitment to the supernatural were both leaders in complete agreement.

Thomas Merton was in a way emblematic of this "renewed" Catholic Church. One of the most influential Christian writers of the twentieth century, he had by now become deeply interested in Buddhism, causing some to believe that, had he lived, he would have converted. For the first of his three meetings with the Precious Protector, the conversation, according to Merton, was all about "religion and philosophy and especially ways of meditation." The Dalai Lama was, he wrote, "most impressive . . . strong and alert, bigger than I expected . . . A very solid, energetic, generous and warm person."

For his part, the Dalai Lama records his gratitude to Merton for introducing him to "the real meaning of the word Christian." The fifty-three-year old Westerner was, he found, a "truly humble and deeply spiritual man," a view that will not surprise any of Merton's many admirers. Yet one wonders what the Dalai Lama would have thought of Merton had he known of the Catholic's recent liaison with a woman three decades his junior. By the same token, one wonders what Merton, a peace activist and critic of the Vietnam War, would have made of the CIA's involvement in Tibet at the time. There is reason to think both would have been horrified.

---

* To be fair to Paul VI, he had inherited most of these reforms from his predecessor, John XXIII. Paul was the one who implemented them.

Merton's journal record of his conversations over several days with the Tibetan monk gives a penetrating insight into the Dalai Lama's real preoccupations. Politics seems to have been mentioned hardly at all, except in relation to the putative compatibility of Marxism and monasticism, the topic of Merton's forthcoming conference contribution: only if Marxism was confined to "the establishment of an equitable economic and social structure," in the Dalai Lama's view. Of greater interest to the Dalai Lama was the question of the stages of the spiritual path within the Catholic tradition. "Having made vows, did the monks continue to progress along a spiritual way, toward an eventual illumination, and what were the degrees of that progress?" Merton does not record his answer, but doubtless would have referred to the writings of mystics such as Saints Teresa of Ávila and Bonaventure. Both describe a seven-stage journey of spiritual development by means of service to others, and prayer. Merton's visit thus alerted the Dalai Lama to the depth of Christian culture in a way that, perhaps, the brisk Anglicanism of some of his other Western visitors had not.

Merton's visit was also significant for the welcome news it brought of the Catholic Church's change in attitude toward mission. Whereas in the past the emphasis had been on obtaining converts, now it was on witness. The issue of conversion is one that still rankles for the Dalai Lama and for Tibetans generally. Buddhism does not seek converts. (When, as has occasionally happened, some of the Dalai Lama's Christian visitors have let their enthusiasm get the better of their good manners and sought to make a convert of him, the insult is thus doubly felt.) The guru teaches only when asked — and asked again. As for mission, the assumption is that as non-Buddhists* come to have a better understanding of what Buddhism is, and in particular when they come to have a better understanding of how things really are, they will naturally seek instruction from a spiritual guide and, in due course, will enter the path to liberation themselves.

It was around the time of Merton's visit that the Dalai Lama and his inner circle had the first indication that the CIA's Tibet program would soon be

---

* In Tibetan, *phyi rol pa,* literally, outsiders — in contrast to *Nang pa,* meaning insiders (where *nang* means "home").

drawing to a close. Gyalo Thondup was alerted by the head of the Russian news agency in Delhi to the fact that moves were afoot in Washington to reach out to the Chinese. As a presidential candidate, Richard Nixon had argued that China could not be kept outside the family of nations, nurturing fantasies in "angry isolation." Now that he was in power, it was clear that President Nixon intended to follow up on his pledge.

To the Dalai Lama personally these developments were not wholly unwelcome. At least, fewer people stood to be killed by the rebels or in retaliation for their attacks. But when it emerged that the CIA's funding of the Tibetan government in exile itself was also under threat, he was persuaded by the more hawkish of his advisers to make loud protestations of commitment to the quest to regain Tibet's independence. In an early speech to mark the anniversary of the "Tibetan National Uprising Day," the Dalai Lama had decried the "inhuman treatment and persecution" of his people at the hands of the Chinese. He had also spoken of their "passive struggle against tyranny and oppression." More recently, the temperature had risen sharply. Speaking of the "naked horror, sufferings and nightmarish hardships" endured by his countrymen in Tibet, he characterized the Chinese as "alien rulers," adding that "not to speak of fundamental human rights, a Tibetan is denied even the right to exist as a human being." Now it was the "great and sacred responsibility" of all Tibetans to commit to the "unmitigated continuation of the national struggle." The Dalai Lama called on his countrymen to "rededicate themselves to this sacred task."

Whether or not this fiery rhetoric had a direct impact on those setting the State Department's budget, we do not know. Nonetheless, for a little while longer, the funding was maintained — as indeed was the rhetoric. In 1971 we find the Dalai Lama speaking of "Tibetan courage" and the people's "determination never to live under alien rule." There should be no doubt that they would "carry on the struggle till we see Tibet once again in its rightful place among the nations of the world." This overt championing of independence for Tibet did not go down well with the Indian administration, for which, as the Dalai Lama reported subsequently to the government in exile, it caused significant "problems."

At this time, Prime Minister Indira Gandhi was in danger of losing control of her Congress Party.* For ideological reasons, Congress retained an instinctive sympathy for the Chinese Communist Party as overthrowers of colonialism — despite the fact that the Communists had shown themselves to be avid colonists. As a result, Mrs. Gandhi could do without further problems stirred up by her country's Tibetan guests. In response to the Dalai Lama's renewed stridency, she let it be known that the future of the Tibetan Special Frontier Force, which, it will be recalled, had been set up following the Sino-Indian War of 1962 and now gainfully employed fully twelve thousand of the refugees, was in the balance.

This was deeply unwelcome news. If both American funding and funding of the SFF were to be withdrawn simultaneously, the viability of the whole community would be threatened. To compound the Dalai Lama's worries, the news from Tibet was deeply concerning. In 1969 and 1970, a wave of revolts and protests had broken out, with significant numbers of casualties inflicted on the Chinese. In retaliation, there had been mass arrests and public executions.

Yet remarkably, in spite of the many obstacles he faced within the temporal realm, on the spiritual plane this was an especially fruitful period for the Dalai Lama. Robert Thurman, with wife and two children in tow, visiting the Dalai Lama in 1971, noticed "an astonishing, exciting change in him . . . He had come alive philosophically." In particular, Thurman noticed, the Dalai Lama "no longer referred every question" to his teachers. Instead, he gave his own "lucid and lyrical explanations of difficult texts." Exactly what spiritual realizations he attained during this period remain secret in accordance with every initiate's vow of silence, but a number of hints suggestive of the Precious Protector's growing stature as a yogin can be gleaned both from his biography of Ling Rinpoché and from the autobiography of Trijang Rinpoché.

From Trijang Rinpoché we gather that toward the end of 1969 the Dalai Lama had a number of auspicious dreams, and that, during a subsequent retreat, he consecrated some long-life pills — "and other substances" — which

* Indira Gandhi, Nehru's daughter; in office 1966–1977 and again from 1980 until her assassination in 1984.

he presented to the junior tutor. The importance of dreams within tantric practice would be hard to overestimate. Because physical sensation is absent in dreams, the practitioner's mental states are considered to be more immediately available, and more readily open to manipulation, during sleep. The majority of dream yoga teachings are "ear-whispered," and therefore secret. But we do know that this remarkable set of practices aims to further the initiate's quest for Enlightenment. To induce lucid dreaming, the practitioner lies on his right side, the right hand cupping the cheek with the thumb pressing a nerve by the cheekbone. The left arm is extended and rests on the left hip. Once the dream is established, there are four principal steps: first, the sleeper, realizing he (or she) is dreaming, takes control of the dream; second, the dreamer "re-describes" the dream such that it becomes a form of spiritual practice; third, the dreamer "multiplies" the dream, imagining himself or herself in a variety of different situations; fourth, the dreamer dissolves the dream into the clear light of mere awareness — one of the features of which is non-duality. Once mastery of the technique is gained, it is said to be possible to travel not just around the terrestrial world but into different worlds, or *loka,* to meet with other spiritual practitioners and to converse with and even take teachings from them. In the Dalai Lama's own case, he has on occasion been able to reconnect with his past lives and has spoken of dreaming that he was once a slave in an ancient Egyptian pharaoh's court.

The Dalai Lama attained another important milestone in his spiritual development toward the end of the following year when he began the completion stage of an advanced tantric practice called *tum mo* — literally, Fierce Woman — yoga. Ordinarily the training involved takes a little over two years, though it may take much longer, depending on aptitude and the ability of the individual to devote himself or herself wholeheartedly to the regime. This includes a requirement to undertake a minimum of 100,000 prostrations, in which the practitioner lays himself or herself down at full stretch, arms out, on the ground while reciting the "refuge" formula (a short prayer to the deity being invoked). An additional ten thousand prostrations are undertaken in case of errors during the practice, plus another thousand in case of further mistakes. It is not surprising to learn that, for best results, besides conducting these exercises very early in the morning (though not before half light, on account of the harmful influences that may beset the practitioner when it is dark), the yogin is advised to adopt meat in his or her diet.* Later in the training, *tum mo* yogins visualize themselves as deities coupled with a consort in the "union of bliss and emptiness." This entails the repetition of 400,000 mantras for the male and 200,000 mantras for the female deity, plus a further 100,000 mantras for the *dakinis* in their retinue. (A *dakini* may be understood most simply as a female spiritual being.)

Of all tantric practices, *tum mo* yoga is capable of producing the most spectacular empirically demonstrable results — results of which the Dalai Lama himself was skeptical at the outset. Though only a byproduct of the training, which is chiefly concerned with pacifying the initiate's afflictive emotions in preparation for experiencing the "union of bliss and emptiness" at which all tantric practice aims, the physical effect of *tum mo* is to raise the body temperature to extraordinary levels. This occurs as a result of the "vase" breathing exercises that form part of the discipline. At the invitation of the Dalai Lama during the early 1980s, a team from the Harvard Medical School led by Dr. Herbert Benson visited Dharamsala to conduct experiments on some adepts. They found that the most proficient meditators could raise their core temperature by up to fifteen degrees Fahrenheit, while in specific areas of the body it went even higher. A popular event, first described by Alexandra David-Néel, the French traveler and religious seeker, is the annual competition held today by hermits high above the snow line in the mountains above Dharamsala. The one who wins is the yogin who can dry out the largest number of sheets soaked in freezing water and draped about his naked torso. Yet when the Americans came to do their research, they "found that without gloves their fingers became numb so quickly that they could not fix the electrodes to the body to obtain their readings. The tests had to be done indoors."

Another feature of *tum mo* yoga is the "levitation" that forms a standard part of the practice, whereby "the practitioner sits in full lotus posture and by means of a downward flip of the legs propels himself upwards in a jump which may reach several feet." When Alexandra David-Néel witnessed the

* This may well be a reason why the Dalai Lama is not wholly vegetarian. The yogas he practices can be very demanding physically.

spectacle for the first time, she was somewhat disappointed, having hoped that she would see something that defied physical laws. Nonetheless, it is startling enough. And while the temptation is to take these remarkable physiological effects as an end in themselves, it is vital to remember that their whole purpose is to enable the yogin to attain direct insight of the nature of mind, which, when undistracted by thought, is seen, according to the tradition, to be clear and limpid as a still lake. When the practitioner attains this level of clarity, the mind is found to be empty of self. What remains is mere awareness.*

The context of this spiritual progress on the part of the Dalai Lama included two conferrals of the Kalachakra initiation, one in Dharamsala in 1970 and the other at one of the south Indian settlements early the following year. Apart from his initiation into Shantideva's *tong len* lineage, one of the most important teachings the Dalai Lama had taken since coming into exile included further initiation into the mysteries of the apocalyptic Kalachakra tantra by its greatest contemporary exponent, the Eleventh Kirti Rinpoché (1926–2006). In a notably vivid dream of Kalachakra's female consort, the Dalai Lama received clear encouragement to spread the peacemaking power of the tantra throughout the world. Accordingly, he made a commitment to serve as the bodhisattva's principal advocate and to offer the Kalachakra initiation as frequently as possible. This was validated during a subsequent retreat when, in a vision he had of Kalachakra in wrathful form, the bodhisattva indicated to the Dalai Lama that he had his full support in this.

How these spiritual events tie in with developments in the temporal sphere can only be guessed at, but it is a fact that the Kalachakra initiation the Dalai Lama conferred in 1971 preceded by only a few months one of the least known but most devastating episodes in the history of his life in exile.

The decade had begun with the worst weather ever recorded on the eastern coast of the Indian subcontinent. A disastrous cyclone killed up to a quarter of a million people in East Pakistan (present-day Bangladesh), flooding huge areas and forcing millions from their homes. The Pakistani government's

* There is an interesting argument to be had here about whether the yogin's experience is merely a psychological state induced by self-hypnosis. Yet for the one who attains such experience, it is evident that there is an attendant indubitability that defies such an easy reduction.

inept handling of the crisis precipitated a level of civil unrest that began to threaten its existence. Following the violent partition of India after independence from Britain in 1947, the predominantly Muslim territories had formed the Islamic Republic of Pakistan, which, at the time, was subdivided into two administrative regions, both governed from Islamabad but separated by more than a thousand miles. By mid-1971, opposition to the Pakistan government had grown to such an extent that civil war began to look likely. Now, millions of refugees from East Pakistan started streaming west toward India, and disease and starvation threatened on an epic scale. To compound the horror, the central government of Pakistan ordered its army to quell the protests in an operation that saw perhaps another quarter of a million — mostly Bengali civilians — dead.

Prime Minister Gandhi meanwhile, seeing both a welcome distraction from her domestic difficulties and an opportunity to seriously weaken India's traditional foe, called in her generals. Among these was S. S. Uban, head of special forces and commander of Establishment 22, the Tibetan Special Frontier Force. Already famous for his alleged exploits as a scout commander in David Stirling's Long Range Desert Patrol (forerunners of Britain's special forces regiment, 22 Special Air Service) during the Second World War, Uban was one of those military men, by no means rare, who manage to combine their commitment to kill when called on with a strong religious faith. Ordering him to "carry out reconnaissance and conduct whatever unconventional warfare [he] deemed necessary," the prime minister made clear to General Uban that she wanted a decisive result in East Pakistan. He in turn asked for an entirely free hand. "Will you allow me to take all my men with me, Tibetans and all?" he demanded. "Tibetans?" she replied. "Goodness! Will you be able to control them?"

"Yes, leave that to me," he replied. "They [will] do anything I ask of them."

Meanwhile, as the world looked on appalled, the tragedy unfolding in East Pakistan inspired what *Rolling Stone* magazine hailed as a "brief incandescent revival of all that was best about the Sixties," the Concert for Bangladesh organized by ex-Beatle George Harrison and featuring many of the artists associated with that decade's counterculture. It is thus one of those cruel ironies of history that, almost at the very moment when forty thousand of New

York's emancipated youth descended on Madison Square Garden for Harrison's concert, Establishment 22's two senior-most Tibetan officers appeared in Dharamsala, carrying with them a letter from the prime minister herself. This, though not addressed personally to the Dalai Lama, set out the Indian position. "We cannot compel you to fight a war for us," Mrs. Gandhi wrote, "but the fact is that General A A K Niazi [the Pakistan army commander in East Pakistan] is treating the people of East Pakistan very badly. India has to do something about it. In a way, it is similar to the way the Chinese are treating the Tibetans in Tibet . . . It would be appreciated if you could help us fight the war for liberating the people of Bangladesh."

There was some force in the Indian argument that Pakistan's suppression of the Bengalis was analogous to Chinese suppression of the Tibetans. There was also no denying that the Pakistani junta's methods were outrageous. But in reality, the Dalai Lama had no option. This was a test of loyalty. It was a test that, should he fail it, could have disastrous consequences, the least of which would be disbandment of the SFF itself. With the greatest reluctance he therefore acquiesced in what can only be described as India's dirty war. Regretfully giving the soldiers his blessing, he consented with only the forlorn caution that they should spare as many lives as possible.

The move was not wholly unsupported by the Dalai Lama's inner circle. Moreover, Trijang Rinpoché had close relations with many in the SFF. During the summer of 1970, he was to be found visiting the soldiers in Chakrata at the invitation of their commander. On succeeding days with the soldiers, the junior tutor granted them a number of tantric permissions — that is, permission to undertake specific practices — as well as a long-life initiation. Thereafter, he gave teachings, transmissions, and advice to individual companies and their commanders according to need.*

By mid-November 1971, and three weeks before hostilities were formally declared, the Tibetans were airlifted to Assam. From there they were infiltrated by canoe into the jungle-covered Chittagong Hills. The plan, known as

---

* Remarkably enough, the British army retains, at least at the time of this writing, at least one Tibetan Buddhist monk on strength as chaplain to its Gurkha regiments. More than half of all Gurkhas are Buddhist.

Operation Eagle, was that they would outflank Pakistan's own special forces and head for the coast, ready to cut off any attempted retreat in the direction of Burma. Wearing unmarked uniforms and armed with Bulgarian assault rifles — this partly to disguise who they really were and partly to confuse the enemy — the Tibetans quickly overran the Pakistani position. "After that," recalled Uban, "they were unstoppable." It was for this action that they earned themselves the sobriquet "the Phantoms of Chittagong."*

On December 3, the Pakistani air force launched what was billed as a preemptive strike against India, as a result of which, as Trijang Rinpoché noted, for the next two weeks "everyone lived in a state of anxiety." In retaliation, India officially declared war. By the sixteenth it was all over thanks largely to the SFF: the Pakistani army was routed, and General Uban was a national hero. "And do you know why Unit 22 was so successful?" he asked afterwards. "Their reputation preceded them. The very idea of Tibetans struck terror in the hearts of the Pakistanis. They heard Unit 22, and the whole bloody world was running away!" As for the Tibetans themselves, "their morale — you should have seen — sky high! They felt they could take back Tibet tomorrow." When he came subsequently to write a memoir of the campaign, Uban dedicated his book to "the gallant officers and men of the SPECIAL FRONTIER FORCE, who made the supreme sacrifice of their lives, braving dangers beyond the call of duty and blazing immortal trails in the history of righteous wars waged against oppression and for the freedom of all mankind."

Victory in Bangladesh was a massive boost to morale for the Indian army generally, and hugely important for the SFF as a demonstration of both its effectiveness and the loyalty of the Tibetan refugees to India. It also demonstrated that, well-armed, well-trained, and well-led, India's clandestine Tibetan army was an extremely potent force. Unfortunately for the Tibetans, because their participation in the war was unofficial — so secret, in fact, that most of the Indian Eastern Army command was unaware that they had already been operating behind enemy lines for three weeks when the war began — there could be no official recognition of their contribution. Instead, all who participated received a bounty of around 500 rupees, but there were to be no

* Uban published a memoir of the same name.

medals, nor any commendations for bravery. When the impossibility of official acclaim became apparent, there was immense disappointment in the ranks. Fearing, perhaps, that dismay at being overlooked might lead to disaffection and from there to open dissent, Uban contacted Dharamsala. The outcome was as welcome as it was unprecedented. The Dalai Lama announced to a parade of the entire unit that, having a few days to himself, he wanted to pay them a personal visit. It was he himself who led the inspection at their base in Chakrata in June 1972.

Although this is the only time that the Dalai Lama is known to have visited the soldiers, that he did not disapprove of the Special Frontier Force is suggested by the fact that his younger brother subsequently became one of its officers.

Back in Dharamsala, the Precious Protector was quick to resume his spiritual training under the direction of the two tutors. From Trijang Rinpoché, he received a number of permissions, "starting with the common torma initiation and the exclusive Cittamani Tara, together with the most secret Heart Absorption Permission," in return for which the Dalai Lama offered his junior tutor "the permissions of the seventeen emanations of Four-Faced Mahakala, Robber of Strength . . . including Split Faces, Striking the Vital Point and Secret Accomplishment," but excluding, for reasons not specified, the "Entrusted Black Brahman." From Ling Rinpoché, too, the Dalai Lama received, "a very special Cittamani initiation."

A year later, the Precious Protector was finally permitted by the Indian government to undertake a six-week, eleven-country tour of Europe during the autumn. This was a welcome development. Not that it was a wholly altruistic move on the part of Prime Minister Gandhi. Against the background of America's thawing relations with the PRC, we might reasonably suspect that unleashing the Dalai Lama was her way of reminding the world that India should not be forgotten amidst the euphoria of rapprochement between the superpowers. It can also be read as a reward for the Dalai Lama's cooperation in the Bangladesh war.

17

"Something beyond the comprehension of the Tibetan people": The Yellow Book *and the Glorious Goddess*

The prospect of his forthcoming trip to the West was a matter of great encouragement not just for the Dalai Lama but for Tibetans generally. Yet while arrangements were being put in place for the now thirty-eight-year-old Dalai Lama's eleven-country itinerary, there occurred a series of events that were to have shattering repercussions both within the exile community and in Tibet.

The first indication of trouble came on the day when the Dalai Lama arrived to consecrate a new statue in the main temple in Dharamsala. To the contemporary reader, the consecration of a statue might seem an unremarkable event, but that would be to ignore the central place that iconography occupies within the Buddhist tradition — as indeed it does in non-secular traditions generally. Gombojav Tsybikov, the Buryato-Russian explorer who visited Lhasa on the cusp of the twentieth century, described how pilgrims would pay a fee to place their own images in the presence of the Jowo, the "self-arisen" statue of the Buddha brought to Tibet in the seventh century by King Songtsen Gampo's Chinese princess bride. Its monk attendants would also sell the bodies of mice that, having gorged themselves on the barley offering made to the statute, had died in its presence. Their meat was considered especially efficacious for expectant mothers facing difficult births. On the occasion in question, the statue was of Padmasambhava, the Lotus-Born — one of the greatest spiritual heroes of the Tibetan Buddhist tradition and, furthermore, the key figure within the Nyingma tradition.

An initiative of the Dalai Lama himself, this project was intended by him to rectify a mistake made during the 1950s. At that time a leading Nyingma master had petitioned the Kashag to have a statue of the Lotus-Born consecrated in the Jokhang Temple as a defense against the Chinese. Significantly, this statue was to portray the sage in the form of Nangsi Zilnon, Overcomer of Obstacles, and it was to be positioned facing east. Although the Kashag accepted the proposal for a statue, when it was erected it was not in the correct form, and it faced south. The dedication now of a statue in the correct form and facing in the right direction in Dharamsala would thus correct the earlier failure.* Another aspect of the undertaking was the Dalai Lama's wish to foster unity among the different schools within the Tibetan tradition. The Lotus-Born is venerated by a large percentage of Tibetans, irrespective of sectarian affiliation, and is thus a unifying figure. Right from the beginning of the exile period, it had been clear to the Precious Protector that the survival of the Tibetan people depended on their coming together as a community. One of his first acts on arrival in Dharamsala had been to convene a meeting of the senior-most representatives of each of the different Tibetan religious traditions. Urging them "to fulfil the . . . welfare of all Tibetans," the Dalai Lama set the tone for increased cooperation among the different schools. Similarly, his founding of the Institute of Buddhist Dialectics in 1973 was another major initiative designed to further his ecumenical vision. Open to students of all backgrounds, the institute sent a clear signal that it was the Mahayana tradition in general, rather than any particular school within it, that was important.

When the day of consecration of the new statue arrived, the Dalai Lama was surprised to see far fewer monks and nuns attending than he would have expected. On making inquiries, he learned that a recently published book had

---

* It can be safely assumed that the Dalai Lama was encouraged in this project by Nechung.

caused many to boycott the ceremony for fear of supernatural consequences. The book, *An Account of the Protective Deity Dorje Shugden, Chief Guardian of the Gelug Order, and of the Punishments Meted Out to Religious and Lay Leaders Who Incurred His Wrath,* better known simply as *The Yellow Book,* had been written by a well-regarded student of Trijang Rinpoché. Little more than a pamphlet — it was originally intended as a supplement to a longer work by Trijang himself — the book opened with an ominous dedication: "Praise to you, Protector of the Yellow Hat tradition, you who grind to dust great adepts, high officials and laymen alike." There followed a list of well-known individuals who had allegedly incurred the wrath of the protector Dorje Shugden for having polluted the pure teachings of the Gelug tradition by venerating objects and individuals associated with other schools or by adopting their practices — particularly those of the Nyingma sect. Among these were many familiar figures of the regency period, including Reting Rinpoché, the former regent, along with Lungshar, whose eyes were put out, and Trimon, a chief minister who lost his mind toward the end of his life.

The word Nyingma means simply "ancient" and is applied to those teachings, lineages, and practices that came to Tibet with the first diffusion of Buddhism, roughly from the seventh to the ninth centuries. This was the time of the religious kings, of whom there were three, each considered a manifestation of Chenresig. Following the apostasy of a later monarch, who persecuted Buddhism to the brink of extinction, Tibet endured a Dark Age for two hundred years before a second diffusion of Buddhism began during the eleventh century. This revival was undertaken by a number of sages working independently of one another and to whom can be traced the later different traditions — the Kadam (from which the Dalai Lama's Gelug school is derived), Sakya, Kargyu, and Jonang traditions.

Within the Buddhist tradition generally, the authority of a given lineage — the lineage being the teacher-to-student relation through which a set of teachings and practices is transmitted — is derived from the ability to trace it back to its origin with the Buddha. This is complicated, particularly in the Mahayana tradition, by the fact that certain of the most highly accomplished masters are said to have received a particular teaching or practice directly, often in a vision of the Buddha, even though they were not his contemporaries. Suffice it to say that some purists hold that all those lineages that claim to derive from the Lotus-Born and the first diffusion of Buddhism in Tibet were in fact broken during the Dark Age and subsequently corrupted. The Lotus-Born's devotees (who make up perhaps a third of the monastic community and an even higher percentage among the laity, for whom adherence to a single sect is less important) believe, however, that many of the lineages brought to Tibet by the Lotus-Born did in fact survive. They hold, moreover, that the Lotus-Born is a manifestation of a fully enlightened being, a "second Buddha."

What is known about the Lotus-Born apart from what the Nyingma tradition says about him is scant. Contemporary records show only that he came to Tibet during the reign of Tibet's second Dharma King and that he was involved with the foundation of Samye, the country's first monastery, toward the end of the eighth century CE. They also tell us that he was expelled from Tibet on the orders of the king and, moreover, that the Lotus-Born foiled an attempt to murder him as he left the court. But the records have nothing to say about his real importance. They do not tell us about the prophecy he uttered on his banishment, to the effect that, in future, the divisions in Tibet would be not between believer and nonbeliever but between the followers of the doctrine themselves. As to the fifty-six years some say that he spent in Tibet following his official banishment, the contemporary records are completely silent. Yet it is to these years that his most important work is said to belong. Secretly, silently, the Lotus-Born waged war on Tibet's indigenous deities, subduing them and binding them over as protectors of the faith. These he put under the command of a certain Pehar, a deity whom he persuaded to leave his abode on the Mongolian steppes to take up residence as the chief protector of Samye Monastery.

Why this is so significant is that it is Pehar who speaks through Dorje Drakden, muse of the Nechung oracle. Pehar himself is a fallen angel. Many eons ago, during an incarnation as a Brahmin priest, he succumbed to the charms of a beautiful girl. For seven days and seven nights they made love in the temple where he lived. Outcast thereafter, Pehar was reborn first in the hell realms, then again as a human being, destined to wander the world homeless until he died. He was then reborn the son of a minor deity, and it was in this incarnation that he took up his vocation as a local god among the Uighur peoples of Central Asia. Why precisely Pehar was chosen by the Lotus-Born to come to Tibet is unclear. But he later emerged as the most important of the dharma protectors. How this came about is significant to our story because it connects the time of the Great Fifth Dalai Lama to the present day.

During the sixteenth century, Pehar had a disagreement with the abbot of Samye Monastery. As a result, the abbot decreed that there was no need for the deity to be depicted in a new chapel then under construction. Incensed, the deity retaliated by manifesting as a boy who came to offer his services as a fresco painter. As recompense for his work, the boy asked only that he be permitted to paint a small monkey holding a stick of incense somewhere on one of the walls. The abbot agreed, the chapel was adorned with the customary religious scenes, and the boy departed. That night, however, Pehar slipped into the image of the monkey and, using the stick of incense, set the building ablaze.

Realizing he had been tricked, the abbot had a demon trap constructed. These devices, still very much a feature of Tibetan Buddhist practice, consist of lengths of yarn stretched in an intricate geometrical pattern over a wooden frame, somewhat in the manner of a giant cat's cradle. The demon is lured in by means of offerings and invocations, and then is unable to find a way out. The deity was subsequently caught, placed in a casket, and pitched into the river. Sometime later, the box washed up on the banks of the Kyichu about half a day's journey from Lhasa, where it was seen by the Great Fifth — though whether in a dream or whether he was alerted to its presence by a third party is obscure. In any case, he ordered the box to be brought ashore, adding that on no account should it be opened. Remarkably, the farther the box was carried from its resting place, the heavier it became, until the monk deputed to the task could carry it no longer. Puzzled, he ignored the instruction not to look inside and opened it up. To his surprise, a pigeon emerged and flew into the branches of a nearby tree. Hearing of this, the Great Fifth admonished the monk and ordered that a shrine be built at the base of the tree. The shrine subsequently became incorporated into Nechung Monastery, and it was among the monks of this foundation that Pehar's oracle began once more to manifest itself. The most important of the dharma protectors can thus be traced unambiguously back to the ministry of the Lotus-Born.

On hearing of the existence of *The Yellow Book* on that day in Dharamsala, the Dalai Lama was deeply affected. Not only was this a public rebuke, and not only did it clearly insinuate that evil would befall him if he continued along his chosen path of rapprochement between the different traditions, but also it was an insult to Nechung, who had sanctioned the admission of the Lotus-Born (in statue form) to the temple. It was one thing to hold reservations about the Dalai Lama's policy of openness to the non-Gelug traditions — he was well aware that some did — but to publish what amounted to a loaded personal criticism without informing him in advance was an insult. The fact that the author was a member of the Dalai Lama's inner circle and a heart disciple of Trijang Rinpoché and could therefore be assumed to have done so with the junior tutor's full knowledge only made matters worse. Nor was this a trivial issue of dharma politics, as the violent events that ensued would show.

The Dalai Lama thus had much on his mind when, during the fall of that year, he embarked on his trip to Europe.

Apart from being an eye-opener, allowing the Dalai Lama to experience what, up until then, he had only heard about, the visit to Europe seems to have had less impact than might have been expected. The Dalai Lama quickly realized that the two hemispheres, East and West, were "not so different after all." From contemporary media coverage of the visit, we learn that the Dalai Lama had been well briefed by the Indian government, which made clear that he was not permitted to engage in political activities but should confine himself strictly to religious matters. An interview on Dutch television shows him laughing at the questions of an interviewer trying to maneuver him into being indiscreet. Since his trip was entirely nonpolitical, he explained, he did "not want to spoil" it. In spite of this, he was nonetheless received by a number of political leaders, including both the president and the prime minister of Ireland. Among senior religious figures, he met with Pope Paul VI, the Archbishop of Canterbury, and the Aga Khan. And in London he was delighted to find a number of elderly ex-officials who had actually served in Tibet during the time of the British Empire and could speak Tibetan. But perhaps most important for the Dalai Lama personally was his meeting with the two hundred Tibetan children who had been adopted post-exile into Swiss families, though he was disappointed to find that most had lost their mother tongue. In view of this, he encouraged monks at the recently founded Rikon Monastery in nearby Zell to provide language classes for them.

On his return to Dharamsala, it was not long before the Dalai Lama was plunged back into the intricacies of supernatural politics. Early in 1974, during the government's annual invocation of the Nechung oracle, the deity handed down a prophecy that shook the Dalai Lama to the core. Something, declared the deity, had upset the mind of Palden Lhamo. As the Precious Protector wrote subsequently, "This was something beyond the comprehension of the Tibetan people." So serious was the matter that "on the following day it was decided it would be right to perform an effective *tsok** ritual propitiation of Palden Lhamo and the five king emanations, to be followed by an invitation to Nechung . . . during which confessions and apologies would be made to Palden Lhamo and Nechung would be asked to clarify what we had done wrong."

The difficulty here was that the Glorious Goddess is far too exalted a being to be contactable by straightforward means. She does not speak through an oracle in the way Pehar speaks through the Nechung oracle. Nor does Dorje Drakden, through whom Pehar speaks, have the right of access to her. He can help in the process, but other than in the most exceptional cases — such as when, during the reign of the Great Fifth, she spoke directly from her *thangka* — Palden Lhamo is accessible only through dream, divination, and inference following careful preparation. The Dalai Lama would have to inquire — something that would take time (months rather than weeks, possibly even years rather than just months) and great diligence. Nonetheless, the importance of the pronouncement cannot be overstated, and investigation of its meaning became a central focus of the Dalai Lama's spiritual practice.

In the meantime, there were important developments on the earthly plane. Now that the CIA had withdrawn all its funding of the Tibetan resistance, the situation with respect to the guerrilla camp in Mustang in northern Nepal came quickly to a head. The guerrillas themselves had declared that they would never give up. But then a new king ascended the throne in Nepal in early 1972. It soon became clear that this monarch would not, as his father had

* A *tsok* offering is a highly charged ritual practice that involves the offering of both material and spiritual substances to the tantric deities as a means to gaining wisdom and merit.

done, simply turn a blind eye to the antics of the Tibetan freedom fighters in Mustang. It was, after all, a province of Nepal, however remote. Following a visit by the new king to Beijing during the autumn of 1973, the Nepalese issued an ultimatum. The camp must either disband voluntarily or face a military contest — with either the Nepalese army, the Chinese, or both.

The terms were generous nonetheless: if the freedom fighters went quietly, the Nepalese government would provide a million dollars (presumably supplied by the Americans) to help resettle the troops. In return, the Nepalese would acquire the Tibetans' weapons. But while the majority of camp residents saw the futility of trying to carry on under these circumstances, a minority still refused to lay down their arms.

Watching with mounting concern over the prospect of an international incident with potentially embarrassing consequences, given that the rebels' financial and other support was being channeled through India, the Indian government contacted the Dalai Lama, requesting that he intervene. It was decided that he should make a voice recording to be played to the diehards. This was duly conveyed to the rebel camp — with disastrous results. On hearing the Dalai Lama's words, the soldiers felt as if the world had been cut from beneath them. For them, the Dalai Lama was their reason for sacrificing not just family but all worldly ambition in the "sacred cause" of which he had spoken so eloquently in his March 10 statement just recently. The tape recording asking the rebels to lay down their arms seemed nothing less than betrayal. Several took their own lives on the spot — one of the commanders slashing so vigorously at his own throat that he completely decapitated himself. Another soldier threw himself wordlessly from the top of a cliff. Others were so dazed that "they wandered around crying, like they didn't even know where they were." It was a tragic end to a project that was, in reality, doomed from the outset.

While on the earthly plane the disbanding of the Mustang guerrilla camp brought to a close Tibetan dreams of an armed liberation of Tibet, on the spiritual plane a similar sundering occurred soon after. During his investigations of the Glorious Goddess's terrifying pronouncement, the Dalai Lama encountered both the Great Fifth and the Great Thirteenth in dreams, and both former incarnations advised him to cease propitiating Dorje Shugden. It emerged that what had upset the mind of the Glorious Goddess two years previously was in fact Shugden's behavior. This was a very serious development, yet it was subsequently given supernatural approval not once but three times when the Dalai Lama conducted separate divinations in front of the Great Fifth's *thangka* of the Glorious Goddess, which, on that never-to-be-forgotten occasion, had spoken directly. The advice was the same in every case: not only should he cease propitiating Shugden in public, but also he should cease doing so in private, too. In fact, as far back as the late 1960s, Pehar, speaking through Nechung, had warned the Dalai Lama and the government that they should beware of the deity. But on that occasion the Dalai Lama had rebuked him for openly criticizing an important fellow protector. After all, had not Shugden played a vital role in the escape into exile? And was he not the guardian of the Gelugpa tradition itself? How could Pehar presume to speak against a colleague in this way?

In the fall of 1976, the Dalai Lama conferred his sixth Kalachakra initiation on a large audience just outside Leh in Ladakh, a remote, ethnically Tibetan province of northern India. Formerly a tributary principality of the Tibetan government, today Ladakh has a Muslim population approaching that of the Buddhist population. But while traditionally Islam is hostile to polytheism, of which Buddhism is considered an example, the Tibetan lamas of the region are widely respected — and the Dalai Lama himself is a popular figure among the Muslim community. On this occasion, it is said that the young daughter of a local mullah, who was taking his family to see the Tibetan holy man, was jokingly told by the grown-ups that she would see that he had four arms like the figures in many of the Buddhists statues. When, however, they asked her afterwards whether she had seen them for herself, she replied that he didn't have four arms. He had a thousand. This was reckoned a marvelous event by Tibetans when they came to hear of it. Chenresig is often depicted as having a thousand arms.

It was on the second day of this Kalachakra initiation that news came of the death of Chairman Mao at the age of eighty-two. The Dalai Lama, greatly moved at the passing of the man he had once admired so greatly, immediately led prayers for him.

No one supposed that this single event would change conditions in Tibet overnight. It was, however, an occasion for hope that life might improve. Credible reports (since corroborated) that a number of Tibetans were executed for showing inadequate remorse at the news of Mao's death quickly dampened expectations. Yet soon after, very different signals began to emerge from Beijing. An early indication of change came when, that same year, a senior American official was invited to visit Tibet. Six months later, Ngabo — the former governor turned collaborator and now a senior government official in Tibet — announced that the Precious Protector would be welcome to return home, "so long as he stood on the side of the people." Both were promising developments. The sudden reappearance of the Panchen Lama at a political conference was yet another hopeful sign. It seemed that the reformers were now in the ascendant, and while open dissent remained impermissible, gradually it became clear that China was seriously intent on liberalization.

As the Dalai Lama watched developments with keen interest, matters relating to the dharma protectors came to a head, culminating in a ceremony at which he summoned Nechung in front of a gathering of high lamas to confirm in public what he had told the Precious Protector in private. Now that he had broken with Shugden, "it would be excellent," proclaimed Nechung, "if the Dalai Lama . . . could receive as many initiations, transmissions and core teachings as possible from all the Tibetan traditions." This meant that, apart from taking Nyingma teachings, the Dalai Lama should also take teachings from masters representing each of the other traditions: Sakya, Kargyu, and Jonang. The Dalai Lama could now consider his determination to help preserve the Tibetan Buddhist tradition in its entirety by taking teachings from each of the different schools as having the approbation of the protectors themselves.

From the Dalai Lama's perspective, the loss of many lineages due to the destruction of the dharma in Tibet had to be limited to the extent possible. One way of helping to do so was for him to take initiations as widely as he was able. This was in keeping with the high lamas' traditional role as custodians of the teaching lineages. Broadening his remit to do so beyond his own school meant that he would be free to explore large areas of the tradition that would otherwise be off limits to him. Among these were the *dzogchen* teachings of the Nyingmapa and the *mahamudra* teachings of the Kargyupa. These *dzogchen* teachings, of which the most well known are to be found in the *Tibetan Book of the Dead,* describe a method of attaining Enlightenment in a single lifetime. In fact, similar methods are also described within the Gelug tradition, but proponents of *dzogchen* claim they are less efficacious than those described in this, arguably the most important of the Treasure Texts. A Treasure is a text, or sometimes an object, believed to have been hidden by the Lotus-Born (though other great masters are also associated with the practice) during his sojourn in Tibet and revealed by a qualified yogin when karmic conditions ripen suitably.

Similarly, *mahamudra** teachings are also to be found within the Gelug corpus, but the Kargyu tradition has a special focus on them and presents them in a unique form that the Dalai Lama was keen to help maintain. This new openness would also allow the Dalai Lama to be initiated into lineages that preserved variations on those maintained by the Gelug school, for example the extraordinary Chod† tradition that is again practiced by both Nyingma and Kargyu, as well as by Gelug yogins. These practices are attributed to an eleventh-century female practitioner by the name of Ma Chig Labdron. When only a girl, and despite her protests that she wanted to become a renunciate, her parents married her off. But so determined was Ma Chig to practice the dharma that she first burned her hands and feet and then, when that did not persuade her husband and parents to let her go, she cut off her own thumbs. Eventually they realized there was no stopping her and she finally had her way. So severe was her asceticism that her hair turned yellow and her eyebrows red, and yet still she was not taken seriously. It was only when the abbot of the monastery close to where she lived came and saw for himself not just these outward signs but signs of her inward realizations that she was accepted as one worthy of the highest respect. As for the Chod teachings, these include a set of visualizations whereby the meditator takes on a series of identities, becoming, among others, a wrathful goddess, a calm purifying god, and finally a fearless yogi, all of whom offer their own flesh and blood as food for the demons. For best results, these visualizations are conducted in a graveyard, or cremation ground, at night. Again, these practices are not unknown within

* The term refers to the union of wisdom and emptiness.

† Correctly *gcod,* which means "cutting through" or "severing" and refers to the hindrances or obstacles that stand in the yogin's way on the path to Enlightenment.

the Gelug tradition, while the habit of practicing among the recently dead is a well-known trope within the tradition as a whole. The Dalai Lama's spiritual lineage includes an incarnation known as the Yogin of the Burning Ground. Prior to his manifestation as King Songtsen Gampo, the first of the religious kings, Chenresig manifested as one known for his habit of frequenting cremation grounds, wearing the shrouds of the deceased, dancing, lying on top of corpses, and eating food left in offering for the dead.

Nechung's approbation of the Dalai Lama's desire to be initiated into practices from across the whole of the Tibetan tradition, not just by Gelug masters, but by other lamas, may seem unremarkable, but it is important to understand the radical nature of this development. One might think of the head of one of the most austere evangelical churches suddenly coming out in favor of inviting Catholic priests to bring their incense, Gregorian chant, communion rails, and confession into church on Sunday. For the majority of Tibetans, it was nonetheless a welcome move. It underlined the fact that this was a Dalai Lama whose wish was to serve all, irrespective of their religious commitments. Yet the change was also to have devastating consequences within the refugee community.

In the meantime, however, the Chinese government began to make overtures to a number of individuals who they thought might be able to influence the Dalai Lama. Among these were Heinrich Harrer and Prince Peter of Denmark and Greece. Having written *Seven Years in Tibet,* Harrer had gone on to make several other notable expeditions. The prince was less well known but had been an important figure in Kalimpong during the 1950s. An anthropologist by training, he had made a special study of the widespread practice of polyandry among Tibetans.* While both Harrer and Prince Peter eventually took up the invitation to revisit Tibet, they found no miraculous transformation for the better under the new regime — quite the contrary in fact — and neither was able to recommend that the Dalai Lama should ask to return, though the Chinese clearly hoped they would.

* His own marital arrangements were much more traditional, except that his marriage to a Russian divorcee four years his senior prevented him from sustaining his claim to the Greek throne.

The Dalai Lama's initial response to China's newfound commitment to openness and reform was muted, therefore. After so many years of the harshest treatment for any Tibetans who resisted Chinese rule, he and the Kashag were skeptical that any fundamental change had occurred. After all, despite some economic liberalization, the basic commitments to communism, to one-party rule, and to the occupation of Tibet were not in question. When, however, Gyalo Thondup — now living in Hong Kong — was approached by some officials of Xinhua, the Chinese state news agency, it became clear that Beijing was in earnest. This was the first contact, if indirect, between the Dalai Lama and the Chinese government in almost twenty years. The party leadership wanted to open a dialogue. With his brother's approval, Gyalo Thondup met with officials in Beijing in March 1979 and, on the twelfth, with Deng Xiaoping himself.

To his surprise, the Chinese leader — whom the Dalai Lama had met when, during the 1950s, Deng was political commissar for the southwestern military district — told Gyalo Thondup that, apart from independence, there was nothing that could not be discussed. And lest the Dalai Lama doubt what he was saying, he should send trusted emissaries to Tibet to investigate the situation for themselves: "Better to see with one's own eyes than to hear something a hundred times from other people."

For his part, Gyalo Thondup, deeply suspicious of Deng — mainly on account of documents he claimed to have seen suggesting that Deng, whom he nicknamed "the Dwarf," had been the very person who authorized the destruction of monasteries in Tibet — put forward three proposals on behalf of the Dalai Lama. The first was that Deng make good on his recent promise that contact between Tibetans inside Tibet and those in exile could be permitted. The second, taking up Deng's offer, was that the exile community be allowed to send representatives to investigate the "new Tibet." Third, the Dalai Lama would like to send some newly qualified teachers to Tibet. To all three proposals Deng responded enthusiastically, asking at once how many teachers were available. When Gyalo Thondup suggested Dharamsala might send "fifty for a start," the Chinese leader complained that was "no good. We need at least one thousand!"

From this encounter was born a plan whereby the Dalai Lama would send a series of fact-finding missions to Tibet to assess the situation on the ground. Should their reports concur with the Panchen Lama's recent speech declaring that "the present standard of living in Tibet is many times better than that of the 'old society,'" the Precious Protector might then accept Deng's further proposal — that he himself return for a visit.

This turn of events was as welcome to the exile community as it was unexpected. Many had given up hope of ever hearing what happened to loved ones who had stayed behind. Yet it was a moment of optimism tempered by dreadful anxiety; much of the news would surely be bad. The Dalai Lama nonetheless instructed his immediate elder brother, Lobsang Samten, recently returned from America, where he had been working anonymously for several years as a janitor at a school in Scotch Plains, New Jersey, to lead the first delegation.* He himself meanwhile set out on a trip to Moscow, the Buryat Republic, and Mongolia. In 1979 Russia still looked like a world superpower, and there was clear merit in developing relations with other players to the greatest extent possible in the field of global politics.

On his arrival in Moscow, the Dalai Lama discovered that Marxist tyranny remained alive and well in Russia. Describing a visit to Lenin's study at the Kremlin, he was later to recall the absurdity of being "watched over by an unsmiling plain-clothes security man who was clearly ready to shoot" at the least provocation. He also noted how out of touch the Russian Communist Party was with the common people. His aides reported how, after he had thanked a doorman in the Kremlin, the man announced that this was the first time in twenty-five years of service that anyone had uttered a word of gratitude. But while the trip to the USSR both sent a signal to China that he was not without friends even in the communist bloc and was a great encouragement to the Buddhists of the Soviet Republics, the trip the Dalai Lama took to the United States in the fall of 1979 was of far greater significance.

---

* Lobsang Samten was, by all accounts that I have heard, the most gentle of souls and his mother's admitted favorite. His decision to return to India may have been influenced by his recent discovery and exposure in the local press.

18

From Rangzen *to* Umaylam: *Independence and the Middle Way Approach*

For several years now, the Dalai Lama's representatives in America had been in touch with sympathetic political figures in Washington, notably Joel McCleary, a student of Geshe Wangyal and then deputy assistant for political affairs at the White House. Although President Ford had regarded the Dalai Lama primarily as the Indian government's "burden," President Carter understood, and was sympathetic to, the human rights angle of the Tibetan issue. The Dalai Lama would be welcome in the United States provided, as usual, that he kept to religious themes.

Arriving on September 3, 1979, the now forty-four-year-old Dalai Lama maintained a schedule that took him on a hectic tour of twenty-two cities over seven short weeks, starting with New York and ending with Washington, DC. Prophetically, the first word uttered in public by the Dalai Lama was "compassion." This was in answer to a question posed at a press conference asking whether he had a message for the United States. Subsequently mixing general talks on spirituality with more-technical discourses on Buddhist philosophy, the Dalai Lama was an immediate hit. Robert Thurman, by now a college professor, later recalled how, on reconnecting with the Dalai Lama, he "almost keeled over." Noting that the Tibetan leader had "always been charming and interesting and very witty," he saw that since their last meeting in 1971, the Dalai Lama had again increased markedly in stature and "opened up some inner wellspring of energy and attention and intelligence," adding, "He was glorious." It seems certain that the Dalai Lama's spiritual progress during the intervening years had given him a powerful self-assurance. Though his life had been — and would continue to be — a struggle in the face of overwhelming odds, nonetheless, sustained by his ever-increasing accomplishments as a yogin, he had grown in confidence and authority. Thurman noticed this, and increasing numbers of people who came into his presence noticed it too. Here was a man who, faced with almost unbearable responsibility from a young age and forced to confront a world for which he had been completely unprepared, nevertheless remained faithful to the spiritual tradition in which he had been raised. In so doing, he found a strength more than equal to the demands of the world in which he now began to move.

That said, this first visit to the United States was a low-key affair, its organization sometimes verging on the chaotic, the flights mostly economy class and the security arrangements less than confidence inspiring. To the alarm of one volunteer, the notional commander of the security detail at one event "intimated that he would be 'packing heat' . . . To call him amateurish would have been a compliment."

Besides visiting many of the country's most famous landmarks, including Thomas Jefferson's Monticello estate, the Dalai Lama also gave teachings at the Buddhist center established by Geshe Wangyal, the CIA's interpreter monk. Among his academic engagements were talks at both Amherst College and Harvard University, where he disarmed and delighted his audiences as he apologized for needing "a walking stick for [his] broken English." Only at the University of Washington did he encounter any opposition, when a number of Maoist students in the audience started yelling at the Dalai Lama.

An important follow-up to this first trip to the United States was the subsequent issue of a compilation of several of the Dalai Lama's talks, published under the title *Kindness, Clarity, and Insight,* edited by Jeffrey Hopkins, who had translated for the Dalai Lama throughout the visit. This was to become the first of dozens of such books. More than anything else, though, the American visit showed the Dalai Lama that while his audiences were sympathetic to the Tibetan cause, they were hungry above all for spiritual and moral guidance. Understanding what Trijang Rinpoché had described as the "lack of spiritual depth" of most Westerners, the Dalai Lama was struck by the climate of "competitiveness" and "insecurity," in which "many people appear[ed] able to show their true feelings only to their cats and dogs." He was also struck by the enthusiasm of the young for what he had to say on a wide variety of topics, not just Buddhism but also "cosmology and modern physics" and questions having to do with "sex and morality." He began to see that, quite apart from acting as a "free spokesman" for Tibet, he might have something to contribute to a people grown apart from their own religious tradition.

The enthusiasm shown toward the exiled Tibetan leader both in the United States and in the USSR's Buddhist territories was not lost on the Chinese, yet it seems they were genuinely confident that what the exile community's missions — which had meanwhile left for Tibet — discovered would persuade the Dalai Lama to go back and, in due course, take up a position within the Chinese administration of his country. It is conceivable that Deng saw the Precious Protector as a future ally in the quest for China's emergence on the world stage. Yet on his return from Tibet, Lobsang Samten could report nothing to assuage the Dalai Lama's fear that, should he go back, he would again be a mere puppet of the central government, while his people continued to suffer discrimination and harassment, their religion disastrously curtailed by the state. Recalling the conditions the first delegation found, Lobsang Samten spoke of the team's intense sorrow: "We were very upset. We were so proud of our people . . . their strength was so encouraging. But it was also very sad. Their poverty was extreme. Most were just in rags, like beggars."

On returning to Dharamsala, carrying many hundreds of letters, the team members were able to give the first comprehensive review of conditions in "China's Tibet." Everywhere they traveled they were greeted by crowds of people, many of them in tears, lamenting their miserable conditions and asking for news of the Dalai Lama. It was clear that Tibetans had become second-class citizens in their own country, that education and health care for Tibetans was poor or nonexistent, and, worst of all, that religion had been all but destroyed. Hardly a single monastery, out of a total estimated at around six thousand, had escaped unscathed. The Three Seats stood in utter ruination, Ganden reduced to a bombed-out hulk.* The Jokhang too had been despoiled.† Both the Potala and the Norbulingka had been robbed of many of their treasures — even though the Potala was protected during the Cultural Revolution, allegedly on the orders of Zhou Enlai. The entire religious establishment had been laid waste, while many structures bore evidence of desecration, the better to inflame the people: temples used in some cases for storing grain, in others even as slaughterhouses.

It was true that some new towns had been erected — consisting almost entirely of Brutalist block buildings — but these were in any case mostly occupied by Chinese settlers. In Tashikiel, for example, the quarter where the Tibetans lived was "little better than an open grave. Its buildings were in total disrepair, its streets muddy and impassable." The people lived in "dark, decaying rooms with barely any furniture or utensils and no running water and only intermittent electricity."

The Dalai Lama was horrified. This was even worse than he had feared. And yet, rather than publicize the delegation's findings, he concluded that the government in exile should continue with plans already in hand to send a further four teams into Tibet.

As it turned out, the second delegation arrived in Tibet shortly before the arrival of Chinese Communist Party secretary general Hu Yaobang, who headed the highest-ranking central government delegation Tibet had seen in thirty years. Evidently he was himself disturbed by what he found. "We feel that our Party has let the Tibetan people down. We feel bad!" he exclaimed,

---

* It was not aerial bomb damage, however, but destruction by artillery fire.

† I saw evidence of this with my own eyes when visiting the Jokhang in April 1988. Giving my tour party's guide the slip, I wandered through its chambers. All were completely empty, their floors swept clean, and on the wall of an upstairs chapel I saw a large hammer and sickle, quite well executed in red paint, superimposed on an ancient fresco.

apparently weeping, in a major speech. Following this, and presumably as a gesture of good faith, the local leader of the Tibet Autonomous Region's Revolutionary Workers' Committee (effectively the party-appointed governor) was removed from his post. Furthermore, it was announced that a large percentage of government cadres would be returned home. Hu subsequently promulgated a new six-point plan for the development of Tibet, which included a tax holiday for farmers and disbanding of the hated (and woefully inefficient) farm collectives. But though welcomed by the people, Hu's initiative was resented by many party cadres. As a result, its implementation was slow and patchy. Tibet was seen as a punishment posting with little attraction for Chinese government officials. As a result, those who took positions there tended to be the less able, the less well educated, and the most open to financial inducement. It is not hard to imagine that more than a few were tyrants in their particular locale. In any case, Hu's proposed reforms threatened them all and were deeply resented.

It has often been suggested that hosting these delegations from the exile community was a public relations disaster for the Chinese, but this is not straightforwardly true. It is clear that the Chinese were hopeful that, after being shown the advances made in Tibet over the past two decades, as well as the irreversibility of the changes, the delegates would advise the Dalai Lama that he should return. Indeed, it seems the Chinese were genuinely concerned that the Dalai Lama's delegates, whom they saw as former "feudal overlords," might be given a hostile reception by the masses. But while it was true that people climbed on the roofs of the cars in which the delegates traveled, this was in hope not of visiting physical violence on them but of obtaining a vicarious blessing from the Dalai Lama.

The fact that what each of the delegations found was a deeply traumatized and largely impoverished people watching helplessly as the large majority of jobs went to Chinese immigrants, while Tibetan children were not even allowed to learn their own language in such schools as there were, suggested to the Dalai Lama that what Mao had ultimately intended was the complete destruction of Tibetan identity. Yet China's apparent willingness to break with the past and to improve the lot of its people, including the Tibetans, presented the Precious Protector with a genuine dilemma. It seemed indeed that the Beijing government had been kept largely ignorant of what had been going on in Tibet these past twenty years, relying to a large degree on inaccurate and self-serving reports. Now, however, it looked as if there was a willingness to treat Tibet more fairly. Given this, and given his wish, deeply felt, to visit his people, the Dalai Lama announced that, all being well, he would do so sometime in 1985.

In the meantime, a second long visit to the United States, during the summer of 1981, further underscored the Dalai Lama's estimation of the spiritual crisis in the West. Besides teaching at a number of different Buddhist centers, the Dalai Lama conferred his first Kalachakra initiation in America on 1,200 mostly young seekers in a field outside Madison, Wisconsin. This was only appropriate, given that the Dalai Lama "had immersed himself in the study and practise of [the] visionary world" of the Kalachakra tantra for a great many years now. Notwithstanding its apocalyptic imagery, he was convinced that promulgating the tantra worldwide could have a positive impact on the cause of universal peace.

The event in Madison caused some local officials to fear they might end up with a Woodstock-style hippie free-for-all on their hands. And it did indeed inspire some responses (for example, June Millington's jazz-funk composition "When Wrong Is Right") that might have raised eyebrows among the more conservative authorities. But on the whole, the event was well received. Attendees appreciated the fact that, while those wishing to take up Kalachakra practice seriously were now initiated into a system that might take half a lifetime of assiduous practice to master, the Dalai Lama made available a daily "six session yoga" for those who could not fit the full practice into their schedule. And for those who merely wanted to attend out of curiosity, there was no obligation to undertake any of the practices at all. This is not always the case. On some occasions the obligations imposed on initiates are quite onerous. The requirement to recite a given mantra one hundred thousand times is by no means rare.

The other major event of this visit to the United States was a series of talks the Dalai Lama gave at Harvard University, subsequently published as *The Buddhist Path to Peace.* Although to some, the Dalai Lama seemed, in the words of Pico Iyer, "like a figure from another planet," and the complexity of his exposition of basic Buddhist principles consisted largely of "philosophical discourses almost none . . . could follow," the main message of the talks — that there can be no world peace in the absence of inner peace — struck a chord. On the one hand, the Dalai Lama showed that peace is the responsibility not so much of governments as of individuals. On the other, he made clear that those who perpetrate violence must take responsibility for their actions, a message that resonated powerfully with his audience.

There was, however, a moment during this trip when the Dalai Lama might have seemed to court controversy. One of the Buddhist centers at which he gave teachings was the Naropa Institute at Boulder, Colorado, the foundation of the popular but eccentric Chogyam Trungpa. Although he doubtless knew that Trungpa had his critics, it is uncertain whether the Dalai Lama was aware of the recent scandal at Naropa. As a self-proclaimed practitioner of so-called Crazy Wisdom, Trungpa modeled his teaching style on the fifteenth-century Kagyu master Drukpa Kunley. Besides having, like Trijang Rinpoché, a genius for spontaneous religious poetry, Drukpa Kunley was also an enthusiastic flute player, *chang* drinker, and fornicator who fathered many children, one of them on a fifteen-year-old nun. But while such behavior may seem extraordinary to the outsider, the antinomian antics of some of the greatest tantric adepts, or *mahasiddi,* are an important and cherished part of the Tibetan tradition. Correctly understood, the shocking behavior of these holy madmen is but the illusory sport, designed to instruct, of a fully enlightened being.

Trungpa had a devoted following, which included, among other well-known figures, Allen Ginsberg. With Trungpa's encouragement, Ginsberg had been a co-founder of the Jack Kerouac School of Disembodied Poetics, whose creative writing program was — as it remains — a key part of the Naropa curriculum.

Ginsberg himself was away when the incident — memorialized in a private-circulation book, *The Great Naropa Poetry Wars* — occurred. At a Halloween party, Trungpa, drunk, ordered all present to strip naked. When W. S. Merwin, a visiting poet, and his new wife refused to join in and returned to their room, the master ordered his bodyguards to bring them back. The guards began to batter the door down. As Merwin recalled: "I was not going to go peacefully. I started hitting people with beer bottles . . . It was a very violent scene." But the bodyguards were too much for him, and the reluctant couple were led back and forcibly undressed.

The incident came to the attention of the national press. One commentator claimed to see an incipient fascism not just in the guru's leadership but in the dharma generally. Coming to Trungpa's defense, Ginsberg argued that the Tibetan teacher was infallible and that this was a lesson whose meaning had not yet become clear.*

The fact that the Dalai Lama visited only a year after the scandal broke suggests either that he was ignorant of what had occurred or that he knew and was prepared to lend his name to Trungpa's center nonetheless. There is no record of any kind of public reprimand from the Dalai Lama. Yet to look for such a reprimand would be to misunderstand the tradition. Because the individual lama is under no authority but his own, a public rebuke by another lama would be an unjustifiable assumption of superiority. Furthermore, given that teachers' spiritual attainments are known only to themselves, to rebuke would be to call these attainments into question. Within the spiritual sphere, the Dalai Lama's authority is moral rather than juridical. That his personal fidelity to the *vinaya,* or monastic code, is exemplary is itself a rebuke to those who flout it. And while not denying the possibility of genuine *siddi* — the exercise of magical power — the Dalai Lama has often referred to the standard test for determining whether an individual lama is sufficiently qualified to engage in these practices: such a person should be able to eat a portion of wholesome food or a portion of excrement with equal indifference. When asked how many people there might be capable of passing this test, he invariably replies by saying that, to the best of his knowledge, at present there are "none."

It was during this, his second long visit to America, that the Dalai Lama began to articulate some of his most appealing insights. Declaring that "happiness comes from within" and that "the purpose of religion is not for arguing," he explained that, beyond any considerations of creed or philosophy, ultimately his religion was "kindness." This resonated powerfully with the many

---

* The late Sogyal Rinpoché, putative author of the multimillion-selling *Tibetan Art of Living and Dying,* is a more recent example of a popular lama falling afoul of that prejudice which favors outward behavior measuring up to claimed inner disposition.

who sought a meaningful inner life without the trappings or commitments of religion, and from now on, the Dalai Lama's simple message of dogma-free spirituality was to be the cornerstone of his ministry to the wider world.

Returning from America to India, the Dalai Lama traveled immediately to Dharamsala to see his mother. The *gyalyum chenmo* had been in slow decline following a stroke several years earlier and was clearly nearing the end of her life. As his sister recalled, on a visit to his mother's bedside, the Dalai Lama "talked to her, just like a little boy coming home . . . He gently told her not to be afraid of dying, but to concentrate on the *thangkas* and say the *mani* prayers." It cannot have been a surprise when, just a short while later in Bodh Gaya, news reached him of her death. Naturally it saddened him. Apart from brief separations, they had been close throughout his adult life, and until recently, she would often send bread and pastry, baked in the Amdo style, up to the Dalai Lama's residence. Yet as he himself admitted, it was the death later that same year of his attendant, Ponpo*, that affected him the more deeply. It was Ponpo whose mole the infant Dalai Lama had sucked for comfort and who had mothered him, during his time at Kumbum, in a way more tenderly than even the *gyalyum chenmo* had been able to — even if, as he so often tells audiences, it was his mother who first introduced him to the meaning of the word "compassion."

As was only to be expected, middle age brought with it increasing numbers of separations. A third came right at the end of 1981, when Trijang Rinpoché also "manifested the act of passing away." Although, following the break with Shugden, the Dalai Lama was not as close to his junior tutor as he had been, the bond between them was by no means broken. When the Dalai Lama heard of his guru's illness, his first act on returning home from giving teachings in Sikkim was to pay the sick man a visit and to ask him "to remain in this world for the welfare of living beings." The Precious Protector was again among the first to pay his respects when, having spent two days in meditation on the "clear light of death," the master abandoned earthly life.

If the passing of his mother, Lobsang Jinpa, and Trijang Rinpoché signaled the beginning of the end of an era, the continued liberalization taking place in

* His real name was Lobsang Jinpa. Ponpo, his nickname, means "the Boss."

Communist China just as clearly signaled the start of a new one. When, during the spring of 1982, a quartet of high-ranking Tibetan government in exile officials traveled to Beijing for what promised to be substantive discussions, all realized that they would soon know how far the party's commitment to reform would go with respect to the Land of Snows.

In accordance with the Dalai Lama's wishes, the officials boldly proposed that from now on, Tibet, as an administrative entity, should include not just the so-called Tibet Autonomous Region but also Kham and Amdo. Second, they proposed that Tibet be granted equivalent status to that proposed for Hong Kong, which would return to Beijing's control when its lease to Great Britain expired in 1997. Tibet would thereby enjoy genuine autonomy through the principle of "one country, two systems."*

The Chinese flatly rejected both proposals. The first, they said, was unrealistic, given that Kham and Amdo had long been subsumed variously within Sichuan, Qinghai, Gansu, and Yunnan provinces. The second suggestion implied a much higher status for Tibet than was plausible, given the fact that it was an economic backwater. Hong Kong was a major trading entity in its own right. Instead the delegation should refer to the five-point plan issued earlier by Hu Yaobang as the basis for any discussion.

Clearly, the Chinese had no interest in any claims made by or on behalf of the government in exile. Only the Dalai Lama's status and future role were up for discussion. It is true that, in former times, a key aspect of the question of Tibet's status with respect to China was the question of the Dalai Lama's status with respect to the emperor. Would the emperor leave his throne and greet the Dalai Lama outside the palace? Must the Dalai Lama kowtow to the emperor? Did the emperor treat the Dalai Lama as a vassal or recognize his authority? Yet having already abandoned any thought of restoring the old system and by fully embracing democracy, the Precious Protector conceived of his role quite differently. Above all, his concern was to serve the Tibetan people as a whole,

* This is the constitutional principle formulated by Deng Xiaoping whereby the former independent Chinese polities (Hong Kong, Macao, and, it was assumed, in due course Taiwan) would retain a large measure of independence following reunification with the Motherland.

not just those living in what China called the Tibet Autonomous Region — effectively just the central and western provinces.

It was this re-envisioning of the role of the Dalai Lama that lay behind his insistence that, henceforth, the three provinces be treated as a single entity. Historically, Lhasa's ability to assert control over and raise taxes from the provinces was distinctly limited. By embracing the non-Gelug schools, however, he had created the conceptual space for a type of leadership that transcended the divisions of the past. The recent exaltation of the Lotus-Born and repudiation of Shugden by the Dalai Lama should thus not be seen as an eccentric throwback to an arcane and irrelevant aspect of Tibetan culture. Instead it was a bold move to break with a narrow, inward-looking metaphysics of government and repurpose it to serve all Tibetans, irrespective of region or religious affiliation. The Dalai Lama had instigated a revolution of his own.

It was during the impasse that followed the meeting of the Dalai Lama's embassy to Beijing that Ling Rinpoché suffered a serious stroke. The previous year, the Precious Tutor had undertaken an arduous tour of America and Europe. Exhorting his Tibetan audiences to remain united in friendship, regardless of regional or doctrinal differences, Ling Rinpoché had used his own — immense — prestige to consolidate this reorientation of the Dalai Lama's role away from narrow concern for the Gelug tradition and its government of Tibet toward a much wider role.

News of Ling Rinpoché's illness reached the Precious Protector while he was on a trip to Switzerland. As he wrote later, the Dalai Lama was at first "tormented with fear" that he would not be able to cope should "the Precious Tutor [show] the act of entering nirvana." On his return to Dharamsala, the Dalai Lama's first act was to visit Ling Rinpoché. He went back many times over the next three months. Sometimes the Precious Tutor showed signs of improvement, and sometimes he appeared to get worse. By the time the Dalai Lama left for Bodh Gaya in December, he was "almost ... used to this awful situation." Thus, when he heard that Ling Rinpoché had entered *tukdam* on December 25, "the earlier fear of not being able to bear the separation was not so strong." In retrospect, the Dalai Lama was convinced that this "taking on" of illness was a deliberate act of generosity on the part of the Precious Tutor, to enable his pupil to become used to the idea of being without the "rock" on which he had leaned his whole adult life.

Clinically speaking, Ling Rinpoché was dead. Yet from the perspective of the Tibetan tradition, the mind stream of the most advanced practitioners does not leave the body at once. Sensing the approach of death, the master begins the prescribed meditation practices and enters a state of mental equipoise such that when the body ceases to function, the mind is absorbed in the clear light held to be the most subtle level of consciousness. This is *tukdam,* wherein the practitioner passes from the earthly realm in what the Western tradition describes as "the odor of sanctity." At the moment of death, the room may be filled with a pleasant smell, sometimes lingering for days, while the body remains for a time incorrupt.* In Ling Rinpoché's case, at precisely the moment when he entered *tukdam,* his attendant and several others also clearly heard the sound of bells and a *damaru* drum.

It was not until half past six in the morning of the eighth day that definitive signs of the Precious Tutor's final passing announced themselves. According to the Dalai Lama's own account, there was a snowstorm with snowflakes in the shape of flowers, and much thunder. During this time the Precious Tutor left his meditation.

> As a sign of this a little urine seeped from his *vajra,* and his complexion changed. However, there was still some warmth on his vest around the chest area, and so the ceremonial washing of the body was postponed for that day. On the seventh at around eleven o'clock, more urine was emitted, and a few tears came from his eyes. At four o'clock the washing ceremony was performed.

The Dalai Lama does not mention post-mortem practices other than the washing and then the salting rituals. Partaking of the body of those masters considered to be enlightened beings who have taken earthly form seven times

* Saints Teresa of Ávila (1515–1582) and, more recently, Thérèse of Lisieux (1873–1897) are well-attested examples.

is held to be effective means of attaining higher realization. To this end, bodily matter may be cut from the corpse for later consumption in the form of so-called "precious pills."* Some of the liquid in which the corpse is washed may also be drunk as a sacrament.

That Ling Rinpoché was a master in the highest degree is in no doubt from the perspective of those closest to him. A fellow adept spoke of how on occasion the Precious Tutor appeared to him in a vision "with a head, nose and so forth that was extraordinarily bright," adding that "behind his ears [were] two small horns radiating blue light . . . with decorations [of] small tongue-like wall hangings." And it was noted by the Dalai Lama himself that "even Palden Lhamo, mistress of the desire realm, could not compete with this great master and had to comply with his wishes." Ling Rinpoché was, or so it seemed to those who knew him best, the veritable manifestation of a fully enlightened being.

Whether or not we accept the truth of this claim, it is undeniable that the senior tutor was the handmaid of the Dalai Lama's role as global teacher of the Buddhadharma. It was out of gratitude to his guru that the Dalai Lama would use his position to make available what he himself had been taught to all who sought it.

If, in fulfilling this role bequeathed to him by Ling Rinpoché, the Dalai Lama was able also to act as a "free spokesman," as he put it, for the people of Tibet, that was to be welcomed. But his reading of the global situation persuaded him that confronting China directly would not succeed. Still less was violence a plausible solution. In view of this, he became increasingly convinced that Tibetans should abandon their claim to complete independence. What mattered was the welfare and happiness of all Tibetans. If his people's happiness could be secured with Tibet as an administrative entity within the People's Republic of China — if, that is, they could enjoy freedom of religion,

---

* This practice is *sKye bdun sgrub pa,* literally "accumulating for the seventh rebirth." While at first sight shocking, it is important to recognize that theophagy — the sacramental eating of a god — lies at the heart of Christian practice: Catholic Christians believe that, in Holy Communion, they too are actually eating the very flesh and drinking the very blood of Jesus, albeit that their outward form of body and blood has changed to those of bread and wine.

association, and speech, and if their material needs were met — he would, as he put it, have "no point to argue." It made sense, therefore, to ignore China's recent rebuff and take Deng Xiaoping at his word. If "anything" could be discussed except independence, he would drop the call for *rangzen* (independence) and adopt instead *umaylam* — a middle-way approach between reaction and surrender.

PART IV

Bodhisattva of Compassion

19

Cutting Off the Serpent's Head: Reaction and Repression in Tibet

Over the decades since the Dalai Lama's first trip to America in 1979, he has made well over four hundred separate visits to foreign countries to teach, to lecture, and to preach. Despite this, only occasionally has he visited a country more than once during the course of a year. What is more, almost invariably these trips have been undertaken at the invitation of a third party, usually a Buddhist group. The only exceptions to this rule have been the occasional private visits for medical purposes or to collect an award. Similarly, he has rarely stayed as a guest in a private house, though he describes one exception in his book *Ethics for the New Millennium.* On this occasion, as he discloses in a disarming confession, he learned an important lesson when, as he was visiting the bathroom, his curiosity got the better of him. Peeking inside a cupboard, he looked through the medicines he found there. To his surprise, he saw that these included antidepressants — and yet this was the house of an exceptionally wealthy family. Evidently wealth and well-being did not always go hand in hand.

When the Dalai Lama makes an overseas trip, it is usual for his hosts to be instructed to book modest accommodations, and, certainly during the earlier visits, this was the rule. During the 1980s, he would travel with a considerably smaller entourage than later, perhaps half a dozen strong, compared with a dozen more recently. Typically this would include two personal attendants, a secretary, two or three security men, and one or two government in exile officials. In recent years, more security has been involved and, on longer trips, more personal attendants. Often, of late, he has also been accompanied by a diarist, the Englishman Jeremy Russell; it is he who compiles the daily reports for the Dalai Lama's (English-language) website.

Of all these overseas trips, only one could be described as a vacation in the accepted sense of the word. This was a ten-day trip to Austria and Switzerland in 1983. After meeting with a small group of scientists in the Tyrolean mountain resort of Alpbach, the Dalai Lama was persuaded to spend a few days sightseeing in Switzerland. It is worth mentioning in this context Trijang Rinpoché's delight on a trip of his own to Switzerland when he witnessed a fireworks display over Lake Geneva. He wrote subsequently that "seeing flowers of every colour appear and fall like sparkling rain from space really helped improve the way I visualized the emission and dissolution of light and the purifying rain of nectar during my daily practices." There is no record of the Dalai Lama's seeing fireworks at Lake Geneva, but it is certain that he himself undertakes just such visualization practices on a daily basis, even when traveling.*

The visit to Alpbach itself brought the Dalai Lama together for the first time with the Chilean biologist and philosopher Francisco Varela. A student of the wayward lama Choegyam Trungpa, Varela was subsequently credited with being the founding father of neuro-phenomenology, a branch of science he described as taking a pragmatic approach to the "hard question" of consciousness. They became friends at once, both agreeing that science and Buddhism were, in essence, entirely compatible methodologies designed to solve the same problem of improving the quality of life for all beings. Before

* I have often thought that a biopic — possibly even an autobiopic — using computer-generated imagery to re-create some of these experiences would be an outstanding way to gain insight of the Dalai Lama's spiritual life.

the gathering was over, the forty-eight-year-old Tibetan, as eager as ever to learn, invited Varela to Dharamsala to initiate him into the mysteries of neuroscience, then Varela's principal area of research. The two subsequently met on many occasions through the Mind and Life Institute, which they co-founded in 1991. Varela died in 2001, but the Dalai Lama keeps a photograph of him on his desk to this day, while the institute itself has become a flourishing multinational forum. Bringing scientists and meditators ("contemplatives") together to study, it researches, among other things, whether Buddhist meditation techniques could benefit society as a whole and, if so, how they might be taught in a secular environment. A major component of the Dalai Lama's efforts to reach out to the scientific community, the Mind and Life Institute has attracted some of the great names in science, including two Nobel laureates: Daniel Kahneman, the Israeli economist and psychologist, and Yuan Tseh Lee, the Taiwanese chemist. Also associated with the institute are world-renowned psychologists Jon Kabat Zin and Daniel Goleman, both of them leaders in the field, who have contributed significantly to the exponential growth of interest in secularized Buddhist meditation techniques associated with the mindfulness movement. The work of neuroscientist Richie Davidson should also be mentioned in this context. Indeed, there have been rich collaborations for many, even if one skeptical early participant quipped that "Buddhist psychology takes people who think they're somebody and helps them understand they're nobody; Western psychology takes people who think they are nobody and helps them understand they're somebody."

From the start, the Dalai Lama found it easier to meet with scientists sympathetic to his ideas than to meet with sympathetic politicians. Although he personally made no special effort to do so, his various representatives abroad did their utmost to develop support for the Tibetan claim to independence — despite the fact that the Dalai Lama himself was moving away from this as a goal. One regular attendee at the press conferences his representatives invariably organized when he arrived in a foreign country recalled how, even in New York City, these were "almost deserted" during the 1980s. And on those occasions when meetings with journalists and others were well attended, there were some embarrassing misconceptions about what the Dalai Lama actually stood for. On an early visit to the United States, a business CEO asked him whether he felt "closer to John Lennon the dreamer, or to Gandhi the politician." The Dalai Lama had never heard of Lennon, and as for dreaming, for him this was not something one did to little or no purpose. More than once, too, he was brought to tears by someone in the audience asking him what was the "quickest, easiest, cheapest" way to attain Enlightenment.

Nonetheless, in spite of these occasional misunderstandings, and in spite of the lack of overt interest in Tibet among politicians, small coalitions of influential supporters did begin to emerge in America and in Europe. At this stage, few people outside Buddhist circles knew much about Tibet. Political support in America at first came as much from Republicans, such as the notoriously right-wing Jesse Helms, and social conservatives, such as *New York Times* editor turned columnist Abe Rosenthal (whose epitaph proclaims that "he kept the paper straight"), as from Democrats. For the right, Tibet was a stick with which to beat the Communist Chinese, a popular stance under the Reagan administration. The Dalai Lama's hoped-for 1985 visit to Tibet not having taken place, that summer ninety-one members of the U.S. Congress wrote an open letter to the Chinese president urging the Communist Party to enter into meaningful negotiations with the Tibetan government in exile. When the Chinese denounced the letter, it was this disparate group of supporters who encouraged the Dalai Lama to follow up their initiative with what became known as his "Five Point Peace Plan for the Future of Tibet."

Invited to address the Congressional Human Rights Caucus in Washington during the fall of 1987, coincidentally at the very moment when Gyalo Thondup arrived in Beijing on business, the Dalai Lama called first for the transformation of the whole of Tibet into what he described as a "zone of peace," whereby his homeland would be completely demilitarized. The Dalai Lama's second proposal was that the Chinese government halt its population transfer policy, whereby large numbers of non-Tibetans were "threatening the very existence of the Tibetans as a distinct people." Instead, his third point, their fundamental human rights should be respected and democratic freedom for Tibetans implemented. Fourth, the natural environment of Tibet—devastated since the Chinese occupation—should be restored, and in particular, the Chinese should desist both from developing nuclear weapons and from dumping nuclear waste in Tibet. Finally, he said, now was the time for "earnest negotiations" on the future status of Tibet and of "relations between the Tibetan and Chinese peoples."

Significantly, there was no mention of independence. Nonetheless, as the Dalai Lama must have feared, the party leadership in Beijing immediately rejected the plan. The Chinese were also pained that Gyalo Thondup had informed them that the Dalai Lama's visit to Washington would be of no importance. Either he had lied, or, if he had been telling the truth and had no foreknowledge of the speech to Congress, he must not be as close to the Dalai Lama and the exile government as he claimed.

But what shocked both sides was the violent protest that erupted in Lhasa the following week. On September 27, a party of monks from one of the Three Seats appeared in Lhasa carrying a Tibetan flag and proceeded to circumambulate the Jokhang Temple, shouting slogans and calling for self-rule (*rangzen* in Tibetan). The monks were quickly arrested and beaten. Four days later — significantly, on China's national day — another group of monks from Sera staged a second demonstration. This was joined by a number of laypeople. Again the demonstrators were rounded up and beaten by police. But as the morning wore on, a large crowd gathered outside the police station where the demonstrators had been detained, demanding their release. A confrontation developed, the outcome of which was that the crowd stormed the station, setting it on fire and freeing the detainees. One of the monk protesters, badly burned in the flames, was carried aloft in front of the crowd, which, further enraged, began pelting the police with stones. In response, law enforcement officers now in position on the roofs of adjacent buildings began to shoot. Up to ten demonstrators were killed.

The Chinese immediately claimed that the Dalai Lama personally was behind the protests. It is conceivable that Dharamsala had alerted some of its contacts inside Tibet that the Dalai Lama would deliver an important speech during his trip to the United States. It seems likely that the Indian government had been informed that something was in the offing, given that, whereas up until now an Indian official had always accompanied the Dalai Lama on his trips abroad, on this occasion he went unaccompanied. So at least some people knew in advance that the Dalai Lama was poised to make an important declaration. Yet, given his attitude toward violence, and in light of the certainty that any protest, however peaceful, would itself be met with violence, it is not credible that he would have issued any such orders.

International coverage of the event nonetheless meant that China was forced to take seriously the resentment to which the riots bore testimony. At once a split arose between those party officials who felt that liberalization in Tibet had gone too far and those who countered that the authorities had "divorced [them]selves from the masses and harmed them." There were calls by the conservative faction to cancel the Great Prayer Festival due to be held the following March, its revival having been recently permitted by the Chinese. Surprisingly, these calls were met with support among the older monks at the Three Seats, fearful that they would not be able to control the younger generation. Yet it was the Chinese head of the Tibet Autonomous Region who insisted that, just as he had attended the previous festival—wearing Tibetan dress—he would do so again. Foreign journalists had been invited, and it would be an embarrassing admission that he was not in control of the situation if the event were to be canceled. In the meantime, as a gesture of reconciliation, the Panchen Lama was sent on a mission to the three major monasteries with news of a generous benefaction from the government. Furthermore, all but a handful of those detained following the late September disturbances were released.

Realizing that the Chinese planned to use the 1988 Monlam Festival in Lhasa as propaganda to demonstrate that local reforms were working, many monks boycotted the proceedings. It was not until the last day that there was any trouble. When the statue of Maitreya, the Buddha to come, was being paraded around the Barkor (the pilgrim's route around the Jokhang Temple), there was a sudden call from one of the participating monks for the release of the remainder of his colleagues still being held since the demonstration the previous fall. When ordered to desist, he was immediately joined by others who shouted pro-independence slogans. Within minutes, a riot was in full swing. The disturbance, involving several thousand people, both lay and monastic, lasted the whole day. A number of police vehicles were overturned and set ablaze, and several shops were set on fire, while the crowd pelted the police with stones. The day ended when security forces stormed the Jokhang Temple, killing, according to Tibetan and foreign eyewitnesses, more than twenty unarmed demonstrators, including a twelve-year-old boy. (Chinese sources claim there were just three casualties — one of them a policeman who had been hiding in a toilet and whose killing in cold blood was independently verified.) The scale of the rioting far exceeded anything that had been seen the previous year.

It was against this background of unrest that the Dalai Lama delivered a second public and again overtly political message to China from another foreign capital. In his "Strasbourg Statement" of June 1988, he gave a clarification and reaffirmation of the Five Point Peace Plan but this time with what appeared to be an explicit modification of his earlier position with regard to independence. Now, he declared, "the whole of Tibet . . . should become a self-governing democratic entity . . . in association with the People's Republic of China."

At first sight, inclusion of the phrase "in association with the People's Republic of China" looked intended to reassure Beijing that the Dalai Lama was willing not merely to pay lip service to giving up the idea of Tibet as an independent country, but actually to give China a recognized role in the governance of Tibet. This time, the Dalai Lama's initiative was not rejected out of hand — at least not by the Chinese. Instead, it provoked a hostile reaction within some Tibetan circles. The Dalai Lama's own eldest brother, Jigme Norbu, by now a respected academic at Indiana University, circulated a letter among the exile community urging his fellow exiles to reject the proposal. The head of the refugee Tibetan Youth Congress likewise denounced the proposal — though he later claimed that he had been encouraged to do so by the Dalai Lama himself. Some have taken this to mean that the Dalai Lama wanted to show the Chinese that he was willing to take on the hard-liners within his own community. In any case, the Tibetan Youth Congress remains to this day opposed to the Dalai Lama's policy of not seeking independence for Tibet. If, therefore, there is doubt as to how hostile some of the reaction really was, there can be no doubt that a great many did see the Strasbourg Statement as a sellout.

When, after some weeks' deliberation, the Chinese again rejected the Dalai Lama's proposal, it was on the grounds that the statement was simply a covert bid for independence: the word "association" did, after all, clearly imply co-equal status. Beijing was also displeased at the inclusion of a foreign legal expert as a member of the proposed Tibetan negotiating team.* Yet it seems that what was really at issue was the Dalai Lama's continued insistence that "Tibet" included both Kham and Amdo, and, moreover, that its people must be accorded freedoms and privileges that were not even in prospect for the domestic population of China. From the Chinese perspective, neither demand seemed remotely realistic.

News of this latest rejection only added to the resentment that had manifested itself in the violent demonstrations of the preceding two years. On International Human Rights Day in December 1988, a demonstration led by monks won immediate support from bystanders in Lhasa. Despite the fact that the demonstrators were unarmed and orderly, two were summarily shot, while a European bystander was also injured. Subsequently, a trial of those deemed to have been the ringleaders was swiftly arranged and deterrent sentences were handed out, including several for life imprisonment and more than one of execution (though in fact no execution took place). In this heightened atmosphere, many Tibetans viewed the sudden and unexpected death of the Panchen Lama just seven weeks later as a politically motivated assassination. Tibet's second-most widely revered incarnation had recently given several speeches openly critical of Beijing, and it seemed certain to many that his death had been ordered as a warning to those who would deviate from the party line. It is hard to see what Beijing would gain by such a move, however. The fact that the Panchen Lama had been cruelly treated following his earlier criticism of Mao seems a far more plausible cause of his premature death aged only fifty. He was by then considerably overweight and was known to have diabetes and high blood pressure.

While Tibetans everywhere remained shocked and in sorrow, an invitation to the Dalai Lama from the official Buddhist Association of China to attend the Panchen Lama's funeral presented him with a troubling dilemma. The invitation could only have come from the very highest level of government. Moreover, it provided both sides with an uncontroversial opportunity

* This was Michael van Walt van Praag, a Belgian-born, US-based international jurist.

to meet which might otherwise have taken years of diplomacy to achieve, even if both sides were willing. And yet the Dalai Lama refused.

In his second autobiography, *Freedom in Exile,* the Dalai Lama makes clear that "personally" speaking, he "wanted to go." Whether his refusal was the decision of the Kashag — perhaps fearing that if he went he would be kidnapped or forced into making some public concession, just as Ngabo had been thirty years before — or whether it was on the advice of Nechung, or perhaps because of an intervention on the part of the Indian government, we do not know.

Yet more unrest in Lhasa broke out a few weeks later, at the turn of the Tibetan New Year, causing the authorities to ban the official celebration of the Great Prayer Festival. In spite of this, large crowds gathered on the day that Monlam was to have been celebrated, and a further three days of rioting ensued. It is unknown how many died in the subsequent crackdown, although one report puts the figure as high as several hundred, including almost a hundred monks. Then, on March 7, 1989, the Chinese authorities decreed that all foreigners residing in Lhasa must leave. The following day, martial law was enacted. It was lifted formally a year later, though it is questionable whether in any meaningful sense it has ever been lifted.

The Dalai Lama was devastated, yet he was impotent to do anything other than pray and protest to the Chinese while reminding Tibetans that any protests must be strictly nonviolent.

If the Panchen Lama's death was arguably a contributory factor in the March riots, the death a month later of Hu Yaobang led to an upheaval in China that made the Lhasa disturbances seem trivial in comparison. One of the more liberal members of the Politburo, Hu had been forced to take responsibility and resign following the anti-CCP student protests that erupted in China during 1985–86. For the six weeks following his demise, Tiananmen Square became the focus of pro-democracy/anti-government demonstrations which, at their height, attracted over a million people. At first the party leadership could come to no decision; but, fearful of the growing unrest in eastern Europe which Soviet Russia was doing nothing to combat, when the protests began to spread outside Beijing and across the whole of China, Deng finally ordered in the military on June 4. Hundreds, possibly thousands, were killed and the protest leaders arrested in a crackdown that drew fierce condemnation from around the world.

It was against this backdrop that, in October, the committee of Norwegian dignitaries responsible for the Nobel Peace Prize selected the Dalai Lama to be the recipient of the 1989 award. When the news broke, it was a joyous moment for Tibetans at home and abroad — a shaft of sunlight illuminating their benighted land, a vindication of their story, a harbinger of the restoration they so earnestly longed for. It was, too, a matter of intense pride that *their* guru, *their* leader, *their* kinsman had been publicly acknowledged in this way. Surely China must now accept democracy, grant the Tibetan people freedom, or remain forever beyond the pale. For the Dalai Lama himself, at that moment traveling in the United States, a report broadcast on the radio suggesting he had won did, he admitted later, excite him a little. But with no further mention on the evening news, he assumed that it had been nothing more than a rumor. When the award was confirmed early the following morning, his attendants waited until after he had completed his meditation before telling him, by which time he was, he said, "no longer excited." He was, however, both surprised and pleased to hear that the prize came with some money. There was a leper colony in India to which he had long wanted to make a donation. He would also use some of the prize money to set up the Foundation for Universal Responsibility, a Delhi-based charity working mainly in education and in interfaith and peace-building projects.

With the award of the Nobel Prize, the "Tibetan issue" became, at a stroke, a global issue, and from this moment on, the Dalai Lama began his ascent to superstardom. Yet as the brutal suppression of the Tiananmen protests made clear, the conservatives within the Politburo had by now reasserted their authority. A siege mentality prevailed, and the government quickly announced its "extreme regret and indignation" concerning the award. For the Chinese, the Nobel committee selection constituted "open support for the Dalai Lama and the Tibetan separatists in their activities to undermine national unity and split China." This was nothing but a collaboration between the Dalai Lama and "hostile foreign forces."

The fall of the Berlin Wall a month later served only to deepen Chinese paranoia. In contrast, it gave the Dalai Lama an opportunity to underscore his status as a world figure by visiting the wall just days after its dismantling. It was a poignant moment for him. "As I stood there," he recalled, "in full view of a still-manned security post, an old lady silently handed me a red candle. With some emotion, I lit it, and held it up. For a moment the tiny dancing flame threatened to go out, but it held and, while a crowd pressed round me, touching my hands, I prayed that the light of compassion and awareness would fill the world and dispel the darkness of fear and oppression."

Returning home to Dharamsala, the fifty-five-year-old Dalai Lama received a rapturous welcome. Yet for him personally, perhaps an even more pleasing event at this time was news of the discovery of the reincarnation of his senior tutor, Ling Rinpoché. When, early the following year, the five-year-old came for a visit, the Dalai Lama was visibly moved. An observer noted how, as the little boy stood to leave the audience chamber, the Dalai Lama "bent down to adjust [Ling Rinpoché's] shoestrap, then stayed down, waving, smiling and blowing kisses like a loving father till the boy was out of sight."

In spite of all the publicity in the immediate aftermath of the award of the Nobel Prize, the Dalai Lama remained at this time relatively unknown both in America and beyond, at least outside Buddhist circles and human rights advocacy groups. His press conferences were better attended than they had been, but as one journalist noted, even now he had "no handlers, advance men, interpreters, press people, or travel coordinators," and he continued to be largely reliant on volunteers when overseas. As a result, the arrangements made on his behalf remained somewhat haphazard. This gave the Dalai Lama the opportunity occasionally to make impromptu changes to his schedule such as one occasion in 1991, while staying in Santa Fe. Having met with a succession of interested people, including "politicians, movie stars, New Age gurus, billionaires and Pueblo Indian leaders," the Dalai Lama announced that he would like to go up into the mountains to watch the skiing. To the consternation of those accompanying him, he insisted on taking a chairlift so that he could get as close to the action as possible. The story is recounted in a delightful article by the writer Douglas Preston.

Sitting quite relaxed, with nothing to hold onto (there was no safety bar), the Dalai Lama "spoke animatedly about everything he saw on the slopes. As he pointed and leaned forward into space [his assistant], who was gripping the arm of the chair with whitened knuckles, kept admonishing him in Tibetan . . . begging His Holiness to please sit back, hold the seat, and not lean out so much."

But the Dalai Lama would not listen.

"How fast they go!" he exclaimed. "And *children* skiing! Look at [that] little boy!" In fact, the slope in question was just a "bunny slope and the skiers weren't moving fast at all. Just then, an expert skier entered from a higher slope, whipping along. The Dalai Lama saw him and said, 'Look — too fast! He [is] going to hit [the] post!' He cupped his hands, shouting down to the oblivious skier, 'Look out for post!' He waved frantically. 'Look out for post!' The skier, who had no idea that the incarnation of the Bodhisattva of Compassion was crying out to save his life, made a crisp little check as he approached the pylon, altering his line of descent, and continued expertly down the hill. With an expostulation of wonder, the Dalai Lama sat back and clasped his hands together . . . 'Ah! This [is] a *wonderful* sport!'" adding that, in a future free Tibet, he was sure that there would be plenty of good skiing to be had.

Many of those who have had the good fortune to travel with the Dalai Lama on his overseas trips have commented on the keen interest he takes in his surroundings, the torrent of questions, his openness to talking to whosoever comes his way, the jokes — often at his own expense — the laughter and his concern for others, especially those in distress. On hearing this, it is all too easy to forget that, throughout it all, his spiritual practice — the three to four hours of meditation he engages in every morning without fail and the hour and more in the evening — remains the most important part of the Dalai Lama's day. But doubtless this is precisely what enables him both to deal with the frequent trials he has to face and to move seamlessly among the vast array of people he encounters, giving each his full attention, "as if," in Preston's words, "he shut out the rest of the world to focus his entire sympathy . . . care and interest on you" alone.* And perhaps this is the secret of his appeal. Here is someone who is manifestly authentic, someone who does exactly and in all circumstances precisely what he urges others to do — and with joy, not gravity, with generosity, never rancor, and all in a spirit of forgiveness of failure.

* Queen Elizabeth II is said to have the same ability.

From Santa Fe the Dalai Lama traveled to Washington, where, in April 1991, he was received for the first time by a serving president of the United States — at that time the elder George Bush. Significantly, their meeting did not take place in the White House itself. It nonetheless provoked a furious response from Beijing. But for the Dalai Lama, an American president was only a warm-up. Among the other world leaders he met in the afterglow of the Nobel award were Pope (now Saint) John Paul II (again), the king of Sweden, Prince Charles of the United Kingdom, and then the presidents of Ireland, Lithuania, Estonia, Bulgaria, Poland, Argentina, and Chile, followed by the prime ministers of Great Britain, Norway, Cambodia, Australia, and New Zealand. Having been a political nonentity up until that moment, with Bush's endorsement he was suddenly the man of the hour. These were heady times both for the Dalai Lama and his growing band of followers — mainly the idealistic young but also many older people who were beginning to wake to a political cause that seemed unarguable. Here was the Tibetan David standing up to the Chinese Goliath, armed only with the rhetoric of nonviolence and compassion.

Later that same year the Dalai Lama returned to New York to confer the Kalachakra initiation on a large audience in an event cosponsored by the actor Richard Gere and Tibet House.* Whether or not there was any direct causal connection between this and the momentum that now gathered behind the movement for a free Tibet is of course impossible to say. Nonetheless, there is little doubt that when he met with President Bill Clinton two years later, the Dalai Lama's campaign on behalf of the Tibetan people had reached a new phase. It was Clinton, perhaps sensing a cause that covered all the bases, who subsequently did the most of any international statesman to make the Tibetan issue a genuine matter of government policy. Indicating support for an earlier State Department report to Congress concerning the forthcoming review of China's most favored nation status, the Clinton administration moved toward endorsing "dialogue with the Dalai Lama or his representatives" as a condition of its extension.

Spiritually, too, the years immediately following the Nobel award were frenetic. There was a total of nine Kalachakra conferrals between 1989 and 1995,

---

* The event was held at Madison Square Garden.

and there were many interfaith encounters besides. In 1994, at the invitation of the World Community for Christian Meditation, the Dalai Lama spoke at a conference dedicated to the dialogue between Buddhism and Christianity. Commenting on passages drawn from the four Christian gospels, the Dalai Lama discussed both similarities and dissimilarities between the two religions. In one memorable analogy he reminded his audience that, in the quest to find common ground, it was important to bear in mind the danger of, as the Tibetan saying has it, "trying to put a yak's head on a sheep's body." Nonetheless, many people present were touched by the manifest humility of the Dalai Lama engaging with a faith tradition other than his own.

But the Chinese know, as the Romans knew, that *cunctando regior mundus:* delay rules the world. Although then less than half a century old, the Communist Party's rule draws on ancient tradition. Its leadership thinks in decades rather than in terms of the few years between presidential elections. If they were successful in turning China into an economic superpower, they understood that it would be only a matter of time before the Dalai Lama became an irrelevance. The Western powers would certainly prioritize trade over human rights. Thus, even as Tibet support groups began to spring up on university campuses around the world, and as increasing numbers of A-listers came forward to support the Dalai Lama's cause — Richard Gere had long been known for his support, but he was now joined by others such as actors Goldie Hawn and Sharon Stone, composer Philip Glass, and hip-hop artist Adam Yauch — the Politburo began planning the Third National Forum for Work in Tibet. This was a conference to be held in Beijing in July 1994 which would review policy and set out strategy into the new millennium. Its main emphasis, at least in the documents made available to the public, was economic: Tibet was a provincial dead end that must be developed. Its real focus, however, centered on fostering the "unity of the nationalities" and the territorial integrity of the Motherland. Not only was there to be no letup in the campaign to identify and root out groups and individuals with "splittist" sympathies, but now the Dalai Lama himself was to be held personally culpable for any challenges to China's claims over Tibet. The Third Forum was thus characterized above all by its unprecedented emphasis on explicitly attacking the Precious Protector, which all officials in Tibet were required to repeat whenever called upon to do so. He was not seeking justice for his people; he was intent on destroying China's territorial integrity and national unity. By internationalizing the Tibetan question, he had "bartered away his honour for Western hostile forces' patronage." People should be in no doubt: "Although sometimes Dalai speaks softly and says nice things to deceive the masses, he has never ceased his splittist activities." For this reason, the "Dalai clique" must be attacked unremittingly: "To kill a serpent, we must first cut off its head."

A further feature of the Third Forum was its focus on religion. This was in response to the fact that it was overwhelmingly members of the *sangha* who had led each of the recent protests. Of those detained following the disturbances, only a third were laypeople — doubly remarkable given the small numbers of monks and nuns now remaining in the population. This observation elicited a response typical of the secular state when confronted with religiously motivated dissent: "The purpose of Buddhism is to deliver all living creatures in a peaceful manner," but "the Dalai and his clique" had "violated the religious doctrine . . . to fool and incite one people against the other," using "godly strength to poison and bewitch the masses," incorporating "Tibetan independence" in his sermons. "Such flagrant deceptiveness and demagoguery constitute a blasphemy to Buddhism."

To counter the Dalai Lama's subversive message, it would be necessary to ensure that all those in positions of authority in Tibet disavow the Precious Protector. All political figures and dignitaries, and all monks and nuns, had to repeat or endorse in writing four sentences explicitly denouncing "the Dalai." No one in public employment could any longer erect an altar in their home, and, within two years, there was a ban on displaying or even possessing pictures of the Dalai Lama, while all Tibetan students were prohibited from visiting monasteries or attending any kind of religious ceremony. It was vital that young people should keep before them a proper understanding of the misery of the masses before liberation. They should be in no doubt about the sources of past suffering and the conditions of present happiness.

The immediate consequence of these new policies announced by the Third Forum was another wave of protests that erupted over the winter of 1994–95.

In that they were again largely led by members of the *sangha,* these were similar to those that had occurred earlier. But there were two important differences. Whereas before the protests were confined to Lhasa, now they spread to outlying regions. And while earlier the monasteries involved in dissent were invariably Gelugpa foundations, now it was evident that the other sects were also involved. This made clear that the Dalai Lama's own policy of openness to all schools within the Tibetan tradition had found support outside circles habitually loyal to him. In the past, the Chinese might have expected the non-Gelug monasteries not to follow the Precious Protector's lead. But no longer.

Further confirmation of the success of the Dalai Lama's efforts at conciliation between the different elements of Tibetan society came during the selection process of the new Panchen Lama. By convention it falls to the Dalai Lama to oversee the procedure, should he be of age. Similarly, the Panchen Rinpoché is, theoretically at least, consulted during the selection of the Dalai Lama (as indeed happened during the search for the present incarnation, although in this case his involvement was limited — on account of the fact that the Panchen Lama died before the process was complete). Selection of the new Panchen Lama (whom the Chinese would doubtless seek to influence) was of critical importance given there was every likelihood that he would play a major role in the selection of the next Dalai Lama.

In light of the historic rivalry between the two sees, it would not have been wholly surprising if the authorities at Tashilhunpo had turned to the Chinese (who had lately provided the monastery with a generous benefaction), rather than to Dharamsala, for assistance in the process. For their part, the Chinese had their own understanding of correct procedure. This involved deployment of the *ser bumba,* the hated Golden Urn. Imposed on Tibet by Qianlong, Qing emperor of China during the late eighteenth century, this was the protocol whereby the final selection of the highest incarnations was to be confirmed by a so-called Divine Lottery whereby the names of rival candidates were to be written on ivory tablets in Tibetan, Manchu, and Mandarin, placed in the urn, and drawn out under supervision of the local Chinese *amban,* or governor. Because of the situation then prevailing, the Golden Urn's use had been dispensed with at the time of both the present Dalai Lama's and the late Panchen Lama's selection: the Chinese were unable to enforce its use. But now the Chinese were certain to insist on its deployment.

In what some Tibetan officials saw as a gesture of conciliation, the Chinese authorities permitted Chadrel Rinpoché, abbot of Tashilhunpo, and as such the person in overall charge of the search, to put a letter seeking the Dalai Lama's guidance into Gyalo Thondup's hands during a visit by the Dalai Lama's brother to Beijing in July 1993. At that moment, it even seemed possible that the authorities might be willing to dispense with use of the Golden Urn. In the end, Chadrel Rinpoché, who had in the meantime had secret word from the Dalai Lama which of the candidates was the authentic reincarnation, was unable to secure dispensation before the day deemed by the Dalai Lama to be the most auspicious on which to make his choice known publicly. To Chadrel Rinpoché's embarrassment and to the fury of the Chinese authorities, the Dalai Lama preempted them by making his own announcement.

It was an extremely risky move, and one that the Dalai Lama must have known would bring serious repercussions. It cannot have come as any great surprise to him when Chadrel Rinpoché was subsequently arrested, along with his chief assistant. What may have caught him by surprise, however, was the speed with which the Chinese authorities detained the little boy declared by the Dalai Lama to be the authentic incarnation and announced another candidate as the "official" Panchen Lama. The Precious Protector's own choice, just six years old, thus became one of the youngest political prisoners in the world. His whereabouts remain unknown.

Why would the Dalai Lama have risked such an outcome? We can but speculate. The only thing we can be certain of is that he did not make the decision lightly. He would, moreover, have consulted closely with Nechung and the other dharma protector, and indeed it is almost certain that their counsel was what clinched the matter.

Whatever the Dalai Lama's intentions, the Panchen Lama controversy clearly impacted the thinking of the Chinese authorities. There was to be no letup in their campaign against the Precious Protector. Those who held the view that the outbreaks of unrest in Tibet were directly attributable to the liberalization of the 1980s were firmly in the ascendant — a position consolidated by further outbreaks of unrest later in the year. To the dismay of the Dalai Lama, who continued to assert the importance of all protest being peaceful, this culminated, in December 1996, with the explosion of a bomb in Lhasa, injuring five people and damaging two hotels and a government building.

Although it was evidently not intended to cause massive loss of life — the device was remotely detonated in the early hours of the morning — this was a shocking development. Up until now, violence, when it had broken out, had done so in the context of civil unrest. But this was malice aforethought. It was now but a short distance to premeditated acts of mass murder. Unless, of course, this was a false flag operation. It is not impossible to imagine that the bomb — much more sophisticated than anything seen thus far in Tibet — was in fact planted and exploded by the authorities themselves. It would be naïve to suppose that a regime capable of administering beatings and electric shocks to detainees as a matter of routine would never undertake such operations.

As a result of both the Panchen Lama debacle and continued unrest in Tibet, one decade removed from the time when a visit to Tibet by the Dalai Lama had seemed a genuine possibility, the political situation was now almost as bad as it had been before Deng's overtures and certainly at any time since Hu Yaobang's intervention in the early 1980s. Given the enormous popularity the Dalai Lama was starting to enjoy on the international scene, and given too the seriousness with which his efforts to bring the situation in Tibet to the attention of political leaders worldwide was being met, this seems cruelly ironic. But the devastating turn that events in the exile community took over the next twelve months was a tragic reminder of the epic scale of the difficulties that the Dalai Lama has faced since the day the search party came knocking at his parents' farmstead door.

20

"An oath-breaking spirit born of perverse prayers": The Murder of Lobsang Gyatso

At the beginning of every year, the Dalai Lama grants a general audience at the main temple in Dharamsala, where he delivers a quasi–State of the Union Address. There follows, soon after, the Precious Protector's spring teachings. During those of 1996, the Dalai Lama surprised his audience by speaking in unusually forceful terms about Dorje Shugden. Over the years since his first public repudiation of him, the Dalai Lama had often repeated his view that the deity was unreliable. Increasingly he had suggested that monks in particular should not have recourse to Shugden. He had, in addition, requested (and requests of the Dalai Lama have the authority of orders within the Tibetan community) that certain statues of Shugden in prominent settings within the major monasteries be removed and, in some cases, replaced with statues of Nechung. On this occasion he issued for the first time a forthright condemnation of Shugden practice, saying that anyone who wished to continue it should no longer consider the Dalai Lama to be their guru. Those in this category should neither attend his teachings nor take any empowerments from him. Beyond this, he made it clear that, on account of the regrettable persistence of Shugden practice, there would, if necessary, have to be follow-up. The matter had reached the point where, if nothing was done, there was danger of harm not just to the Ganden Phodrang government but to his own life, which could be shortened as a result.

The speech was greeted with general dismay. Shugden remained a popular figure, especially among Khampas and traders as well as with the late Trijang Rinpoché's many followers. Of all the supernatural beings venerated by Tibetans, he is the one to whom ordinary people can most easily relate. Besides his claimed role as principal protector of the Gelug school, Shugden is also known for facilitating the prosperity of his followers. But to many, the most shocking aspect of all was the fact of Shugden's perceived pivotal role in the successful escape of the Dalai Lama from Lhasa in 1959.

The dismay was not just on the part of Shugden devotees, however. People were also appalled that there were some within the community who would disregard the Dalai Lama's requests with respect to the practice. It was well understood that the Dalai Lama would not speak out without just cause, and since nothing is more precious than the life of the Precious Protector, if it was the case that his life was endangered, those who continued to defy him were guilty of serious wrongdoing. With this in mind, some reacted with zealous indiscretion. Taking advantage of the absence of the abbess, they threw out as rubbish the Shugden statue kept in Dharamsala's Ganden Choeling Nunnery. Later, a number of departments within the Tibetan exile administration took it on themselves to mount a campaign to root out from government employ any who maintained a connection with the deity—even if this amounted to no more than the usual monthly ritual offering. The Department of Health, among others, circulated a notice requiring all employees and their families to sign a letter of abjuration. At the same time, representatives of the Dalai Lama visited the monasteries in southern India to apprise them of the Precious Protector's directive. Worrying reports began to spread that those who refused to sign or comply were beaten up. By early summer, resistance groups started to emerge, and demonstrations against the Dalai Lama's proclamation were held at both the Ganden and Sera Monasteries.

As tensions began to mount, a number of devotees found their businesses boycotted, while signs began to appear in shop windows announcing that Shugden supporters would not be welcome. The question of loyalty was on everyone's lips.

No doubt part of the government in exile's zeal can be attributed to the desire to be seen to be doing something. Recent events in Dharamsala had already heightened tensions within the exile community. Not long before, a man had been found working in the Dalai Lama's kitchen who had links with the Chinese government. In the previous two years, a total of five spies had allegedly been uncovered in Dharamsala by Indian intelligence. There was also a rumor that the Tibetan administration's internal security had recently foiled a plot that called for a female agent, posing as a new arrival from Tibet, to put nerve agent in her hair so that when the Dalai Lama touched her in blessing, he would be poisoned. On top of this, following the recent fatal stabbing of a young Indian by a Tibetan youth, relations between Dharamsala's immigrant and resident Gaddi communities had fallen to a disastrous low.* There was even talk of the Indian government's relocating the entire Tibetan population to an area south of Delhi, while the Dalai Lama himself had declared that he would move to southern India if his continued presence in Dharamsala was inconvenient.

The possibility of another move was hugely unsettling to the exile community, and there can be little doubt that the McCarthyite paranoia that gripped many of those in authority can be attributed to the tense atmosphere then prevailing. But what was most toxic of all was the response of a small but well-organized cell of Shugden devotees within the Gelugpa establishment. Posters denouncing the Dalai Lama's declaration appeared in Dharamsala and elsewhere, and a court case was brought in the wake of the government's campaign, while Amnesty International was appealed to on the grounds that Shugden's devotees were being denied the right to freedom of religious belief.

As the crisis worsened, an anonymous letter circulated in Dharamsala

---

* The Gaddi are an Indian hill tribe of pastoralists who have farmed the foothills of the Himalayas since time immemorial.

threatening the Dalai Lama with a "bloodbath." At the same time, death threats were issued against the young incarnation of Trijang Rinpoché and another senior Shugden lineage holder, Song Rinpoché. Simultaneously, an attempt was made on the life of a former abbot of one of the Ganden colleges by Shugden supporters. Then, at a séance during which the Dalai Lama invoked Nechung and several other oracles, one of the mediums (in a trance) accused a lama in attendance of being an unrepentant Shugden devotee and attacked him. A fracas broke out, and the lama subsequently threatened to sue, until the Dalai Lama personally intervened. In January 1997 a respected *geshe* was beaten up in Delhi.

But even the best-informed observer could not have predicted what would happen next. The Venerable Lobsang Gyatso was a close associate of the Dalai Lama. It was he whom the Tibetan leader had chosen to be founder-director of the School of Buddhist Dialectics when it was inaugurated in 1973. An example of one of the Dalai Lama's many forward-looking initiatives, the school (now Institute) was set up with the purpose of offering an advanced education grounded in Buddhism's ancient Nalanda tradition but outside the traditional monastic setting. By this time, it had integrated modern science and English language classes into the curriculum, alongside courses designed to introduce students to the full range of the Tibetan Buddhist tradition. With a towering reputation as a scholar-practitioner, Lobsang Gyatso — invariably referred to as Gen-la (honorable teacher) — was known as a kind but strict disciplinarian whose way of life was as austere as it was exemplary. Notoriously outspoken, somewhat rough in his diction and combative in his manner, he nevertheless inspired the greatest loyalty among his students. To the fury of some, he was also a notable supporter of the Dalai Lama's pronouncements on Shugden.

On a bitter cold night right at the end of the Tibetan year (in 1997 it fell during February), at the very moment when it is traditional to banish ritually the evils and spiritual defilements of the past twelve months before welcoming in the next, four visitors called at Gen-la's room. Earlier in the day he had met with the Dalai Lama, and now he was working with two students who were translating a religious text into Chinese. Situated within the precincts of the main temple, his room was within earshot of the Dalai Lama's private compound — though no one reported hearing anything. When the visitors left a short while later, Lobsang Gyatso and his two companions lay dead or dying with multiple knife wounds. Renowned as a fighter in his youth, he must have put up a struggle. There was blood high up the walls. But his assailants had stabbed him in the eye, slashed him in the throat, and plunged a blade deep into his heart. His companions fared no better, though one survived to gasp his life away soon after arriving at the Delek Hospital, half a mile down the hill, where he was taken as soon as the alarm was raised. From there he was sent to the Chandigarh hospital, but he died en route.

The whole of Dharamsala reeled in shock. Among foreign residents and local journalists, rumors began to circulate to the effect that Lobsang Gyatso had been murdered for the large amount of cash he had brought back with him from a recent fund-raising trip to Hong Kong. Another story was that a drunken brawl in the basement of the building (where there was a small restaurant) had somehow spun out of control. But the truth is, most Tibetans knew perfectly well what lay behind the tragedy. This was an attempt by the deity's supporters to intimidate the Dalai Lama into dropping his policy on Shugden practice. By way of confirmation, an open letter to the Dalai Lama published in the name of the Delhi-based Shugden Supporters Society which circulated a few days later issued a stark warning: "We have already offered you three corpses, you will find others if you continue with your approach."

Ultimately, the controversy over Shugden's status is a theological one. Within Buddhism, "church" and state, or rather *sangha* and state, have not come apart as they have in the West. As a result, theological controversy very quickly finds its way out of the monastery and into the political arena, often with immediate and far-reaching consequences. In the case of Shugden, what was at stake was not merely the question of what status should correctly be assigned to a certain deity — in particular whether he is simply a minor being or one of the protector deities, as his followers proposed. It was also the question of who should govern Tibet. According to devotees of Dorje Shugden, the present Dalai Lama had shown by his actions that he himself was unqualified to occupy the Lion Throne.

In the immediate aftermath of the murder, confusion reigned. It was several hours before the police were called — long enough for the killers to make good their escape. The Indian criminal investigation concluded eventually that the suspects had fled abroad. For months afterwards, Dharamsala remained paralyzed. The Dalai Lama, however, maintained his position regarding the Shugden issue. On his behalf the letter-writing campaigns continued, and both monks and laymen were required to sign a statement declaring that they had no connection with Shugden.

During the fall of that same year (1997), the Dalai Lama gave a long and careful explanation, subsequently published, justifying his position. Its main thrust was to argue that it was not Shugden the practitioner should worry about offending, but the Buddha. To the outsider, the speech gives a moderately worded and clear exposition of the Dalai Lama's thinking behind his injunction. To Shugden's devotees, it was a tissue of falsehoods and outright lies. For them, the crux of the matter was as much the purity of the Gelugpa teachings that, in their view, the Dalai Lama's advocacy of Padmasambhava, the Lotus-Born, and the Nyingma tradition generally, threatened, as it was the insult to the deity himself that upset them. For devotees of Shugden, a powerful minority of the Gelug school, the teachings of their founder, Tsongkhapa, were to be practiced and preserved without taint. For the Dalai Lama, Shugden threatened the ecumenical approach he wanted to take toward the other Tibetan schools.

Yet far more was at issue here than the "lama politics" of which the Dalai Lama sometimes speaks. For the tradition, and hence for him, the gods and protectors are not mere fictions. They are both real and powerful. While the gods have limited abilities, the dharma protectors are vastly more capable and can influence events not only in the world but within other realms too. The protectors are considered to be manifestations of different bodhisattvas, just as the Dalai Lama himself is a manifestation of Chenresig, and their main function is to keep the dharma itself from harm. And while the Dalai Lama characterizes Shugden as nothing but the lowest form of godling, to Shugden devotees he is the wrathful manifestation of Manjushri, Bodhisattva of Wisdom.

We can understand the Dalai Lama's insistence that worship of Shugden cease only when we see that for him, Shugden, like Nechung (the great rival of Shugden), is not merely a projection or imaginative construct but as real as the flesh and blood in which human beings manifest. It is precisely this construal of the deities and the protectors as real that lies behind the Dalai Lama's relationship with Nechung. As he recounts in his autobiography: "When I was small, it was touching. Nechung liked me a lot and always took great care of me. For example, if he noticed I had dressed carelessly or improperly, he would come over and rearrange my shirt, adjust my robe and so on." As to his character, "he is very reserved and austere, just as you would imagine a grand old man of ancient times to be." To be clear, the Dalai Lama is referring not to the medium through whom Dorje Drakden manifests but to Dorje Drakden himself.

As a rule, the Dalai Lama consults with Nechung formally only once or twice a year, always during the Great Prayer Festival and sometimes on other important occasions. But he also consults with him privately on a more frequent basis. When he does so informally, the medium does not wear the full regalia of his office, which is reserved for the great occasions of state. Although there exist a number of YouTube videos of Nechung and other oracles in a trance, to appreciate fully their importance to the tradition, it is necessary to witness the phenomenon at first hand, a privilege granted to few outsiders.

The Dalai Lama, sumptuously clad in yellow silk over his habitual maroon robe, sits on an elaborately decorated throne while he presides over the entirety of the Namgyal monastic community. It will be recalled that Namgyal is the monastery that exists to serve the Dalai Lama and to conduct rituals on behalf of the Tibetan government. This community is divided into the choir, made up of a majority of the monks — perhaps forty of them — and the orchestra, which comprises perhaps a dozen. Many are, like the Dalai Lama, swaddled in the yellow outer robe of the Gelug school, while the more senior wear the tall, forward-curving headdress that is adopted only for the most important liturgies.

Before the ceremony begins, the medium looks small and vulnerable, clearly conscious that what he is about to undertake will test him to the utmost limits of his strength. His ordeal begins with the impossible bass of the *umze,* the cantor, who leads the monastic choir and whose voice is joined shortly by the steady beat of a pair of drums. These drums are of shallow construction and are held vertical on a short pole and struck with a curved stick. In response, there is an immediate contraction around the medium's jaw, and it is clear the possession is already beginning. The look of vulnerability is gone, and now, after another minute and to a sudden trembling of cymbals and oboes thrilling, two attendants come forward and proceed to fasten in place a breastplate of burnished silver about the size of a small salver. As they do so, the *kuten,* or medium, tries to help, but he fumbles ineffectually, no longer in full control of his limbs.

The Dalai Lama, meanwhile, has withdrawn his attention inward and his demeanor has become more serious. Rocking gently back and forth, he joins in the chant, as the orchestra beseeches the presence of the deity with mounting insistence. But again, after a clamoring crescendo, the monks fall silent before the chant begins anew to the tap of the drums and a slow rumble of voices following the cantor's lead.

All at once there is a palpable sense — of what? — that something momentous is under way. But more than that — of a *mysterium et tremendum fascinans,* a mystery before which the onlooker stands in awe, both fearful and fascinated.

The chant starts to swell once more. The medium, now fully dressed, remains seated as the Dalai Lama looks on. One senses a definite rapport between him and Nechung — the deity, though, not the medium. This is evidently a meeting of familiars. Indeed, there is nothing to suggest that, for the Precious Protector, anything untoward or remarkable is about to take place. The same may be said of the congregation as a whole: many people are quietly chatting to one another, even as they tell their rosaries. The medium sits quite peacefully now, his eyes closed and his hands upon his knees. But again there is a sudden increase in the tempo of the drums and an outburst of oboe — and trumpet, the famed *gang ling,* crafted from human femur, which accompanies first a quivering, then a clashing of the cymbals in climax. The Precious Protector, eyes cast down, rocks forward and back faster and with shorter, more abrupt movements.

Without any sign from the medium himself, two attendants bring the oracle's headdress. This consists of a huge helmet, its wide brim supporting a superstructure of intricate religious symbols, each of these studded with precious stones, while sprays of what look like horsehair burst from the crown, falling at least the length of a man's arm behind. It is hard to believe anyone could wear such a thing unsupported. To an observer it looks as if it must weigh thirty pounds or more — though it is said that, in former times, it was more than twice as heavy. Once it is tied in place, an improbably thin strap passing under his chin, the *kuten* stops grimacing, and his expression assumes a look of deep serenity as the next cycle of invocations begins. It is indeed so hypnotic, this sound, its strong, steady, rhythmic flow so overwhelming, that it seems surprising that more people do not succumb. And in fact, they sometimes do. What is more, the tempo of chant and music has a profound impact on the experience of the medium himself, who must visualize, while it progresses, first the mandala — the symbolic representation of his dwelling place — corresponding to the deity and then the arrival of the deity as he steps out of his mandala. On this occasion, evidently attuned to the least sign that all is not as it must be, one of the attendants — there are four altogether — comes forward and reties the headdress.

After the five minutes or so that the chant cycle takes, yet another begins. Now the medium begins to jerk spasmodically, his whole body quaking. The Dalai Lama, who has been following this part of the proceedings silently, joins in the chant briefly. The *kuten* is leaning back, his mouth forced wide, his breathing stentorian, as oboe, horn, and cymbal combine once more in clashing crescendo. An attendant now brings what looks as if it must be a sword, covered with a red cloth, together with a bow but no arrows. In times past, when the ceremony took place outside, the oracle would generally loose off several. He did so when indicating the direction in which the search parties looking for the present incarnation of the Dalai Lama should conduct their search. And it is said that, once, long ago, one struck and killed a child.

The timbre and tempo of the chant change. One of the trumpeters keeps time by tapping his finger on his instrument, while the oracle, still seated and partially screened by a ministering attendant, continues to tremble and twitch. The Dalai Lama, hitherto bareheaded, dons a tall, forward-curving yellow headpiece with long silken earflaps reaching to his shoulders, and at that moment there is a faint sound of tinkling bells. Could this be the deity announcing himself?

The *kuten* remains seated, clutching his weapons, one leg trembling with increasing violence. All of a sudden he begins to emit short, sobbing grunts

— "ah-ah-ah" — as the orchestra rises once more in a crescendo. And now, taking his accoutrements firmly in hand, Nechung rises from his throne, its tiger-skin covering visible for the first time. As he does so, the whole congregation — though not the choir and not the Dalai Lama — stands too.

The Precious Protector, eyes cast down, sways gently in silent prayer.

With Dorje Drakden clearly in full possession of the medium, the first part of the ceremony is over. It is now for individual members of the government to greet him, each rising in turn to go forward and present a *kathag,* a white silk scarf representing an offering of one subordinate to his or her superior.

It is only when the last *kathag* has been presented that Nechung turns to the Dalai Lama. There is something matter-of-fact about the manner in which he responds to the oracle. The choir continues its chant, and after this brief acknowledgment, it is the turn of three successive monastic officials to speak with Dorje Drakden. Bending low toward the *kuten,* they put their questions to him, and he replies in a voice unexpectedly high-pitched and sobbing almost as if he were on the verge of tears, like a coerced child. It is impossible not to feel enormous concern for the human being thus used. The observer has the impression that he can barely contain the enormous force to which he has granted temporary residence. Small wonder these men do not often survive beyond middle age.

After the last question, the *kuten* resumes his throne but continues to quake and to emit a curious hissing sound while the officials confer with one another. Occasionally it looks as if the oracle wishes to stand but is unable to, the vast headdress turning from side to side as he twists his neck, his lower lip pulled down in rictus gape. And every so often he speaks, apparently repeating himself as if frustrated that he has not been properly understood. The officials, having spoken among themselves, now return, evidently seeking further clarification.

At last the interviews are complete. Dorje Drakden has imparted his augury of the year ahead, and the oracle gesticulates with his hand, stabbing the air with an index finger. He stands once more as oboe, trumpet, and cymbal rise again. Turning to the Dalai Lama, he takes a pace or two forward, with his sword in one hand and, in the other, a peacock feather — a symbol of purity —

which he proceeds to offer to the Precious Protector. The exchange is perfunctory and yet unaccountably moving.

Only now does the Dalai Lama himself rise. He places a *kathag* around the oracle's neck before they consult together privately for perhaps a minute, after which the Precious Protector reassumes his throne. Almost at once the deity abandons its earthly confinement, and the medium falls back into the arms of his waiting attendants. Deftly they untie the enormous headdress before carrying out the medium's inert and rigid body.

In any consideration of the Shugden controversy, it is thus essential to keep in mind the intimate relationships that the protectors have with earthbound mortals, relationships that we see most vividly as they are played out in these consultations with the oracles. For not only do Nechung and Shugden speak through mediums, but also there are many other deities that speak through oracles besides these two. Even today, there are many mediums who channel deities, both within Tibet and in exile, though only a handful are conduits for the supra-mundane protectors. The remainder give voices to more minor beings. But they are by no means rare.

Aside from the question of the reality of the protectors and their communications with human beings, with respect to the issue of Shugden himself, we also need to understand something of the role that Tsongkhapa — whose teachings it is allegedly Shugden's special responsibility to protect — plays within the Gelug tradition, at the pinnacle of which the Dalai Lama stands.

The fourteenth-century founder of the Dalai Lama's own Gelug tradition, Tsongkhapa (literally, and somewhat deflatingly, the Man from the Land of Onions) is unquestionably the most important figure to have emerged in Tibet in the past six hundred years. He was, most educated Tibetans would agree, Aristotle, Shakespeare, Saint Francis, and Einstein all rolled into one. Showing early signs of brilliance, Tsongkhapa began his monastic career in a small monastery close to the present Dalai Lama's birthplace in Amdo. As a child, he was said to be capable of memorizing seventeen folios of scripture a day — approximately fifteen hundred words — and to have perfect recall ever after. Once ordained, he adopted the life of a wandering hermit, taking teachings from many different masters — though none of them Nyingma. One of his early devotions was to recite the mantra of his principal meditational deity a hundred million times. Gifted with a laser-sharp intelligence, he was able at once to grasp the most abstruse arguments in metaphysics and to reconcile apparently contradictory theses. He was a poetic genius, too, with an extraordinary facility with words. Much of his most important and difficult philosophy is framed in perfectly metered verse, while his spiritual songs and praises are said to be without compare for their ability to move the heart of the one who recites them. If, though, he had one virtue that crowned all others, it was his proficiency in the meditative practices of a yogin. He was a visionary whose personal relationship with Manjushri, Bodhisattva of Wisdom, would mark him as the outstanding practitioner of the Buddhadharma of his — and, many would argue, of any — age since that of the Buddha Shakyamuni himself.

As well as being a stickler for the rules of personal conduct, Tsongkapa brought to the monastic movement itself a renewed emphasis on the life and works of the historical Buddha. The annual celebration of the Great Prayer Festival in Lhasa was one of his key innovations. He also established Ganden Monastery, which — together with its sister foundations at Drepung and Sera — came to be the single most important religious foundation in Tibet. From his own time up to the present, Tsongkhapa continues to inspire not only young Tibetans but also, increasingly, people from all over to renounce the world and dedicate themselves to the monastic life. Yet Tsongkhapa is not without his critics. There are those who question the authenticity of his self-proclaimed relationship with the bodhisattva Manjushri. Others are suspicious of the way in which he totally ignored the earlier Tibetan tradition of which the Lotus-Born is the key figure. Yet for the present Dalai Lama himself, Tsongkhapa is the scholar-saint of the Tibetan tradition to whom he feels closest, and he regularly gives teachings on the master's Great Treatise on the Stages of the Path to Enlightenment.

With respect to Shugden, as the Dalai Lama explained in his 1997 talk, the origins of the deity's cult lie in the seventeenth century, during the lifetime of the Great Fifth Dalai Lama. It was this incarnation — the one to whom the present Dalai Lama has often said he identifies with most closely — who acquired for the Dalai Lama institution its temporal power. Until his alliance with Gushri Khan, the Mongolian warlord who became chief patron of the

Gelugpas, the Dalai Lamas were merely one among several reincarnation lineages renowned for their spiritual attainments. His predecessor the Fourth Dalai Lama, Yonten Gyatso, can, by virtue of his Mongolian princely ancestry, be regarded as an earlier attempt at gaining political power for the (still relatively young) Gelugpa sect. But the Fourth Dalai Lama died a failure, unimpressive in either the temporal or the spiritual realm. As a result, during the interregnum that followed his death, the Gelugpas, having no reliable backing, struggled for survival "like a butter lamp flickering in a raging storm." It was only when, through the diplomacy of his chamberlain, the (not yet deemed Great) Fifth Dalai Lama forged an alliance with Gushri Khan, head of the Qoshot Mongols, that Gelug fortunes were transformed. Sweeping all before them, the Mongolians destroyed first the resurgent Bonpos of the kingdom of Beri in eastern Tibet. It is the Bonpos who claim to be the guardians of the original religion of Tibet (though they have adopted many Buddhist practices). Then, despite the Dalai Lama's deep misgivings, and after a lengthy siege, the Mongolians toppled the Kargyu-supporting king of Tsang in central Tibet.

When, subsequently, the Dalai Lama established his headquarters in Lhasa, he oversaw a major expansion of the Gelug establishment. Yet for all his dedication to the legacy of Tsongkhapa, and despite being the incarnation of its most important lineage, he was himself a master of the Nyingma tradition and an initiate of many of its most secret and occult practices, notably the art of war magic.

Even in the seventeenth century, there was considerable opposition within Gelug circles to the Dalai Lama's enthusiasm for the Nyingma tradition. This opposition coalesced around a gifted lama by the name of Drakpa Gyaltsen, who had in fact been a candidate when the Fifth Dalai Lama was being searched for. Both sides agree that matters eventually came to a head when Drakpa Gyaltsen died, though how he did so is a matter of dispute. According to devotees of Shugden, the two met in a debate, which, humiliatingly, the Dalai Lama lost. The following day, the victor was found dead with the silk offering scarf the Dalai Lama had been compelled to present to him in recognition of his triumph rammed down his throat. Exactly what happened next is also a matter of controversy, although there is broad agreement at least as to the outcome.

As we saw earlier, it is well understood that victims of violent crime are likely to be reborn as *shi dre,* a kind of ghost that often causes harm to those with whom it comes into contact. Something similar seems to have happened with Drakpa Gyaltsen. When his remains came to be cremated, it is said that a thick pall of black smoke rose from the pyre, assuming the shape of an open hand, which hung suspended in the air. Soon after, strange events began to be reported in central Tibet: the silver casket into which his ashes had been deposited started to emit a buzzing sound; animals became unaccountably sick and many died; crops failed. More troubling still, the dishes on which the Dalai Lama's food was set overturned themselves spontaneously, and there came the sound of stones crashing onto the roof of the Potala. The noise could be drowned out only by monks blowing on the huge *dung chen* horns normally used to summon the faithful to prayer. Exasperated, the Dalai Lama summoned the abbot of the recently founded Mindroling Monastery (a Nyingma foundation), who presided over construction of a demon trap. On this occasion, however, the abbot was distracted at a critical moment during the ritual, enabling the spirit to escape. In the end, the best that could be done was to lure it to a lonely spot where a small shrine was built in its honor.*

Shugden devotees claim that, at this point, the Dalai Lama was forced to accept that this was no ordinary spirit but that Drakpa Gyaltsen, having been reborn in a heavenly realm, was revealed to be a dharma protector, whose real name was Dorje Shugden.† It is even alleged that the Great Fifth wrote prayers in his honor, though, as the present Dalai Lama pointed out in his 1997 speech, there is no evidence for this in any of the eighteen volumes of the collected works. On the contrary, these make clear that, far from settling at the shrine, Shugden's "harmful activities only intensified." In response, the Great Fifth ordered a huge ritual onslaught, culminating in a fire ceremony during which ef-

* This was at the Trode Khangsar, which still stands in Lhasa today.

† There is, however, another tradition, which holds that the real origins of Shugden lie with the maleficent activity of a seventeenth-century Kargyu lama. It is alleged that, owing to friction between the Gelug and Kargyu schools at that time, this lama succeeded in "hacking" Drakpa Gyaltsen's spirit, then sending him off to another realm and substituting an evil spirit in its place to masquerade as a dharma protector but in fact to do maximum harm to the Gelugpas.

figies of the "perfidious interfering spirit" and his entourage were burnt. A sign of success was "the smell of burning flesh that everybody witnessed."

Unfortunately for the Dalai Lama, despite this promising sign, ultimately his campaign failed and the spirit survived. By the time of the Great Thirteenth Dalai Lama, Shugden's cult had spread to Kham, where, thanks to the enthusiastic advocacy of one of the greatest and most famous lamas of this time, Phabongka Rinpoché, guru to both Ling Rinpoché and Trijang Rinpoché and a teacher of legendary charisma, he acquired an enormous following. This was further bolstered by Shugden's spectacular manifestation through the Panglung oracle. Joseph Rock, the Austro-American botanist and explorer who reported on the massacre of Tibetan children by Hui bandits, recounted in *National Geographic* how, during a séance he witnessed in 1928, the oracle "took a sword handed to him, a strong Mongolian steel blade . . . [and] [i]n the twinkling of an eye . . . twisted it with his naked hands into several loops and knots!"

The Great Thirteenth likewise had severe reservations about the deity. Formally reprimanding Phabongka, he required him to desist from spreading the practice. But by now it was too late. So when the Great Thirteenth Dalai Lama died in 1933, some said that Shugden had a hand in his demise. In spite of this, the cult of the deity continued to spread, especially among the laity in Kham. So powerful did he become that it is said the western gate of Nechung Monastery was kept permanently locked, as it was there that Shugden waited, poised to move in the moment Pehar attained final liberation.

Part of the discomfort Shugden's devotees feel about the present Dalai Lama's attempted proscription of his cult is the thought that he is calling the commitment of many great masters of the Gelug tradition into question. Also, by implication, that he is willing to abrogate the *samaya* — the sacred bond established when a pupil takes a teaching from a lama — that exists between himself and those Shugden devotees, notably Trijang Rinpoché and the regent Taktra Rinpoché, whose student he was. The bond further requires that the student sees the teacher as the actual embodiment of the Buddha. This means that to criticize the teacher in any way is to criticize the Buddha himself. Yet the Dalai Lama is quick to point out that while he had just such a relationship with Reting Rinpoché, no one argues that Reting did not make mistakes. For him to deny these would be to contradict the evidence — the letters the ex-regent wrote asking for Chinese support — that he saw with his own eyes. Furthermore, just because he has come to the conclusion that Trijang Rinpoché's Shugden practice was mistaken, he emphasizes that this should in no way be seen as disrespecting either the high spiritual attainments or the great contribution of his junior tutor. He even confided that his regard for Trijang Rinpoché remains so deep that, on one occasion, he even dreamt of "lapping up" his teacher's urine as the junior tutor relieved himself. To the outsider this seems a surprising — even shocking — anecdote to share, but to a monastic audience, it will have put them in mind of a relatively common practice whereby small quantities of the bodily waste of high lamas are ritually imbibed as a means to furthering one's own spiritual progress.*

Over the years since his 1997 address, the Dalai Lama has maintained his position on Shugden (whom he refers to as *dolgyal* — the king demon) with consistency, explaining that, when it comes to matters of such importance, "being a fairly forthright person, I just don't know how to be courteous and discreet." Fortunately, there have been no more killings, though there is anecdotal evidence of continuing friction between the two factions. More destructive has been the internationalization of the issue. This has been seen in protests, such as those that occurred during high-profile visits by the Dalai Lama to the University of Oxford in 2008 and, in 2015, to the University of Cambridge. Organized by an alliance of Shugden groups in the West, these incidents bear eloquent testimony to the power of metaphysics to move human beings; this is, after all, a deity that, until at most a century ago, had not been heard of beyond the reaches of a relatively small number of Himalayan communities. Yet it is in Tibet that the greatest damage has been done. The controversy has not gone unnoticed by the Chinese authorities, and it is unsurprising

---

* When Father Johannes Grueber, the first European known to have visited Lhasa, reached the capital in 1661, he was scandalized to discover that the most highly prized remedy in the Tibetan pharmacopoeia was the Dalai Lama's and other high lamas' excrement, desiccated and incorporated into "Precious Pills." While Precious Pills continue to be manufactured, it is remarkable to see that medical opinion has lately turned in favor of a similar practice (fecal microbiota transplant) for treatment of certain intestinal conditions.

to learn that a number of Shugden-supporting monasteries have been, in recent years, recipients of generous funding from Chinese government sources.

Without question, the Shugden controversy highlights the single most challenging aspect of the encounter between Tibetan tradition and contemporary secular society. The Dalai Lama is fully committed to introducing the natural sciences not only into the ordinary school curriculum but into the monastic curriculum as well. He is similarly committed to the advancement of women, to full democracy, and to institutional transparency.* At the same time, it is clear that the Dalai Lama remains fully immersed in the traditional Buddhist worldview — even if he regards the cosmological texts as needing interpretation — and to the dharma protectors and their supernatural enemies central to that worldview.

At the time of writing, there appears to be an uneasy truce between declared Shugden supporters and those who follow the Dalai Lama on the issue. Among the exile population, anecdotal evidence suggests that the proportion of Shugdenpa is unlikely to be more than 10 to 15 percent at the most. A similar figure is probably true of Tibetans in Tibet itself. Nevertheless, both Ganden and Sera Monasteries in exile have seen breakaway groups opening separate Shugden monasteries, and there are several other, smaller monasteries in exile that have opened separate Shugden houses too. It is thus not impossible that Shugden numbers could grow during a future regency period. From the Precious Protector's point of view, it is fortunate that the one person who might have emerged to take on leadership of the pro-Shugden faction, the new Trijang Rinpoché, has shown no inclination to do so. Indeed, the young man discovered himself to be at the center of a plot to discredit the Precious Protector. It emerged that a group of Shugden devotees planned to murder his chief assistant with the intention of laying the blame on Dalai Lama loyalists. Even so, there are signs that such leadership could yet emerge.

When the 101st Ganden Throne Holder, the highest authority within the Gelug establishment, retired in 2009, observers were stunned when news

* It is true that the government in exile (the Central Tibetan Administration) has some quite obvious shortcomings in both respects, but this is a very young institution as well as a very new idea in terms of the tradition.

emerged that he had joined the breakaway Shugden-supporting Shar Ganden Monastery in southern India. If true, this meant that, throughout his six-year incumbency, he had been in undeclared opposition to the Dalai Lama all along—a revelation made all the more remarkable for his impeccable scholarly and spiritual conduct. This defiance of the Dalai Lama at the very highest level suggests that there might be other, similarly highly placed opponents of the Precious Protector waiting for a safe moment to declare themselves. At the very least, it suggests that there is likely to be further turmoil in the community when the Dalai Lama chooses to manifest the act of passing away.

A demeanor of "great calmness" in the eyes of some, "such a hard, expressionless face" in the eyes of others: the Great Thirteenth Dalai Lama, Calcutta, circa 1907. *Courtesy of Dominic Winter Auctioneers*

"No different from our urchin friends": one of the earliest known images of the Fourteenth Dalai Lama, Kumbum Monastery, 1939. *Courtesy of the Center for Asian Studies at Arizona State University*

Brother and sister (Gyalo Thondup and Jetsun Pema) with their mother and father, the *gyalyum chenmo* and the *yabshi kung*, 1939. *Courtesy of the Center for Asian Studies at Arizona State University*

Lhasa's western gate, photographed in 1938. *Royal Geographical Society (with IBG)*

Fond of dogs and horses, the regent, Reting Rinpoché, in a serious mood following a reception at the British mission in Lhasa, 1940. © *Pitt Rivers Museum, University of Oxford*

The Norbulingka Palace, 1938. *Royal Geographical Society (with IBG)*

A “solid, solemn . . . very wide-awake boy, red-cheeked and closely shorn.” Lhasa, 1944. *Courtesy of the Center for Asian Studies at Arizona State University*

Aged eighteen, photographed in Chamdo en route to Beijing, 1953. *Jan Vanis*

View of the Potala Palace from Chakpori, Lhasa, 1936. © *Pitt Rivers Museum, University of Oxford*

At an entertainment in Chamdo, 1953. Note the People's Liberation Army personnel in the background.
Jan Vanis

Exchanging pleasantries at the Tibetan delegation's farewell banquet in Beijing, 1955. From left to right: Zhou Enlai, the Panchen Lama, Mao, the Dalai Lama, Zhu De.
Keystone-France/Getty Images

Being received by the Chögyal of Sikkim while the Panchen Lama, seen here to the left of the Dalai Lama, looks on. Gangtok, 1956. *Office of His Holiness the Dalai Lama*

With the two tutors: Ling Rinpoché (left) and Trijang Rinpoché. India, 1956. *Courtesy of the Office of H.E. Kyabje Ling Rinpoché*

Into exile: a moment of respite, 1959. *Office of His Holiness the Dalai Lama*

How the tradition sees him: detail from a fresco in the Potala Palace, 1956. *Photo © by Thomas Laird, 2018, "Murals of Tibet, TASCHEN"*

With schoolchildren, Mussoorie, late 1959 or early 1960. *© Tibet Documentation/ Tibetan Children's Village School*

With a local family in Dharamsala, 1960. The Dalai Lama is wearing the "well-pressed" trousers that he donned occasionally in the early days of exile. *Courtesy of Tibet Documentation*

With Lhasa apsos. On the left is Tashi, a gift of Tenzing Norgay, the Everest mountaineer. On the right is Senge, noted for his huge appetite. Actually, though, the Dalai Lama prefers cats. Dharamsala, 1970s. *Office of His Holiness the Dalai Lama*

A cruel irony of history: inspecting the secret Tibetan troops of India's Special Frontier Force, Establishment 22, in Chakrata, 1972. The photograph, rumored to have been taken by a Chinese spy, in fact originates from General Uban's personal collection. He stands to the left of the Dalai Lama. *© Ken Conboy*

Receiving the 1989 Nobel Peace Prize in Oslo. *Eystein Hanssen/ Scanpix Norway/PA Images*

"Look, no hands!" Getting ideas for a future free Tibet. Santa Fe, 1991. *Photo by Bob Shaw, courtesy of Project Tibet*

How the West sees the Dalai Lama, complete with badly photoshopped teeth, on the cover of *Vogue,* winter 1992–93. © *Vogue Paris*

What a coincidence! "Interrupted" by President Bill Clinton at the White House, April 1994. *Courtesy of the Clinton Presidential Library*

An "old ham," or a genuine sense of fun? With students attending a Tibetan medicine course. Dharamsala, 2014. *Office of His Holiness the Dalai Lama*

Precious Protector, the Victor, Lion Among Men, Wish-Fulfilling Jewel, Ocean of Wisdom, earthly manifestation of Chenresig, Bodhisattva of Compassion. Dharamsala, 2018. *Office of His Holiness the Dalai Lama*

21

Tibet in Flames: The Beijing Olympics and Their Aftermath

If the violence of the Shugden controversy has to some extent overshadowed the latter years of the Dalai Lama's biography, it has had little impact on his reputation internationally. Following the award of the Nobel Peace Prize, public recognition of the Precious Protector has continued to grow — as has appreciation of his message of universal compassion.

One moment when this surging popularity might have suffered came in 1997, when the Dalai Lama's private office received an open letter from a prominent gay activist seeking clarification over some remarks the Precious Protector had recently made. The Dalai Lama had given an interview during which he had expounded the classical Buddhist view of active same-sex relationships — that they are impermissible — apparently contradicting a more liberal stance he had taken earlier. In response, the Dalai Lama agreed to meet a small group of gay and lesbian Buddhists in San Francisco during the summer of that year. Later, one of the participants wrote of how, "stepping into the June sunlight [afterward, he] felt tired, calm, enormously grateful — and disappointed." The

Dalai Lama had explained that, while for non-Buddhists the strictures did not apply, for followers of the Buddhadharma, certain sexual practices were indeed forbidden. He explained further that the prohibition against these activities applied equally to non-same-sex couples. It followed, therefore, that it was not same-sex relationships themselves that were proscribed but only the physical expression of them. He added, however, that the matter was one of tradition and that this tradition reflected the moral codes of the time, allowing the possibility that change could come about "in response to science, modern social history and discussion within the various Buddhist *sanghas*." As for himself, while he was open to the possibility of such change, he had no authority to bring it about single-handedly even if he wanted to. The activists should therefore advocate for their interests according to the Buddhist principles of "rigorous investigation and non-violence" — presumably remaining chaste while doing so.

The notion that the Dalai Lama could be persuaded to change his mind if the tradition itself changed its mind, while not quite what the group was looking for, was enough to satisfy most people that the highest Tibetan spiritual authority was not closed to the possibility of a development of doctrine — even if this was an example, noted by one commentator, of how the Dalai Lama "delights listeners everywhere by being the rare spiritual figure who says there is no need for temples or scripture" but then "disappoints them, often, by suggesting that there is a need for old-fashioned ethics and all the things your grandmother told you were good for you." Yet it is clear that this tendency to disappoint does not diminish the Dalai Lama's appeal to those attracted to his identification with nonviolence and compassion, and to his insistence that warmheartedness is of greater value than which religious tradition people do or do not adhere to. This, surely, is what is behind his emergence, during the closing years of the twentieth century, as a universal "doctor of the soul" — Pico Iyer's evocative soubriquet — even though it is also true that Buddhism explicitly denies the existence of the soul.

At the close of the twentieth century, this growing appreciation of the Dalai Lama was augmented by high-profile appearances at events such as a rock concert celebrating the fiftieth anniversary of the Universal Declaration of Human Rights. Here, alongside the likes of Bruce Springsteen and the surviving members of Led Zeppelin, the Dalai Lama took to the stage in Paris to declare his own commitment to human rights — infuriating the Shugden devotees who were, at that moment, making a case to Amnesty International that he had infringed theirs by proscribing worship of the deity.

Arguably the most important element in securing the Dalai Lama's reputation as a "doctor of the soul" was the publication in 1998 of *The Art of Happiness.* Marketed as being jointly authored by the Dalai Lama, the book was based on a series of interviews granted to the American psychiatrist Dr. Howard Cutler. In presenting and interpreting the Dalai Lama's outlook to Westerners educated in the norms of contemporary society, the work succeeded brilliantly in presenting not so much the profundity of its subject's thinking as the notion that happiness (admittedly never precisely defined) could be attained by "assembling" the causes and conditions of happiness — which, the book further suggested, did not necessarily include the strict discipline of the religious life. The book was an immediate — and enduring — success, selling more than a million copies in its first year of publication in America alone.

With the Dalai Lama's increasing popularity came increasing requests for talks and teachings. Most continued to be at the invitation of different Buddhist groups around the world. In fulfilling these, the Dalai Lama would often drive himself so hard that he would return to Dharamsala utterly exhausted. Although his public talks are generally given extemporaneously, he prepares meticulously for every teaching he gives. His principal translator, the brilliant Cambridge-educated (now former) monk Thupten Jinpa, recalls once catching sight of the Dalai Lama's heavily annotated copy of a notoriously abstruse text. Jinpa later noticed that, during an enforced wait at the airport, he "delved into his small shoulder bag and . . . launched into deep study," approaching the text almost like a young student.

Not all invitations came from Buddhist groups, however. In 2000 the Dalai Lama visited Northern Ireland to participate in, among other events, one billed as "testimonials from victims of sectarian violence." This was organized by the Catholic monk Father Laurence Freeman, who had also organized the Good Heart conference where the Dalai Lama commented on the Christian gospels. Besides meeting, and being photographed with, Gerry Adams, the Irish Sinn Fein leader whom many believe to have been a senior member of the terrorist Irish Republican Army, the Dalai Lama also met with the man he has since described as his "hero," Richard Moore. One of three speakers to give their testimonial, Moore had been blinded as a ten-year-old boy by a rubber bullet fired by a British soldier, which hit him between the eyes. Prior to the event, the Dalai Lama placed Moore's hand on his head and face, inviting him to picture what he felt. A few years afterwards, Moore met with his assailant and made an unlikely friend of him. At the Dalai Lama's invitation, the two men then traveled to Dharamsala, where the Tibetan leader presented them to a large audience of refugee schoolchildren, explaining that their story exemplified what he meant by compassion, reconciliation, and forgiveness.*

There were some light moments, such as when, having been gifted a "vineyard" — claimed to be the smallest in the world, and consisting of precisely four vines — the Dalai Lama was invited in front of a crowd of a thousand onlookers to fire a pistol in the air, as tradition demanded, on completion of the "harvest." He took the gun from the previous owner (a Catholic monk), looked at it, hesitated for a moment, then kissed it and handed it back.

By now, the Dalai Lama's popularity was such that, shortly after the two-year anniversary of 9/11, a crowd of 65,000 came to Central Park to hear him declare that "the very concept of war is out of date." And as an example of the seriousness with which Buddhist thought is now beginning to be taken by the scientific community, during the winter of 2005 the Dalai Lama was invited to address the American Society for Neuroscience. The invitation to do so was not without controversy. A five-hundred-signature petition (largely, it seems, from among scientists with a connection to China) urged the organizers to withdraw it, on the grounds that his proposed lecture on the value of meditation "is of poor scientific taste because it will highlight hyperbolic claims, limited research and compromised scientific rigour." One delegate was critical of the Dalai Lama's belief that the mind and the body are separable and that, moreover, it is possible for the consciousness of one individual to be trans-

* Moore founded the charity Children in Crossfire, of which the Dalai Lama is now patron. He is a gifted musician and as a young man played lead guitar in the musical *Jesus Christ Superstar* when it opened in Dublin. He often jokes that in holding him up as any kind of hero, the Dalai Lama shows that he is a terrible judge of character.

ferred into the body of another. The reference here is to the Buddhist practice of *phowa,* whereby the practitioner transfers his or her consciousness into the body of another, either recently deceased or who desires to practice the dharma in another realm.*

The Dalai Lama's lecture was well received nonetheless, even if many remained skeptical of some of his claims about the benefits of meditation. But few would have wished to argue with the Dalai Lama's further claim that, while countless billions of dollars were spent annually on exploring outer space, it was time to devote proper resources to probing the "inner space" of consciousness.

If these examples of the Dalai Lama's mounting stature throughout the world are impressive, the devotion he continues to inspire among Tibetans in Tibet is arguably even more so. A striking instance of this occurred in 2006, when a comment, picked up from a speech he gave in Bodh Gaya, electrified the whole country when word of it was somehow circulated in Tibet. In view of the threat to the long-term survival of several rare species indigenous to Tibet, the Dalai Lama had suggested that it would be a good idea if Tibetans ceased to wear or to use animal fur. They responded by the hundreds and thousands. Himalayan tiger and leopard skin, otter pelts, sable and bear skin, all highly prized both as clothing and as furnishings in religious ceremonies, were brought from their places of safekeeping and publicly burned. Had the Chinese doubted for a moment where the loyalty of the vast majority of Tibetans lay, this was a forceful reminder of how things stood. In vain did they try to halt the bonfires; to no effect were the arrests of the organizers.

Between 1995 and 2002, from the disappearance of the Panchen Lama until the time of Beijing's confirmation as the venue for the Games, there had been no official contact between the Chinese authorities and the Tibetan government in exile, recently recast as the Central Tibetan Administration. This was despite — perhaps even because of — America's enthusiastic advocacy of dialogue between the two sides. In October 1997, Bill Clinton had urged his Chinese counterpart, Jiang Zemin, to initiate meaningful talks with the Dalai

* The sign of successful transference is said to be the appearance of a small hole at the crown of the head, into which it is traditional to push a blade of kusha grass.

Lama, and on a visit to Beijing the following year, the American president confronted Jiang during a live press conference, saying of the Dalai Lama, "I believe him to be an honest man, and I believe that if he had a conversation with President Jiang, they would like each other very much." Whether the laughter from the audience that followed was generous or nervous is unclear.

Nonetheless, with the Olympics looming, and perhaps due to China's concern following more than one visit by the Dalai Lama to Taiwan, contact between Beijing and Dharamsala was reestablished, and one or more government-level meetings took place each year from 2002 in the run-up to the Games, with increasing signs of progress. These followed a potentially difficult moment occasioned, during 2000, by the dramatic flight from Tibet of the fourteen-year-old Ogyen Trinley Dorje, head of the Karma Kargyu tradition, who, having walked from his monastery in Tibet to the Nepalese border and subsequently flown to Kathmandu by helicopter, arrived in Dharamsala in early January. Rumors that he was a spy were put about by those whom his presence in exile threatened. In particular this included a rival to his leadership position who already occupied substantial property assets belonging to the Kargyu in India. For his part, however, the Dalai Lama recognizes the "Tibetan" candidate and has since taken a close, even avuncular interest in the young man's education and welfare, saying more than once that he expected the Karmapa to play an important role in the future of the refugee community.

When the controversy occasioned by this unexpected arrival had abated, and following successive rounds of talks between officials from Dharamsala and Beijing, in 2007 the Dalai Lama's chief negotiator announced that, although the differences in viewpoint on the question of the Tibetan issue were "numerous," they had, he said, "reached the stage where, if there is political will on both sides, we have an opportunity to finally resolve this issue." This was an extraordinary development, and even though the Chinese responded to the Dalai Lama's Congressional Gold Medal, awarded that year by the Bush administration, by describing it as a "farce," optimism within the exile community rose to its highest since the Deng era. In fact, the award, made by an act of Congress, which must be cosponsored by two-thirds of the membership of both the House of Representatives and the Senate, was a matter of immense significance not only for the Tibetan exile leadership but also for the Chinese, to whom it looked like a major upgrading of the Dalai Lama's political status by the United States. The perception was further reinforced when Congress authorized the president to confer the award on the Dalai Lama in person.

In Tibet, meanwhile, China's denunciation of the award, along with, for example, continued restrictions on display of photographs of the Dalai Lama, caused serious resentment. If anyone expected the Tibetan masses to turn the other cheek to this latest insult following the Congressional award, and to the continued demonization of the Dalai Lama in the months leading up to the Beijing Olympics, they were tragically disappointed. Once more, Tibet erupted in flames and in fury.

On March 10, 2008, monks staged a protest against Chinese rule that centered on the Ramoche Temple in Lhasa. Here it needs to be understood that, besides this date being significant as the one on which the Dalai Lama fled Tibet, it also falls during the first month of the Tibetan New Year, which itself commemorates *chorul dawa:* the Month of Miracles. These signs were performed by the Buddha in answer to the gibes and abuse of nonbelieving heretical teachers before a crowd of more than ninety thousand. Making the miracles of Christ look like the trivial deeds of a minor *siddha,* the Buddha began by flying through the air. He then produced a stunning display of fire and water emanating from his body. Next, he planted his toothpick in the ground and it grew into a vast tree, laden with fruit and fragrant flowers. On the following day, he "manifested" two mountains made of the most precious stones. Thereafter, he produced a lake. Next he manifested a voice that sounded throughout the world, expounding the dharma. The day after, he radiated a light which filled the universe. On the penultimate day, he made his patrons world rulers. On the last day, the Buddha pressed down on his seat with the fingers of his right hand, and from beneath arose Vajrapani, a wrathful bodhisattva, who scattered the heretics and smashed their thrones. Then the Buddha radiated eighty-four thousand beams of light from each pore of his skin. On the tip of each ray reposed a lotus, on which was seated another Buddha preaching the dharma. Given the resonance of these events and of this time in the Buddhist psyche, it is hardly surprising that the New Year is a time of heightened emotion for Tibetans, especially within the monasteries.

Also, it is important to remember that the Dalai Lama's identification with Chenresig is not, for Tibetans, merely an abstract theological proposition. It is built into their self-understanding. As every child knows, Chenresig is the father of the Tibetan race, first manifesting in the guise of a monkey. One day he was importuned by an ogress who lived among the mountains and was at that moment mourning the death of all her children. Moved by pity, the monkey accepted the ogress's request to become her mate. It was their offspring who were the first Tibetans. Thus it stands to reason that Chenresig, as his name implies — translated literally it means the One Who Looks Down with Compassion — takes special care of the successors of his own progeny. Moreover, that he has since taken human form in the Dalai Lamas and their predecessors is only to be expected, given the bodhisattva's relationship with the Tibetan people. The relationship between Chenresig and the Tibetan people is thus a feature of the way the world is.

When we understand how the tradition conceives the Dalai Lama, we begin to see why it is so hard for Tibetans to hear him slandered. We also see why it is so hard for communism to make real converts among the Tibetan people. And indeed why, six decades since his flight into exile, the Dalai Lama's picture still cannot be shown in his homeland.

The forced dispersal of the demonstration at the Ramoche Temple in March 2008 was the trigger of a disastrous riot. Many in the crowd, including a number of monks, went on a rampage. Over a period of several days, mobs of Tibetans attacked both ethnic Chinese and Hui Muslims, killing, it is thought, up to eighteen innocent civilians. At one point an attempt was made to storm the Lhasa mosque, the rioters setting its gate ablaze, while large numbers of businesses owned both by Han Chinese and the Hui minority were torched. Foreign eyewitnesses spoke of stabbings and stonings as shops burned and were looted, and several non-Tibetan hotels were also set ablaze and vandalized. Not only were men involved but women and children, too. There were dozens of police injuries, and large numbers of vehicles — including a fire engine — were destroyed. In all, the number of separate incidents ran into the dozens, possibly hundreds, as the city erupted. Among other measures, the Chinese authorities responded by cutting off the water supply to the Three Seats, whose personnel were implicated in the disturbances, preventing food and medical deliveries to the monasteries. But news of the unrest spread quickly and was followed by riots in Kham and Amdo, a number of them turning violent and resulting in several deaths, both of Chinese and Tibetans, and the destruction of property.

It seems hard to deny that the viciousness of the 2008 uprising harmed the Tibetan cause in the eyes of the world. Yet it is true that claims about video shot in various locations during the protests suggested that some of the rioters were operating under a false flag as *agents provocateurs.* That the weapons and dress of a number of the individuals involved did not correspond to the area in which the incidents took place is taken as evidence they were planted by the Chinese. And it is indeed also true that it would have been extremely helpful to the central government if the rioters could be portrayed as racist thugs. Nevertheless, even if some of these accusations of deception on the part of the Chinese are correct, it seems unlikely that they could account for all the violence. Nor can we say that the memory of those little Tibetan boys and girls, their heads strung like a garland of flowers about the Hui military garrison eighty years earlier, nor even the memory of the casual brutality of the Cultural Revolution forty years before, could possibly justify what occurred, even if it does contextualize it.

For most people worldwide, Tibet was hardly a major issue. Many had heard of the Dalai Lama, but few know much about his homeland. It was therefore a matter of deepest regret to the Tibetan leader that, when news of the Land of Snows did finally make headlines, the picture it presented should be so dismal. Nevertheless, at the time, it did not prevent the Chinese president from announcing to international media just before the Olympics: "Our attitude towards contacts and consultation with the Dalai Lama is serious." This was taken by sympathizers as a sign that the main effect of the riots was to show the Chinese the strength of Tibetan discontent. While it certainly did that, once the Games safely passed without major protest — despite earlier suggestions, no head of state apart from Poland's stayed away in solidarity with the Tibetan people — Tibet abruptly vanished from the world's consciousness. A proposal on autonomy presented by negotiators from Dharamsala that autumn met with nothing more than derision. By the end of the year, the Dalai Lama was admitting that all his efforts of the past thirty years to find a political solution agreeable both to Tibet and to the Chinese had failed.

Since then, the Dalai Lama has made repeated admissions of the failure of his policy of rapprochement with China. From his perspective, his determination to meet Beijing halfway by demanding autonomy but not independence for Tibet has resulted in nothing other than cynical maneuvering on the part of the Chinese government. When the spotlight was on China at the time of the Olympics, its officials let drop one or two hopeful remarks for the benefit of those listening but then failed to act on them. And yet, in admitting the failure of his Middle Way policy, the Dalai Lama did not disavow it. Instead, he immediately responded with a plan to call a referendum to learn the will of the people. Did they or did they not want to continue with the policy in spite of its manifest failure? At first the vote was to have included all Tibetans, but the impracticality of a full plebiscite meant that, in the end, it was confined only to the diaspora. Unsurprisingly, it was found that the vast majority were indeed in favor of accepting the Dalai Lama's views and continuing with the policy.

Of course, such a referendum was only ever going to yield one result, given that the Middle Way was still the Dalai Lama's preferred option. But it is important to recognize here the Dalai Lama's openness to dissent. To the dismay of many, some Tibetans in exile even had the temerity to do so. Both the Tibetan Youth Congress, long a source of rumblings in favor of direct, even violent action, and Amnye Machen (a Dharamsala-based research institute) made clear their rejection of the Dalai Lama's policy, albeit expressing full confidence in his spiritual authority. A small number of elected politicians also broke ranks. To this, traditionalists reacted with outrage at what they saw as open expressions of disloyalty, some even calling for violence to be visited on the offenders.

It is often imagined that genuine democracy, once established, must, by virtue of its own internal logic, succeed as soon as it is implemented. That this view is naïve is shown by several recent attempts to initiate rule by the people, for the people, in countries where, historically, other systems have traditionally prevailed. In the case of the Tibetan diaspora (as no doubt would also be the case if ever democracy came to Tibet itself), loyalty to the Precious Protector is seen — even by many educated young people — as having greater value than the free expression of opinion. Yet for all this, most recognize the wisdom of the Dalai Lama's position. To make violence a component of policy is unthinkable for him. But beyond this, it is obvious that, even if every man, woman, and child were to take up arms, a few million Tibetans could not possibly succeed against the might of all China. The effect of conflict would only be more pain and more suffering for more people. The Dalai Lama's Middle Way policy thus prevails.

And yet, tragically, a new and still more desperate expression of discontent erupted among Tibetans just a few months after the Beijing Olympics as a young monk from Kirti Monastery in Kham poured gasoline over himself and lit a match. When, in 1963, a Vietnamese monk had done the same in protest against the Diem government, President John F. Kennedy said of the Pulitzer Prize–winning photograph of the event that no other news picture in history had aroused such emotion around the world. But though also photographed, the incident in Tibet was barely remarked on by the world's media.

Although at first this looked like an isolated incident, it was followed by a shocking spate of fourteen more self-immolations in 2011 and a staggering eighty-six in 2012. The figure dropped to twenty-eight the year after and eleven the year after that, and, since then, only a handful more have been recorded. But just when it seems the last flames have died down, more leap into Tibetans' collective consciousness as some (usually) young man or some young woman undertakes the ultimate protest and another name is added to the martyrs' memorial in Dharamsala. At the time of writing, more than 150 cases have been recorded.

The statistics are as sorrowful as they are startling. But it is the Dalai Lama's reaction to them that seems to many to be almost as remarkable, if differently so. While one might expect him firmly to oppose such horror, at no point has he come forward categorically to condemn the practice. In fact, self-sacrifice, usually by burning but also by other methods, such as starvation, is an attested component of Buddhist tradition with scriptural warrant — in both the Jataka Tales and the Lotus Sutra, for example. When, therefore, the Dalai Lama is called upon by the Chinese to repudiate self-immolation, it is actually not surprising that he refrains from doing so definitively — even though he discourages it. For him, the question is one of motivation. To the extent that the act is motivated by compassion (a motivation that the Dalai Lama has said would be extremely hard to maintain in the circumstances), it may be considered licit nonetheless. We should also remember that, from the point of view of the families and loved ones of those who have made what they see as the ultimate sacrifice, an edict from the Precious Protector condemning the practice would seem a cruel repudiation.

For an outsider, it is almost impossible to imagine the depths of despair, coupled with love for the Dalai Lama, that, even after all these years, a majority of Tibetans continue to feel in the depths of their hearts. If, though, we look at some of the photographs taken during the first half of the twentieth century — or, better still, some of the silent film shot by Sir Basil Gould on his 1940 expedition to Lhasa for the enthronement of the Dalai Lama — perhaps we can attain an inkling of it. Though somewhat grainy, the best frames give a vivid sense of the tradition that still has such a grip on the Tibetan imagination. There we catch a glimpse of the culture before the ill winds of industrialism blasted the country's fragile landscape. There we see the world ordered aright: the high-ranking members of the Ganden Phodrang government, the length of pendant in their left ear denoting their rank, standing swathed in delicious golden brocade shot with turquoise and green, vermillion and violet, the womenfolk adorned with fabulous headdresses on which are displayed lapis, coral, and jade, while around their necks they sport strings of *gzi,* the strange "heaven pearls" said to have been made by the gods themselves.* There we see the leading lamas of the day, likewise sumptuously clad, as befits their status, and the serried ranks of religious — testimony to the indispensability of the *sangha* in public life — while we can almost hear the whirl of prayer wheels spinning in the hands of the faithful to affirm the primacy of religion in the lives of the laypeople. But we note, too, signs of the feudal character of the old society: the grooms trotting alongside their masters' palfreys, the servants standing mutely expectant at their beck and call.

If it is true that in this film and in old photographs we get an inkling of what has been lost, it would be quite wrong to suppose that it is the outward

* Though these have been identified as a form of agate, there has been no definitive classification of the natural bead that I am aware of. Genuine stones now change hands for thousands of dollars apiece.

expression of this loss that people mourn. The often opium-addicted, often weak, conniving, and morally corrupt aristocrats are not missed. Still less does anyone regret the abolition of the feudal system, the exploitation of the many by the few, and the lifelong obligations to monastic and manorial estates. No, it is neither the pomp nor the circumstance of the old days that is regretted. Rather, it is the right-ordering of the world — a world where the Potala's Lion Throne is occupied by the Precious Protector and in which the rites and remembrances of religion occupy their proper place at the heart of public life — that is so keenly lamented.

Very likely those young men and women who sacrifice themselves have little idea what the return of the Dalai Lama would entail; they merely sense that it would be enough. And they would be right. The fact is, it is unthinkable that he would do so without some guarantee of basic liberties for his people: education in their own language, freedom of association, equality of opportunity, and, above all, the lifting of restrictions on religious practice. Of course, no such rights were recognized in the old Tibet. Outside the monasteries there was little, if any, education available, and none for free. There was no freedom of association or opinion, as Lungshar learned to his terrible cost. As for equality of opportunity, the concept had no meaning — even if it was true that a good number of lamas, such as Reting Rinpoché himself, were of humble background and that one or two who came to the Dalai Lama's attention were promoted to the aristocracy. In general, if you were born to a low estate, that was your karma. If, then, you ran away from a master, you were justly liable to punishment — even though you had no means of paying debts incurred by your forebears many generations ago. Far from bringing about a return to the old ways, the Dalai Lama's reinstallation at the Potala would signify a radical departure from the past. Yet while all this would of course be welcome, it is the mere fact of Chenresig residing among his people for which most Tibetans yearn before all else.

22

The Magical Play of Illusion

In April 2011 the Dalai Lama announced his full retirement from office as leader of the Tibetan government in exile.* Henceforth it would be headed by a democratically elected first minister. In thus handing over political power, the Precious Protector brought to an end three and a half centuries of theocratic rule — albeit that power had for long periods been vested in regents acting in the name of the Dalai Lama. It was a reform not universally applauded by Tibetans, but it had clearly been among the Precious Protector's plans from the moment he decided in favor of democracy on first coming into exile.

The Dalai Lama effected extraordinary change with this move. When Altan Khan, the Mongol strongman of sixteenth-century Central Asia, proclaimed Sonam Gyatso, abbot of Drepung, to be Taleh (the Mongolian term

* By chance, I happened to be in audience with the Dalai Lama when the document enacting his resignation was brought for signature. He left the room for a few minutes and returned with the air of a man in whom relief mingled with awe at what he had wrought.

for ocean, from which the word "Dalai" is derived) Lama, the Tibetan was head of a monastery comprising several thousand monks. But although this conferred immense prestige and great wealth, the direct political power attaching to him personally was limited to the sway he held over the Gelug establishment in general and over Drepung and its sister monasteries and their estates in particular. It was not until the Great Fifth secured the patronage of another of the Khans that the institution of the Dalai Lama attained such prestige that, in combination with his viceroy and backed by the military might of the Mongols, he could exercise political power across the Tibetan Buddhist world as a whole. In so doing, the Great Fifth forged the Tibetan people into a broadly harmonious society in a way that had not been seen since the fall of the religious kings in the ninth century. Moreover, his imaginative recapitulation of the Tibetan empire brought the spiritual realm of gods, demons, and protectors together with the earthly realm of human beings, their landed property, and their possessions, and made both answerable to a single authority.

What the present Dalai Lama brought about with his retirement was thus not just his withdrawal from politics but the end of the dispensation whereby, in effect, the Dalai Lama united within himself the functions of both priest and patron. This, it will be remembered, was the paradigmatic relationship whereby the priest, or lama, guaranteed the legitimacy of the king, while the king in turn supported the lama temporally. Under the new dispensation, the Dalai Lama continues to rule the supernatural realm while earthly matters are placed under the authority of a secular establishment. What is especially innovative about this maneuver is the elevation of the people themselves to the role of patron.

The withdrawal of the Dalai Lama's authority from the temporal realm was almost as important for its psychological as for its political value. No longer should Tibetans look to the Dalai Lama for answers to every question of a practical nature that, in theory at least, they had hitherto been free to put to him. Instead, they would stand on their own feet. The Dalai Lama and his successors could thus concern themselves with what they are actually trained for, namely, spiritual direction, even if, to the end of this life, he would remain a symbolic figurehead for his people.

Given that the Precious Protector's every word is held by most of his people to have divine authority, it presumably takes considerable restraint on his part not to speak out on earthly matters from time to time. But save for his handling of the Shugden controversy, insofar as it is a political matter, the Dalai Lama has so far shown little inclination to intervene in affairs of state. Instead, the former leader has dedicated himself to fulfilling what he describes as his three "main commitments." These are, first, as a human being, by helping others to be happy; second, as a Buddhist monk, by working to bring about harmony among the world's various religious traditions; and third, as a Tibetan, by helping to preserve his country's unique language and culture. In this last, he emphasizes the enormous debt the Tibetan tradition owes to what it inherited from the Indian scholar-saints of Nalanda, the Buddhist monastic university that flourished from the fifth to the twelfth century and provided the blueprint for the monastic universities of Tibet.

A major component of these commitments is the Dalai Lama's dedication to the environmentalist cause. The destruction of wildlife in Tibet since 1950 is a continuing sorrow to him, though his attitude toward the environment generally is neither sentimental nor a function of his religiosity. There is nothing "sacred or holy" about nature, he writes in his autobiography; rather, "taking care of our planet is like taking care of our houses." Similarly, while he is a ready advocate of compassion in farming and has said on occasion that he would like to be the "world spokesman for fish," he does not go so far as to deny categorically the possibility that animal experimentation might, in certain circumstances, be justifiable — provided that the motive in doing so is altruistic. It is characteristic of the Buddhist approach to avoid absolutes. Also to the dismay of some, the Dalai Lama, though he has often spoken in favor of vegetarianism, is, as we have seen, not a vegetarian himself. Moreover, he recognizes the difficulty of living in an environmentally responsible way and does not make a fetish of doing so. While eschewing baths, he admits that, in taking a shower morning and evening, there might be little difference in his water consumption.

With respect to his commitment to helping others find happiness, the Dalai Lama includes scientific research as an important component in the human search for felicity. To this end, he continues to meet and to engage in dialogue with scientists from around the world. Whether a consequence of this is that he has himself "become one of the world's greatest scientists," as

Robert Thurman has suggested, may be open to question. It is certainly not a claim he would make for himself. But his patronage of a compendium of Buddhist scientific texts demonstrates his wish to see Buddhist inquiry, especially into the nature of consciousness, given serious consideration by outsiders. Noting the congruence between the Buddhist and the scientific worldviews, the Dalai Lama wonders why "the impulse for helping and kindness are not recognized as drivers for human behaviour and . . . flourishing?" If scientists were to ask these questions honestly, he believes that they would find the answers provided by Buddhist thinkers compelling.

In the field of interreligious dialogue, the Dalai Lama has, since retiring from office, continued to meet and to pray with religious leaders and prominent spiritual figures from around the world. Setting aside his vow to refrain from intoxicating beverages, he once partook of Holy Communion administered by Archbishop Desmond Tutu. On another occasion, he donned an apron to serve food in a church-run homeless shelter in Australia. Despite hostility from some quarters, the Dalai Lama has visited Israel more than once; in 2006, he met with both the Sephardi and Ashkenazi chief rabbis. He has also visited several Islamic countries, notably Jordan, again more than once, meeting with Prince Ghazi bin Mohammed, a leading figure in Islamic interfaith dialogue, later that same year.

Besides advocating pluralism with respect to other religions, it is evident that the Dalai Lama also wishes to strengthen his followers in their faith. As a rule, he counsels people to remain within their own faith tradition, remarking that if a person is a poor practitioner of one, changing to another will do nothing to improve matters. Referring to his visit to the monastery of Le Grand Chartreuse, where he noticed the monks' feet cracked with cold from wearing only sandals, he praises the dedication of followers of non-Buddhist religions. At the same time, he speaks of his concern about Tibetan teachers abroad who live luxuriously or flout their vows. Yet his concern about behavior inappropriate to prelates is not confined to Buddhists. When Pope Francis removed a German ecclesiastic for the ostentatious restoration of his residence, the Dalai Lama wrote to congratulate the Roman pontiff.* Whether or not it is true

* This was Franz-Peter Tebartz-van Elst, the so-called "Bishop of Bling."

that, of all the other religions, the Dalai Lama feels closest to Catholicism is an open question. On the one hand, for him it is given a priori that there is no Creator. On the other hand, the superficial similarities between many of the liturgical practices of Rome and Lhasa cause him to wonder if there was not earlier contact between the two traditions. Both religions practice ritual eating and drinking, and both venerate the relics of saints. It is also true that the Dalai Lama has been hosted many times by ecumenically minded Catholic organizations, and if he is not mistaken, the Dalai Lama enjoys divine approval for fostering links with the Catholic Church. On a visit to Fatima in 2001, he experienced a vision of the Virgin Mary, whose statue turned and smiled at him. In this context, it is not entirely clear how we are to interpret his remark that one of the biggest surprises of his life came when Pope Benedict XVI proclaimed the indispensability of reason to religious faith. In the Dalai Lama's view, if people would only think hard enough, they would come to see the truth of *how things really are*—and thus the falsity of the pope's position and the correctness of his own.

The Dalai Lama's dedication to these three main commitments has meant that his retirement from politics has not resulted in any more leisure than before. He continues to receive dozens of invitations to talk or teach even though, when his office accepts any of these on his behalf nowadays, it is on the proviso that the Dalai Lama's public appearances are limited to two hours a day. Meanwhile, he continues to take spiritual teachings and instruction from other lamas as often as his schedule permits, while he maintains rigorously his own practice and study. When traveling abroad, he makes no concession to jet lag and always rises at the same time of day. His one real recreation is to attend monastic debates and follow the progress of the rising generation of scholars, particularly on his visits to the great monastic universities refounded in the south of India. A particular source of joy to him on such occasions is that he is able to do so not, as is generally supposed by non-monastics, as a "great authority" but rather as a supremely well-informed student eager to learn from those who, unlike him, have been able to devote their whole lives to study.

He continues to take the opportunity while traveling to visit places of interest or special significance. He prayed at the site of Martin Luther King's assassination on one trip to America. On another, he announced his wish to visit an active volcano. As a bonus, on that particular occasion he was delighted to spot a plant species that he had cultivated at home in Dharamsala. "Suddenly," recalls Thurman, "with a whoop of glee, he leaped off the roadway and across a ditch . . . and clambered up the opposite embankment . . . He then asked to be photographed holding out a leaf . . . He stood there in his goofy hat, grinning from ear to ear . . . 'Next life,' he announced, 'I will be a naturalist!'"

Since retiring, the Dalai Lama has continued to confer the Kalachakra initiation — both at home in India and abroad. In 2014 he did so for the third time in Ladakh, where a new palace was built for him toward the end of the last century, onto a crowd estimated at a quarter of a million. At the time of writing, he has conducted the Kalachakra ceremonies thirty-four times since his initiation into the practice.

With regard to those invitations to speak in public that the Dalai Lama accepts, it is of course true that they are the ones that his closest advisers deem suitable to recommend to him. Any that are proposed directly may be lobbied against by the same individuals. It is also natural that, sometimes, personal connections and preferences on their part come into play. And it is true that, over the years, there have been a number of missteps. One of the most embarrassing was the series of audiences granted in the late 1980s to Shoko Asahara, the Japanese cult leader and future mass murderer. Since Asahara's emergence as the mastermind of the gas attack on a Tokyo subway station, the Dalai Lama has often pointed out that, if he was, as a manifestation of a bodhisattva, perfectly omniscient, he would not have been hoodwinked by the cult leader.

A more recent embarrassment was the Dalai Lama's public talk in Albany, New York, partially sponsored by the controversial group known as NXIVM (pronounced Nexium). It was alleged that the organization, besides conducting dubious financial activities, was also a sex cult, an allegation that has since been proven correct. It has also been claimed that, as a condition of the Dalai Lama's participation in the event, a large sum of money changed hands. The Dalai Lama's office was quick to point out that the Dalai Lama never charges a fee for appearing, a fact attested to by many who have organized events at which he has been featured.* It should also be said that the Dalai Lama mentioned in his talk that he was aware that there was controversy about NXIVM, which, he suggested, should be investigated properly. Nonetheless, it is apparent that there was a link between the Dalai Lama and the Tibetan monk working in a semiofficial capacity, subsequently removed from office, who had facilitated his appearance. This individual was subsequently reinstated and exonerated, although his position was then almost immediately abolished by the Dalai Lama, suggesting some uncomfortable behind-the-scenes maneuvering. It has struck some that the Precious Protector may not always be well served by those closest to him.

There have also been several occasions when a portion of the Dalai Lama's supporters have been disappointed by the choice of events that his advisers have arranged for or encouraged him to attend. His appearance on the Australian *Master Chef* TV show was a case in point. Another was his appearance at Glastonbury Festival in Britain. In the latter case, however, the Dalai Lama did say that he had enjoyed himself—despite being kissed on stage by singer Patti Smith, to the outrage of many Tibetans. Unless, however, we are prepared to say (as indeed the Chinese do say) that the approbation of dozens of world leaders who have welcomed him, numerous chancellors of universities who have conferred honorary degrees on him, and each of the (certainly hundreds and probably thousands of) mayors and community leaders who have made civic awards to the Dalai Lama—to say nothing of the millions of ordinary people who have been encouraged by and have drawn inspiration from the Dalai Lama—has been, in every single case, misinformed and misguided, it would be hard to argue that these occasional lapses tell us more about the man than his many successes. And even those who do hold a negative view must acknowledge the Dalai Lama's fidelity to his role. After all, what was to stop him as a young man from forsaking his robes and gravitating to the fleshpots of the free world?

It is true nonetheless that the Dalai Lama has attracted the ire of some

* I am one of them. The rule explained at the outset was that organizers could charge to cover the costs of hosting the Dalai Lama and his entourage. Any surplus should be donated to one or more local charities.

commentators in the Western media. One such was Christopher Hitchens, who criticized him for, among other reasons, seeming to support India's testing of thermonuclear weapons. Furthermore, he has drawn dismay in some quarters for suggesting that Europe is for Europeans and that, while migrants should be welcomed, they should plan to return home to build their countries as soon as they are in a position to do so. Some have accused him of exploiting his audiences, of being a "ham," as one put it, and the "crowd-pleaser to end all crowd-pleasers." Against this, others have noted that he often makes a point of addressing and embracing the mentally disturbed, including those who seem likely to be violent, who attend events at which he appears. Besides, the Dalai Lama has been known to make artless remarks that have, on occasion, deeply offended people. On a visit to Norway, he once pointed to a teenaged girl and told her, giggling, that she was "too fat." These are hardly the actions of a "ham." The Dalai Lama has also been criticized for some of his friendships. His affection for George W. Bush (who painted the Dalai Lama's portrait) causes difficulty for some. His personal regard for Nancy Pelosi perhaps causes difficulty for others. Yet his unaffected charm and evident humanity have won him countless admirers.

As to the future, while it is clear that, functionally, the Dalai Lama's retirement from his leadership role is genuine, it remains to be seen whether his reforms will survive him. It is not impossible to imagine an ambitious future incumbent of the office — or, perhaps more likely, a weak successor manipulated by ambitious staff — re-appropriating political power. This is a particular danger should the Precious Protector "manifest the act of passing away" sooner rather than later. It would be surprising to learn that he has not had exactly the same thought, however. From what he has said about his succession, besides repeating that there will be a Fifteenth Dalai Lama only if that is the wish of the Tibetan people as a whole (which, undoubtedly, it will be), he has made clear that, as one of a number of options, he is already considering the possibility of appointing a successor while still living, by identifying a *ma de tulku.* This is an incarnation appointed when the previous incumbent remains alive.

Usually the procedure for anointing such an incarnation entails an elderly lama declaring that the *bodhi* which resides with himself has been identified as residing with someone younger, usually a disciple or spiritual friend, though sometimes an assistant or even (somewhat less plausibly) a relative. The one so named then occupies the lama's position within both the spiritual and the temporal realms, taking on all property, tithes, and title of the one making the appointment while the incumbent himself retires, often moving to a hermitage and going on permanent retreat. One huge advantage of success in identifying and confirming the new Dalai Lama in this way is that it would greatly complicate any attempt on the part of the Chinese authorities to interfere in the succession. Should this not come to pass, however, and should the Dalai Lama not appoint his successor personally, it is certain that the traditional methods of identification will be used, and in anticipation of his death outside Tibet, the Dalai Lama has made clear that his incarnation should also be sought outside Tibet. It is even rumored that Palden Lhamo, the Glorious Goddess, has been invited to move her residence from the visionary lake in Tibet to another lake, somewhere in Ladakh.*

But if the Precious Protector has, potentially, settled the question of what form the Dalai Lama institution will take in the future, and if he finds a way to finesse the succession problem (though understanding full well that the Chinese are sure to anoint their own "official" candidate), there remains at least one important obstacle to securing his ultimate vision. While he wishes the Dalai Lama to be an inclusive figure, able to speak for all Tibetans irrespective of their regional origin (whether they hail from Ü-Tsang, Kham, or Amdo), and irrespective of which denomination they belong to, the Shugden challenge remains. What this amounts to, practically speaking, is the age-old question faced by all ancient institutions under pressure from events in the world: whether to turn toward it and risk annihilation, or whether to turn away and retreat to first principles, or some version thereof, in the hope of weathering the storm until a full-scale revival can be brought about. As we have seen, the

* When I put this to the Dalai Lama in April 2019, he did not answer directly but conceded that, on a recent visit to Ladakh, many had observed an unusual cloud formation roll over the mountains from Tibet during a teaching he was giving. As soon as the ceremonies were concluded, the cloud went back the way it came, leaving a rainbow in its wake. "So, something mysterious," he said.

outcome of the contest between these two impulses, the one represented by Shugden, the other by Nechung, has yet to be finally settled, and the problem remains a thorn in the Precious Protector's flesh.

Let us suppose, however, that the present Dalai Lama lives, as he has suggested he might, to be well over a hundred, and that he succeeds both in implementing his vision of the Dalai Lama institution as a unifying force for all and in settling the question of his succession. What are the prospects for his people?

It is difficult to be optimistic. The Chinese Communist Party's policy of economic expansion as a means of preserving its position has been an outstanding success. It has shown that liberal democracy is by no means an inevitable entailment of capitalism. On the contrary, the panoptico-Leviathan state the party has created looks very much able to face down any merely ideological challenge to its existence. What it cannot assimilate, it will surely destroy. Thus China's ascent as a world superpower looks set to continue into the foreseeable future, while, just as the party's planners forecast long ago, fewer and fewer countries will dare risk their trading relations with China for the sake of a few million Tibetans.

Indeed, this is already happening. The Dalai Lama has been refused visas to South Africa and Botswana. As early as 2008 the British Foreign Office ceased (after more than a century) to recognize China's suzerainty over Tibet and instead acknowledged Tibet as an "integral part of China." For the foreseeable future, and assuming no radical change in attitude on the part of Beijing, it looks certain, therefore, that Tibetans will continue to face political and cultural subjugation in their own homeland. It is an open question how long this can be sustained before the notion that the Tibetan people might one day be emancipated ceases to have real meaning. It might well have passed already. If this is true, the further question is whether the culture can survive. This is really the question of whether Tibetan Buddhism is able to do so. Here, too, the signs are not all encouraging. The religious impulse among Tibetans in Tibet seems undeniably to be declining as young people concern themselves more with this life than the next. Although the combined population of the Three Seats in exile today is said to equal their historic numbers, with upwards of twenty thousand monks in residence, numbers are down from their peak a decade or so ago, partly a result of the fact that China now prevents easy migration from Tibet, but partly because it is less and less usual for families to send children to the monasteries as a matter of course. A further worry is whether the tradition can again produce individual practitioners of the stature of, for example, the Dalai Lama's tutors.

As for the prospects of a full restoration of religion in Tibet under Chinese rule, unquestionably the biggest impediment to this is the tradition's association with the idea of Tibetan independence. For the Precious Protector, however, the survival of the Buddhadharma in Tibet is more important than nationhood. He clearly hopes that with the Dalai Lama institution decoupled from government, it will cease to be a focal point for nationalism. Whether or not this translates into a less political *sangha* within Tibet remains to be seen. But there are reasons to be cautiously optimistic for the survival of the tradition on other grounds. The growth of interest in religion generally, and in Buddhism in particular, is one of the most important, if also one of the least documented, features of modern China. We are compelled to rely on anecdotal evidence, but it seems clear that a major revival is under way. To take one example, the mixed-sex monastic settlement at Larung Gar in a remote part of Kham was home, until recently, to around forty thousand monks and nuns living consecrated lives. In 2016 the authorities ordered that this be reduced to just two thousand nuns and fifteen hundred monks (the disparity in numbers being perhaps a reflection of the perception that women religious are less likely to cause trouble than their male counterparts), and demolition of many dwellings began soon after. At the time of writing, the exact status of Larung Gar is unclear. But what is known is that, both at its height and now, approximately half the numbers were, as they remain, made up by ethnic Chinese.

Religious revivals are one thing of which, historically, the Chinese authorities have been extremely wary. The White Lotus Rebellion, followed by the Taiping Rebellion — both of them inspired by charismatic religious leaders — were important factors in the demise of the Qing dynasty. Given this, the likelihood is that there will continue to be friction between state and *sangha* in both Tibetan- and Han-dominated territories. Already recognition of new incarnations is technically forbidden, and at the time of writing, there are severe restrictions on the activities of the monasteries generally.

As for the thought that the present, or a future, Chinese leader might experience a Constantinian-style spiritual conversion (Constantine being the fourth-century Roman Emperor who became a Christian): while intriguing, the reality is that such a turn of events would be unlikely to have much impact. Even Chairman Mao was unable invariably to dictate terms to the Politburo. And while it is not impossible that the party could tolerate a Buddhist premier, what it could not tolerate is any move that threatened its grip on Tibet. It is, therefore, hard to imagine a Chinese president inviting the Dalai Lama even for a short visit to his homeland. That said, there does appear to have been a moment (though later denied) in 2014 when the Dalai Lama and the general secretary of the Chinese Communist Party (and thus paramount leader of China), Xi Xinping, might have met. It is believed by many Tibetans that Xi's wife is a practicing Buddhist and that he himself is personally sympathetic toward both Buddhism and the Dalai Lama, perhaps on account of the fact that his father was stationed in Tibet during the 1950s. While the Chinese leader was on a visit to Delhi, the Dalai Lama's office contacted the Chinese embassy to see whether a personal meeting between the two men might arranged. It transpired that Xi was willing. But, allegedly after an intervention by the Indian government, the meeting did not in fact take place. Yet even had it done so, it is difficult to imagine any radical change of policy on China's part.

If it is true that China is unlikely to make political concessions with respect to Tibet, the question that must be faced is whether there is any realistic hope for the survival of a distinct Tibetan identity. Of course, dynasties come and go, but so too do whole peoples. The Celts dominated western and central Europe for perhaps a thousand years before the coming of the Romans. The Phoenicians were earlier and lasted longer. The Aztecs are a more recent people that once flourished and have since disappeared. It is not wrong to fear, as the Dalai Lama fears, for the long-term future of the Tibetan people under such a regime as the Chinese have brought into being. There is nevertheless one entity that has shown itself consistently able to endure harassment, persecution, and even genocidal hatred: the human spirit itself. Here we might think of that of the Jewish people, who for so much of their history have been persecuted. If the experience of the Jews, whose endurance has been underpinned by religious faith, is anything to go by, the prospects for survival of the Tibetan people look more secure, especially given leadership by an individual who eschews the ordinary inducements of the world — the fame (which the present Dalai Lama has shown himself entirely willing to give up over the Shugden controversy) and the fortune (there is little doubt the Dalai Lama would be content with nothing more than a room in which to meditate) which are the perennial temptations of those in power. Indeed, the Dalai Lama's own spirit — his life-force, his character, his resolve in the face of overwhelming odds — shows that where unshakeable faith meets with wholehearted renunciation of self, human beings are capable of surmounting even the most abject circumstances. (This, surely, is the secret of the Dalai Lama's personal magnetism: the aura that he exudes, at all times and in every circumstance, of an absolute conviction, rooted deep within a tradition that is itself both rich and profound, a conviction that is yet worn lightly and grounded in a generous — and palpable — good-naturedness.)

The greatest threat to the Tibetan people is thus the same as the threat to the Dalai Lama institution itself: that the onslaught of the contemporary world proves too much for the individual who takes up the present incarnation's mantle. So intimately connected is the Dalai Lama institution with Tibetan identity that it is impossible to think of this identity surviving long should the Dalai Lama himself (or, less plausibly but, according to the present incarnation, possible, herself) be less than fully rooted in the tradition and less than wholly committed to the role. Already there are signs of weakening within the Karmapa institution. One of the claimants to the title of Karmapa, in defiance of tradition, has married. The other has spoken of his battle with depression. And while the Dalai Lama institution has shown itself capable of enduring wayward behavior, as in the case of the lovelorn Sixth Dalai Lama, and even lack of direction over long periods, such as the century and more that elapsed between the demise of the Seventh and the coming of age of the Great Thirteenth Dalai Lama, it is doubtful it could survive a thoroughgoing apostasy — either of an individual Dalai Lama or of the people themselves.

And yet, all this being said, even if there are just a few families surviving on the Himalayan plateau in the days and years following the collapse of the present Chinese empire — which, if history is any guide, must surely come — it is almost impossible to imagine them forgetting the One Who Looked

Down with Compassion on their forefathers. Remembering this, will they not look for signs and wonders in nature and go searching for his face among the newborn children in their black horsehair tents, those miraculous emblems of human endurance against the wind and the cold and the depredations of ghost and demon, in the harsh uplands of the Land of Snows? This could happen after a lengthy hiatus and seems all the more likely when we consider the myth that is sure to be woven out of the achievements of the present incarnation.

Consider the extraordinary reversal of ill fortune that the Fourteenth has brought about. When he was followed into exile by eighty thousand destitute refugees, one might have hoped, at best, for their rapid absorption into Indian society while the Dalai Lama himself went on to establish one or more small Buddhist centers either in India or elsewhere. For him to have presided over the establishment of a widely successful, broadly cohesive diaspora that numbers now perhaps a quarter of a million individuals scattered across the world, and besides this to have won for Buddhism in the Tibetan tradition a following numbering in the millions worldwide, is quite astonishing and certainly without parallel in the modern world.*

Whereas fifty years ago the number of Tibetan Buddhist centers outside Tibet — the first of them set up by the amiable beer-drinking CIA translator Geshe Wangyal — could be counted on the fingers of one hand, today there are certainly thousands. The present Dalai Lama has also established close links with Buddhist communities outside his own tradition such that his counsel and benediction are frequently sought by monks and nuns from Korea, Vietnam, Taiwan, Mongolia, Thailand, Japan, and even mainland China itself. Absent the leadership of the farmer's son from Taktser, it is almost impossible to imagine such a state of affairs.

It is arguably true that the upsurge of interest in Buddhism generally is only partly due to the Dalai Lama, and that it might have occurred anyway, but it seems overwhelmingly unlikely that it would have done so to the extent it has without the tireless work of the Precious Protector. It seems indeed, just

* To this achievement might also be added the extraordinary success of Tibetan studies as an academic discipline. From this has come a vast literature of translations and other secondary literature.

as he foresaw, the Buddha's prophecy that, two and a half millennia after his parinirvana, the teachings would flourish in the land of the red-faced people has been fulfilled, in large part through his own efforts. Beyond this, though, we can consider the contribution by the Dalai Lama to humanity's growing familiarity with the concept of compassion. It is remarkable that, on the best measure available, the frequency of usage of the word "compassion" during the past half century has increased more than 200 percent in English, while in some European languages (German, for example) the increase has been substantially greater. In a way that was certainly not true half a century ago, compassion is now seen as a cornerstone of health care, as a goal of education, as a precondition of peace, and as of significance to the world of business. It is increasingly accepted that even prisoners merit being shown compassion. It is hard to imagine the preeminent position the virtue of compassion has come to occupy within public discourse without the Dalai Lama's advocacy. This, too, is a towering achievement that will surely animate his memory within the tradition.

What, though, of his legacy to the world itself? Arguably his most significant contribution has yet to be widely appreciated. For many, if not most, the word "compassion" is synonymous with empathy. If, however, the Dalai Lama's relationship with Chenresig, Bodhisattva of Compassion, is to be taken seriously, it surely follows that the Precious Protector's whole life is, in an important sense, an object lesson in the meaning of compassion. And it turns out that, on this view, there is more to being compassionate than is ordinarily supposed.

Considering his life's work, we see that, for the Dalai Lama, compassion consists first and foremost in generosity — not just generosity in the sense of gift giving, though even in this sense he is generous to a fault. His immediate gift of the prize money that accompanied both the Nobel and the Templeton awards is testimony to this. It should also be mentioned that he has made numerous — often substantial — donations to charities around the world for such causes as disaster relief. All royalties from his many books (over two hundred separate titles in all, several of them million-sellers) are paid directly into one of several charitable foundations that he has caused to be set up. Beyond this, he is also personally generous. He recycles gifts as a matter of course, but has been known to make cash gifts and interest-free loans to family and friends —and not exclusively to Tibetans. When the New Zealand–born Theosophist known throughout Dharamsala affectionately (if also somewhat fearfully) as Auntie Joyce needed full-time care at the end of her life, having for decades volunteered her secretarial service to the government in exile, it was the Dalai Lama who, hearing that she was in want, settled her bills. He is also notoriously generous with his time, often inconveniencing himself by extending both public talks and private audiences in order to answer questions. Yet from a Buddhist perspective, his generosity is made manifest most forcefully and most valuably through his service to the Buddhadharma: the countless talks he has given, the thousands of teachings and initiations he has granted, the tens of thousands of rituals in which he has participated and ordinations he has conferred.

While generosity in this sense of serving others through furthering appreciation and understanding of the Buddhadharma represents the full flowering of the Dalai Lama's compassion, it is also important to recognize that there are other—indispensable—aspects to his exemplification of the virtue of compassion. If it is right to say that the Precious Protector's whole life can be seen as living out what it means to be compassionate, we see that it also embraces the virtue of prudence in practical matters. Looking back on his life, we see that it meant, for example, not becoming involved either in the CIA's operations in Tibet or in the Chushi Gangdruk resistance during the 1950s and 1960s. At the same time, his living out of compassion did not cause him categorically to prohibit their endeavors. Similarly, it has not precluded a certain pragmatism, as, for example, when he acquiesced in India's request to send Establishment 22 to war in Bangladesh—however much it pained him to do so.

It is also clear from the Dalai Lama's biography that compassion entails a willingness both to compromise and, where appropriate, to exercise resolve. Giving up the quest for independence for Tibet is an obvious example of a judicious compromise, while his fidelity to Buddhist doctrine is testament to his resolve. The Four Noble Truths are not open to negotiation. Nor are the basic Buddhist insights into the ultimate nature of reality: the doctrines of karma, of dependent origination, of emptiness, and, as a corollary of these, of no-self. But if defending what is a priori may not demand much in the way of effort, there are times when being compassionate entails holding the line in the face of determined opposition. Thus compassion is clearly related to courage. With respect to the Shugden controversy, it would have been easy to make concessions. Instead, the Precious Protector has risked his entire reputation in defending what he judges to be the correct position in regard to the deity — not for his own good, but for the good of all. Less obviously, but just as important, the Dalai Lama also shows, in his dealings with the protectors, that being compassionate means upholding the truth of the supernatural realm. It is not the case, in his view, that Buddhism can be stripped of the supernatural or that the protectors can be dispensed with. The Buddhadharma cannot simply be reduced to ethics and mindfulness meditation, notwithstanding the paramount importance of both right conduct and inner calm. Helping others to see this is, again, part of what it means to be compassionate — even if it is true that the Dalai Lama does not emphasize protector practice among neophyte Buddhists.

When we take seriously the claim that the Precious Protector is the earthly manifestation of Chenresig, we see also that compassion is, in many respects, a conservative virtue. Not that the Dalai Lama himself can be pigeonholed as a conservative. His advocacy of democracy in the political sphere and his ecumenism in the religious sphere make this plain. So too does his consideration of women. The Dalai Lama has been a staunch supporter of the recent introduction of the *geshema* degree for nuns, even though he has made clear that the tradition is such that women cannot actually be ordained. It is also true that some lighthearted comments about the need for a possibly female future Dalai Lama (not ruled out entirely, although a necessary condition of full Enlightenment is that the individual is male) to be attractive caused disappointment in some areas. Similarly, the Dalai Lama's encouragement of science as part of the monastic curriculum shows his commitment to the betterment of the world through technology. He has often said that if he had had to choose a career other than monasticism, he would have wanted to be an engineer.

Another vital feature of the Precious Protector's exposition of compassion is his insistence that it is not pompous. As anyone who has had the privilege of meeting him knows, the ever present smiles and the irrepressible laughter are wholly unforced. One is reminded of Chesterton's remark about there being "some one thing that was too great for God to show us when he walked upon our earth and I have sometimes fancied that it was his mirth." In contrast, the Dalai Lama, having plumbed the depths of consciousness through his daily meditation practice, shows no such restraint.

But if there is one thing above all that the Dalai Lama shows, it is that compassion is the fruit of *bodhichitta,* the determination to work unstintingly for the Enlightenment of all sentient beings — all humans, gods, demigods, animals, hungry ghosts, and denizens of the hell realms. It is this aspiration that finally determines the Dalai Lama's conduct: his every thought, word, and deed. All his teaching, all his writings, all his public talks, all his media appearances and interviews with journalists, all his charitable works, all the rituals in which he participates, all the divinations he undertakes, all his private prayer and meditation, even all his political endeavors are expressions of this single aim. By teaching and by example, his ultimate goal is to help others understand the way things really are and thus to set them on the path to liberation. It turns out that, in this, his wish to help people overcome ignorance and to cease grasping at the existence of a substantial self, the Dalai Lama is a much more radical figure than is generally supposed. And yet to miss this is to miss the whole point of his ministry. Unlike the Christ who taught selflessness, the Buddha taught self-lessness. The Dalai Lama wants us to understand that, ultimately, there is no self and no other, indeed no Dalai Lama, no Precious Protector, no Tibet — that in the end there is only the magical play of illusion.

AFTERWORD AND ACKNOWLEDGMENTS

One of the biggest challenges in writing this book was having to confront the yawning gap between the Tibet of historical record and what might be called the Facebook image of Tibet. What strikes us most forcibly about the Tibet of historical record is, echoing the words of Johan Huizinga, the great Dutch historian, writing of the European Middle Ages, the "violent tenor of life" that characterizes it. As we have seen, justice was often summary and, by modern standards, cruel. Offense was easily given and easily taken, meeting all too often with revenge, while grudges might be borne for centuries, given new life every so often by a ferment of religious belief. Yet the fact is there have always been two Tibets. On the one hand, there is Tibet as it is perceived by the tradition, a tradition expressed in the culture and customs of the people but also grounded in the landscape, the flora and fauna of the roof of the world. On the other, there is Tibet as it is perceived from outside the tradition.

The Tibet that tradition sees is one where, whatever the failings of individual men and women — and none would wish to say that the blinding of Lungshar or the murder of Reting Rinpoché was anything but iniquitous — theirs was a society that nonetheless prized and often practiced compassion. From the perspective of the tradition, the existence of the monasteries and the dedication of the people to their religion is all the proof that is needed, since to practice the Buddhadharma *is* to be compassionate. With respect to Tibet as it is seen from outside, there is a greater variety of opinion. To some, Tibet before the Chinese takeover of the middle years of the twentieth century was the "wisdom heart of the world," its emptiness was "sacred space," its people were "guardians of a storehouse of spiritual treasures" whose religion was an "inner science" while they, as its practitioners, were "exponents of sacred technology." To others, it was simply and without remainder a "hell on earth" where the masses "groaned under the tyranny of serfdom."

If, at first sight, the tradition's view of itself is unjustifiably optimistic, neither of these outside perspectives stands up to scrutiny either. Although doubtless many suffered at the whims of their masters, there is scant evidence that the majority considered their way of life hellish. What came afterwards was more nearly hell. Furthermore, it is clear that the Dalai Lama, the very personification of the Tibetan tradition, was himself intent on the abolition of feudalism from early on. Equally, the historical record shows that the two-dimensional characterization of Tibet as a land of monks meditating in the mystic fastness of the Himalayan Mountains while the laity lived in serene harmony with one another and with nature is completely untenable. Neither extreme serves the cause of the Tibetan people, who, if they are to be served at all, would profit most from a sober analysis of their grievances and sufferings.

Moreover, if we content ourselves with saying that the truth lies somewhere in between, there is a danger of overlooking the way in which both the Tibetan tradition and the Dalai Lama himself radically challenge contemporary society. In a way, we could call this the challenge of the natural world to the scientific world. From the perspective of the tradition, the existence — and willingness to use — not just weapons of mass destruction but weapons that kill indiscriminately seems a disastrous state of affairs. A society that would permit, let alone condone, such a thing must be barbarous in the extreme. Similarly, the fact of what, from the perspective of the tradition, is nothing less than infanticide being practiced on an industrial scale (the millions of abortions carried out annually) seems atrocious beyond imagining, while, at the other end of life, the treatment of the elderly and infirm, abandoned in nursing homes outside the family, seems heartless and ungrateful. And the mechanized slaughter of untold numbers of animals on a daily basis looks obscene. From a contemporary standpoint, these seem normal and rational solutions to the challenges of modern living. Yet against these features of the modern world, the occasional and always to be regretted failings of individuals in the history of Tibet look, from the perspective of the tradition, altogether easier to forgive.

. . .

I have to thank a large number of people for their help over the years that this project has been under way. First and foremost, I would like to thank His Holiness the Dalai Lama himself for kindly inviting me to stay at the SOS Tibetan Youth Hostel during December 2014 so that he might be available to answer the great many questions I had for him at the outset of this work. Subsequently, the Dalai Lama generously met with me on several occasions, culminating in a lengthy interview granted on what was supposed to be a day of complete rest in April 2019. This should not be taken to imply that I had the opportunity to clear up every doubt or query, or that this is in any sense an authorized biography. Nevertheless, I can claim to have had well in excess of my fair share of access to the Dalai Lama during the writing and research of this book.

Ippolite Desideri, the eighteenth-century missionary to Tibet, notes that, as a generality, the Tibetans he met with were "kindly, clever, and courteous by nature." This is certainly true of all those of the Dalai Lama's compatriots who so generously gave of their time to help me with this project. In particular, I should like to mention and thank Mr. Tendzin Choegyal (Ngari Rinpoché), Yangten Rinpoché, Mrs. Rinchen Khando, Mr. Tenzin Geyche Tethong, Dr. Thupten Jinpa (who read and commented on parts of the manuscript: I was especially gratified that he "really enjoyed" the last chapter), Mrs. Namgyal Taklha, the late Mr. Rinchen Sadutsang, Mrs. Sadutsang, the late Mr. Tsering Gongkatsang, the late Mr. Tsewang Norbu, Professor Samten Karmay, Mr. Paljor Tsarong, Mr. Tenzin Namgyal Tethong, Mr. Jamyang Choegyal Kasho, and, especially, Mr. Tenzin Choepel — each of whom gave invaluable support and generously helped whenever asked.

I also thank Mr. Jeremy Russell for answering questions and pointing the way whenever I asked; Mr. Aniket Mandavagane for his insights from his position as Indian government liaison officer to the Dalai Lama; Dr. Jianglin Li for sharing unpublished material and entering into a lengthy correspondence about the Chinese occupation of Tibet during the 1950s; Mr. Ralf Kramer for many discussions, for sharing his encyclopedic knowledge of sources and where to find them, for his help with obtaining many of the images in this book, and for his work on the bibliography and notes; Dr. George FitzHerbert, in particular for sharing his paper on Tibetan war magic; Professor Ulrike Roesler for several introductions; Professor Mel Goldstein for sharing sources and unpublished material relating to the Dalai Lama's escape from Lhasa and kindly entering into a lengthy correspondence about these; and Dr. Jan Westerhoff for an illuminating discussion about Indo-Tibetan logic. From within the walls of academia, I am indebted above all to Professor Robbie Barnett for his acute reading of, and corrections to, substantial parts of the text. He saved me from many mistakes.

There are many other people who have, over many years, helped shape my thinking on Tibet's history and culture, but for more general discussions of a philosophical nature, I wish to thank in particular Mr. Stephen Priest; Dr. Ralph Weir (who was good enough to read and comment on the manuscript); Dr. Samuel Hughes; and Professor Benedikt Goecke. For his theological reading of the manuscript, I thank Mr. Nikolas Prassas.

Despite all this help, I am quite certain that there remain many errors. These I claim as my own.

Finally, for her assistance in sourcing photographs, I thank Ms. Jane Moore, while, for his readiness to share unpublished manuscripts, I am especially indebted to Mr. David Kittlestrom of Wisdom Books. For her unfailing and sorely tested patience, and for her critical acumen, I should like to thank my editor at Houghton Mifflin Harcourt, Ms. Deanne Urmy.

For their patience I would also like to thank my wife and my children, Rosie, Edward, and Theo. Finally, I must single out my daughter for the insight expressed in the penultimate sentence of the last chapter.

THE FOURTEEN DALAI LAMAS

The First Dalai Lama: Gendun Drub (1391–1474) Posthumously recognized, he was one of the "heart disciples" of Tsongkhapa. Especially esteemed for his writings on the *vinaya,* he is nonetheless not so highly regarded as his contemporary Khedrup Je, who is associated with the Panchen Lama lineage.

The Second Dalai Lama: Gendun Gyatso (1475–1542) Noted especially for his spiritual songs, he referred to himself as a "mad beggar monk" and became abbot first of Tashilhunpo and then of Drepung Monastery. In terms of spiritual attainment, he is regarded as one of the most accomplished of the Dalai Lamas.

The Third Dalai Lama: Sonam Gyatso (1543–1588) The first Dalai Lama to be recognized in his lifetime but, because he was considered the reincarnation of Gendun Gyatso, who was himself accepted as the reincarnation of Gendun Drup, it followed that when Altan Khan bestowed on him the title Dalai Lama, he must in fact be the Third. It is largely thanks to his efforts that Mongolia became a major component of the Gelug establishment.

The Fourth Dalai Lama: Yonten Gyatso (1589–1617) A direct descendant of Genghis Khan, the Fourth is regarded as one of the least successful Dalai Lamas. He never learned to speak Tibetan well, and his spiritual attainments were negligible. According to a story heard by Tsybikov, the Russo-Buryat explorer, he died from poisoning.

The Great Fifth: Nawang Lobsang Gyatso (1617–1682) Unifier of Tibet under the government of the Ganden Phodrang thanks to the patronage of the Mongolian warlord Gushri Khan. An ecumenist who sought to engage each of the different schools within the Tibetan tradition, the Great Fifth was an initiate of many Nyingma practices, a matter of controversy during his lifetime and later. When he died, the event was concealed from the public for almost fifteen years while the Sixth Dalai Lama grew to maturity. It was the Great Fifth who established Nechung as state oracle.

The Sixth Dalai Lama: Tsangyang Gyatso (1683–1706) Refused to take monastic vows and lived as a layman. He is chiefly remembered for his love songs—and for bedding the daughters of most of the aristocratic houses of his day.

The Seventh Dalai Lama: Kelzang Gyatso (1708–1757) Criticized by the Fourteenth Dalai Lama for his narrowly sectarian bias, the Seventh Dalai Lama is nonetheless highly regarded both for his writings and for his spiritual attainments. It was during his reign that a relationship was forged with the Qing emperors.

The Eighth Dalai Lama: Jamphel Gyatso (1758–1804) Although fully ordained, the Eighth Dalai Lama was reluctant to assume temporal power, relying instead on his regent even when he came of age. It was during his reign that Tibet fought, and lost, a disastrous war against the Gorkhas of Nepal.

The Ninth Dalai Lama: Lungtok Gyatso (1805–1815) The first Dalai Lama known to have contact with a European, he was visited by the eccentric British traveler Thomas Manning. He showed signs of great promise as a spiritual practitioner. There is some suspicion that he was murdered.

The Tenth Dalai Lama: Tsultrim Gyatso (1816–1837) Plagued with ill health, he seems not to have assumed temporal power and in any case died before having any impact. Some believe that he was slowly poisoned at the behest of the Chinese *amban.*

The Eleventh Dalai Lama: Khedrup Gyatso (1838–1856) A promising scholar, he was invested with temporal power at the age of seventeen. His death just three years later is believed by many to have been orchestrated by his ex-regent.

The Twelfth Dalai Lama: Trinley Gyatso (1857–1875) Invested with temporal power as an infant following a coup against the regent, he ruled for only a short time and showed little promise as a scholar before his demise—many believe at the hands of two of his attendants, who in any case were arrested, tortured, and exiled.

The Great Thirteenth: Thubten Gyatso (1876–1933) The Great Thirteenth was the first Dalai Lama since the Eighth to dodge the machinations of his regent and of the Qing *ambans* and attain both spiritual and temporal power. He was forced to flee Lhasa for exile, first in Mongolia and then in China, by a British military expedition under Colonel Younghusband (see Glossary). Almost no sooner had he returned than he was pushed out by Qing military forces. This time he fled south to British-controlled India. On the fall of the Qing dynasty in 1912, he returned and set about restoring his authority. Opposition from the Three Seats thwarted his plans to establish an independent military.

The Fourteenth Dalai Lama: Tenzin Gyatso (b. 1935) The subject of this book.

GLOSSARY OF NAMES AND KEY TERMS

Here I give brief definitions of some key terms alongside thumbnails of leading figures in the story. While I give Tibetan both phonetically and in Wylie, the Sanskrit terms are given only phonetically. Note that in the text itself, I have also used phonetics for most Tibetan words.

Amdo (A mDo) The eastern province of historical Tibet. Since 1950 absorbed variously into Sichuan, Qinghai, Gansu, and Yunnan provinces of the People's Republic of China.

Amdowa (A mdo ba*)* One who hails from Amdo (such as the present Dalai Lama).

bodhichitta The spontaneous wish, rising out of Great Compassion, to attain Enlightenment for the benefit of all sentient beings.

bodhisattva A being with the wish to facilitate the liberation of all other sentient beings before taking Enlightenment; more generally, anyone who has generated *bodhichitta.*

Buddha Literally, one who is awakened; one who knows the Truth (of the way things really are).

Buddhadharma The path to liberation taught by the Buddha.

CCP Chinese Communist Party.

Chiang Kai-shek (1887–1975) Leader of the Chinese Nationalists (Guomindang), president of the Republic of China 1928–1975, from 1928 to 1949 within China proper, latterly on the island of Taiwan. Raised a Buddhist, he converted to Christianity on marrying his fourth wife, Soong Mei-ling

(Madame Chiang, ca. 1898–2003). Inheriting the ideology of Sun Yat-sen, he saw Tibetans as a minority Chinese ethnic group.

Chenresig (sPyan ras gzigs) (in Sanskrit, Avalokitesvara) Bodhisattva of Compassion.

Chushi Gangdruk (Chu bzhi sgang drug) The Kham Four Rivers, Six Ranges Tibetan Defenders of the Faith Volunteer Army.

Cultural Revolution (1966–1969) Motivated by Mao's desire to restore his own power following the Great Leap Forward, and to secure his legacy, the Great Proletarian Cultural Revolution was a period of violent class struggle during which the "bourgeoisie," allegedly intent on restoring capitalism, were to be eliminated. In Tibet, not only was all private property confiscated, but also it was impermissible even to cook at home. Arguably its chief achievement was the destruction of many monuments and artifacts held to symbolize the "four olds": old customs, old culture, old habits, and old ideas.

dharma A Sanskrit term meaning, literally, "the way": Buddhism in particular; religion more generally.

dob dob (rDob rdob) Fraternities of monks from whose ranks were drawn the monastery "police," noted also for their sporting, fighting, and homosexual activities.

Dorje Drakden (rDo rje grags ldan) A deity who is a minister in the retinue of the dharma protector Pehar, and who communicates with the Dalai Lama and members of the Ganden Phodrang via the medium of the Nechung oracle.

Dorje Shugden (rDo rje shugs ldan) His proponents hold him to be a wrathful emanation of Manjushri, Bodhisattva of Wisdom, and as such a dharma protector; his opponents maintain that he is merely a worldly spirit.

Enlightenment The state attained by one who has achieved liberation from samsara and is thus fully awakened as to the way things really are.

emptiness (sTong pa nyid) The ultimate nature of reality.

Four Noble Truths

1. The truth of suffering

2. The truth of the cause of suffering
3. The truth of the cessation of suffering
4. The truth of the Path to the cessation of suffering

Gadong (dGa' gdong) One of the oracles consulted by the Dalai Lama and members of the Ganden Phodrang for auguries of the future. A recent medium was mute when in trance. He could only simper.

Ganden (dGa' ldan) Monastery founded by Tsongkhapa in 1409; mother house of the Gelug school.

Ganden Phodrang (dGa' ldan pho brang) Name used to refer to the government of the Dalai Lamas.

Ganden Throne Holder The senior-most position within the Gelug school.

Gelug (dGe lugs) Literally, the Way of Virtue. Sometimes known as the New Kadam tradition, also as the Yellow Hat sect; the Gelug tradition, to which all Dalai Lamas have belonged, was founded by Tsongkhapa in the fifteenth century.

Gelugpa One who follows the Gelug tradition.

geshe (dGe bshes) An academic degree awarded to monks.

geshema (dGe bshes ma) An academic degree awarded to nuns (an innovation of the current Dalai Lama).

Geshe Wangyal (dGe bshes Ngag dbang dbang rgyal) (1901–1983) The Kalmykian monk student of the Great Thirteenth's favorite, Agvan Dorjieff, Geseh Wangyal founded the first Tibetan Buddhist center in America while working as a CIA agent.

Glorious Goddess (dPal ldan lha mo) Palden Lhamo, one of the most powerful protector deities, closely associated both with Tibet in general and the Dalai Lama lineage in particular.

Gonpo Tashi Andrugtsang (A 'brugs mgon po bkra shis) (1905–1964) Freedom fighter and founder of Chushi Gangdruk.

Gould, Sir Basil (1883–1956) British political officer of Sikkim, Bhutan, and Tibet. Attended the enthronement of the present Dalai Lama as representative of the viceroy of India and of the British Crown.

Great Compassion (sNying rje chen po) The wish or aspiration to facilitate the liberation of all sentient beings from samsara (*see* samsara).

guru A spiritual guide or teacher (*see* lama).

Gyalo Thondup (rGya lo don 'grub) (b. 1928) Second-eldest brother of the present Dalai Lama, protégé of Chiang Kai-shek, and a CIA agent.

gyalyum chenmo (rgyal yum chen mo) Title of the Dalai Lama's mother.

Harrer, Heinrich (1912–2006) Austrian-born mountaineer, student ski champion, and adventurer. His BA was in geography, and he qualified as a teacher before becoming a member of the SS and subsequently joining the Nazi Party. He saw the Dalai Lama regularly during the first half of 1950 and wrote about his experiences in the classic travelogue *Seven Years in Tibet.*

Hinayana Literally "Lesser Vehicle" in contrast to Mahayana "Great Vehicle" Buddhism; arguably a derogatory term for non-Mahayana Buddhism.

hungry ghost or ***yidag*** (Yi dwags) A being belonging to the realm below that of animals and insects but above that of hell beings.

Jetsun Pema (rJe btsun pad ma) (b. 1940) Younger sister of the Dalai Lama. For over four decades she served as president of the Tibetan Children's Villages, the school system founded by the Dalai Lama for the education of Tibetan refugee children.

Jokhang (Jo khang) The most important temple in Tibet, it stands at the eastern end of Lhasa and is sacred to each of the different Buddhist traditions indigenous to Tibet.

Kalachakra tantra Literally the "Wheel of Time" tantra, known since the eleventh century, this is a complex system of practices claimed by the Dalai Lama to be beneficial to the cause of world peace. It features explicit sexual imagery and an apocalyptic "theology" in which barbarian hordes are put to the sword by an invincible army emanating from Shambala, a hidden kingdom located within the Himalayas.

Kargyu (bKa' brgyud) Founded in the eleventh century, the tradition is particularly associated with Marpa and his famous disciple Milarepa. It split subsequently into several different schools centered on different incarnation lineages.

karma (Kar ma) Its literal meaning is "action," and it refers to the positive, negative, or neutral imprint of a given action on the actor's mental continuum. It is the sentient being's negative karma that keeps it within samsara.

Kashag (bKa' shag) The four-member council of ministers, or cabinet, of the Dalai Lamas and their regents. Traditionally, two members were monks. In recent times there have also been women Kashag members.

kathag (kha dags) A length of (generally) white silk offered to a person or object (such as an image) to whom respect is due. These are of varying lengths and quality. The method of offering is to drape the *kathag,* which resembles a scarf, over the wrists with the arms outstretched, the hands open, and the palms turned upward.

khabse (Kham zas) Traditional New Year cookies.

Kham (Khams) Eastern province of historical Tibet, presently absorbed variously into the PRC's Tibet Autonomous Region and its Sichuan, Qinghai, Gansu, and Yunnan provinces.

Khampa (Khams pa) One who hails from Kham, such as Gonpo Tashi Andrugtsang (*see* Gonpo Tashi Andrugtsang).

kuten (sku rten) Literally, the basis. A medium through whom one or more deities may speak.

lama (bLa ma) A teacher or spiritual guide (the word translates the Sanskrit term *guru*).

liberation

1. From samsara, the necessary condition of Enlightenment
2. From the "living hell" of serfdom by the Chinese Communist Party

Ling Rinpoché (Gling rin po che) (1903–1983) Ninety-seventh Ganden Throne holder and senior tutor to the Fourteenth Dalai Lama.

Lobsang Samten (bLo bsang bsam gtan) (1933–1985) Immediate elder brother of the Fourteenth Dalai Lama. Educated with the Dalai Lama, 1940–1945; Lord Chamberlain; school janitor in Scotch Plains, New Jersey; leader of first delegation to Tibet.

Losar (Lo sar) Tibetan New Year (calculated according to the lunar calendar).

Lotus-Born, The (Sanskrit: Padmasambhava) Eighth-century Kashmiri-born sage and thaumaturge. He was present at the founding of Samye, Tibet's first monastery, but was subsequently banished from the kingdom. Surviving an assassination attempt, he is said to have spent the next fifty-six years in Tibet subduing its indigenous deities and binding them over to serve the Buddhadharma.

Mahakala (Ma ha ka la) Protector deity, considered a wrathful emanation of Chenresig. He is closely associated with the Dalai Lamas, having protected the infant First Dalai Lama in the form of a raven.

Mahayana Literally "Great Vehicle" (in contrast to "Lesser Vehicle" Buddhism); the earliest Mahayana teachings, which propound the way of the bodhisattvas, have been dated to around the first century CE.

Maitreya The Buddha to come.

Manchu The "barbarian" race of Manchuria, now subsumed as part of the People's Republic of China, from which originated the Qing dynasty.

mandala A two- or sometimes three-dimensional symbolic representation of the cosmos, or some part of it.

Manjushri The Bodhisattva of Wisdom.

Mao Zedong (1893–1976) Popularly known as the Great Helmsman, he was a Communist revolutionary and guerrilla leader who became the founding father of the People's Republic of China. The Fourteenth Dalai Lama once composed a prayer in his honor.

mo (Mo) Common form of divination that may use, for example, dough balls, inside of which paper with different possible answers are concealed, or dice.

Monlam Chenmo (sMon lam chen mo) The Great Prayer Festival that celebrates the Month of Miracles of the Buddha, held at the beginning of the Tibetan New Year.

National Assembly Traditionally comprising the aristocratic families of Tibet.

Nechung (gNas chung) A monastery situated outside Lhasa and close to Drepung where resides the medium who channels Dorje Drakden. Also an alternative name for the deity himself.

Nehru, Jawaharlal (1889–1964) According to the sometime US ambassador to India Loy Henderson, he was the "vain, sensitive, emotional, and complicated" ex-British public schoolboy and Cambridge-educated lawyer who became prime minister of India from independence in 1947 until his death in 1964.

Ngabo, Nawang Jigme (Nga phod gnag dbang 'jigs med) (1910–2009) Tibetan aristocrat and former governor of Chamdo, he was a member of the delegation that signed the Seventeen Point Agreement. According to Gyalo

Thondup, he was the "biggest traitor of all time," but Ngabo was nonetheless trusted by the Dalai Lama, who often sought his opinion and advice.

nirvana The state beyond suffering in which all those who have attained final liberation subsist.

Norbulingka (Nor bu ling kha) Literally the Jewel Park, founded by the Seventh Dalai Lama in the mid-eighteenth century, it became the summer retreat of subsequent Dalai Lamas, although both the Great Thirteenth and the Fourteenth both based themselves there permanently.

Nyingma (rNying ma) Literally the "old" or "ancient" tradition, associated with the Lotus-Born during the first diffusion of Buddhism to Tibet.

Nyingmapa (rNying ma) A follower of the Nyingma tradition.

oracle There were many oracles in Tibet, those of Nechung Monastery and Panglung Hermitage being only the most famous. Most monasteries and most villages had their own medium who would channel one or more deities.

Padmasambhava *See* Lotus-Born.

Palden Lhamo (dPal ldan lha mo) *See* Glorious Goddess.

Panchen Lama (Pan chen la ma) The second-most important reincarnation lineage within the Gelug tradition, centered on Tashilhunpo Monastery in southern Tibet.

Pehar (Pe har) More correctly Gyalpo Pehar, the protector deity of the Tibetan government who communicates with Dorje Drakden (*see* Dorje Drakden).

Phabongka Rinpoché (Pha bong rin po che) (1878–1941) Guru to Taktra Rinpoché, Ling Rinpoché, and Trijang Rinpoché, among others, Phabongka Rinpoché was a charismatic teacher and is credited with popularizing the cult of Dorje Shugden as protector of the Gelug tradition.

Phuntsog Wangyal (Phun tsogs dbang rgyal) (1922–2014) An early member of the CCP, Phunwang, as he was known, interpreted for the Dalai Lama during his visit to China. He was subsequently purged following the One Hundred Flowers campaign, spending nineteen years in prison.

PLA The People's Liberation Army, the standing army of the People's Republic of China.

Potala (Po ta la) Palace built during the seventeenth century to house the Dalai Lama and the government of Tibet.

Preparatory Committee for the Autonomous Region of Tibet This was the precursor to the modern-day Tibet Autonomous Region. Its nominal head was the Dalai Lama, who was succeeded in 1959 by the Tenth Panchen Lama.

protector deity (Srung ma) Of these there are two classes: the worldly protectors and the dharma protectors.

Qing dynasty (1644–1912) Established by the Manchu Aisin Gioru clan, it revived the empire of the earlier T'ang dynasty.

rebirth The doctrine of transmigration. When a sentient being dies, it is reborn in one of the Six Realms unless it has succeeded in attaining Enlightenment. When first encountered by the Jesuit missionaries in Tibet, it was castigated for justifying infanticide: if a child was unwanted (usually because it was female), it might be exposed and left to die in the pious hope that it would obtain a more favorable rebirth.

reincarnation The means by which the most highly evolved spiritual masters are able to choose the manner and timing of their rebirth.

Religious Kings (Chos rgyal) Of these there were three. First, **Songtsen Gampo** (Srong btsan sgam po) (604–649/50). Though he was a warrior chieftain, it is he who is credited with bringing Buddhism to Tibet. Famously, he married both Chinese and Nepalese princesses. Second, **Trisong Detsen** (Khri srong lde'u btsan) (742–797), who oversaw expansion of the Tibetan empire to its greatest extent and was on the throne when Tibetan forces briefly toppled the T'ang emperor. Third, **Rapalchen** (Ral pa can) (802–836), whose piety was such that he is said to wear woven hair extensions which his monastic advisers would sit on when in his presence. It is related that he was murdered by having his head twisted until his neck broke.

Reting (Rwa sgreng) Monastery founded by Drom Thonpa, an earlier incarnation of Chenresig, in the eleventh century, as headquarters of the Kadam tradition.

Reting Rinpoché (Rwa sgreng rin po che) (1912–1947) The Dalai Lama's root guru and first regent, regarded as a great mystic and seer, he was almost certainly murdered.

Richardson, Hugh (1905–2000) The last British political officer to serve in Tibet, he was both an outstanding scholar and an accomplished linguist, said to have spoken impeccable Lhasa Tibetan with the slight trace of an Oxford accent.

Rinpoché (Rin po che) An honorific title meaning, literally, "Precious One," generally reserved for reincarnate lamas.

samaya May either refer to the commitment of an initiate or to the sacred bond established between master and pupil wherein the master is seen as an embodiment of the Buddha himself.

samsara Or cyclic existence, the always unsatisfactory state in which all sentient beings suffer and remain until they attain Enlightenment, at which point they are liberated from samsara.

sangha The monastic community.

Shakyamuni Literally the sage of the Shakyas, ca. fifth-century BCE historical Buddha, born Prince Gautama in present-day Nepal and also known as Siddhartha (the one who accomplishes).

shi dre (Shi "dre) A type of ghost into which victims of violent death may transform.

Six Realms In descending order:

1. The heavenly realm (within which there are many heavens or grades of heaven)
2. The realm of demigods or demons
3. The human realm
4. The animal realm
5. The realm of hungry ghosts
6. The hell realm (within which there are many hells or grades of hell)

skillful means (Thabs; *upaya* in Sanskrit) The practice whereby a teacher adapts his words and deeds to the level of spiritual attainment of his audience.

Songtsen Gampo (Srong btsan sgam po) *See under* Religious Kings.

tantra A set of esoteric practices intended to speed the initiate's progress on the path to full Enlightenment.

Tashilhunpo (bKra shis lhun po) Monastery in southern Tibet, seat of the Panchen Lama, founded in 1447 by the First Dalai Lama.

Taktra Rinpoché (sTag brag rin po che) (1874–1952) Regent of Tibet, 1941–51.

thangka A religious painting on a scroll, usually framed with silk brocade, that may contain relics and/or other ritually consecrated substances.

Theravada Tradition regarded by its proponents as authentically preserving the original teachings of the Buddha. In general, Theravadins do not accept the Mahayana scriptures. The tradition remains dominant in Southeast Asia and Sri Lanka.

Three Seats (gDan sa gsum) Ganden, Drepung, and Sera Monasteries: the Harvard, Princeton, and Yale of Tibet.

torma (gTor ma) Butter sculpture: at Losar, different monasteries would compete with one another to produce the finest examples. Up to thirty feet high, they were paraded around the Barkhor on the last day of the Monlam Chenmo.

TPA Tibetan People's Association, a grassroots movement that grew up in opposition to the Chinese during the 1950s.

Trijang Rinpoché (Khri byang rin po che) (1901–1981) Junior tutor to the Dalai Lama and leading advocate of Dorje Shugden.

tsampa Roasted barley flour, a staple of the Tibetan diet.

Tsongkhapa (Tsong kha pa) (1357–1419) Also known as Je Rinpoché, founder of the Gelug school.

tukdam (Thugs dam) The meditative state whereby the most accomplished practitioners attain the clear light (*od gsal*) of primordial consciousness as they transition from embodied life to the heavenly realms from which they will again take rebirth for the benefit of sentient beings.

tulku (sPrul sku) Literally "emanation body," the technical term for a reincarnate lama.

TWC Tibet Work Committee, front of the Chinese central government that carries out its policies in Tibet.

Ü-Tsang (dBus gTsang) The combined southern provinces of Tibet.

Vajryana The Diamond Path. Some scholars regard Vajryana Buddhism as a distinct tradition, alongside the Theravada and Mahayana traditions, others hold simply that it is the apotheosis of the Mahayana tradition.

vinaya ("Dul ba) The monastic code or set of precepts by which the renunciate lives. For monks there are 253, for nuns 364.

yabshi (Yab gzhis) Term referring to the Dalai Lama's household, including his family.

yabshi kung (Yab gzhis khang) The Dalai Lama's father, in which *kung* is a title roughly equivalent to duke.

yoga Perhaps best translated as "discipline," yoga denotes both the practice and the set of practices whereby the yogin/yogini trains the mind in the quest for Enlightenment.

yogin Male practitioner of yoga.

yogini Female practitioner of yoga.

Younghusband, Colonel Sir Francis (1863–1942) British army officer and explorer turned mystical writer who led the expedition that captured Lhasa in 1904.

Zhou Enlai (1989–1976) Premier of the People's Republic of China from its inception until his death, Zhou was the famously suave diplomat who managed affairs of state, including foreign affairs, while Mao struggled against perceived enemies of the Revolution.

NOTES

Introduction: Waldorf Astoria Hotel, New York, August 1989

page

xx *Tibetan humor:* Sir Basil Gould, the political officer for Sikkim, Bhutan, and Tibet, thought the same thing. See Basil Gould, *The Jewel in the Lotus: Recollections of an Indian Political* (London: Chatto & Windus, 1957), p. 207: "Tibetans laugh at the same things and in the same tone, and appreciate beauty in just the same things as Englishmen."

xxi *"feeling it between finger and thumb":* Charles Bell, *Portrait of the Dalai Lama* (London: Collins, 1946), p. 88.

1. The Travails of the Great Thirteenth

7 *fifty shrapnel shells:* Patrick French, *Younghusband: The Last Great Imperial Adventurer* (London: HarperCollins, 1995), p. 224.
those taken prisoner: Tsepon W. D. Shakabpa, *Tibet: A Political History* (New Haven: Yale University Press, 1967), p. 212.

8 *"one of great calmness":* Petr Kuz'mich Kozlov, *Tibet I Dalai Lama* (St. Petersburg, 1920). I have changed the last word of Mark Belcher's translation of this passage from "nervousness" to "emotion," which seems more apt.

9 *"Tibet," she wrote:* First Historical Archives of China, vol. 30 (1996), quoted in Jung Chang, *Empress Dowager Cixi: The Concubine Who Launched Modern China* (London: Jonathan Cape, 2013), p. 366.

10 *"the hospitable and venerable":* Philip Short, *In Pursuit of Plants: Experiences of Nineteenth and Early Twentieth Century Plant Collectors* (Portland, OR: 2004), p. 108. Forrest's account was originally told in his paper, its title splendidly understated, "The Perils of Plant Hunting" in the *Gardeners' Chronicle* of May 1910.

11 *"eventually run to ground":* Short, *In Pursuit of Plants,* p. 114. Forrest himself only just survived. At one point in the course of his three-week ordeal, much of it passed at 16–17,000 feet, he trod on an inch-wide spike in a booby trap, which, "passing through the bones of my foot," protruded "half a hand's width" from the other side.

He accepted that capital punishment: Charles Bell, *Portrait of the Dalai Lama* (London: Collins, 1946), p. 157.

12 *The Chinese* amban*:* Xiuyu Wang, *China's Last Imperial Frontier: Late Qing Expansion in Sichuan's Tibetan Borderlands* (Lanham, MD: Lexington Books, 2011), p. 124.
in a cauldron of "cold water": Albert Leroy Shelton, *Pioneering in Tibet: A Personal Record of Life and Experience in Mission Fields* (New York: F. H. Revell Company, 1921), pp. 93–94. See also Eric Teichman, *Travels of a Consular Officer in North-west China* (Cambridge: Cambridge University Press, 1921), p. 228.
"resemble living demons": Sam van Schaik, *Tibet: A History* (New Haven: Yale University Press, 2011), p. 84.
"only made confusion worse": Short, *In Pursuit of Plants,* p. 108.

13 *"in order to curry favour":* Flora Beal Shelton, *Shelton of Tibet* (New York: George H. Doran, 1923), 171–72.
a "shrieking" and "diabolical" noise: W. N. Fergusson, *Adventure, Sport and Travel on the Tibetan Steppes* (New York: Charles Scribner's Sons, 1911), pp. 2–3.

14 *"a kind people":* Fergusson, *Adventure, Sport and Travel,* p. 3.
"welcoming smile ": Bell, *Portrait,* p. 103.
"Many monks": Gyalo Thondup with Anne F. Thurston, *The Noodle Maker of Kalimpong: The Untold Story of My Struggle for Tibet* (London: Rider, 2015), p. 7.

2. A Mystic and a Seer

17 *a white dragon:* Khemey Sonam Wangdu, Basil J. Gould, and Hugh E. Richardson, *Discovery, Recognition and Enthronement of the 14th Dalai Lama: A Collection of Accounts* (Dharamsala: Library of Tibetan Works and Archives, 2000), p. 3.

18 *forced it on him:* Melvyn C. Goldstein, *A History of Modern Tibet: 1913–1951,* vol. 1, *The Demise of the Lamaist State* (Berkeley: University of California Press, 1989), p. 141. See also the account in Charles Bell, *Portrait of the Dalai Lama* (London: Collins, 1946), chap. 68.

19 *If we are not able:* Sam van Schaik, *Tibet: A History* (New Haven: Yale University Press, 2011), p. 204.

22 *stamping his right foot:* Lest anyone doubt the veracity of this story, one can, according to the regent's niece, who visited his monastery in 2006, still see the imprint carefully preserved in a chapel. Tseyang Sadutshang, *My Youth in Tibet: Recollections of a Tibetan Woman* (Dharamsala: Library of Tibetan Works and Archives, 2012), p. 37.
one of his nieces: His niece remembers him at the start of an important religious ceremony smiling and waving at her and then, during an interval, toying with her fingers. When a smallpox epidemic broke out in the region of Reting Monastery, she was taken to see the Rinpoché while he undertook a spiritual retreat at a hermitage in the mountains. There he gave her some powder which included the desiccated skin of a cousin who had contracted and survived the disease. This, the great lama explained, was to be inhaled up the nose like snuff. When she did so and duly sneezed, he "very kindly let down the folded sleeve of his yellow silk shirt" and allowed her to blow her nose on it.

Sadutshang, *My Youth in Tibet,* pp. 37, 45. A delicate fragrance is a well-attested characteristic of Christian holy men too: Saint Philip Neri was one of them, Saint Pio of Pietrelcina another.

"gauche," "self centred," and "immature": Hugh E. Richardson, *High Peaks, Pure Earth: Collected Writings on Tibetan History and Culture* (London: Serindia, 1998), p. 715.

"a very mediocre personage": Philip Neame, *Playing with Strife: The Autobiography of a Soldier* (London: George G. Harrap, 1947), p. 159. See also Philip Neame, "Tibet and the 1936 Lhasa Mission," *Journal of the Royal Central Asian Society* 26 (April 1939): 234–46.

"new things": Isrun Engelhardt, *Tibet in 1938–1939: Photographs from the Ernst Schäfer Expedition to Tibet* (Chicago: Serindia, 2007), p. 29.

25 *chief minister's wife:* Bell, *Portrait,* p. 54. The full story of Lungshar's fall is given in chap. 6 of Melvyn C. Goldstein, *A History of Modern Tibet: 1913–1951,* vol. 1, *The Demise of the Lamaist State* (Berkeley: University of California Press, 1989), chap. 6. Apparently Lungshar did not resent his punishment. He took it as karmic retribution for having once blinded a sheep with a nonfatal shot from his sling.

3. A Child Is Born

27 *took to be significant:* The most authoritative account of the events described in this chapter is to be found in Khemey Sonam Wangdu, Basil J. Gould, and Hugh E. Richardson, *Discovery, Recognition and Enthronement of the 14th Dalai Lama: A Collection of Accounts* (Dharamsala: Library of Tibetan Works and Archives, 2000).

28 *strange star-shaped fungi:* See the account in Mary Taring, *Daughter of Tibet* (London: John Murray, 1970). Basil Gould visited Lhasa in August 1936, so it seems possible he actually saw the fungi. But he says they looked more like antlers; see his *Jewel in the Lotus: Recollections of an Indian Political* (London: Chatto & Windus, 1957).

29 *in her right hand:* Adapted from Réne de Nebesky-Wojkowitz, *Oracles and Demons of Tibet* (Delhi: Book Faith India), p. 22.

30 *"It is not known":* The story is told in more detail in Alexander Norman, *Secret Lives of the Dalai Lama* (New York: Random House, 2008), p. 352.

31 *"singular sweetness":* Charles Bell, *Portrait of the Dalai Lama* (London: Collins, 1946).

32 *the search party:*The full account of the search party is given in Wangdu, Gould, and Richardson, *Discovery, Recognition and Enthronement,* pp. 14–15.

33 *" a kind of "jump-suit":* Wangdu, Gould, and Richardson, *Discovery, Recognition and Enthronement,* p. 15.

34 *"No," they replied:* Robert Thurman recounts a story about the Dalai Lama's mother having a dream about a bright blue dragon escorted by two playful green snow lions, but I have not seen this corroborated anywhere. Robert Thurman, *Why the Dalai Lama Matters* (New York: Atria, 2008), p. 14.

"even for a moment": Gyalo Thondup with Anne F. Thurston, *The Noodle Maker of Kalimpong: The Untold Story of My Struggle for Tibet* (London: Rider, 2015), pp. 15, 19.

35 *"utter no words":* Quoted in Françoise Pommaret, *Lhasa in the Seventeenth Century: The*

Capital of the Dalai Lama, trans. Howard Solverson (Leiden: Brill, 2003), p. 69. See also Samten Karmay's translation of the relevant passage in the Great Fifth's autobiography, *The Illusive Play* (Chicago: Serindia, 2014).
"very sarcastic": Personal interview.

4. The View from the Place of the Roaring Tiger

36 *"grinding poverty":* Gyalo Thondup with Anne F. Thurston, *The Noodle Maker of Kalimpong: The Untold Story of My Struggle for Tibet* (London: Rider, 2015), p. 4.

37 *"one of the best":* Thondup, *Noodle Maker,* pp. 6–13. The Dalai Lama's extended family owned forty-five acres, while his parents owned approximately six and a half acres of land themselves — enough to be classified as landlords, and therefore "class enemies" by the Communists. Jianglin Li, "When the Iron Bird Flies: The 1956–1962 Secret War on the Tibetan Plateau," unpublished ms., trans. Stacey Mosher.

38 *"happy and contented life":* Adapted from Thubten Jigme Norbu, *Tibet Is My Country* (London: Rupert Hart Davis, 1960), p. 51.

40 *"strung about the walls":* Gary Geddes, *Kingdom of Ten Thousand Things: An Impossible Journey from Kabul to Chiapas,* illustrated ed. (New York: Sterling Publishing Company, 2008), p. 175.
"slipped to the door": Diki Tsering, *Dalai Lama, My Son: A Mother's Story* (London: Virgin, 2000), pp. 37–38. Although the provenance of this work might cause the strictest biographers to raise their eyebrows, it was first taken down in note form by one grandchild as a series of stories and subsequently turned into a continuous narrative by another before it received the ministrations of its English editor. The book's artlessness and charm nonetheless give it the ring of authenticity.
"and stood beside me": Tsering, *Dalai Lama, My Son,* pp. 40–41.

41 *guarded by trolls:* With respect to Laplanders, see, for example, Andrew Brown, "Gods and Fairytales," *The Spectator,* February 14, 2015.
"nameless religion": Starting with the great French Tibetologist R. A. Stein. See his *Tibetan Civilisation,* trans. J. E. Stapleton Driver (London: Faber and Faber, 1972).
celestial dragons: Tsewang Y. Pemba, *Young Days in Tibet* (London: Jonathan Cape, 1957), p. 146. For a useful Tibetan account, see Norbu Chophel, *Folk Culture of Tibet* (Dharamsala: Library of Tibetan Works and Archives, 1983); for a scholarly analysis of the different classes, see Geoffrey Samuel, *Civilized Shamans: Buddhism in Tibetan Societies* (Washington, DC: Smithsonian Institution Press, 1993).
"dreadful and tedious solitude": Although he was wrong on this point, Desideri's *relazione* of his seven-year sojourn in Tibet (available in *Mission to Tibet: The Extraordinary Eighteenth-Century Account of Father Ippolito Desideri SJ,* ed. L. Zwilling, trans. M. Sweet [Somerville, MA: Wisdom Publications, 2010]) is extremely valuable for its many insights of the time. The quotation is from the earlier translation of Desideri's *relazione, An Account of Tibet: The Travels of Ippolite Desideri di Pistoia, SJ, 1712–1727,* ed. Filippo de Filippi, rev. ed. (London: G. Routledge, 1937), p. 353; the whole of his "Report on Tibet and Its Routes" gives an extraordinary perspective on both eighteenth-century

Tibet and Counter-Reformation Europe. Desideri himself was a linguistic genius. It took him less than two years to master the language sufficiently well to write the first of his three books in Tibetan (one of them a catechism of the Christian faith, two of them philosophical works designed to refute Buddhism). See Donald S. Lopez and Thupten Jinpa, *Dispelling the Darkness: A Jesuit's Quest for the Soul of Tibet* (Cambridge: Harvard University Press, 2017).

42 *"strange jealous creatures"*: Robert B. Ekvall, *Tents Against the Sky* (London: Gollancz, 1954), p. 188.

43 *"almost as a pet"*: The full story is told in Pemba, *Young Days in Tibet,* pp. 148–50. *human scapegoat:* Practices such as these were not confined to treatment of the sick. It is said that at the great Nyingma foundation at Samye there was "a special room where the bodies that get lost in the Bardo, the realm between successive lives, were chopped up and [in which] the weighing of souls for punishment occurred . . . [O]ccasionally it became politically necessary for a man to be put in this room as a ransom for the sins of Tibet." John Crook and James Low, *The Yogins of Ladakh: A Pilgrimage Among the Hermits of the Buddhist Himalayas* (1997; repr., Delhi: Motilal Banarsidass, 2012), p. 199 and n. 65.

44 *"found out that"*: Pemba, *Young Days in Tibet,* p. 149.

5. "Lonely and somewhat unhappy"

46 *"A last attempt"*: Thubten Jigme Norbu, *Tibet Is My Country* (London: Rupert Hart Davis, 1960), p. 128.

47 *"lonely" and "somewhat unhappy"*: Dalai Lama, *Freedom in Exile: The Autobiography of His Holiness the Dalai Lama of Tibet* (London: Hodder & Stoughton, 1990), p. 12.
suck a mole: Raimondo Bultrini, *The Dalai Lama and the King Demon,* trans. Maria Simmons (New York: Tibet House US, 2013), p. 338.
"no one to play with": *My Land and My People: The Autobiography of His Holiness the Dalai Lama* (London: Weidenfeld and Nicolson, 1962), p. 27.
"a childish dislike": Dalai Lama, *Freedom in Exile,* p. 14.

48 *"for the most part"*: Dalai Lama, *Freedom in Exile,* p. 14.
Ma Bufang: Neither the Tibetan nor the Chinese historians have been kind to Ma. To the Tibetans he was "so devious and scandalous in his behaviour that it was beyond description." The Dalai Lama's elder brother recalled how, on tax-collecting missions, Ma's officials would hunt down the local people, string them up by the ankles, and beat them with bamboo sticks if they tried to evade payment. Gyalo Thondup with Anne F. Thurston, *The Noodle Maker of Kalimpong: The Untold Story of My Struggle for Tibet* (London: Rider, 2015), p. 26. To the victorious Communists, Ma, as a supporter of the Nationalist Guomindang, was a counterrevolutionary and a traitor to the nation. But anecdotal evidence suggests that he was affable, good-humored, and forward-thinking. An American government official visiting Qinghai province praised his leadership as one of the most efficient in China, and one of the most energetic. Ma was particularly concerned with reforestation and gave free seeds and instructions for planting to the

peasantry, saying that the tree was the "salvation of the desert." As onetime leader of the great mosque of Xining, he might be expected to have been socially conservative, but in fact Ma Bufang set up a modern school for girls that provided a secular education. On the Communists' accession to power, ostensibly on pilgrimage to Mecca, he fled to Saudi Arabia, where he died in 1975.

49 *100,000 silver dollars:* Melvyn C. Goldstein, *A History of Modern Tibet: 1913–1951,* vol. 1, *The Demise of the Lamaist State* (Berkeley: University of California Press, 1989), p. 321.

via India: See Goldstein, *History of Modern Tibet,* 1:323. This fact shows that, while Amdo itself was outside Lhasa's control, the Chinese government could not dictate terms to the Tibetans with respect to central Tibet.

50 *"began to look":* Dalai Lama, *Freedom in Exile,* p. 14.

"a strikingly pretty girl": Heinrich Harrer, *Seven Years in Tibet* (London: R. Hart-Davis, 1953), p. 205.

"We spent a great deal": Dalai Lama, *Freedom in Exile,* p. 15.

51 *"the vast herds":* Dalai Lama, *Freedom in Exile,* p. 15.

"thousands of": Thondup, *Noodle Maker,* p. 33.

52 *"the officials, secretaries and monks":* Thondup, *Noodle Maker,* p. 35.

53 *"as it might be poisoned":* Diki Tsering, *The Dalai Lama, My Son: A Mother's Story* (London: Virgin, 2000), p. 93.

"the stars of heaven": Michael Aris, *Hidden Treasures and Secret Lives: A Study of Pemalingpa (1450–1521) and the Sixth Dalai Lama (1683–1706)* (London: Kegan Paul International, 1989), p. 149.

54 *these outer manifestations:* One of the best single collections of photographs of premodern Tibet can be seen at the Pitt Rivers Museum in Oxford. This is viewable in its entirety online at http://tibet.prm.ox.ac.uk/tibet_project_summary.html.

"with big bulging eyes": Thomas Laird, *The Story of Tibet: Conversations with the Dalai Lama* (London: Atlantic, 2006), pp. 269–70.

6. Homecoming

57 *"a town full of animation":* Alexandra David-Néel, *My Journey to Lhasa* (Harmondsworth: Allen Lane, Penguin Books, 1940), p. 273.

58 *"metropolis of filth":* Ekai Kawaguchi, *Three Years in Tibet* (London: Theosophical Publishing Society, 1909), p. 407. Though he was a devout pilgrim, the city evidently disgusted Kawaguchi. He spoke of "the filth, the stench, the utter abomination of the streets."

"squatting or lying": William Stanley Morgan, *Amchi Sahib: A British Doctor in Tibet, 1936–37* (Charlestown, MA: Acme Bookbinding, 2007), p. 73. Dr. Morgan was attached to the 1936–37 British mission to Lhasa under Sir Basil Gould. His lively memoir is notable for its description of the syphilis clinic he ran. Monks from the local monasteries made up a large percentage of his patients. On venereal disease among Tibetans, see also Harrer, *Seven Years,* p. 176.

"They were at once": Frederick Spencer Chapman, *Lhasa: The Holy City* (London: Chatto & Windus, 1938), p. 148.
"The ordinary residents": Tsewang Y. Pemba, *Young Days in Tibet* (London: Jonathan Cape, 1957), p. 76.
stumps "immersed": Pemba, *Young Days in Tibet,* p. 86.
59 *"an Amazon with breasts"*: Pemba, *Young Days in Tibet,* p. 109.
settled population: Estimates vary, but most agree that the population was around ten thousand. W. S. Morgan puts it at a mere eight thousand (*Amchi Sahib,* p. 86).
Within a few hours' walk: Remarkably enough, a common way of measuring both time and distance was to give the number of cups of tea that could be drunk over the course of a given interval. Tibetans at this time drank spectacular quantities. Charles Bell reports that many people he knew would consume "sixty or seventy cups daily," though the Great Thirteenth limited himself to "about forty cups, of ordinary tea cup size, each day." Charles Bell, *Portrait of the Dalai Lama* (London: Collins, 1946), p. 303.
"from sunrise to sunset": David-Néel, *My Journey to Lhasa,* p. 273.
60 *"a herd of tame musk deer"*: Dalai Lama, *Freedom in Exile: The Autobiography of His Holiness the Dalai Lama of Tibet* (London: Hodder & Stoughton, 1990), p. 38.
until that moment: Thomas Laird, *The Story of Tibet: Conversations with the Dalai Lama* (London: Atlantic, 2006), p. 271.
61 *habitual opium smokers:* See Henrich Harrer's foreword in Dorje Yudon Yuthok, *House of the Turquoise Roof* (Ithaca: Snow Lion Publications, 1990), p. 12.
take the measure: Sir Basil Gould, in *Jewel in the Lotus: Recollections of an Indian Political* (London: Chatto & Windus, 1957), p. 220, described him as "a man of quiet and gentle poise." Hugh Richardson once described him to me as "a dreadful old horse coper."
warmly affectionate: Describing her to me, Tenzin Geyche Tethong, scion of an old and senior aristocratic family, asserted that the *gyalyum chenmo* was "really something . . . quite a remarkable person." Similarly, Gould described her as "surely one in a million, the worthy mother of a Dalai Lama" (*Jewel in the Lotus,* p. 220). Heinrich Harrer also has many good things to say of her.
62 *"One saw many of these people"*: Pemba, *Young Days in Tibet,* p. 84.
marched with a peculiar gait: Pemba, *Young Days in Tibet,* p. 98.
"really let themselves go": Pemba, *Young Days in Tibet,* p. 115.
63 *"one of the best moments"*: Dalai Lama, *Freedom in Exile,* p. 45. The Casting-Out *(smon lam gdor rgyag)* was celebrated on February 7 in 1940, the year in question. For a full description, see Hugh Richardson, *Ceremonies of the Lhasa Year* (London: Serindia Publications, 1993).
Consisting of "wooden frames": Pemba, *Young Days in Tibet,* p. 114.
65 *"The sight of all those people"*: Dalai Lama, *Freedom in Exile,* p. 48.
"This tended to result": Dalai Lama, *Freedom in Exile,* p. 49. See also Alexandra David-Néel's account in *My Journey to Lhasa,* chap. 8. She adds that most of the spectators were drunk by this time.
A "solid, solemn": Gould, *Jewel in the Lotus,* p. 218.

66 *He was more eager:* Gould, *Jewel in the Lotus,* p. 231.

67 *"The contrasts and rhythms":* Knud Larsen and Amund Sinding-Larsen, *The Lhasa Atlas: Traditional Tibetan Architecture and Townscape* (London: Serindia, 2001), p. 104.
around 1.3 million square feet: Gyurme Dorje, *Tibet Handbook,* 4th ed. (Bath: Footprint, 2008), p. 97.

69 *200,000 pearls:* Dorje, *Tibet Handbook,* p. 102. I wonder who counted them.
"devotion and love": Khemey Sonam Wangdu, Basil J. Gould, and Hugh E. Richardson, *Discovery, Recognition and Enthronement of the 14th Dalai Lama: A Collection of Accounts* (Dharamsala: Library of Tibetan Works and Archives, 2000), p. 79.
"ancient and decrepit": Dalai Lama, *Freedom in Exile,* p. 22.
ran with urine: Dalai Lama, *Freedom in Exile,* p. 23.

70 *millions of mantras:* When, for example, the Great Fifth Dalai Lama fell ill in 1681, the monks of Doenye Ling Monastery recited the *mig tse ma* no fewer than 21,750,000 times. This was followed by a complete recitation of the 108 volumes of the *kangyur* a total of 108 times by thousands of novice monks throughout the country, recitation of the Perfection of Wisdom in Eight Thousand Lines three times, the *bhadracari* 199,500 times, the *namasangiti* 59,300 times, the Sadhana of the Goddess of the White Umbrella 105,500 times, the Heart of the Perfection of Wisdom 149,300 times, the Hymn to Tara 1,043,600 times, and the Life Dharani 9,533,000 times. See *Sans-rgyas rgya-mtsho: Life of the Fifth Dalai Lama,* trans. Ahmed Zahiruddin (New Delhi: Academy of Indian Culture, 1999). According to Georges Dreyfus, the monasteries are indeed "first and foremost ritual communities." Georges B. J. Dreyfus, *The Sound of Two Hands Clapping: The Education of a Tibetan Buddhist Monk* (Berkeley: University of California Press, 2003), p. 44.
"lazy, stupid": Pemba, *Young Days in Tibet,* p. 80.

71 dob dob: The best descriptions of *dob dob* culture are to be found in Tashi Khedrup, *Adventures of a Tibetan Fighting Monk,* ed. Hugh Richardson (Bangkok: Orchid Press, 2003). See also Melvyn C. Goldstein, "A Study of the Ldab Ldob," *Central Asiatic Journal* 9, no. 2 (1964): pp. 123–41; and Kawaguchi, *Three Years in Tibet,* esp. the chapter titled "Warrior Priests of Sera." According to Kawaguchi, "the beauty of young boys was a frequent cause" of fighting, "and the theft of a boy [would] often lead to a duel" (p. 292). Kawaguchi, himself an ordained *bhikku,* speaks of "nights . . . abused as occasions for indulging in fearful malpractices. They [the *dob dob*] really seem to be the descendants of the men of Sodom and Gomorrah mentioned in the bible" (p. 470).
tough looking: Pemba, *Young Days in Tibet,* pp. 80–81. According to Dreyfus, *dob dob* are forbidden in the monasteries in exile (*Two Hands Clapping,* p. 345, n. 25).

7. Boyhood

74 *"death held no fears":* Tsewang Y. Pemba, *Young Days in Tibet* (London: Jonathan Cape, 1957), pp. 112, 113.

75 *a "raised seat":* The account of Ling Rinpoché is drawn from Dalai Lama, *The Life of My*

Teacher: A Biography of Kyabje Ling Rinpoché (Somerville, MA: Wisdom Publications, 2017), pp. 147–48, 371, 129, 101, 120.

76 *A relatively recent:* I do not remember who told me this story, but I have no difficulty believing it. Georges B. J. Dreyfus, *The Sound of Two Hands Clapping: The Education of a Tibetan Buddhist Monk* (Berkeley: University of California Press, 2003), provides the best account of the life and culture of a modern Tibetan monastery.

77 *From your place:* Free translation by the author, with acknowledgments to Dr. T. J. Langri.

78 *the hand of a high lama:* Melvyn C. Goldstein, *A History of Modern Tibet: 1913–1951,* vol. 1, *The Demise of the Lamaist State* (Berkeley: University of California Press, 1991), p. 465. The Dalai Lama is himself an accomplished marksman. In days gone by, he would use an air rifle to scare any cats he caught stalking birds.

79 *After eating:* Goldstein, *History of Modern Tibet,* 1:344.
these rumors: See Goldstein, *History of Modern Tibet,* vol. 1, chap. 9. Further details are supplied in Jamyang Choegyal Kasho, *In the Service of the 13th and 14th Dalai Lamas* (Frankfurt am Main, Tibethaus Deutschland, 2015), chap. 10.
homosexual relationships: When one is considering the issue of homosexuality within the monasteries, it is important to be clear that traditional Tibetan culture does not recognize homosexuality either as an identity or as a category of human nature. It is only homosexual acts that are acknowledged. Similarly, so far as the *vinaya,* or code of conduct for monastics, is concerned, only those acts involving penetration are actually considered an infraction of the root vow of chastity. Non-penetrative acts are considered lesser infractions and were generally overlooked. It was by no means unusual for older monks to take younger monks as sexual consorts. But while this was generally consensual it need not imply that the passive partner regarded the activity as anything more than a duty. The authoritative account is in Melvyn C. Goldstein, *The Struggle for Modern Tibet: The Autobiography of Tashi Tsering* (London: Routledge, 1997), pp. 28–29. See also Heinrich Harrer, *Seven Years in Tibet* (London: R. Hart-Davis, 1953), p. 194; and Tashi Khedrup, *Adventures of a Tibetan Fighting Monk,* ed. Hugh Richardson (Bangkok: Orchid Press, 2003), p. 50.

80 *"the orphan's box":* Kasho, *In the Service,* p. 118.

81 *"a very gentle man":* Dalai Lama, *Freedom in Exile: The Autobiography of His Holiness the Dalai Lama of Tibet* (London: Hodder & Stoughton, 1990), p. 19.
dictatorial: See, for example, Thomas Laird, *The Story of Tibet: Conversations with the Dalai Lama* (London: Atlantic, 2006), p. 277. Archibald Steele, *In the Kingdom of the Dalai Lama* (Sedona, AZ: In Print Publishing, 1993), p. 60, describes him as "a paragon of conservatism."

82 *"perverted intentions": The Magical Play of Illusion: The Autobiography of Trijang Rinpoche,* trans. Sharpa Tulku Tenzin Trinley (Somerville, MA: Wisdom Publications, 2018), pp. 100, 114, 91.

83 *"His Holiness seemed":* Trijang, *The Magical Play of Illusion,* p. 148.

introduced the sport: Basil Gould, *Jewel in the Lotus: Recollections of an Indian Political* (London: Chatto & Windus, 1957), p. 207.

Thomas Manning: For his remarkable story, see my *Secret Lives of the Dalai Lama* (New York: Random House, 2008), pp. 318–21.

"immediately impressed": Ilia Tolstoy, "Across Tibet from India to China," *National Geographic* 90, no. 2 (1946): 169–222.

84 *"such a happy time":* Dalai Lama, *Freedom in Exile,* p. 51.

85 *publicly censured:* The edict was seen and included in translation by the British mission in its weekly dispatch to India. Goldstein, *History of Modern Tibet,* 1:373.

86 *"They came to treat me":* Gyalo Thondup with Anne F. Thurston, *The Noodle Maker of Kalimpong: The Untold Story of My Struggle for Tibet* (London: Rider, 2015), p. 73. Madam Chiang seems to have been genuinely solicitous of Gyalo Thondup. It was apparently she who, following the death of the *yabshi kung*, arranged for a private aircraft to fly the brothers' grandmother and sister to India. See Diki Tsering, *The Dalai Lama, My Son: A Mother's Story* (London: Virgin, 2000), p. 127.

8. Trouble in Shangri-La

88 *"When he left":* Dalai Lama, *Freedom in Exile: The Autobiography of His Holiness the Dalai Lama of Tibet* (London: Hodder & Stoughton, 1990), p. 21.

"They were full of fun": Thomas Laird, *The Story of Tibet: Conversations with the Dalai Lama* (London: Atlantic, 2006), pp. 277, 274.

Arko Lhamo: Laird, *The Story of Tibet,* p. 278.

90 *"laughed uncontrollably": The Magical Play of Illusion: The Autobiography of Trijang Rinpoche*, trans. Sharpa Tulku Tenzin Trinley (Somerville, MA: Wisdom Publications, 2018), p. 163.

91 *gave him a warm welcome:* Melvyn C. Goldstein, *A History of Modern Tibet: 1913–1951,* vol. 1, *The Demise of the Lamaist State* (Berkeley: University of California Press, 1991), pp. 441–42. The abbot eventually returned to Tibet as a collaborator of the Communists.

he would support them: Goldstein, *History of Modern Tibet,* 1:466.

92 *"misinforming" her son:* Diki Tsering, *The Dalai Lama, My Son: A Mother's Story* (London: Virgin, 2000), p. 120.

whether or not the accusation: Jamyang Norbu, for one, disputes it. See his "Shadow Tibet" blog post for June 29, 2016, "Untangling a Mess of Petrified Noodles," jamyang norbu.com.

93 *incontrovertible evidence:* See the section of a speech where the Dalai Lama mentions Reting Rinpoché at https://www.dalailama.com/messages/dolgyal-shugden/speeches-by-his-holiness-the-dalai-lama/dharamsala-teaching. I discussed the Reting episode at length with H. E. Richardson, British political officer for Tibet at the time, at his home in St. Andrews, Scotland. He admitted that he had absolutely no inkling of what was going on in government circles before the affair erupted.

94 *a horse called Yudrug:* Goldstein, *History of Modern Tibet,* 1:486.

he hesitated: Goldstein, *History of Modern Tibet,* 1:488.

95 *"At last":* Dalai Lama, *Freedom in Exile,* p. 33.

alert to the danger: Laird, *The Story of Tibet,* p. 185.

"like the call": Goldstein, *History of Modern Tibet,* 1:499.

96 *Around thirty:* Goldstein, *History of Modern Tibet,* 1:505. With respect to the government's losses, I include the sixteen soldiers subsequently killed at Reting. See also the account in Jamyang Choegyal Kasho, *In the Service of the 13th and 14th Dalai Lamas* (Frankfurt am Main: Tibethaus Deutschland, 2015), chap. 10.

no room to maneuver: Goldstein, *History of Modern Tibet,* 1:505. See also Laird, *The Story of Tibet,* p. 287.

"my position was hopeless": Laird, *The Story of Tibet,* p. 287.

98 *"The officials started bullying him":* Laird, *The Story of Tibet,* p. 279.

his first attempt at driving: The story is charmingly told by the Dalai Lama in *Freedom in Exile,* pp. 42–43.

9. The Perfection of Wisdom

99 *"did his best":* Dalai Lama, *The Life of My Teacher: A Biography of Kyabje Ling Rinpoché* (Somerville, MA: Wisdom Publications, 2017), p. 153. I think it fair to assume that in likening himself to a boat cut adrift, the Dalai Lama has in mind the perils of a Himalayan torrent.

107 *"smiled when asked":* Lowell Thomas, *Out of This World* (London: Macdonald and Co., 1951), p. 155.

a Catholic missionary: This was Father Maurice Tournay, a Swiss priest later declared Blessed by Pope John Paul II for having died "in odium fidei" — at the hand of one motivated by hatred of the faith. His story is told in Robert Loup, *Martyr in Tibet* (Philadelphia: D. McKay and Co., 1956). The actual date of his martyrdom was August 11, 1949.

a link between the Nazis: An entertaining account may be found in Mark Hale, *Himmler's Crusade: The True Story of the Nazis' 1938 Expedition into Tibet* (London: Bantam Books, 2003).

108 *Schaefer and his men:* One of these was Bruno Beger, convicted in 1974 of having helped select a group of Jews whose skulls were to form the basis of a collection designed to show the subhuman characteristics of their possessors. An anthropologist by training, Beger was sentenced to a mere three years in prison, which in fact he never served. He subsequently became a regular, if embarrassing, attendee at Tibet-related events in Germany and abroad. I met him at a luncheon given by the Dalai Lama at London's five-star Grosvenor House Hotel in 1992. Although this was before the age of Wikipedia, it is nonetheless somewhat surprising that Beger should have been invited. I remember being told that he had been a Nazi, but presumably the details of his service were unknown to the organizers of the event, which was designed to bring together all those surviving Europeans who had visited Tibet prior to 1949. In retrospect, Beger struck me in conversation as both shamefaced about his past and unrepentant. Subsequent research shows

him to have been a deeply unpleasant character; see Heather Pringle's excellent and disturbing book *The Master Plan: Himmler's Scholars and the Holocaust* (London: Fourth Estate, 2006), pp. 260–62. Also present at the luncheon was Archie Jack, who as a young man had been a competitor at Hitler's Olympics and subsequently visited Lhasa. It was Jack who was responsible for setting free the flock of doves that the Führer was to have released at the opening ceremony. Furiously anti-Nazi, he told me later that at dinner with Tsarong Shapé, the Great Thirteenth's favorite, they had discussed the possibility of assassinating Hitler. Tsarong told him that if he could procure a lock of the German leader's hair, the matter could easily be arranged by monks adept at black magic.

an unambiguous link: See a useful article by Kalachakra scholar Alexander Berzin at https://studybuddhism.com/en/advanced-studies/history-culture/shambhala/the-nazi-connection-with-shambhala-and-tibet.

109 *"seemed less like":* Heinrich Harrer, *Seven Years in Tibet* (London: R. Hart-Davis, 1953), p. 248. The book was a huge best-seller when first published and has been continuously in print ever since. Harrer was modest and generous enough to point out that it was vastly more successful in English than in any other of the more than fifty languages into which it was translated, a success he attributed to his translator, Richard Graves — brother of the poet Robert Graves. It is certainly true that *Return to Tibet,* the book he published three decades later, reads as if written by somebody else entirely, and with greatly inferior literary talent.

"He seemed to me": Harrer, *Seven Years,* p. 249. Harrer was of humble background. Although he was university educated himself, his father had been a postal worker. I met Harrer on a number of occasions. Though well into his eighties by then, he was still full of life and interested in all matters Tibetan and struck me as down-to-earth and affable, just as the Dalai Lama describes him.

110 *"the utmost trouble":* Harrer, *Seven Years,* p. 249.

"he came running": Harrer, *Seven Years,* p. 257.

111 *caused him to change his mind:* This is the opinion expressed by Messner, the great Italian mountaineer, who knew Harrer. In an interview with *Die Welt,* he speaks of how Harrer's conduct after the war was quite different from his conduct before the war. See https://www.welt.de/print-welt/article189698/Einer-der-Zaehesten-seiner-Generation.html.

the romantic strain in fascist ideology: See Nicholas Goodrick-Clarke, *Black Sun: Aryan Cults, Esoteric Nazism, and the Politics of Identity* (New York: NYU Press, 2001), p. 4.

"elegant Tibetan characters": Harrer, *Seven Years,* pp. 253, 258.

mechanical devices: Harrer, *Seven Years.* p. 249.

"did not know": Harrer, *Seven Years,* pp. 253, 258.

112 *"convinced that by virtue":* Harrer, *Seven Years,* p. 255.

10. "Shit on their picnic!"

114 *"double-edged steel": The Magical Play of Illusion: The Autobiography of Trijang Rinpoche,* trans. Sharpa Tulku Tenzin Trinley (Somerville, MA: Wisdom Publications, 2018),

pp. 187–88. A highly placed source assures me that these "support substances" would have been actual rather than merely symbolic.

"the honourable": India Office Records quoted in Melvyn C. Goldstein, *A History of Modern Tibet: 1913–1951,* vol. 1, *The Demise of the Lamaist State* (Berkeley: University of California Press, 1991), p. 624.

115 *"in order that":* There are various translations. The earliest known is into Russian, dating from 1827; the earliest in English dates from 1880 (that of S. W. Bushell in *The Early History of Tibet from Chinese Sources*).

117 *"approached the microphone reverently":* Robert Ford, *Captured in Tibet* (London: G. Harrap and Co., 1957), p. 64.

"thirty or forty" dull explosions: See Heinrich Harrer, *Seven Years in Tibet* (London: R. Hart-Davis, 1953), p. 259; Dalai Lama, *Freedom in Exile: The Autobiography of His Holiness the Dalai Lama of Tibet* (London: Hodder & Stoughton, 1990), p. 55.

"blazing summer weather": Harrer, *Seven Years,* p. 260.

"Give the Dalai Lama": Harrer, *Seven Years,* p. 263.

119 *"Right now":* Goldstein, *History of Modern Tibet,* 1:692.

120 *"people . . . running":* Ford, *Captured,* p. 127.

charged with being a British spy: All quotations are drawn from his obituary in the *Daily Telegraph,* October 6, 2016; but see also his memoir *Captured in Tibet* (London: G. Harrap and Co., 1957).

122 *"If you don't make good offerings":* Goldstein, *History of Modern Tibet,* 1:705.

123 *For as long:* Dalai Lama, *Freedom in Exile,* p. 314.

124 *a famous oracle:* The story of how the oracle was (quite recently) identified is instructive. The phenomenon of people — not just monks — falling into a trance during religious ceremonies is common, but not all of them communicate intelligibly. I recall hearing someone do so during a dawn ceremony on the roof of the Tsuglhakang in Dharamsala. It sounded like the hoarse barking of a fox. Nor is it the case that when they do communicate intelligibly they are channeling anyone important. It could be just a ghost impersonating one of the protector deities. In the case of the Dungkhar oracle, it is said that a pilgrim who had traveled all the way from Mongolia asked for admittance at the monastery but was refused. Not only was he thrown out by one monk, but also he was abused and beaten by four others from whom he implored help. At this he left, uttering a curse that the five monks who had ill-treated him would all be dead within a year. Sure enough this came to pass, but not before another monk had fallen into a trance and begun "to jump about, beating his breast and making weird noises through clenched teeth." It was not until the five were dead that the deity could be understood. It turned out to be the spirit of the Mongolian pilgrim, through which no fewer than six different deities subsequently manifested. See Tsewang Y. Pemba, *Young Days in Tibet* (London: Jonathan Cape, 1957), p. 40.

the end of their natural life: The Second Dalai Lama's mother, Ma Cig Kinga, a famous renunciate, is an example. He kept her skull for use as a ritual chalice. See

Alexander Norman, *Secret Lives of the Dalai Lama* (New York: Random House, 2008), p. 173.

"followed its normal course": Harrer, *Seven Years,* p. 275.

"You are not allowed": Adapted from Melvyn C. Goldstein, *A History of Modern Tibet,* vol. 2, *The Calm Before the Storm, 1951–1955* (Berkeley: University of California Press, 2007), p. 182.

126 *"ever filled a man's belly":* Thubten Jigme Norbu, *Tibet Is My Country* (London: Rupert Hart Davis, 1960), p. 211.

bandits: Almost every European traveler mentions these, but so too does Dr. Pemba; see *Young Days in Tibet,* p. 51.

"petty injustices": Dalai Lama, *Freedom in Exile,* p. 64.

"It was heartbreaking": Trijang, *Magical Play,* p. 181.

Dungkar Monastery: When Archie Jack visited the monastery en route to Gyantse and then Lhasa just over a decade earlier, it had left a poor impression: "The monks were suspicious, filthy dirty (many of the young boys covered in large running sores). No photographs could be taken and altogether one had a very unpleasant, unclean, nauseating feeling on emerging from the place." Archibald Jack, unpublished Tibet journal, Royal Geographical Society, London. Against this, traveling the same route, Robert Byron, his near contemporary, wrote in his *First Russia, Then Tibet* (London: Macmillan, 1933), p. 206, that "from the monks we received nothing but hospitality and smiles," although it is clear that Byron did not actually visit Dungkar Monastery itself.

127 *horribly disfigured:* Pemba, *Young Days in Tibet,* p. 58.

"usual routine": Dalai Lama, *Freedom in Exile,* p. 65.

tantras are considered: The tantras are also associated with a system of sexual practices, their centrality to the tradition attested in the frequent depictions of the protectors united in sexual congress with a consort. Unsurprisingly, these practices are the source of much misunderstanding, but it is important to acknowledge that the Dalai Lama asserts their validity, going so far as to say that undertaking them physically during at least one lifetime is necessary for Enlightenment. Within the Gelug tradition generally, however, the practices are confined to the mental, not the physical plane.

The theory behind the sexual practices owes much to how the human being is conceived in relation to the cosmos. The tantras envisage a correspondence between the two such that the mind-body composite is in fact a microcosm of the universe itself. And just as the sun and the moon, the planets and the stars are held aloft by cosmic winds, so too the mind is held to be sustained by infinitesimally subtle internal winds that pass along the body's "wind channels." These winds are held to carry "drops" or seeds of potential, which, correctly utilized, enable the practitioner to have direct experience of non-duality. This in itself is an essential preparation for the ultimate attainment of full Enlightenment.

In mundane terms, what is required for the sexual practices actually to contribute toward the individual's spiritual progress is that one be able to engage in the most advanced meditative techniques. Without such ability, it will not be possible to exercise the necessary control over the body. It is not enough for the male merely to be able to prevent the release of seminal fluid, nor for the female to be able to control her climax. To obtain the highest spiritual insights, the practitioner must be in full control of the subtlest energies that are activated during sexual congress. Of the males, it is said that the most accomplished are able actually to reverse the flow of semen from the tip of the sex organ and withdraw it back down the shaft.

For an account by June Campbell of her experiences as a consort, see *Traveller in Space: Gender, Identity and Tibetan Buddhism* (London: Athlone, 1996). From Campbell's perspective, her relationship with Kalu Rinpoché, the Kagyu master, was ultimately exploitative. It is remarkable to learn that Kalu Rinpiche's reincarnation reports that he himself was sexually abused when a minor.

the kiss of a beautiful woman: John Crook and James Low, *The Yogins of Ladakh: A Pilgrimage Among the Hermits of the Buddhist Himalayas* (1997; Delhi: Motilal Banarsidass, 2012), p. 279.

128 *"that if they were so arrogant":* Rinchen Sadutshang, *A Life Unforeseen: A Memoir of Service to Tibet* (Somerville, MA: Wisdom Publications, 2016), p. 144.

129 *in radio contact:* Sadutshang, *A Life Unforeseen,* p. 145.

130 *"so great and powerful":* Gyalo Thondup with Anne F. Thurston, *The Noodle Maker of Kalimpong: The Untold Story of My Struggle for Tibet* (London: Rider, 2015), p. 146.

131 *"three men":* Dalai Lama, *Freedom in Exile,* p. 72.

11. Into the Dragon's Lair

133 *"many present":* Dalai Lama, *The Life of My Teacher: A Biography of Kyabje Ling Rinpoché* (Somerville, MA: Wisdom Publications, 2017), p. 163.

human flesh eaters: Melvyn C. Goldstein, *A History of Modern Tibet,* vol. 2, *The Calm Before the Storm, 1951–1955* (Berkeley: University of California Press, 2007), p. 206.

"in a short time": Goldstein, *History of Modern Tibet,* 2:206.

134 *"willing to help":* Goldstein, *History of Modern Tibet,* 2:149.

"challenged and confronted": Goldstein, *History of Modern Tibet,* 2:188 (quoting Lhalu), 181.

136 *"grand salvation":* Melvyn C. Goldstein, *A History of Modern Tibet: 1913–1951,* vol. 1, *The Demise of the Lamaist State* (Berkeley: University of California Press, 1989), p. 684.

unwilling to allow: Dalai Lama, *Freedom in Exile: The Autobiography of His Holiness the Dalai Lama of Tibet* (London: Hodder & Stoughton, 1990), p. 84.

"the Dalai Lama belongs": Goldstein, *History of Modern Tibet,* 2:442.

"if you take away the pastures": Jianglin Li, *Tibet in Agony: Lhasa, 1959* (Cambridge: Harvard University Press, 2016), p. 73.

137 *hold off:* Goldstein, *History of Modern Tibet,* 2:370.

"an ocean fraught": Dalai Lama, *Kalachakra Tantra: Rite of Initiation,* trans., ed., and with an introduction by Geoffrey Hopkins, enlarged ed. (Somerville, MA: Wisdom Publications, 1999), p. 178.

"lotus": Dalai Lama, *Kalachakra Tantra,* p. 95.

138 *"When we passed fourteen"*: Mary Craig, *Kundun: A Biography of the Family of the Dalai Lama* (London: HarperCollins, 1997), pp. 184–85.

139 *social convention:* Jamyang Choegyal Kasho, *In the Service of the 13th and 14th Dalai Lamas* (Frankfurt am Main, Tibethaus Deutschland, 2015), p. 193.

"The aeroplane": Goldstein, *History of Modern Tibet,* 2:482.

140 *"shabby tents"*: Trijang, *Magical Play,* p. 204.

spittle-smeared: Dalai Lama, *Freedom in Exile,* p. 93.

"Brahmins, outcasts and pigs": Trijang, *Magical Play,* p. 318.

141 *"The craft"*: Dalai Lama, *Freedom in Exile,* p. 94.

taken to a house: Diki Tsering, *The Dalai Lama, My Son: A Mother's Story* (London: Virgin, 2000), p. 140.

"required to attend": Diki Tsering, *The Dalai Lama, My Son,* p. 140.

142 *the hypocrisy he witnessed:* Melvyn C. Goldstein, Dawei Sherap, and William R. Siebenschuh, *A Tibetan Revolutionary: The Political Life and Times of Bapa Phüntso Wangye* (Berkeley: University of California Press, 2004), pp. 53, 90.

"elegantly dressed": Goldstein, Sherap, and Siebenschuh, *A Tibetan Revolutionary,* p. 72.

143 *"anyone who couldn't pay"*: Goldstein, Sherap, and Siebenschuh, *A Tibetan Revolutionary,* pp. 72, 55.

"act like the great leader": Goldstein, Sherap, and Siebenschuh, *A Tibetan Revolutionary,* p. 191.

144 *"one of the main fabrications"*: Goldstein, *History of Modern Tibet,* 2:494–95.

"when dealing with": https://www.dalailama.com/messages/dolgyal-shugden/speeches-by-his-holiness-the-dalai-lama/dharamsala-teaching (accessed March 21, 2019).

145 *"not to let the lamas dance"*: Goldstein, Sherap, and Siebenschuh, *A Tibetan Revolutionary,* p. 191.

"extremely alert": Goldstein, Sherap, and Siebenschuh, *A Tibetan Revolutionary,* p. 191.

"Meeting often": Goldstein, Sherap, and Siebenschuh, *A Tibetan Revolutionary,* pp. 191, 193.

146 *"silly. Wasteful"*: Goldstein, *History of Modern Tibet,* 2:504.

"extremely interested": Goldstein, Sherap, and Siebenschuh, *A Tibetan Revolutionary,* p. 192.

film footage: It is easily found on YouTube; see www.youtube.com.

"eager to learn": Goldstein, Sherap, and Siebenschuh, *A Tibetan Revolutionary,* p. 192.

"From morning till evening": Diki Tsering, *The Dalai Lama, My Son,* p. 140.

147 *"I could plainly read"*: Rinchen Sadutshang, *A Life Unforeseen: A Memoir of Service to Tibet* (Somerville, MA: Wisdom Publications, 2016), p. 180.

bag of tsampa*:* Sadutshang, *A Life Unforeseen,* p. 182.

"with a mischievous expression": Dalai Lama, *Freedom in Exile,* pp. 107, 108.

12. The Land of the Gods

148 *"had become wretched":* Diki Tsering, *The Dalai Lama, My Son: A Mother's Story* (London: Virgin, 2000), p. 145.

149 *June 30, 1955:* Several different dates have been proposed for the Dalai Lama's homecoming. I use the one he himself gives in *The Life of My Teacher: A Biography of Kyabje Ling Rinpoché* (Somerville, MA: Wisdom Publications, 2017), p. 191.

"miraculous iron pills": *The Magical Play of Illusion: The Autobiography of Trijang Rinpoche,* trans. Sharpa Tulku Tenzin Trinley (Somerville, MA: Wisdom Publications, 2018), pp. 336, 343.

"lord": Melvyn C. Goldstein, *A History of Modern Tibet,* vol. 3, *The Storm Clouds Descend, 1955–1957* (Berkeley: University of California Press, 2014), p. 31.

news started: Rinchen Sadutshang, *A Life Unforeseen: A Memoir of Service to Tibet* (Somerville, MA: Wisdom Publications, 2016), p. 189.

150 *"liberation, Tibet could see":* Alan Winnington, *Tibet: Record of a Journey* (London: Lawrence and Wishart, 1957), p. 132.

"harboured a low opinion": Trijang, *Magical Play,* p. 340.

"even the insects": Goldstein, *History of Modern Tibet,* 3:71–72.

152 *the all-powerful British:* While there was undoubtedly much to draw inspiration from, remarkably, the British population of India, including wives, children, and traders, along with government and military personnel, was only around 150,000 at the end of the nineteenth century, while the general population approached 300 million. The British population may have increased somewhat during the early twentieth century, but it seems never to have risen above 250,000. See, e.g., https://history.stackexchange.com/questions/15298/how-many-britons-lived-in-india-during-the-british-raj-1858-1947. The skill of the British had been to flatter the Indian princes and play the different states off against one another with minimal effort on their part. The other crucial ingredient for Mahatma Gandhi's success was, arguably, the conquerors' residual allegiance to the teachings of Christ's Sermon on the Mount, which the Mahatma had made central to his political philosophy.

"On this matter": Goldstein, *History of Modern Tibet,* 3:95.

the nomad chieftain: The chieftain's name was Yoenrupoen. See Goldstein, *History of Modern Tibet,* 3:133ff.

153 *"If someone supported the CCP":* Goldstein, *History of Modern Tibet,* 3:139.

"stabbed to death": Goldstein, *History of Modern Tibet,* 3:230.

correct motivation: There are other supports for compassionately motivated violence; see, for example, Jacob Dalton, *Taming the Demons* (New Haven: Yale University Press, 2011).

"where the motive is good": Roger Hicks and Chogyam Ngakpa, *Great Ocean, an Authorised Biography: The Dalai Lama* (Shaftesbury, Dorset: Element Books, 1984), p. 162.

154 *"the Tibetans were going out":* Goldstein, *History of Modern Tibet,* 3:234.
the damage: Incorrectly, it was inferred that this had been inflicted by the bombers, mentioned in the article accompanying the photograph. This was further conflated with rumors (which turned out to be true) that Batang Monastery had also been bombed. Melvyn C. Goldstein, *A History of Modern Tibet,* vol. 2, *The Calm Before the Storm, 1951–1955* (Berkeley: University of California Press, 2007), p. 238.
"I cried": Dalai Lama, *Freedom in Exile: The Autobiography of His Holiness the Dalai Lama of Tibet* (London: Hodder & Stoughton, 1990), p. 121.

155 *"How are Tibetans":* Dalai Lama, *Freedom in Exile,* pp. 121–22.
"filled with awe": Sadutshang, *A Life Unforeseen,* p. 159.
"anxious to leave": John Kenneth Knaus, *Orphans of the Cold War: America and the Tibetan Struggle for Survival* (New York: PublicAffairs, 1999), p. 131.

156 *no attempt had been made:* See the description in Trijang, *Magical Play,* p. 351.
"It must be anticipated": Goldstein, *History of Modern Tibet,* 3:338–39.
"probably perished": Tsewang Y. Pemba, *Young Days in Tibet* (London: Jonathan Cape, 1957), p. 131.
"their real feelings": Dalai Lama, *Freedom in Exile,* p. 127.
"was not made easier": Nari Rustomji, *Enchanted Frontiers: Sikkim, Bhutan and India's North-Eastern Borderlands* (Oxford: Oxford University Press, 1971), pp. 123, 215.

157 *We had hardly passed:* Rustomji, *Enchanted Frontiers,* pp. 215, 216.

158 *"It was evident":* Rustomi's observation regarding the Panchen Lama was perceptive. The lama subsequently married the daughter of a senior Chinese Nationalist army officer. I had the honor once of meeting the Panchen Lama's daughter, whose business card, printed on pink stock, identified her unexpectedly as a princess.
"Their views": Goldstein, *History of Modern Tibet,* 3:343.

159 *"It was a calm and beautiful":* Dalai Lama, *Freedom in Exile,* p. 127.
did not share: That said, there were undoubtedly some modernists within the Nehru government who thought Tibetan Buddhism was a hilarious concoction of falsehoods. See the remarks of Apa Pant quoted in Goldstein, *History of Modern Tibet,* 3:364.
"as full of charm": Dalai Lama, *Freedom in Exile,* p. 129.
happy to supply: Goldstein, *History of Modern Tibet,* 3:377.

160 *"but one scholar": The Political Philosophy of the XIVth Dalai Lama: Selected Speeches and Writings* (Delhi: Tibetan Parliamentary and Policy Research Centre, 1998), p. 5.
made it back: Sadutshang, *A Life Unforeseen,* pp. 196–97.

161 *"At first he listened":* Dalai Lama, *Freedom in Exile,* pp. 128, 129. As I recall, the Dalai Lama originally said in his book that Nehru did in fact drift off briefly, but it was decided during the editing process to spare the blushes of his Indian readers. Ted Heath, the former British prime minister, whom he met during the early 1980s, likewise fell asleep during a meeting with the Dalai Lama.
the (Chinese) transcripts: See Goldstein, *History of Modern Tibet,* vol. 2, chap. 11, "The Dalai Lama Visits India."

"At first when you say": Goldstein, 3:422.

162 *enjoyed a vision:* William Meyers, Robert Thurman, and Michael G. Burbank, *Man of Peace: The Illustrated Life Story of the Dalai Lama of Tibet* (New York: Tibet House, 2016), p. 84. I am assuming he saw this vision while meditating.

"hell realms": Trijang, *Magical Play,* pp. 355–56.

163 *"There was a lot of submissiveness":* Kenneth Conboy and James Morrison, *The CIA's Secret War in Tibet* (Lawrence: University Press of Kansas, 2002), p. 33.

"please arrange": Knaus, *Orphans of the Cold War,* p. 297.

164 *"When men become desperate":* Dalai Lama, *Freedom in Exile,* p. 132.

165 *such a plot:* Goldstein, *History of Modern Tibet,* 3:431. The only written account is that of General Fan Ming himself in his autobiography.

"being returned to prison": Trijang, *Magical Play,* p. 218.

13. "Don't sell the Dalai Lama for silver dollars!"

166 *Zhou Enlai's promises:* Melvyn C. Goldstein, *A History of Modern Tibet,* vol. 3, *The Storm Clouds Descend, 1955–1957* (Berkeley: University of California Press, 2014), pp. 445–51.

far fewer: see Jianglin Li, "When the Iron Bird Flies: The 1956–1962 Secret War on the Tibetan Plateau," unpublished ms., trans. Stacey Mosher, p. 117.

167 *performing the ritual:* Goldstein, *History of Modern Tibet,* 3:44. See also *The Magical Play of Illusion: The Autobiography of Trijang Rinpoche,* trans. Sharpa Tulku Tenzin Trinley (Somerville, MA: Wisdom Publications, 2018), p. 359.

"a very bad show": Goldstein, *History of Modern Tibet,* 3:44. In fact, many Tashilhunpo monks did attend in the end, but that was clearly not the monastery authorities' intention.

168 *"with tears filling my eyes":* Dalai Lama, *The Life of My Teacher: A Biography of Kyabje Ling Rinpoché* (Somerville, MA: Wisdom Publications, 2017), p. 189.

The work of: See http://www.jamyangnorbu.com/blog/2014/09/27/the-political-vision-of-andrugtsang-gompo-tashi/ (accessed November 1, 2017).

169 *"brave, honest and strong":* Kenneth Conboy and James Morrison, *The CIA's Secret War in Tibet* (Lawrence: University Press of Kansas, 2002), p. 55.

170 *"completely non-committal":* Conboy and Morrison, *Secret War,* p. 69.

"gesturing in the direction": See opening sequence of the documentary *The Shadow Circus: The CIA in Tibet.*

"to ward off colds": Conboy and Morrison, *Secret War,* p. 81.

171 *"monastery religious personnel":* Jianglin Li, *Tibet in Agony: Lhasa, 1959* (Cambridge: Harvard University Press, 2016), p. 50.

"we took a great leap": Li, *Tibet in Agony,* p. 55. The original population of Namthang township was just under two thousand.

"excellent": Li, "When the Iron Bird Flies," pp. 377, 164.

172 *an ambitious raid:* Conboy and Morrison, *Secret War,* p. 78.

progressed to Sera: See Dalai Lama, *Life of My Teacher,* pp. 190–91.

173 *"troubled state of mind":* Trijang, *Magical Play,* p. 228. Here I prefer the more literal translation of the first redaction.

geshe *exams:* For a description of the final examination of a Gelug monk, see Georges B. J. Dreyfus, *The Sound of Two Hands Clapping: The Education of a Tibetan Buddhist Monk* (Berkeley: University of California Press, 2003), pp. 256–59.

cabled a message: International Commission of Jurists, *The Question of Tibet and the Rule of Law* (Geneva, 1959), p. 9.

174 *had been canceled:* Here I follow Li, *Tibet in Agony,* pp. 100–101.

"cream of scholars": Dalai Lama, *Life of My Teacher,* p. 193.

175 *"hatching a plot":* Li, *Tibet in Agony,* p. 101.

"make short work": Li, *Tibet in Agony,* p. 105.

176 *"Maybe this isn't":* The autobiography of Phuntsog Tashi Taklha, the Dalai Lama's chief of security, quoted in Li, *Tibet in Agony,* p. 111. I had the honor of knowing Phuntsog Tashi when he lived in London. He was not a man of obvious military bearing.

"all-knowing Guru": Li, *Tibet in Agony,* p. 112. One might object here that if the Dalai Lama really was all-knowing, he would not need this or indeed any advice from the oracle. But actually the epithet "all-knowing" or "omniscient" is a common one used of high lamas to refer rather to their mastery of the doctrine.

177 *already been abducted:* Tsering Shakya, *The Dragon in the Land of Snows: A History of Modern Tibet Since 1947* (New York: Columbia University Press, 1999), p. 192.

beat him to death: Shakya, *Dragon in the Land of Snows,* p. 192. Goldstein also covers the incident in detail.

178 *"Don't forget":* Li, *Tibet in Agony,* p. 129.

179 *Tibet has always been free!:* Li, *Tibet in Agony,* p. 157.

"sitting anguished": Li, *Tibet in Agony,* pp. 135, 177.

volunteers congregated: Tubten Khetsun, *Memories of Life in Lhasa Under Chinese Rule,* trans. Matthew Akester (Delhi: Penguin for Columbia University Press, 2009), p. 29.

"not in any fear": My Land and My People: The Autobiography of His Holiness the Dalai Lama (London: Weidenfeld and Nicolson, 1962), p. 189.

"stop holding": Phuntsog Tashi Takhla, quoted in Li, *Tibet in Agony,* p. 150.

180 *"The reactionaries":* Li, *Tibet in Agony,* p. 178.

"the Tibetan people": Li, *Tibet in Agony,* pp. 162, 163.

181 *"He looked haggard":* Li, *Tibet in Agony,* pp. 179, 157.

"snatch the egg": From my conversations with Tenzin Geyche Tethong and Tendzin Choegyal, November 2018.

issued an order: Li, *Tibet in Agony,* p. 159.

"keep open the dialogue": Dalai Lama, *Freedom in Exile: The Autobiography of His Holiness the Dalai Lama of Tibet* (London: Hodder & Stoughton, 1990), p. 148.

"If you think it necessary": Li, *Tibet in Agony,* p. 184.
182 *"Someone bearing the name"*: Trijang, *Magical Play,* p. 245.
183 *"a large gold brick"*: Li, *Tibet in Agony,* p. 200.
184 *"no one looked up"*: Dalai Lama, *Freedom in Exile,* p. 151.

14. On the Back of a Dzo

187 *It turns out:* I am immensely grateful to Dr. Jianglin Li and to Professor Melvyn Goldstein, both of whom not only shared much unpublished material with me but also took the trouble to enter into lengthy discussions with respect to the question as to whether, as some have claimed, the Chinese deliberately allowed the Dalai Lama to escape. Professor Goldstein inclines to this view; Dr. Li inclines the other way.

Both, surely, are right, albeit in different ways. It is true, as Professor Goldstein points out, that Mao made clear as early as 1956 that he was not worried about the Dalai Lama quitting Lhasa to live abroad. Mao maintained this position consistently, at least until March 16. As Dr. Li points out, however, it is evident that, at the Politburo meeting on March 17, the day the Dalai Lama fled the Norbulingka, this policy had changed. In essence, now it was "best to try to keep the Dalai Lama in Lhasa. *However, if he leaves, it is not a big deal*" (Wen Feng, "Tan Guansan Jiangjun Zhihui Lasa Pingpan Shimo" [The Complete Story of How General Tan Guansan Put Down the Rebellion], *Wenshi Jinghua* 228 [May 2009]: 4–13). No minutes of this meeting have been published, but the three accounts of it that we do have all concur on this point. What is not entirely clear is whether this was Mao's directive, communicated to Zhang Jingwu, Zhang Guohua, and Huang Kecheng, whom he had summoned to his temporary headquarters at Wuhan, and who had arrived back in Beijing on the train that day, or whether this was the Politburo's collective view. Either way, it is clear that there had been a change of plan. What we also do not know is when General Tan was made aware of this change. There is no paper trail. The Politburo meeting took place during the afternoon of March 17. It could be that its instructions were communicated immediately afterwards via telephone. It could also be that a cable was sent either on the evening of the same day or sometime the following day. What is clear is that if Tan did receive the instruction on the seventeenth, he did nothing about it. Although he would have had only a few hours to act, he could at least have sent out one or more night patrols that evening; he could have alerted the informants he would certainly have had on the ground to look out for and report any suspicious movements around the Norbulingka; he could have ordered one or more checkpoints to be established on the road leading away from the Norbulingka. It is evident that he did not.

It is thus correct to say that the Chinese allowed the Dalai Lama to escape, but this was rather an act of omission than an act of commission. They were clearly aware that he might attempt to withdraw from Lhasa, but they did not knowingly permit him to do so — unless we accept at face value the anecdote supplied by Professor Goldstein's interviewee Li Zuomin, who recounted that an official at the Norbulingka, Goshampa, had contacted Ngabo (by what means is not stated) on the seventeenth to inform him that the Dalai Lama planned to leave that night. Ngabo is said to have passed the message by telephone to Li, who in turn informed General Tan. Tan then called Beijing for instructions. He was told to let the Dalai Lama go.

The trouble here is that for this to be correct, Tan's interlocutor in Beijing would have had to ignore the Politburo's instruction issued earlier that day. This seems implausible. From other evidence, it also clear that Tan did not, in fact, learn until the nineteenth that the Dalai Lama had fled, and indeed it was not until that day that he informed Beijing. There is also no other evidence to corroborate Li Zuomin's claim. Could he have been lying? It is certainly not unknown even for retired officials to fabricate evidence to save face for the institution they served.

To me, the most likely sequence is that the Chinese maintained a permissive policy toward the possibility of the Dalai Lama's withdrawing right up until the seventeenth, changing it only on that day. Very likely General Tan was made aware of this change in the early evening of the same day, but, following receipt of the Dalai Lama's letter saying that he would like to take up the general's offer to come to the PLA for safety, Tan did not act on his new instructions immediately.

Subsequently no effort was made to capture the Precious Protector on account of the instruction "not to worry" should he in fact succeed in getting away. But with the caveat regarding the putative evidence supplied by Li Zuomin, this does not amount to the Chinese leadership knowingly permitting the Dalai Lama to leave. If Li Zuomin's evidence is true, why have the Chinese not published the communiqués between Lhasa and Beijing that were sent on March 18? The reason is surely that it would be embarrassing to do so.

"and his cohorts": Mao's cable of March 12 has not been published in its entirety, but a summary is quoted in Jianglin Li, *Tibet in Agony: Lhasa, 1959* (Cambridge: Harvard University Press, 2016), p. 167.

"do everything possible": Jianglin Li, "When the Iron Bird Flies: The 1956–1962 Secret War on the Tibetan Plateau," unpublished ms., trans. Stacey Mosher, p. 264.

"the least harm": The Magical Play of Illusion: The Autobiography of Trijang Rinpoche, trans. Sharpa Tulku Tenzin Trinley (Somerville, MA: Wisdom Publications, 2018), p. 245.

188 *"I found it extremely difficult":* Dalai Lama, *Freedom in Exile: The Autobiography of His Holiness the Dalai Lama of Tibet* (London: Hodder & Stoughton, 1990), p. 152.

mixed up: This story is told by Trijang Rinpoché in his autobiography but not in the published English-language version, *Magical Play.*

189 *"must deliberate profoundly":* See Sumner Carnahan and Lama Kunga Rinpoche, *In the Presence of My Enemies: Memoirs of Tibetan Nobleman Tsipon Shuguba* (Santa Fe, NM: Heartsfire Books, 1998), p. 4.

seal off: Li, *Tibet in Agony,* pp. 234, 243, 235.

190 *"countless guns":* Carnahan and Lama Kunga Rinpoche, *In the Presence,* p. 4.

191 *One alternative they considered:* http://www.atimes.com/article/dalai-lama-prefer-exile-myanmar-india/ (accessed December 10, 2018).
a full six days: Carnahan and Lama Kunga Rinpoche, *In the Presence of My Enemies,* pp. 4–5.

192 *A famous photograph:* See Jamyang Choegyal Kasho, *In the Service of the 13th and 14th Dalai Lamas* (Frankfurt am Main: Tibethaus Deutschland, 2015), p. 205.
Prisoners caught saying prayers: Besides the oral histories collected by various organizations, such as the International Commission of Jurists and the Library of Tibetan Works and Archives, there are several good firsthand accounts of the period available in English. One of the most thorough is that of Tubten Khetsun (*Memories of Life in Lhasa Under Chinese Rule,* trans. Matthew Akester [Delhi: Penguin for Columbia University Press, 2009]), a minor aristocrat who served in the Dalai Lama's administration. Also useful is the biography of Kabshoba, a minister, by his son Jamyang Choegyal Kasho (*In the Service*). The autobiographies of Phuntsog Wangyal and Tashi Tsering give a flavor of the miseries of life in prison in Beijing. Probably the most famous is that of Palden Gyatso (*Fire Under the Snow: The True Story of a Tibetan Monk* [London: Harvill Press, 1997]), kept a prisoner for three decades, but other useful accounts are given in Shuguba (Carnahan and Lama Kunga Rinpoche, *In the Presence of My Enemies*) and Khetsun. David Patt, *A Strange Liberation: Tibetan Lives in Chinese Hands* (Ithaca: Snow Lion Publications, 1993), provides the stories of Ama Adhe, a nomad woman and mother of two incarcerated for over twenty years, and Tenpa Soepa, a government official jailed for a similar period. Of course, these should all be read with a critical eye, but the increasing availability of Chinese sources, especially those provided by Jianglin Li (*Tibet in Agony* and "When the Iron Bird Flies"), goes a long way toward substantiating even the more horrific of the claims made.

193 *This made plain:* See Li, *Tibet in Agony,* p. 301.

194 *most surprised:* See the report for April 5, 1959, of Har Mander Singh, the Indian political officer based at Tawang, http://www.claudearpi.net/wp-content/uploads/2018/03/April-5-Report-on-the-entry-of-His-Holiness-the-Dalai-Lama-into-India.pdf (accessed December 11, 2018).
an airplane might be sent: Li, *Tibet in Agony,* p. 304.
the last Tibetan villages: This second night was in fact passed at a monastery a short distance away from the fortress. Li, *Tibet in Agony,* p. 305.
a large aircraft: Amazingly, the moment was captured on film. It can be seen near the beginning of the documentary *The Shadow Circus,* part 3.
no markings: Dr. Jianglin Li concurs that the lack of markings means that it could not have been Chinese.

15. Opening the Eye of New Awareness

196 *"We do not yet know":* http://www.archieve.claudearpi.net/maintenance/uploaded_pics/590330_Nehru_to_Rajedra_Prasad.pdf (accessed November 21, 2018).

197 *no interviews: Time* nonetheless put the story on its cover for April 15, 1959, under the headline "THE ESCAPE THAT ROCKED THE REDS." An early account can be found in Noel Barber, *The Flight of the Dalai Lama* (London: Hodder & Stoughton, 1960).
"for their spontaneous": The full text may be read in *The Political Philosophy of the Dalai Lama: Selected Speeches and Writings,* ed. Dr. Subash C. Kashyap (New Delhi: Rupa, 2014), pp. 3–5.
"The so-called statement": Dalai Lama, *My Land and My People: The Autobiography of His Holiness the Dalai Lama* (London: Weidenfeld and Nicolson, 1962), p. 218.
"to invoke the commitment": Dalai Lama, *The Life of My Teacher: A Biography of Kyabje Ling Rinpoché* (Somerville, MA: Wisdom Publications, 2017), p. 200.
"immediately one of irritation": Quoted in Lobsang Gyatso Sither, *Exile: A Photo Journal, 1959–1989* (Dharamsala: Tibet Documentation, 2017), p. 15.

198 *"his lower lip":* Dalai Lama, *Freedom in Exile: The Autobiography of His Holiness the Dalai Lama of Tibet* (London: Hodder & Stoughton, 1990), p. 161.
"focus . . . on religious practice": The Magical Play of Illusion: The Autobiography of Trijang Rinpoche, trans. Sharpa Tulku Tenzin Trinley (Somerville, MA: Wisdom Publications, 2018), p. 253.

200 *"tyranny and oppression":* International Commission of Jurists, *The Question of Tibet and the Rule of Law* (Geneva, 1959), pp. 197–98.
"one of the most impressive": Mikel Dunham, *Buddha's Warriors: The Story of the CIA-Backed Tibetan Freedom Fighters, the Chinese Invasion, and the Ultimate Fall of Tibet* (New York: Jeremy P. Tarcher/Penguin, 2004), p. 332. For an unexpected account of the resistance fighters, see also Chris Mullin, *Hinterland* (London: Profile Books, 2017).

201 *generous supply of war matériel:* Among the supplies were 370 M1 rifles with 192 rounds for each one, four machine guns with a thousand rounds apiece, and two radio sets. A month later, a second drop delivered a similar quantity of weapons, including this time three recoilless rifles (or bazookas). A third delivery, on the night of the next full moon, comprised 226 pallets with eight hundred rifles, twenty cases of hand grenades, 113 carbines (presumably M4 close-quarter rifles), and two hundred cases of ammunition, each containing ten thousand rounds. A final drop onto Pemba in January 1960 was the largest of all. Three aircraft dropped a total of 657 pallets, which, in addition to a proportionately similar number of arms as the previous three drops, also included thirty cases of various first aid items, a dozen crates of food, and a mimeograph machine for producing propaganda. Among the food rations was a special *tsampa,* formulated for mountain warfare by Kellogg's. John Kenneth Knaus, *Orphans of the Cold War: America and the Tibetan Struggle for Survival* (New York: PublicAffairs, 1999), p. 280.
"At first we didn't believe": Dunham, *Buddha's Warriors,* p. 339.

202 *"one of the greatest intelligence hauls":* John Kenneth Knaus, speaking in the documentary *The Shadow Circus.*
"a remarkably effective": Knaus, *Orphans of the Cold War,* p. 2.
"Tibet had been": Knaus, *Orphans of the Cold War,* p. 330.

203 *"Dharamsala water":* Dalai Lama, *Freedom in Exile,* p. 173.
"his mother, his two sisters": John F. Avedon, *In Exile from the Land of Snows* (London: Michael Joseph, 1984), p. 86.

204 *suddenly able to enjoy:* Although rumors that he occasionally listened to Beatles records and that he wore jeans in private are false, it is true that he would sometimes forsake monastic robes and don a pair of "well-pressed" (as he once mentioned to me) trousers.
a small trekkers' hut: Avedon, *In Exile from the Land of Snows,* p. 86.
televised interviews: Both may be found on the Internet.

205 *"We exiled Tibetans": Speeches of His Holiness the XIVth Dalai Lama (1959–1989),* trans. Sonam Gyatso, vol. 1 (Dharamsala: Library of Tibetan Works and Archives, 2011), pp. 7–8, 3.
"The 'written oath'": Speeches of His Holiness, 1:14–15, 118.

206 *"Our foreign": Speeches of His Holiness,* 1:29, 31.
"They are, by nature": Speeches of His Holiness, 1:9, 36.

207 *"our worst mistake":* Pico Iyer, *The Open Road* (London: Bloomsbury, 2008), p. 228.
"We still have faults": Speeches of His Holiness.

208 *fifty-eight villages:* The number I use is that provided by the Central Tibetan Administration; see its Department of Home website, https://tibet.net/department/home/.
"many of the Tibetans": Avedon, *In Exile from the Land of Snows,* pp. 67, 85.

209 *"to be cautious":* Gyalo Thondup with Anne F. Thurston, *The Noodle Maker of Kalimpong: The Untold Story of My Struggle for Tibet* (London: Rider, 2015), p. 213.
less than a third: See Rinchen Sadutshang, *A Life Unforeseen: A Memoir of Service to Tibet* (Somerville, MA: Wisdom Publications, 2016), p. 241.

210 *four members:* Ginsberg, author of *Howl,* both the most celebrated and the most widely excoriated American poem of the 1950s, was a self-confessed pederast and early member of the North American Man/Boy Love Association. He later became a prominent member of the Buddhist community associated with Chogyam Trungpa. Orlovsky is probably best remembered, if indeed he is remembered at all, other than for his association with Ginsberg, for his strikingly titled collection *Clean Asshole Poems and Smiling Vegetable Songs.* Snyder gained a reputation as the poetic voice of Deep Ecology. Kyger, also a poet, taught for many years at Trungpa's Naropa community. It is not entirely clear whether Orlovsky was in fact present at the audience, as he was in the habit of "lock[ing] himself in the bathroom all night and smok[ing] opium" preparatory to vomiting "all the next morning." Joanne Kyger, *The Japan and India Journals, 1960–1964* (New York: Tombouctou Books, 1981), p. 193.
We met the Dalai Lama: Kyger, *The Japan and India Journals,* entry for April 11, 1962; letter to Nemi April 10, 1962, pp. 193–96.

211 *"a cadre of":* Stuart Gelder and Roma Gelder, *The Timely Rain* (London: Hutchinson and Co., 1964), p. 61.
"in the socialist paradise": A Poisoned Arrow: The Secret Report of the 10th Panchen Lama (London: Tibet Information Network, 1997), p. xvii.

212 *"poisoned arrow": A Poisoned Arrow,* pp. xx–xxi.
214 *protective talismans:* Trijang, *Magical Play,* p. 260.

16. "We cannot compel you"

215 *a "villain," a "liar":* Dalai Lama, *Freedom in Exile: The Autobiography of His Holiness the Dalai Lama of Tibet* (London: Hodder & Stoughton, 1990), pp. 199–200.

216 *deemed to have married:* Tubten Khetsun, *Memories of Life in Lhasa Under Chinese Rule,* trans. Matthew Akester (Delhi: Penguin for Columbia University Press, 2009), p. 138.

as the disparity: Khetsun, *Memories,* p. 107.

"the last priests": Stuart Gelder and Roma Gelder, *The Timely Rain* (London: Hutchinson and Co., 1964), p. 50. One wonders what the Gelders would have made of Drepung today, with its ten thousand mostly young monks.

217 *"because they knew":* Melvyn C. Goldstein, Dawei Sherap, and William R. Siebenschuh, *A Tibetan Revolutionary: The Political Life and Times of Bapa Phünto Wangye* (Berkeley: University of California Press 2004), p. 245.

tens of millions died: Today, the Chinese government admits to around 15 million, though, for example, Frank Dikotter in *Mao's Great Famine: The History of China's Most Devastating Catastrophe, 1958–1962* (London: Bloomsbury, 2010) argues for a figure three times higher.

218 *"three years":* Sumner Carnahan and Lama Kunga Rinpoche, *In the Presence of My Enemies: Memoirs of Tibetan Nobleman Tsipon Shuguba* (Santa Fe, NM: Heartsfire Books, 1998), p. 162.

we began to look for: David Patt, *A Strange Liberation: Tibetan Lives in Chinese Hands* (Ithaca: Snow Lion, 1993), p. 182.

Great Leap: Another story from this time that deserves to be better known is that of Tashi Tsering. Born into a polyandrous peasant farming family in 1929, Tashi Tsering was sent off at the age of ten as a candidate for the Dalai Lama's personal dance troupe. His district was one of those obliged to supply young boys as a sort of tax. But although this tax was hugely resented, a position in the troupe was a sure way of entering government service once the term of engagement was up, even if conditions were harsh. As he explained, "the teachers' idea of providing incentives was to punish us swiftly and severely for each mistake. They constantly hit us on the faces, arms and legs." As a way both to escape these harsh conditions and to further improve his prospects, Tashi Tsering accepted the offer of becoming a senior monk official's *drombo,* or catamite.

This relationship enabled him to obtain an education that would not otherwise have been available to him, such that, when his term in the dance troupe came to an end on passing his eighteenth birthday, he was able to obtain a good job as a clerk in the Potala treasury. Subsequently, he married then divorced before traveling to India during the 1950s with the intention of learning English. There he came into contact with Gyalo Thondup and, through him, became involved in the oral histories project of the

International Commission of Jurists. As a result of this work, Tashi Tsering came to know a wealthy young American who agreed to help him continue his education in America.

Although he did well in his studies, Tashi Tsering decided that above all he wanted to serve his people in their hour of need. He dreamed of setting up a kindergarten for his home village. Deciding that he must return to Tibet, he relinquished a comfortable academic's life in America in exchange for a place at the Chinese-run Tibetan Minority Institute, not far from the Dalai Lama's birthplace in Amdo. Subsequently he taught at a remote provincial school before falling under suspicion of being a spy. In 1970 he was denounced as a counterrevolutionary and imprisoned.

Writing of his experiences later, he recounted how he was interrogated "day after day" before being compelled to write and rewrite accounts of his life in America, of his relationship with Gyalo Thondup, and of his reason for wanting to return to Tibet. When finally sentenced, he was transferred to a prison for political prisoners. "Our daily routine was rigorous," he recalled. "We were made to get up early in the morning, given some watery rice soup, and then sent to the fields to do intentionally demeaning manual labour. We worked in the pig pens or carried human excrement or urine . . . to the fields, where it was used as fertiliser. We also, of course, were still subject to relentless and systematic indoctrination to correct our thinking." This entailed giving an account of their "daily, hourly and minute-by-minute mental activities." Small wonder that many broke under the strain. Tashi Tsering's story is told in Melvyn C. Goldstein, William Siebenschuh, and Tashi Tsering, *The Struggle for Modern Tibet: The Autobiography of Tashi Tsering* (New York: M. E. Sharpe, 1997), p. 121. Finally released, Tashi Tsering went on to found more than seventy schools in central Tibet.

219 *a certain "guardedness":* Robert Thurman, *Why the Dalai Lama Matters* (New York: Atria, 2008), p. 5.

"he would invariably": Thurman, *Why the Dalai Lama Matters,* p. 6.

"strong" disappointment: Robert A. F. Thurman, "The Dalai Lama's Roles and Teaching," in *Understanding the Dalai Lama,* ed. Rajiv Mehrotra (Delhi: Viking India, 2004), p. 12. Leary himself had been briefly encountered by some of the CIA's Tibetan recruits. Recognizing that "one of the most serious problems facing the Tibetans [was] a lack of trained officials equipped with linguistic and administrative abilities," the agency funded a program whereby selected candidates were enrolled at Cornell University. On one occasion they attended a seminar given by Leary, a psychologist and advocate of hallucinogenic drug use, during which he "raced around a darkened auditorium chanting and beating drums." This, we are told, left his Tibetan audience "completely baffled." See John Kenneth Knaus, *Orphans of the Cold War: America and the Tibetan Struggle for Survival* (New York: PublicAffairs, 1999), p. 285.

220 *lack of "spiritual depth": The Magical Play of Illusion: The Autobiography of Trijang Rinpoche*, trans. Sharpa Tulku Tenzin Trinley (Somerville, MA: Wisdom Publications, 2018), p. 292.

"We divided our culture": John F. Avedon, *In Exile from the Land of Snows* (London: Michael Joseph, 1984), p. 92.

221 *"religion and philosophy":* Thomas Merton, *The Asian Journals* (London: Sheldon Press, 1974), pp. 100–101.
"the real meaning": Dalai Lama, *Freedom in Exile,* p. 207.
recent liaison: See Mark Shaw, *Beneath the Mask of Holiness* (New York: St. Martin's Press, 2009).

222 *"the establishment":* Merton, *The Asian Journals,* pp. 125, 124.

223 *"inhuman treatment ":* Speech of March 10, 1962, https://www.dalailama.com/messages/Tibet.
"passive struggle": Speech of March 10, 1963, https://www.dalailama.com/messages/Tibet.
"naked horror": Speech of March 10, 1969, https://www.dalailama.com/messages/Tibet.
"Tibetan courage": Speech of March 10, 1971, https://www.dalailama.com/messages/Tibet.
significant "problems": Speeches of His Holiness the XIVth Dalai Lama (1959–1989), trans. Sonam Gyatso, vol. 1 (Dharamsala: Library of Tibetan Works and Archives, 2011), p. 65.

224 *casualties inflicted on the Chinese:* The March 10 statement for 1971 claims at least a thousand; https://www.dalailama.com/messages/Tibet.
"an astonishing, exciting": Thurman, *Why the Dalai Lama Matters,* p. 7.
"lucid and lyrical": Thurman, "The Dalai Lama's Roles and Teaching," p. 12.
"and other substances": Trijang, *Magical Play,* p. 336.

225 *To induce lucid dreaming:* John Crook and James Low, *The Yogins of Ladakh: A Pilgrimage Among the Hermits of the Buddhist Himalayas* (1997; repr., Delhi: Motilal Banarsidass, 2012), p. 196.

226 *coupled in the "union of bliss":* Crook and Low, *The Yogins of Ladakh,* p. 196.
skeptical at the outset: Crook and Low, *The Yogins of Ladakh,* p. 69.
raise their core temperature: Herbert Benson, *Your Maximum Mind* (New York: Avon Books, 1991), pp. 16–22.
"found that without gloves": Crook and Low, *The Yogins of Ladakh,* p. 90. What "amused the monks very much was that the Americans . . . never asked them how to do it!" It should be noted that a later study by other scientists found that heat gains could be produced by non-meditators just using the breathing exercises. It was found that the main effect of meditation was to prolong the effects of the exercises. See https://www.ncbi.nlm.nih.gov/pmc/articles/PMC3612090/.
"the practitioner sits": Crook and Low, *The Yogins of Ladakh,* p. 220.

227 *startling enough:* See, for example, https://www.youtube.com/watch?v=Kelb5IGbLXM.
in a vision: William Meyers, Robert Thurman, and Michael G. Burbank, *Man of Peace: The Illustrated Life Story of the Dalai Lama of Tibet* (New York: Tibet House, 2016), pp. 135, 161–65. Each bodhisattva is considered to have one or more wrathful forms. These they manifest when required to clear accretions of karmic negativity.

228 *one of those military men:* When he met the Dalai Lama for the first time, General Uban touched the monk's feet and ever afterwards wore a ring that the Dalai Lama gave him;

https://talesfromanoasis.wordpress.com/2014/09/08/indias-phantom-warriors-part-ii-maj-gen-uban-and-his-beloved-two-twos/. The centurion mentioned in chapter 7 of the Gospel of Luke and chapter 8 of the Gospel of Mark was presumably another such soldier. Yet although Uban's career with the Special Air Service is widely cited, the archivist of 22 SAS regiment informs me that no one of this name is known to have served either in the regiment or in its predecessor, the Long Range Desert Group.

"carry out reconnaissance": Adapted from Mikel Dunham, *Buddha's Warriors: The Story of the CIA-Backed Tibetan Freedom Fighters, the Chinese Invasion, and the Ultimate Fall of Tibet* (New York: Jeremy P. Tarcher/Penguin, 2004), p. 385. See also Claude Arpi, "A Two Two as Army Chief," *Indian Defence Review,* http://www.indiandefencereview.com/news/a-two-two-as-army-chief/ (accessed March 28, 2019).

229 *"We cannot compel you":* http://tibetwrites.in/index.html%3FNot-their-own-wars.html (accessed January 24, 2018).

Regretfully giving: See *The Autobiography of Dasur Ratruk Ngawang of Lithang,* vol. 2 (Dharamsala: Amnye Machen Institute, 2008), p. 131.

230 *"After that":* Kenneth Conboy and James Morrison, *The CIA's Secret War in Tibet* (Lawrence: University Press of Kansas, 2002), pp. 244–45.

"everyone lived": Trijang, *Magical Play,* p. 341.

"And do you know why": Dunham, *Buddha's Warriors,* pp. 385–86.

"the gallant officers": Sujan Singh Uban, *Phantoms of Chittagong* (New Delhi: Allied Publishers, 1985), p. iv.

231 *From Trijang Rinpoché:* Trijang, *Magical Play,* pp. 345, 346.

"a very special Cittamani initiation": Dalai Lama, *The Life of My Teacher: A Biography of Kyabje Ling Rinpoché* (Somerville, MA: Wisdom Publications, 2017), p. 275.

17. "Something beyond the comprehension of the Tibetan people"

232 *the Buryato-Russian explorer:* Tsybikov is quoted in Isabelle Charleux, *Nomads on Pilgrimage: Mongols on Wutaishan (China), 1800–1940* (Leiden: Brill, 2015), p. 36.

233 *"to fulfil": Speeches of His Holiness the XIVth Dalai Lama (1959–1989),* trans. Sonam Gyatso, vol. 1 (Dharamsala: Library of Tibetan Works and Archives, 2011), p. 3.

234 *The book:* See Raimondo Bultrini, *The Dalai Lama and the King Demon* (New York: Tibet House US, 2013), p. 122.

237 *"not so different":* Dalai Lama, *Freedom in Exile: The Autobiography of His Holiness the Dalai Lama of Tibet* (London: Hodder & Stoughton, 1990), p. 215.

"not want to spoil": https://www.youtube.com/watch?v=Qwwfj_5A3S8.

238 *upset the mind:* Dalai Lama, *The Life of My Teacher: A Biography of Kyabje Ling Rinpoché* (Somerville, MA: Wisdom Publications, 2017), p. 298.

239 *"they wandered around crying":* Mikel Dunham, *Buddha's Warriors: The Story of the CIA-Backed Tibetan Freedom Fighters, the Chinese Invasion, and the Ultimate Fall of Tibet* (New York: Jeremy P. Tarcher/Penguin, 2004), pp. 388–89, tells the story, which the Dalai Lama partially corroborates in *Freedom in Exile,* p. 211.

advised him to cease: William Meyers, Robert Thurman, and Michael G. Burbank, *Man of Peace: The Illustrated Life Story of the Dalai Lama of Tibet* (New York: Tibet House, 2016), p. 138.

241 *"so long as he stood":* Quoted in Tsering Shakya, *The Dragon in the Land of Snows: A History of Modern Tibet Since 1947* (New York: Columbia University Press, 1999), p. 370.

"it would be excellent": Dalai Lama, *Life of My Teacher,* p. 310. In so doing, the protector was encouraging the Dalai Lama to align himself with the *ris med,* or nonsectarian, movement, which had flourished during the first third of the twentieth century.

242 *Ma Chig Labdron:* Her story is told in, e.g., John Crook and James Low, *The Yogins of Ladakh: A Pilgrimage Among the Hermits of the Buddhist Himalayas* (1997; Delhi: Motilal Banarsidass, 2012), chap. 15.

244 *"Better to see":* Shakya, *Dragon in the Land of Snows,* p. 376.

"fifty for a start": Mary Craig, *Kundun: A Biography of the Family of the Dalai Lama* (London: HarperCollins, 1997), pp. 308.

245 *"the present standard":* Craig, *Kundun,* p. 306.

"watched over": Dalai Lama, *Freedom in Exile,* p. 296.

His aides reported: Daniel Goleman, *A Force for Good: The Dalai Lama's Vision for Our World* (London: Bloomsbury, 2015), p. 56.

18. From *Rangzen* to *Umaylam*

246 *"burden":* See John Kenneth Knaus, https://case.edu/affil/tibet/tibetanSociety/documents/usstuff.PDF, p. 78 (accessed March 28, 2019).

a message for the United States: Marcia Keegan, *The Dalai Lama's Historic Visit to North America* (New York: Clear Light Publications, 1981), unpaginated.

247 *"almost keeled over":* Pico Iyer quoting Thurman in "Making Kindness Stand to Reason," in *Understanding the Dalai Lama,* ed. Rajiv Mehrotra (Delhi: Viking India, 2004), p. 54.

"intimated that he": Barry Boyce, *The Many Faces of the Dalai Lama,* https://www.lionsroar.com/the-many-faces-of-the-dalai-lama/ (accessed March 28, 2019).

"a walking stick": Pico Iyer, *The Open Road* (London: Bloomsbury, 2008), p. 66.

248 *spiritual and moral guidance:* Iyer, *The Open Road,* pp. 75, 219, 220.

"We were very upset": John F. Avedon, *In Exile from the Land of Snows* (London: Michael Joseph, 1984), p. 333.

249 *bombed-out hulk:* Avedon, *In Exile from the Land of Snows,* p. 349.

"little better than": William Meyers, Robert Thurman, and Michael G. Burbank, *Man of Peace: The Illustrated Life Story of the Dalai Lama of Tibet* (New York: Tibet House, 2016), p. 189.

"We feel that our Party": Tsering Shakya, *The Dragon in the Land of Snows: A History of Modern Tibet Since 1947* (New York: Columbia University Press, 1999), pp. 381, 382.

251 *"had immersed himself":* Meyers, Thurman, and Brinkman, *Man of Peace,* p. 162.

"six session yoga": Dalai Lama, *Kalachakra Tantra: Rite of Initiation,* trans., ed., and intro. by Geoffrey Hopkins, enlarged ed. (Somerville, MA: Wisdom Publications, 1999), p. 382.

subsequently published: The Dalai Lama at Harvard: Lectures on the Buddhist Path to Peace (Ithaca: Snow Lion, 1988).

"like a figure": Iyer, *The Open Road,* p. 74. This is a somewhat surprising admission from someone who won a Congratulatory Double First from the University of Oxford.

252 *a private-circulation book:* Tom Clark, *The Great Naropa Poetry Wars* (Santa Barbara: Cadmus Editions, 1980). Trungpa can be seen in action in a number of films on YouTube. See, for example, https://www.youtube.com/watch?v=YgviVWanZgc.

"I was not going": https://archive.nytimes.com/www/nytimes.com/books.99/04/04/specials/merwin-own.html?_r=1 (accessed May 14, 2018).

253 *incipient fascism:* https://www.cadmuseditions.com/naropa.html (accessed May 14, 2018).

there are "none": For one instance, see https://www.youtube.com/watch?v=owP4rsM7AZQ.

254 *dogma-free spirituality:* For his message more generally, see, for example, his book *Beyond Dogma: The Challenge of the Modern World* (London: Souvenir Press, 1996).

"talked to her": Mary Craig, *Kundun: A Biography of the Family of the Dalai Lama* (London: HarperCollins, 1997), p. 323.

"manifested the act": The Magical Play of Illusion: The Autobiography of Trijang Rinpoche, trans. Sharpa Tulku Tenzin Trinley (Somerville, MA: Wisdom Publications, 2018), p. 376.

255 *five-point plan:* See Shakya, *Dragon in the Land of Snows,* p. 384, for details.

256 *Exhorting his Tibetan audiences:* See Dalai Lama, *The Life of My Teacher: A Biography of Kyabje Ling Rinpoché* (Somerville, MA: Wisdom Publications, 2017), p. 328.

"tormented with fear": Dalai Lama, *Life of My Teacher,* p. 363.

257 *absorbed in the clear light:* A clear and detailed account of the process is given in the hagiography of the Ninth Dalai Lama. See Glenn H. Mullin, *The Fourteen Dalai Lamas: A Sacred Legacy of Reincarnation* (Santa Fe, NM: Clear Light Books, 2000).

clearly heard: Dalai Lama, *Life of My Teacher,* p. 364.

As a sign of this: Dalai Lama, *Life of My Teacher,* p. 364.

258 *may also be drunk:* For an account of the practice, see Nyoshul Khenpo, *A Marvelous Garland of Rare Gems: Biographies of Masters of Awareness in the Dzogchen Lineage* (Junction City, CA: Padma Publishing, 2005), pp. 211–12. Somewhat hair-raisingly, it describes an occasion when some visitors were so enthusiastic for spiritual nourishment that they literally tore at the flesh of a recently deceased high master.

"with a head": Dalai Lama, *Life of My Teacher,* p. 299.

"free spokesman": Speech of March 10, 1980.

19. Cutting Off the Serpent's Head

263 *one exception:* See Dalai Lama, *Ethics for the New Millennium* (New York: Riverhead Books, 2000), p. 7.

264 *"Seeing flowers of every colour": The Magical Play of Illusion: The Autobiography of*

Trijang Rinpoche, trans. Sharpa Tulku Tenzin Trinley (Somerville, MA: Wisdom Publications, 2018), p. 291.

265 *"Buddhist psychology takes people.":* William Meyers, Robert Thurman, and Michael G. Burbank, *Man of Peace: The Illustrated Life Story of the Dalai Lama of Tibet* (New York: Tibet House, 2016), p. 197.

"almost deserted": Pico Iyer, "Making Kindness Stand to Reason," in *Understanding the Dalai Lama,* ed. Rajiv Mehrotra (Delhi: Viking India, 2004), p. 53.

266 *"closer to John Lennon":* Pico Iyer, *The Open Road* (London: Bloomsbury, 2008), pp. 75, 158.

"zone of peace": The speech was delivered on September 21, 1987. The full text may be found at https://www.dalailama.com/messages/tibet/five-point-peace-plan.

267 *In response:* This was witnessed by several foreigners. Various contemporary accounts of these events exist, of which the reports in the *New York Times* are the most comprehensive.

It seems likely: An overview of events may be found in Tsering Shakya, *The Dragon in the Land of Snows: A History of Modern Tibet Since 1947* (New York: Columbia University Press, 1999), pp. 414–16.

268 *"divorced":* Chinese source quoted in Shakya, *Dragon in the Land of Snows,* p. 422.

Within minutes: See Melvyn C. Goldstein, *The Snow Lion and the Dragon,* new ed. (Berkeley: University of California Press, 1999), p. 83.

269 *one of them a policeman*: I am grateful to Professor Robbie Barnett for drawing this incident to my attention.

"the whole of Tibet": The full text of the Strasbourg Statement is available on the Dalai Lama's official website at https://www.dalailama.com/messages/tibet/strasbourg-proposal-1988.

later claimed: See Goldstein, *The Snow Lion and the Dragon,* p. 139, n. 24. For others openly critical of the Dalai Lama, see Shakya, *Dragon in the Land of Snows,* p. 524, n. 88.

271 *"personally" speaking:* Dalai Lama, *Freedom in Exile: The Autobiography of His Holiness the Dalai Lama of Tibet* (London: Hodder & Stoughton, 1990), p. 287.

unknown how many died: https://www.nytimes/com/1990/08/14/world/chinese-said-to-kill-450-tibetans-in-1989.html (accessed May 24, 2018).

272 *"no longer excited":* Adapted from Mary Craig, "A Very Human Being," in *Understanding the Dalai Lama,* ed. Rajiv Mehrotra (Delhi: Viking India, 2004), p. 72. His actual words were "no more excited."

Nobel Prize: One pleasing bonus of his subsequent visit to Norway to attend the award ceremony was the opportunity it afforded the Dalai Lama to fulfill a lifelong wish to ride in a reindeer sleigh when he visited the Sami people in Lapland. Meyers, Thurman, and Burbank, *Man of Peace,* p. 219.

"extreme regret": See *Christian Science Monitor,* October 10, 1989, https://www.csmonitor.com/1989/1010/odali.html (accessed February 7, 2019).

273 *"As I stood there":* Dalai Lama, *Freedom in Exile,* p. 290.

"bent down to adjust": Craig, "A Very Human Being," p. 72.

"no handlers, advance men": Douglas Preston's article about the Dalai Lama's visit to Santa Fe in April 1991, from which this account is drawn, is widely available on the Internet; see, e.g., "The Dalai Lama's Ski Trip," Slate.com.

275 *"dialogue with the Dalai Lama":* A May 28, 1993, White House report to Congress on China's most favored nation status extension lists "seeking to resume dialogue with the Dalai Lama or his representatives" as a favorable step China should take to ensure MFN renewal. See https://www.savetibet.org/policy-center/chronology-of-tibetan-chinese-relations-1979-to-2013/ (accessed April 29, 2019).

276 *manifest humility:* I was one of them. See Dalai Lama, *The Good Heart: A Buddhist Perspective on the Teachings of Jesus* (London: Rider, 1996).

277 *"bartered away his honour":* Article by Li Bing in *Tibet Daily,* quoted in *Cutting Off the Serpent's Head: Tightening Control in Tibet, 1994–1995* (New York: Human Rights Watch, March 1996), p. 18.

"To kill a serpent": This saying was the inspiration for the title of a 1996 report published jointly by the Tibet Information Network and Human Rights Watch, Asia. Its author (now Professor), Robbie Barnett, kindly drew my attention to weaknesses in an earlier version of this paragraph.

"The purpose of Buddhism": Cutting Off the Serpent's Head, p. 18.

279 *an extremely risky move:* The story is told variously in Dalai Lama, *Freedom in Exile; Cutting Off the Serpent's Head;* Goldstein, *The Snow Lion and the Dragon;* and, most authoritatively, in Isabel Hilton, *The Search for the Panchen Lama* (New York: W. W. Norton, 2000). Chadrel Rinpoché was sentenced to six years in prison.

280 *explosion of a bomb:* https://www.nytimes.com/1996/12/30/world/bomb-at-government-offices-wounds-5-in-tibetan-capital.html. See also the relevant Tibet Information Network reports.

beatings and electric shocks: For firsthand accounts, see "Torture," section 2 of part 2, in *Cutting Off the Serpent's Head.* See also Palden Gyatso, *Fire Under the Snow: The True Story of a Tibetan Monk* (London: Harvill Press, 1997).

20. "An oath-breaking spirit born of perverse prayers"

282 *threw out as rubbish:* Raimondo Bultrini, *The Dalai Lama and the King Demon* (New York: Tibet House US, 2013), p. 198.

283 *by Indian intelligence:* Bultrini, *The Dalai Lama and the King Demon,* p. 242.

284 *"bloodbath":* Bultrini, *The Dalai Lama and the King Demon,* pp. 201, 292–93.

A fracas broke out: Bultrini, *The Dalai Lama and the King Demon*, p. 201.

285 *"We have already offered":* Bultrini, *The Dalai Lama and the King Demon,* p. 352.

286 *justifying his position:* See https://www.dalailama.com/messages/dolgyal-shugden/speeches-by-his-holiness-the-dalai-lama/dharamsala-teaching.

287 *"When I was small":* Dalai Lama, *Freedom in Exile: The Autobiography of His Holiness the Dalai Lama of Tibet* (London: Hodder & Stoughton, 1990), p. 234.

292 *a hundred million times:* If, as seems plausible, he was able to do so at a speed of one hundred recitations per minute, this would have taken a little under seventeen thousand

hours — two entire years of his life. For an authoritative biography, see Thupten Jinpa, *Tsongkhapa: A Buddha in the Land of Snows* (Boulder: Shambala, 2019).

294 *"harmful activities":* http://www.dalailama.com/messages/dolgyal-shugden/historical-references-historical-references-fifth-dalai-lama. See also the relevant section in Samten Karmay, *The Illusive Play: The Autobiography of the Fifth Dalai Lama* (Chicago: Serindia Publications, 2014).

295 *"took a sword":* Joseph F. Sungmas Rock, "The Living Oracles of the Tibetan Church," *National Geographic* 68 (1935): 475–86. In the article, Rock uses his own phonetics and a Sinicized version of his name, but it is clear that he is referring to the Shugden oracle. He refers to the gurgling sound, said to represent the *kathag* stuffed down Drakpa Gyaltsen's throat, that the medium emitted. Rock published photographic evidence of several knotted swords in the magazine.

poised to move in: René von Nebesky-Wojkowitz, *Where the Gods Are Mountains* (London: Weidenfeld and Nicholson, 1956), p. 210.

296 *"lapping up" his teacher's urine:* https://www.dalailama.com/messages/dolgyal-shugden/speeches-by-his-holiness-the-dalai-lama/dharamsala-teaching. See also the quotation in Georges B. J. Dreyfus, *The Sound of Two Hands Clapping: The Education of a Tibetan Buddhist Monk* (Berkeley: University of California Press, 2003), p. 62, where the anecdote is mentioned of a high lama drinking from his guru's chamber pot.

unsurprising to learn: A Reuters report published in December 2015 offers hard evidence of China's involvement in the Shugden controversy: https://www.reuters.com/investigates/special-report/china-dalailama.

297 *planned to murder:* Bultrini, *The Dalai Lama and the King Demon,* pp. 310–12.

21. Tibet in Flames

299 *"stepping into":* https://www.lionsroar.com/gays-lesbians-and-the-definition-of-sexual-misconduct/ (accessed March 29, 2019).

300 *"delights listeners":* Pico Iyer, *The Open Road* (London: Bloomsbury, 2008), p. 146.

301 *making a case:* Amnesty subsequently found that the issue fell outside its purview of "grave violations of fundamental human rights." See https://www.amnesty.org/download/Documents/152000/asa170141998en.pdf (accessed April 29, 2019).

"delved into his small shoulder bag": Thupten Jinpa, "The Dalai Lama and the Tibetan Monastic Academia," in *Understanding the Dalai Lama,* ed. Rajiv Mehrotra (Delhi: Viking India, 2004), p. 200.

302 *some light moments:* The story is told at https://www.nzz.ch/schweiz/warum-der-dalai-lama-einen-weinberg-im-wallis-besitzt-ld.1397292 and https://www.deutschlandfunk.de/schweizer-wallis-der-weinberg-des-dalai-lama.1242.de.html?dram:article_id=336905.

"is of poor scientific taste": https://www.theguardian.com/world/2005/jul/27/research.highereducation (accessed February 21, 2019).

303 *"inner space":* Yudhijit Bhattacharjee, "Neuroscientists Welcome Dalai Lama with Mostly Open Arms," *Science* 310 (November 18, 2005).

304 *"I believe him to be":* https://www.nytimes.com/1998/06/28/world/clinton-china-overview-clinton-jiang-debate-views-live-tv-clashing-rights.html (accessed April 13, 2019).

a rival: The story of the two rival candidacies is well told in Mick Brown, *The Dance of Seventeen Lives: The Incredible Story of Tibet's 17th Karmapa* (London: Bloomsbury, 2005). Arguably there is room for a second edition, given that the "Tibetan" Karmapa has acquired a Dominican passport, to the evident annoyance of the Indian government, while the "Indian" Karmapa, in defiance of tradition, has taken a wife. The controversy over who should inherit the previous Karmapa's wealth continues at this writing.

"numerous": https://www.savetibet.org/policy-center/chronology-of-tibetan-chinese-relations-1979-to-2013/.

306 *the Lhasa mosque*: See *The Economist,* March 19, 2008.

307 *claims about video*: I recall the Dalai Lama himself telling me about this at the time, though whether he had seen them himself is not clear.

it seems unlikely: The best account of the unrest available in English, which is also a political manifesto, is *The Division of Heaven and Earth: On Tibet's Peaceful Revolution* by Shokdung, trans. Matthew Akester (London: C Hurst Publishers, 2017). There are also several authoritative eyewitness accounts in contemporary newspapers, notably the *New York Times, The Guardian,* and *The Economist.*

the Dalai Lama was admitting: See the *Daily Telegraph,* November 3, 2008.

310 *extremely hard to maintain:* I am grateful to Professor Robbie Barnett for drawing this remark to my attention.

the silent film: The Gould film is accessible on YouTube.

22. The Magical Play of Illusion

313 *his viceroy:* Widely believed to have been the Great Fifth's natural son, Desi Sangye Gyatso, known to his contemporaries as Flat-Head, was a great figure in his own right. Formerly a monk, he was a polymath and a lifelong scholar. He was also an accomplished athlete and archer. It is further reported that "of the noble ladies of Lhasa and those who came there from the provinces, there was not a single one whom [he] did not take to bed." Michael Aris, *Hidden Treasures and Secret Lives: A Study of Pemalingpa (1450–1521) and the Sixth Dalai Lama (1683–1706)* (London: Kegan Paul International, 1989), p. 123.

314 *"sacred or holy":* Dalai Lama, *Freedom in Exile: The Autobiography of His Holiness the Dalai Lama of Tibet* (London: Hodder & Stoughton, 1990), p. 296.

not a vegetarian himself: He explains that this is on advice of doctors, following a bout of hepatitis. His continued meat eating may also have something to do with the fact that it is recommended for those engaging in the practices of highest yoga tantra. See John Crook and James Low, *The Yogins of Ladakh: A Pilgrimage Among the Hermits of the Buddhist Himalayas* (1997; repr., Delhi: Motilal Banarsidass, 2012), p. 89.

he admits that: Daniel Goleman, *A Force for Good: The Dalai Lama's Vision for Our World* (London: Bloomsbury, 2015), p. 146.

"become one of": Robert Thurman, *Why the Dalai Lama Matters* (New York: Atria, 2008), p. 57.

315 *"the impulse for helping":* Dalai Lama, *Science and Philosophy in the Indian Buddhist Classics,* ed. Thupten Jinpa (Somerville, MA: Wisdom Publications, 2017), p. 16.

partook of Holy Communion: Dalai Lama and Desmond Tutu with Douglas Abrams, *The Book of Joy: Lasting Happiness in a Changing World* (London: Hutchinson, 2016), p. 182.

homeless shelter: Goleman, *Force for Good,* p. 146.

changing to another: See Dalai Lama, *Ethics for the New Millennium* (New York: Riverhead Books, 2000), p. 238.

316 *contact between the two traditions:* It is well known that there were Christian communities living in both China and Central Asia during the first millennium. There is also written evidence of a Christian mission to Tibet as early as the eighth century. The Chaldean Christian patriarch Timothy I, writing to his friend Severus, mentions that he is preparing to anoint a metropolitan for the "Land of the Tibetans." See Alexander Norman, *Secret Lives of the Dalai Lama* (New York: Random House, 2008), p. 30 and note.

smiled at him: Personal communication.

one of the biggest surprises: Pico Iyer, *The Open Road* (London: Bloomsbury 2008), p. 77.

"great authority": Thupten Jinpa, "The Dalai Lama and the Tibetan Monastic Academia," in *Understanding the Dalai Lama,* ed. Rajiv Mehrotra (Delhi: Viking India, 2004), p. 205.

317 *"Suddenly":* Thurman, *Why the Dalai Lama Matters,* p. 189.

319 *Christopher Hitchens:* In *Salon* magazine (https://www.salon.com), July 1998.

Europe is for Europeans: https://www.independent.co.uk/news/world/europe/dalai-lama-europe-refugee-crisis-immigration-eu-racism-tibet-buddhist-a8537221.html. His saying so recalls the seventh-century stone pillar in Lhasa which claims that China is for the Chinese and Tibet for the Tibetans, as well as the slogan "Tibet is for Tibetans" chanted outside the Norbulingka in March 1959.

being a "ham": Ann Treneman, writing in *The Times* of London, May 23, 2008. See also the summary at the end of a Xinhua News Agency article referencing the *Daily Mail,* http://www.gov.cn/english/2008-12/12/content_1176383.htm.

mentally disturbed: Iyer, *Open Road,* p. 238; Thupten Jinpa, *A Fearless Heart: Why Compassion Is the Key to Greater Wellbeing* (London: Piatkus, 2015), p. 44.

320 *It is even rumored*: I am grateful to Professor Robbie Barnett for drawing this to my attention.

323 *might have met:* See https://www.ndtv.com/book-excerpts/president-xi-was-to-meet-me-in-delhi-in-2014-but-dalai-lama-exclusive-2037863?fbclid=IwAR1vEKVngMFlEKdsjTIzUkOTr-D2FwazSohTo6d4eejvifu8gWmiVI6I-H8. It should be noted that the Dalai Lama's office has since downplayed the significance of the story.

326 *the best measure available:* See https://books.google.com/ngrams and search under

"compassion." If one further analyzes the number of references to the Dalai Lama in relation to the number of references to Buddhism and compassion, it is notable that the references that associate him with compassion amount to a full 50 percent of the number of references that associate Buddhism with compassion.

329 *"some one thing":* This is the last sentence of G. K. Chesterton's *Orthodoxy* (1908).

BIBLIOGRAPHY

(A more comprehensive bibliography providing background and history may be found in my *Secret Lives of the Dalai Lama.*)

An Account of Tibet: The Travels of Ippolito Desideri di Pistoia, SJ, 1712–1727. Edited by Filippo de Filippi, revised ed. London: G. Routledge, 1937.

Aris, Michael. *Hidden Treasures and Secret Lives: A Study of Pemalingpa (1450–1521) and the Sixth Dalai Lama (1683–1706).* London: Kegan Paul International, 1989.

Avedon, John F. *In Exile from the Land of Snows.* London: Michael Joseph, 1984.

Barber, Noel. *The Flight of the Dalai Lama.* London: Hodder & Stoughton, 1960.

Bell, Charles. *Portrait of the Dalai Lama.* London: Collins, 1946.

Benson, Herbert, *Your Maximum Mind.* New York: Avon Books, 1991.

Brown, Mick. *The Dance of Seventeen Lives: The Incredible Story of Tibet's 17th Karmapa.* London: Bloomsbury, 2005.

Bultrini, Raimondo. *The Dalai Lama and the King Demon.* New York: Tibet House US, 2013.

Byron, Robert. *First Russia, Then Tibet.* London: Macmillan, 1933.

Carnahan, Sumner, and Lama Kunga Rinpoche. *In the Presence of My Enemies: Memoirs of Tibetan Nobleman Tsipon Shuguba.* Sante Fe, NM: Heartsfire Books, 1998.

Chang, Jung. *Empress Dowager Cixi: The Concubine Who Launched Modern China.* London: Jonathan Cape, 2013.

Chapman, Frederick Spencer. *Lhasa: The Holy City.* London: Chatto & Windus, 1938.

Charleux, Isabelle. *Nomads on Pilgrimage: Mongols on Wutaishan (China), 1800–1940.* Leiden: Brill, 2015.

Chophel, Norbu. *Folk Culture of Tibet.* Dharamsala: Library of Tibetan Works and Archives, 1983.

Conboy, Kenneth, and James Morrison. *The CIA's Secret War in Tibet.* Lawrence: University Press of Kansas, 2002.

Craig, Mary. *Kundun: A Biography of the Family of the Dalai Lama.* London: HarperCollins, 1997.

Crook, John, and James Low. *The Yogins of Ladakh: A Pilgrimage Among the Hermits of the Buddhist Himalayas.* 1997. Reprint. Delhi: Motilal Banarsidass, 2012.

Cutting Off the Serpent's Head: Tightening Control in Tibet, 1994–1995. New York: Human Rights Watch, March 1996.

Dalai Lama XIV. *My Land and My People: The Autobiography of His Holiness the Dalai Lama.* London: Weidenfeld and Nicolson, 1962.

———. *Freedom in Exile: The Autobiography of His Holiness the Dalai Lama of Tibet.* London: Hodder & Stoughton, 1990.

———. *The Good Heart: A Buddhist Perspective on the Teachings of Jesus.* London: Rider, 1996.

———. *Kalachakra Tantra: Rite of Initiation.* Translated, edited, and introduced by Geoffrey Hopkins. Enlarged edition. Somerville, MA: Wisdom Publications, 1999.

———. *Ethics for the New Millennium.* New York: Riverhead Books, 2000.

———. *Speeches of His Holiness the XIVth Dalai Lama (1959–1989).* Translated by Sonam Gyatso. Dharamsala: Library of Tibetan Works and Archives, 2011.

———. *The Political Philosophy of the Dalai Lama: Selected Speeches and Writings.* Edited by Dr. Subash C. Kashyap. New Delhi: Rupa, 2014.

———. *The Life of My Teacher: A Biography of Kyabje Ling Rinpoché.* Somerville, MA: Wisdom Publications, 2017.

———. *Science and Philosophy in the Indian Buddhist Classics.* Edited by Thupten Jinpa. Vol. 1. *The Physical World.* Somerville, MA: Wisdom Publications, 2017.

Dalai Lama and Desmond Tutu with Douglas Abrams. *The Book of Joy: Lasting Happiness in a Changing World.* London: Hutchinson, 2016.

Dalton, Jacob. *Taming the Demons.* New Haven: Yale University Press, 2011.

David-Néel, Alexandra. *My Journey to Lhasa.* Harmondsworth: Allen Lane, Penguin Books, 1940.

Dikotter, Frank. *Mao's Great Famine: The History of China's Most Devastating Catastrophe, 1958–1962.* London: Bloomsbury, 2010.

Dorje, Gyurme. *Tibet Handbook.* 4th edition. Bath: Footprint, 2008.

Dreyfus, Georges B. J. *The Sound of Two Hands Clapping: The Education of a Tibetan Buddhist Monk.* Berkeley: University of California Press, 2003.

Dunham, Mikel. *Buddha's Warriors: The Story of the CIA-Backed Tibetan Freedom Fighters, the Chinese Invasion, and the Ultimate Fall of Tibet.* New York: Jeremy P. Tarcher/Penguin, 2004.

Ekvall, Robert B. *Tents Against the Sky.* London: Gollancz, 1954.

Engelhardt, Isrun. *Tibet in 1938–1939: Photographs from the Ernst Schäfer Expedition to Tibet.* Chicago: Serindia, 2007.

Fergusson, W. N. *Adventure, Sport and Travel on the Tibetan Steppes.* New York: Charles Scribner's Sons, 1911.

FitzHerbert, S. G. "Rituals as War Propaganda in the Establishment of the Ganden Phodrang State." *Cahiers d'Extrême Asie,* EFEO, 27 (2018): 49–119.

Ford, Robert. *Captured in Tibet.* London: G. Harrap and Co., 1957.

French, Patrick. *Younghusband: The Last Great Imperial Adventurer.* London: HarperCollins, 1995.

Gelder, Stuart, and Roma Gelder. *The Timely Rain.* London: Hutchinson and Co., 1964.

Goldstein, Melvyn C. *A History of Modern Tibet: 1913–1951.* Vol. 1. *The Demise of the Lamaist State.* Berkeley: University of California Press, 1989.

———. *A History of Modern Tibet.* Vol. 2. *The Calm Before the Storm, 1951–55.* Berkeley: University of California Press, 2007.

———. *A History of Modern Tibet.* Vol. 3. *The Storm Clouds Descend, 1955–57.* Berkeley: University of California Press, 2014.

Goldstein, Melvyn C., Dawei Sherap, and William R. Siebenschuh. *A Tibetan Revolutionary: The Political Life and Times of Bapa Phüntso Wangye.* Berkeley: University of California Press, 2004.

Goleman, Daniel. *A Force for Good: The Dalai Lama's Vision for Our World.* London: Bloomsbury, 2015.

Goodrick-Clarke, Nicholas. *Black Sun: Aryan Cults, Esoteric Nazism, and the Politics of Identity.* New York: NYU Press, 2001.

Gould, Basil J. *The Jewel in the Lotus: Recollections of an Indian Political.* London: Chatto & Windus, 1957.

Gyatso, Palden. *Fire Under the Snow: The True Story of a Tibetan Monk.* London: Harvill Press, 1997.

Hale, Mark. *Himmler's Crusade: The True Story of the Nazis' 1938 Expedition into Tibet.* London: Bantam Books, 2003.

Harrer, Heinrich. *Seven Years in Tibet.* London: R. Hart-Davis, 1953.

———. *Return to Tibet.* London: Penguin, 1985.

Hicks, Roger, and Chogyam Ngakpa. *Great Ocean, an Authorised Biography: The Dalai Lama.* Shaftesbury, Dorset: Element Books, 1984.

Hilton, Isabel. *The Search for the Panchen Lama.* New York: W. W. Norton, 2000.

Iyer, Pico. *The Open Road.* London: Bloomsbury, 2008.

Jinpa, Thupten. *A Fearless Heart: Why Compassion Is the Key to Greater Wellbeing.* London: Piatkus, 2015.

———. *Self, Reason and Reality in Tibetan Philosophy: Tsongkhapa's Quest for the Middle Way.* London: Routledge Curzon, 2002.

———. *Tsongkhapa: A Buddha in the Land of Snows.* Boulder: Shambala, 2019.

Karmay, Samten. *The Illusive Play: The Autobiography of the Fifth Dalai Lama.* Chicago: Serindia Publications, 2014.

Kasho, Jamyang Choegyal. *In the Service of the 13th and 14th Dalai Lamas.* Frankfurt am Main: Tibethaus Deutschland, 2015.

Kashyap, Dr. Subash C., ed. *The Political Philosophy of the Dalai Lama: Selected Speeches and Writings.* New Delhi: Rupa, 2014.

Kawaguchi, Ekai. *Three Years in Tibet.* London: Theosophical Publishing Society, 1909.

Keegan, Marcia. *The Dalai Lama's Historic Visit to North America.* New York: Clear Light Publications, 1981.

Khedrup, Tashi. *Adventures of a Tibetan Fighting Monk.* Edited by Hugh Richardson. Bangkok: Orchid Press, 2003.

Khetsun, Tubten. *Memories of Life in Lhasa Under Chinese Rule.* Translated by Matthew Akester. Delhi: Penguin for Columbia University Press, 2009.

Kilty, Gavin. *The Case against Shukden: The History of a Contested Tibetan Practice.* Somerville, MA: Wisdom Publications, 2019.

Knaus, John Kenneth. *Orphans of the Cold War: America and the Tibetan Struggle for Survival.* New York: PublicAffairs, 1999.

Kyger, Joanne. *The Japan and India Journals, 1960–1964.* New York: Tomboctou Books, 1981.

Laird, Thomas. *The Story of Tibet: Conversations with the Dalai Lama.* London: Atlantic, 2006.

Larsen, Knud, and Amund Sinding-Larsen. *The Lhasa Atlas: Traditional Tibetan Architecture and Townscape.* London: Serindia, 2001.

Li, Jianglin. *Tibet in Agony: Lhasa, 1959.* Translated by Susan Wilf. Cambridge: Harvard University Press, 2016.

———. "When the Iron Bird Flies: The 1956–1962 Secret War on the Tibetan Plateau." Unpublished manuscript. Translated by Stacey Mosher.

Loup, Robert. *Martyr in Tibet.* Philadelphia: D. McKay and Co., 1956.

Mehrotra, Rajiv, ed. *Understanding the Dalai Lama.* Delhi: Viking India, 2004.

Merton, Thomas. *The Asian Journals.* London: Sheldon Press, 1974.

Meyers, William, Robert Thurman, and Michael G. Burbank. *Man of Peace: The Illustrated Life Story of the Dalai Lama of Tibet.* New York: Tibet House, 2016.

Mission to Tibet: The Extraordinary Eighteenth-Century Account of Father Desideri SJ. Translated by M. Sweet. Edited by L. Zwilling. Somerville, MA: Wisdom Publications, 2010.

Morgan, William Stanley. *Amchi Sahib: A British Doctor in Tibet, 1936–37.* Charlestown, MA: Acme Bookbinding, 2007.

Mullin, Glenn H. *Path of the Bodhisattva Warrior: The Life and Teachings of the Thirteenth Dalai Lama.* Ithaca: Snow Lion Publications, 1988.

———. *The Fourteen Dalai Lamas: A Sacred Legacy of Reincarnation.* Santa Fe, NM: Clear Light Books, 2000.

Neame, Philip. *Playing with Strife: The Autobiography of a Soldier.* London: George G. Harrap, 1947.

Nebesky-Wojkowitz, René de. *Oracles and Demons of Tibet.* Delhi: Book Faith India, 1993.

Nebesky-Wojkowitz, René von. *Where the Gods Are Mountains.* London: Weidenfeld and Nicholson, 1956.

Norbu, Thubten Jigme. *Tibet Is My Country.* London: Rupert Hart Davis, 1960.

Norman, Alexander. *Secret Lives of the Dalai Lama.* New York: Random House, 2008. (Published in the UK as *Holder of the White Lotus.* London: Little, Brown, 2008.)

Nyoshul Khenpo. *A Marvelous Garland of Rare Gems: Biographies of Masters of Awareness in the Dzogchen Lineage.* Junction City, CO: Padma Publishing, 2005.

Patt, David. *A Strange Liberation: Tibetan Lives in Chinese Hands.* Ithaca: Snow Lion Publications, 1993.

Pemba, Tsewang Y. *Young Days in Tibet*. London: Jonathan Cape, 1957.

A Poisoned Arrow: The Secret Report of the 10th Panchen Lama. London: Tibet Information Network, 1997.

Pringle, Heather. *The Master Plan: Himmler's Scholars and the Holocaust*. London: Fourth Estate, 2006.

The Question of Tibet and the Rule of Law. Geneva: International Commission of Jurists, 1959.

Rahula, Walpola Sri. *What the Buddha Taught*. 1959. Reprint. Oxford: One World Publications, 2008.

Richardson, Hugh. *Ceremonies of the Lhasa Year*. London: Serindia Publications, 1993.

Rustomji, Nari. *Enchanted Frontiers: Sikkim, Bhutan and India's North-Eastern Borderlands*. Oxford: Oxford University Press, 1971.

Sadutshang, Tseyang. *My Youth in Tibet: Recollections of a Tibetan Woman*. Dharamsala: Library of Tibetan Works and Archives, 2012.

Samuel, Geoffrey. *Civilized Shamans: Buddhism in Tibetan Societies*. Washington, DC: Smithsonian Institution Press, 1993.

Sans-rgyas rgya-mtsho: Life of the Fifth Dalai Lama. Translated by Ahmed Zahiruddin. New Delhi: Academy of Indian Culture, 1999.

Santideva. *The Bodhischaryavatara*. Translated with an introduction and notes by Kate Crosby and Andrew Skilton. Oxford: Oxford University Press, 1995.

Schaeffer, Kurtis, and Matthew Kapstein. *Sources of Tibetan Tradition*. New York: Columbia University Press, 2013.

Shakabpa, Tsepon W. D. *Tibet: A Political History*. New Haven: Yale University Press, 1967.

Shakya, Tsering. *The Dragon in the Land of Snows: A History of Modern Tibet Since 1947*. New York: Columbia University Press, 1999.

Shelton, Albert Leroy. *Pioneering in Tibet: A Personal Record of Life and Experience in Mission Fields*. New York: F. H. Revell Company, 1921.

Shelton, Flora Beal. *Shelton of Tibet*. New York: George H. Doran, 1923.

Shokdung. *The Division of Heaven and Earth: On Tibet's Peaceful Revolution*. Translated by Matthew Akester. London: C. Hurst Publishers, 2017.

Short, Philip. *In Pursuit of Plants: Experiences of Nineteenth and Early Twentieth Century Plant Collectors*. Portland, OR: Timber Press, 2004.

Sither, Lobsang Gyatso. *Exile: A Photo Journal, 1959–1989*. Dharamsala: Tibet Documentation, 2017.

Steele, Archibald. *In the Kingdom of the Dalai Lama*. Sedona, AZ: In Print Publishing, 1993.

Stein, R. A. *Tibetan Civilisation*. Translated by J. E. Stapleton Driver. London: Faber and Faber, 1972.

Strong, Anna Louise. *When Serfs Stood Up in Tibet*. Peking: New World Press, 1960.

Teichman, Eric. *Travels of a Consular Officer in North-west China*. Cambridge: Cambridge University Press, 1921.

Thomas, Lowell. *Out of This World*. London: Macdonald and Co., 1951.

Thondup, Gyalo, with Anne F. Thurston. *The Noodle Maker of Kalimpong: The Untold Story of My Struggle for Tibet*. London: Rider, 2015.

Thurman, Robert. *Why the Dalai Lama Matters.* New York: Atria, 2008.

Trijang Rinpoche. *The Magical Play of Illusion: The Autobiography of Trijang Rinpoche.* Translated by Sharpa Tulku Tenzin Trinley. Somerville, MA: Wisdom Publications, 2018.

Tsering, Diki. *The Dalai Lama, My Son: A Mother's Story.* London: Virgin, 2000.

Uban, Sujan Singh. *Phantoms of Chittagong.* New Delhi: Allied Publishers, 1985.

van Schaik, Sam. *Tibet: A History.* New Haven: Yale University Press, 2011.

Wang, Xiuyu. *China's Last Imperial Frontier: Late Qing Expansion in Sichuan's Tibetan Borderlands.* Lanham, MD: Lexington Books, 2011.

Wangdu, Khemey Sonam, Basil J. Gould, and Hugh E. Richardson. *Discovery, Recognition and Enthronement of the 14th Dalai Lama: A Collection of Accounts.* Dharamsala: Library of Tibetan Works and Archives, 2000.

Williams, Paul. *Mahayana Buddhism: The Doctrinal Foundations.* 2nd ed. London: Routledge, 2009.

INDEX

ABOUT THE AUTHOR

ALEXANDER NORMAN has collaborated with the Dalai Lama on several of his bestselling books, including the autobiography *Freedom in Exile*, and *Beyond Religion*. He is the author of a critically acclaimed history of the Dalai Lamas, *Holder of the White Lotus*.

30 Years *of*

HarperCollins *Publishers* India

At HarperCollins, we believe in telling the best stories and finding the widest possible readership for our books in every format possible. We started publishing 30 years ago; a great deal has changed since then, but what has remained constant is the passion with which our authors write their books, the love with which readers receive them, and the sheer joy and excitement that we as publishers feel in being a part of the publishing process.

Over the years, we've had the pleasure of publishing some of the finest writing from the subcontinent and around the world, and some of the biggest bestsellers in India's publishing history. Our books and authors have won a phenomenal range of awards, and we ourselves have been named Publisher of the Year the greatest number of times. But nothing has meant more to us than the fact that millions of people have read the books we published, and somewhere, a book of ours might have made a difference.

As we step into our fourth decade, we go back to that one word – a word which has been a driving force for us all these years.

Read.